Microsoft® Office 365™
WORD 2016

INTRODUCTORY

Microsoft® Office 365™
WORD 2016

INTRODUCTORY

Misty E. Vermaat

CENGAGE
Learning®

SHELLY CASHMAN SERIES®

Australia • Brazil • Japan • Korea • Mexico • Singapore • Spain • United Kingdom • United States

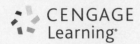

Microsoft Word 2016: Introductory
Misty E. Vermaat

SVP, GM Skills & Global Product Management:
Dawn Gerrain

Product Director: Kathleen McMahon

Senior Product Team Manager: Lauren Murphy

Associate Product Manager: Melissa Stehler

Senior Director, Development: Marah
Bellegarde

Product Development Manager: Leigh Hefferon

Managing Content Developer: Emma F.
Newsom

Developmental Editor: Lyn Markowicz

Product Assistant: Erica Chapman

Manuscript Quality Assurance:
Jeffrey Schwartz, John Freitas,
Serge Palladino, Susan Pedicini,
Danielle Shaw, Susan Whalen

Senior Production Director: Wendy Troeger

Production Director: Patty Stephan

Senior Content Project Manager: Matthew
Hutchinson

Manufacturing Planner: Julio Esperas

Designer: Diana Graham

Text Design: Joel Sadagursky

Cover Template Designer: Diana Graham

Cover image(s): Piotr Zajc/Shutterstock.com;
Mrs. Opossum/Shutterstock.com

Compositor: Lumina Datamatics

Vice President, Marketing: Brian Joyner

Marketing Director: Michele McTighe

Marketing Manager: Stephanie Albracht

For product information and technology assistance, contact us at
Cengage Learning Customer & Sales Support, 1-800-354-9706

For permission to use material from this text or product,
submit all requests online at **www.cengage.com/permissions.**
Further permissions questions can be e-mailed to
permissionrequest@cengage.com

Library of Congress Control Number: 2015958834

ISBN: 978-1-305-87099-4

Cengage Learning
20 Channel Center Street
Boston, MA 02210
USA

Cengage Learning is a leading provider of customized learning solutions with employees residing in nearly 40 different countries and sales in more than 125 countries around the world. Find your local representative at **www.cengage.com.**

Cengage Learning products are represented in Canada by Nelson Education, Ltd.

To learn more about Cengage Learning, visit **www.cengage.com**
Purchase any of our products at your local college store or at our preferred online store **www.cengagebrain.com**

Printed in the United States of America
Print Number: 01 Print Year: 2016

Microsoft® Office 365™
WORD 2016

INTRODUCTORY

Contents

Microsoft **Office 365 & Word 2016**

MODULE ONE
Creating, Formatting, and Editing a Word Document with a Picture

MODULE TWO
Creating a Research Paper with References and Sources

Productivity Apps for School and Work

Corinne Hoisington

Lochlan keeps track of his class notes, football plays, and internship meetings with OneNote.

Zoe is using the annotation features of Microsoft Edge to take and save web notes for her research paper.

Nori is creating a Sway site to highlight this year's activities for the Student Government Association.

Hunter is adding interactive videos and screen recordings to his PowerPoint resume.

© Rawpixel/Shutterstock.com

Being computer literate no longer means mastery of only Word, Excel, PowerPoint, Outlook, and Access. To become technology power users, Hunter, Nori, Zoe, and Lochlan are exploring Microsoft OneNote, Sway, Mix, and Edge in Office 2016 and Windows 10.

In this Module

Learn to use productivity apps!
Links to companion **Sways**, featuring **videos** with hands-on instructions, are located on www.cengagebrain.com.

Introduction to OneNote 2016

notebook | section tab | To Do tag | screen clipping | note | template | Microsoft OneNote Mobile app | sync | drawing canvas | inked handwriting | Ink to Text

As you glance around any classroom, you invariably see paper notebooks and notepads on each desk. Because deciphering and sharing handwritten notes can be a challenge, Microsoft OneNote 2016 replaces physical notebooks, binders, and paper notes with a searchable, digital notebook. OneNote captures your ideas and schoolwork on any device so you can stay organized, share notes, and work with others on projects. Whether you are a student taking class notes as shown in **Figure 1** or an employee taking notes in company meetings, OneNote is the one place to keep notes for all of your projects.

Figure 1: OneNote 2016 notebook

Each **notebook** is divided into sections, also called **section tabs**, by subject or topic.

Use **To Do tags**, icons that help you keep track of your assignments and other tasks.

Type on a page to add a **note**, a small window that contains text or other types of information.

Personalize a page with a **template**, or stationery.

Write or draw directly on the page using drawing tools.

Pages can include pictures such as **screen clippings**, images from any part of a computer screen.

Attach files and enter equations so you have everything you need in one place.

Creating a OneNote Notebook

OneNote is divided into sections similar to those in a spiral-bound notebook. Each OneNote notebook contains sections, pages, and other notebooks. You can use One-Note for school, business, and personal projects. Store information for each type of project in different notebooks to keep your tasks separate, or use any other organization that suits you. OneNote is flexible enough to adapt to the way you want to work.

When you create a notebook, it contains a blank page with a plain white background by default, though you can use templates, or stationery, to apply designs in categories such as Academic, Business, Decorative, and Planners. Start typing or use the buttons on the Insert tab to insert notes, which are small resizable windows that can contain text, equations, tables, on-screen writing, images, audio and video recordings, to-do lists, file attachments, and file printouts. Add as many notes as you need to each page.

Syncing a Notebook to the Cloud

OneNote saves your notes every time you make a change in a notebook. To make sure you can access your notebooks with a laptop, tablet, or smartphone wherever you are, OneNote uses cloud-based storage, such as OneDrive or SharePoint. **Microsoft OneNote Mobile app**, a lightweight version of OneNote 2016 shown in **Figure 2**, is available for free in the Windows Store, Google Play for Android devices, and the AppStore for iOS devices.

If you have a Microsoft account, OneNote saves your notes on OneDrive automatically for all your mobile devices and computers, which is called **syncing**. For example, you can use OneNote to take notes on your laptop during class, and then open OneNote on your phone to study later. To use a notebook stored on your computer with your OneNote Mobile app, move the notebook to OneDrive. You can quickly share notebook content with other people using OneDrive.

Figure 2: Microsoft OneNote Mobile app

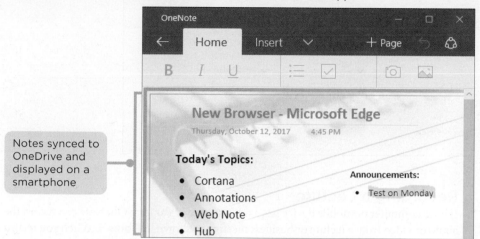

Notes synced to OneDrive and displayed on a smartphone

Taking Notes

Use OneNote pages to organize your notes by class and topic or lecture. Beyond simple typed notes, OneNote stores drawings, converts handwriting to searchable text and mathematical sketches to equations, and records audio and video.

OneNote includes drawing tools that let you sketch freehand drawings such as biological cell diagrams and financial supply-and-demand charts. As shown in **Figure 3**, the Draw tab on the ribbon provides these drawing tools along with shapes so you can insert diagrams and other illustrations to represent your ideas. When you draw on a page, OneNote creates a **drawing canvas**, which is a container for shapes and lines.

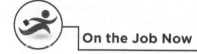

On the Job Now

OneNote is ideal for taking notes during meetings, whether you are recording minutes, documenting a discussion, sketching product diagrams, or listing follow-up items. Use a meeting template to add pages with content appropriate for meetings.

Figure 3: Tools on the Draw tab

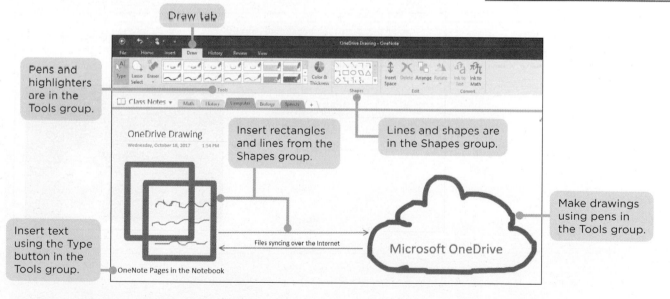

Pens and highlighters are in the Tools group.

Insert rectangles and lines from the Shapes group.

Lines and shapes are in the Shapes group.

Insert text using the Type button in the Tools group.

Make drawings using pens in the Tools group.

Converting Handwriting to Text

When you use a pen tool to write on a notebook page, the text you enter is called **inked handwriting**. OneNote can convert inked handwriting to typed text when you use the **Ink to Text** button in the Convert group on the Draw tab, as shown in **Figure 4**. After OneNote converts the handwriting to text, you can use the Search box to find terms in the converted text or any other note in your notebooks.

Figure 4: Converting handwriting to text

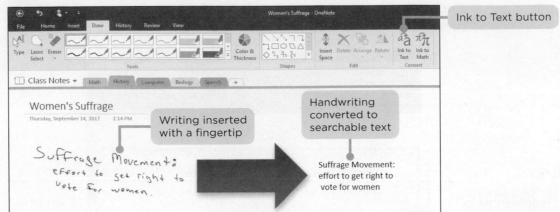

On the Job Now

Use OneNote as a place to brainstorm ongoing work projects. If a notebook contains sensitive material, you can password-protect some or all of the notebook so that only certain people can open it.

Recording a Lecture

If your computer or mobile device has a microphone or camera, OneNote can record the audio or video from a lecture or business meeting as shown in **Figure 5**. When you record a lecture (with your instructor's permission), you can follow along, take regular notes at your own pace, and review the video recording later. You can control the start, pause, and stop motions of the recording when you play back the recording of your notes.

Figure 5: Video inserted in a notebook

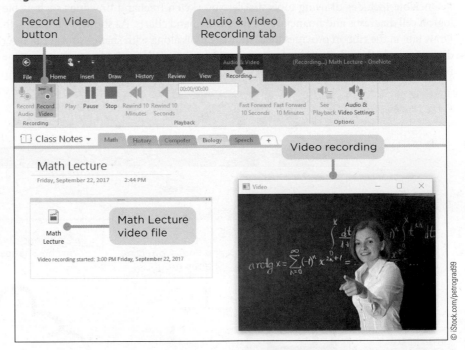

Try This Now

1: Taking Notes for a Week

Learn to use OneNote!
Links to companion **Sways**, featuring **videos** with hands-on instructions, are located on www.cengagebrain.com.

As a student, you can get organized by using OneNote to take detailed notes in your classes. Perform the following tasks:

a. Create a new OneNote notebook on your Microsoft OneDrive account (the default location for new notebooks). Name the notebook with your first name followed by "Notes," as in **Caleb Notes**.

b. Create four section tabs, each with a different class name.

c. Take detailed notes in those classes for one week. Be sure to include notes, drawings, and other types of content.

d. Sync your notes with your OneDrive. Submit your assignment in the format specified by your instructor.

2: Using OneNote to Organize a Research Paper

You have a research paper due on the topic of three habits of successful students. Use OneNote to organize your research. Perform the following tasks:

a. Create a new OneNote notebook on your Microsoft OneDrive account. Name the notebook **Success Research**.

b. Create three section tabs with the following names:

- **Take Detailed Notes**
- **Be Respectful in Class**
- **Come to Class Prepared**

c. On the web, research the topics and find three sources for each section. Copy a sentence from each source and paste the sentence into the appropriate section. When you paste the sentence, OneNote inserts it in a note with a link to the source.

d. Sync your notes with your OneDrive. Submit your assignment in the format specified by your instructor.

3: Planning Your Career

Note: This activity requires a webcam or built-in video camera on any type of device.

Consider an occupation that interests you. Using OneNote, examine the responsibilities, education requirements, potential salary, and employment outlook of a specific career. Perform the following tasks:

a. Create a new OneNote notebook on your Microsoft OneDrive account. Name the notebook with your first name followed by a career title, such as **Kara - App Developer**.

b. Create four section tabs with the names **Responsibilities, Education Requirements, Median Salary**, and **Employment Outlook**.

c. Research the responsibilities of your career path. Using OneNote, record a short video (approximately 30 seconds) of yourself explaining the responsibilities of your career path. Place the video in the Responsibilities section.

d. On the web, research the educational requirements for your career path and find two appropriate sources. Copy a paragraph from each source and paste them into the appropriate section. When you paste a paragraph, OneNote inserts it in a note with a link to the source.

e. Research the median salary for a single year for this career. Create a mathematical equation in the Median Salary section that multiplies the amount of the median salary times 20 years to calculate how much you will possibly earn.

f. For the Employment Outlook section, research the outlook for your career path. Take at least four notes about what you find when researching the topic.

g. Sync your notes with your OneDrive. Submit your assignment in the format specified by your instructor.

Introduction to Sway

Sway site | responsive design | Storyline | card | Creative Commons license | animation emphasis effects | Docs.com

Expressing your ideas in a presentation typically means creating PowerPoint slides or a Word document. Microsoft Sway gives you another way to engage an audience. Sway is a free Microsoft tool available at Sway.com or as an app in Office 365. Using Sway, you can combine text, images, videos, and social media in a website called a **Sway site** that you can share and display on any device. To get started, you create a digital story on a web-based canvas without borders, slides, cells, or page breaks. A Sway site organizes the text, images, and video into a **responsive design**, which means your content adapts perfectly to any screen size as shown in **Figure 6**. You store a Sway site in the cloud on OneDrive using a free Microsoft account.

Figure 6: Sway site with responsive design

You can display a Sway presentation in a web browser.

Sway uses responsive design to make sure pages fit perfectly on any device.

The Market for Commercial Drones

Medical Defibrillator

- Ambulance drone can help heart attack victims in under 2 minutes with

© iStock.com/marinello, © iStock.com/marekuliasz

Creating a Sway Presentation

You can use Sway to build a digital flyer, a club newsletter, a vacation blog, an informational site, a digital art portfolio, or a new product rollout. After you select your topic and sign into Sway with your Microsoft account, a **Storyline** opens, providing tools and a work area for composing your digital story. See **Figure 7**. Each story can include text, images, and videos. You create a Sway by adding text and media content into a Storyline section, or **card**. To add pictures, videos, or documents, select a card in the left pane and then select the Insert Content button. The first card in a Sway presentation contains a title and background image.

Figure 7: Creating a Sway site

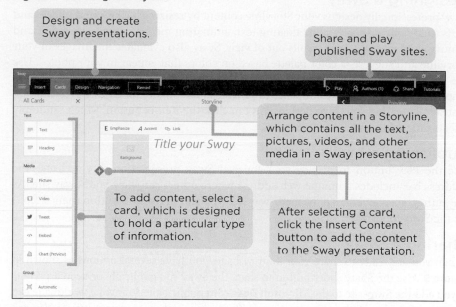

Design and create Sway presentations.

Share and play published Sway sites.

Arrange content in a Storyline, which contains all the text, pictures, videos, and other media in a Sway presentation.

To add content, select a card, which is designed to hold a particular type of information.

After selecting a card, click the Insert Content button to add the content to the Sway presentation.

Adding Content to Build a Story

As you work, Sway searches the Internet to help you find relevant images, videos, tweets, and other content from online sources such as Bing, YouTube, Twitter, and Facebook. You can drag content from the search results right into the Storyline. In addition, you can upload your own images and videos directly in the presentation. For example, if you are creating a Sway presentation about the market for commercial drones, Sway suggests content to incorporate into the presentation by displaying it in the left pane as search results. The search results include drone images tagged with a **Creative Commons license** at online sources as shown in **Figure 8**. A Creative Commons license is a public copyright license that allows the free distribution of an otherwise copyrighted work. In addition, you can specify the source of the media. For example, you can add your own Facebook or OneNote pictures and videos in Sway without leaving the app.

On the Job Now

If you have a Microsoft Word document containing an outline of your business content, drag the outline into Sway to create a card for each topic.

Figure 8: Images in Sway search results

Select the source of media objects

Information about Creative Commons licenses

Storyline title

The Market for Commercial Drones

Drag an image to the picture placeholder box

Suggested images in the search results

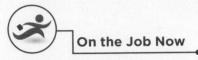

On the Job Now

If your project team wants to collaborate on a Sway presentation, click the Authors button on the navigation bar to invite others to edit the presentation.

Designing a Sway

Sway professionally designs your Storyline content by resizing background images and fonts to fit your display, and by floating text, animating media, embedding video, and removing images as a page scrolls out of view. Sway also evaluates the images in your Storyline and suggests a color palette based on colors that appear in your photos. Use the Design button to display tools including color palettes, font choices, **animation emphasis effects**, and style templates to provide a personality for a Sway presentation. Instead of creating your own design, you can click the Remix button, which randomly selects unique designs for your Sway site.

Publishing a Sway

Use the Play button to display your finished Sway presentation as a website. The Address bar includes a unique web address where others can view your Sway site. As the author, you can edit a published Sway site by clicking the Edit button (pencil icon) on the Sway toolbar.

Sharing a Sway

When you are ready to share your Sway website, you have several options as shown in **Figure 9**. Use the Share slider button to share the Sway site publically or keep it private. If you add the Sway site to the Microsoft **Docs.com** public gallery, anyone worldwide can use Bing, Google, or other search engines to find, view, and share your Sway site. You can also share your Sway site using Facebook, Twitter, Google+, Yammer, and other social media sites. Link your presentation to any webpage or email the link to your audience. Sway can also generate a code for embedding the link within another webpage.

Figure 9: Sharing a Sway site

Share button

Drag the slider button to Just me to keep the Sway site private

Post the Sway site on Docs.com

Options differ depending on your Microsoft account

Send friends a link to the Sway site

> Play   Authors (1)   Share
>
> Share ◯ Just me
>
> Share with the world
>   Docs.com - Your public gallery
>
> Share with friends
>   f twitter g+ y share ...
>   https://sway.com/JQDFrUaxmg4lEbbk
>
> ▲ More options
>
> ☑ Viewers can duplicate this Sway
>
> Stop sharing

Try This Now

Learn to use Sway!
Links to companion **Sways**, featuring **videos** with hands-on instructions, are located on www.cengagebrain.com.

1: Creating a Sway Resume

Sway is a digital storytelling app. Create a Sway resume to share the skills, job experiences, and achievements you have that match the requirements of a future job interest. Perform the following tasks:

a. Create a new presentation in Sway to use as a digital resume. Title the Sway Storyline with your full name and then select a background image.

b. Create three separate sections titled **Academic Background, Work Experience**, and **Skills**, and insert text, a picture, and a paragraph or bulleted points in each section. Be sure to include your own picture.

c. Add a fourth section that includes a video about your school that you find online.

d. Customize the design of your presentation.

e. Submit your assignment link in the format specified by your instructor.

2: Creating an Online Sway Newsletter

Newsletters are designed to capture the attention of their target audience. Using Sway, create a newsletter for a club, organization, or your favorite music group. Perform the following tasks:

a. Create a new presentation in Sway to use as a digital newsletter for a club, organization, or your favorite music group. Provide a title for the Sway Storyline and select an appropriate background image.

b. Select three separate sections with appropriate titles, such as Upcoming Events. In each section, insert text, a picture, and a paragraph or bulleted points.

c. Add a fourth section that includes a video about your selected topic.

d. Customize the design of your presentation.

e. Submit your assignment link in the format specified by your instructor.

3: Creating and Sharing a Technology Presentation

To place a Sway presentation in the hands of your entire audience, you can share a link to the Sway presentation. Create a Sway presentation on a new technology and share it with your class. Perform the following tasks:

a. Create a new presentation in Sway about a cutting-edge technology topic. Provide a title for the Sway Storyline and select a background image.

b. Create four separate sections about your topic, and include text, a picture, and a paragraph in each section.

c. Add a fifth section that includes a video about your topic.

d. Customize the design of your presentation.

e. Share the link to your Sway with your classmates and submit your assignment link in the format specified by your instructor.

Introduction to Office Mix

add-in | clip | slide recording | Slide Notes | screen recording | free-response quiz

To enliven business meetings and lectures, Microsoft adds a new dimension to presentations with a powerful toolset called Office Mix, a free add-in for PowerPoint. (An **add-in** is software that works with an installed app to extend its features.) Using Office Mix, you can record yourself on video, capture still and moving images on your desktop, and insert interactive elements such as quizzes and live webpages directly into PowerPoint slides. When you post the finished presentation to OneDrive, Office Mix provides a link you can share with friends and colleagues. Anyone with an Internet connection and a web browser can watch a published Office Mix presentation, such as the one in **Figure 10**, on a computer or mobile device.

Figure 10: Office Mix presentation

Adding Office Mix to PowerPoint

To get started, you create an Office Mix account at the website mix.office.com using an email address or a Facebook or Google account. Next, you download and install the Office Mix add-in (see **Figure 11**). Office Mix appears as a new tab named Mix on the PowerPoint ribbon in versions of Office 2013 and Office 2016 running on personal computers (PCs).

Figure 11: Getting started with Office Mix

Capturing Video Clips

A **clip** is a short segment of audio, such as music, or video. After finishing the content on a PowerPoint slide, you can use Office Mix to add a video clip to animate or illustrate the content. Office Mix creates video clips in two ways: by recording live action on a webcam and by capturing screen images and movements. If your computer has a webcam, you can record yourself and annotate the slide to create a **slide recording** as shown in **Figure 12**.

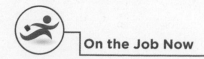

On the Job Now

Companies are using Office Mix to train employees about new products, to explain benefit packages to new workers, and to educate interns about office procedures.

Figure 12: Making a slide recording

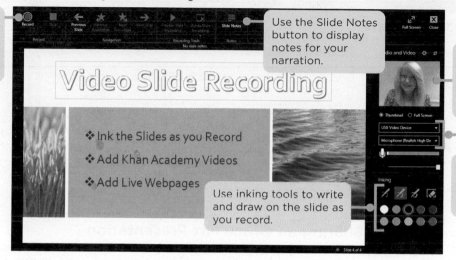

Record your voice; also record video if your computer has a camera.

Use the Slide Notes button to display notes for your narration.

For best results, look directly at your webcam while recording video.

Ink the Slides as you Record

Add Khan Academy Videos

Add Live Webpages

Use inking tools to write and draw on the slide as you record.

Choose a video and audio device to record images and sound.

When you are making a slide recording, you can record your spoken narration at the same time. The **Slide Notes** feature works like a teleprompter to help you focus on your presentation content instead of memorizing your narration. Use the Inking tools to make annotations or add highlighting using different pen types and colors. After finishing a recording, edit the video in PowerPoint to trim the length or set playback options.

The second way to create a video is to capture on-screen images and actions with or without a voiceover. This method is ideal if you want to show how to use your favorite website or demonstrate an app such as OneNote. To share your screen with an audience, select the part of the screen you want to show in the video. Office Mix captures everything that happens in that area to create a **screen recording**, as shown in **Figure 13**. Office Mix inserts the screen recording as a video in the slide.

On the Job Now

To make your video recordings accessible to people with hearing impairments, use the Office Mix closed-captioning tools. You can also use closed captions to supplement audio that is difficult to understand and to provide an aid for those learning to read.

Figure 13: Making a screen recording

Record the action on the screen within the red dashed outline.

Record audio while capturing your on-screen actions.

Select Area button

Inserting Quizzes, Live Webpages, and Apps

To enhance and assess audience understanding, make your slides interactive by adding quizzes, live webpages, and apps. Quizzes give immediate feedback to the user as shown in **Figure 14**. Office Mix supports several quiz formats, including a **free-response quiz** similar to a short answer quiz, and true/false, multiple-choice, and multiple-response formats.

Figure 14: Creating an interactive quiz

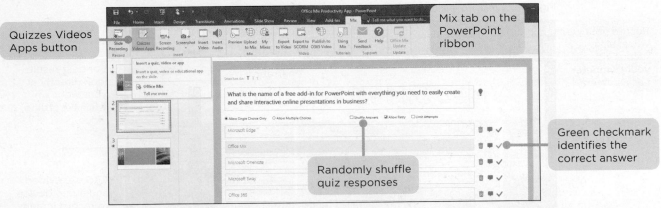

Quizzes Videos Apps button

Mix tab on the PowerPoint ribbon

Green checkmark identifies the correct answer

Randomly shuffle quiz responses

Sharing an Office Mix Presentation

When you complete your work with Office Mix, upload the presentation to your personal Office Mix dashboard as shown in **Figure 15**. Users of PCs, Macs, iOS devices, and Android devices can access and play Office Mix presentations. The Office Mix dashboard displays built-in analytics that include the quiz results and how much time viewers spent on each slide. You can play completed Office Mix presentations online or download them as movies.

Figure 15: Sharing an Office Mix presentation

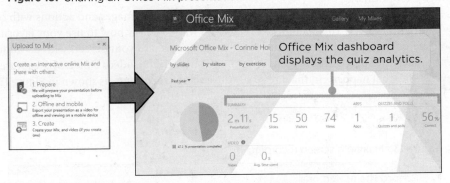

Office Mix dashboard displays the quiz analytics.

Try This Now

1: Creating an Office Mix Tutorial for OneNote

Note: This activity requires a microphone on your computer.

Office Mix makes it easy to record screens and their contents. Create PowerPoint slides with an Office Mix screen recording to show OneNote 2016 features. Perform the following tasks:

a. Create a PowerPoint presentation with the Ion Boardroom template. Create an opening slide with the title **My Favorite OneNote Features** and enter your name in the subtitle.
b. Create three additional slides, each titled with a new feature of OneNote. Open OneNote and use the Mix tab in PowerPoint to capture three separate screen recordings that teach your favorite features.
c. Add a fifth slide that quizzes the user with a multiple-choice question about OneNote and includes four responses. Be sure to insert a checkmark indicating the correct response.
d. Upload the completed presentation to your Office Mix dashboard and share the link with your instructor.
e. Submit your assignment link in the format specified by your instructor.

2: Teaching Augmented Reality with Office Mix

Note: This activity requires a webcam or built-in video camera on your computer.

A local elementary school has asked you to teach augmented reality to its students using Office Mix. Perform the following tasks:

a. Research augmented reality using your favorite online search tools.
b. Create a PowerPoint presentation with the Frame template. Create an opening slide with the title **Augmented Reality** and enter your name in the subtitle.
c. Create a slide with four bullets summarizing your research of augmented reality. Create a 20-second slide recording of yourself providing a quick overview of augmented reality.
d. Create another slide with a 30-second screen recording of a video about augmented reality from a site such as YouTube or another video-sharing site.
e. Add a final slide that quizzes the user with a true/false question about augmented reality. Be sure to insert a checkmark indicating the correct response.
f. Upload the completed presentation to your Office Mix dashboard and share the link with your instructor.
g. Submit your assignment link in the format specified by your instructor.

3: Marketing a Travel Destination with Office Mix

Note: This activity requires a webcam or built-in video camera on your computer.

To convince your audience to travel to a particular city, create a slide presentation marketing any city in the world using a slide recording, screen recording, and a quiz. Perform the following tasks:

a. Create a PowerPoint presentation with any template. Create an opening slide with the title of the city you are marketing as a travel destination and your name in the subtitle.
b. Create a slide with four bullets about the featured city. Create a 30-second slide recording of yourself explaining why this city is the perfect vacation destination.
c. Create another slide with a 20-second screen recording of a travel video about the city from a site such as YouTube or another video-sharing site.
d. Add a final slide that quizzes the user with a multiple-choice question about the featured city with five responses. Be sure to include a checkmark indicating the correct response.
e. Upload the completed presentation to your Office Mix dashboard and share your link with your instructor.
f. Submit your assignment link in the format specified by your instructor.

Introduction to Microsoft Edge

Reading view | Hub | Cortana | Web Note | Inking | sandbox

Microsoft Edge is the default web browser developed for the Windows 10 operating system as a replacement for Internet Explorer. Unlike its predecessor, Edge lets you write on webpages, read webpages without advertisements and other distractions, and search for information using a virtual personal assistant. The Edge interface is clean and basic, as shown in **Figure 16**, meaning you can pay more attention to the webpage content.

Figure 16: Microsoft Edge tools

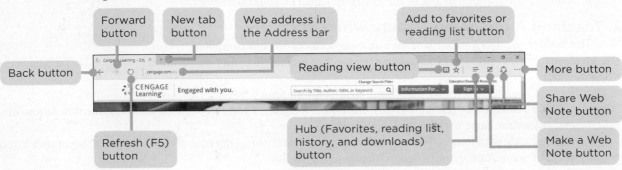

- Forward button
- New tab button
- Web address in the Address bar
- Add to favorites or reading list button
- Reading view button
- Back button
- More button
- Share Web Note button
- Refresh (F5) button
- Hub (Favorites, reading list, history, and downloads) button
- Make a Web Note button

Browsing the Web with Microsoft Edge

One of the fastest browsers available, Edge allows you to type search text directly in the Address bar. As you view the resulting webpage, you can switch to **Reading view**, which is available for most news and research sites, to eliminate distracting advertisements. For example, if you are catching up on technology news online, the webpage might be difficult to read due to a busy layout cluttered with ads. Switch to Reading view to refresh the page and remove the original page formatting, ads, and menu sidebars to read the article distraction-free.

Consider the **Hub** in Microsoft Edge as providing one-stop access to all the things you collect on the web, such as your favorite websites, reading list, surfing history, and downloaded files.

Locating Information with Cortana

Cortana, the Windows 10 virtual assistant, plays an important role in Microsoft Edge. After you turn on Cortana, it appears as an animated circle in the Address bar when you might need assistance, as shown in the restaurant website in **Figure 17**. When you click the Cortana icon, a pane slides in from the right of the browser window to display detailed information about the restaurant, including maps and reviews. Cortana can also assist you in defining words, finding the weather, suggesting coupons for shopping, updating stock market information, and calculating math.

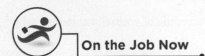

Figure 17: Cortana providing restaurant information

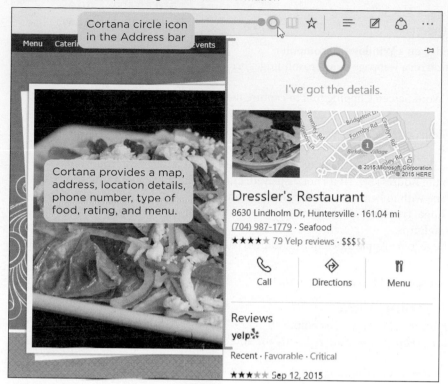

Cortana circle icon in the Address bar

Cortana provides a map, address, location details, phone number, type of food, rating, and menu.

I've got the details.

Dressler's Restaurant
8630 Lindholm Dr, Huntersville · 161.04 mi
(704) 987-1779 · Seafood
★★★★★ 79 Yelp reviews · $$$$$

| 📞 Call | ◈ Directions | 🍴 Menu |

Reviews
yelp

Recent · Favorable · Critical
★★★★★ Sep 12, 2015

Annotating Webpages

One of the most impressive Microsoft Edge features are the **Web Note** tools, which you use to write on a webpage or to highlight text. When you click the Make a Web Note button, an **Inking** toolbar appears, as shown in **Figure 18**, that provides writing and drawing tools. These tools include an eraser, a pen, and a highlighter with different colors. You can also insert a typed note and copy a screen image (called a screen clipping). You can draw with a pointing device, fingertip, or stylus using different pen colors. Whether you add notes to a recipe, annotate sources for a research paper, or select a product while shopping online, the Web Note tools can enhance your productivity. After you complete your notes, click the Save button to save the annotations to OneNote, your Favorites list, or your Reading list. You can share the inked page with others using the Share Web Note button.

On the Job Now

To enhance security, Microsoft Edge runs in a partial **sandbox**, an arrangement that prevents attackers from gaining control of your computer. Browsing within the **sandbox** protects computer resources and information from hackers.

Figure 18: Web Note tools in Microsoft Edge

Inking toolbar with Web Note tools for making annotations

Writing and drawing created with the Pen tool

Highlighted text

Save a copy of the webpage with annotations

Typed note

Try This Now

Learn to use Edge!
Links to companion **Sways**, featuring **videos** with hands-on instructions, are located on www.cengagebrain.com.

1: Using Cortana in Microsoft Edge

Note: This activity requires using Microsoft Edge on a Windows 10 computer.

Cortana can assist you in finding information on a webpage in Microsoft Edge. Perform the following tasks:

a. Create a Word document using the Word Screen Clipping tool to capture the following screenshots.

- Screenshot A—Using Microsoft Edge, open a webpage with a technology news article. Right-click a term in the article and ask Cortana to define it.
- Screenshot B—Using Microsoft Edge, open the website of a fancy restaurant in a city near you. Make sure the Cortana circle icon is displayed in the Address bar. (If it's not displayed, find a different restaurant website.) Click the Cortana circle icon to display a pane with information about the restaurant.
- Screenshot C—Using Microsoft Edge, type **10 USD to Euros** in the Address bar without pressing the Enter key. Cortana converts the U.S. dollars to Euros.
- Screenshot D—Using Microsoft Edge, type **Apple stock** in the Address bar without pressing the Enter key. Cortana displays the current stock quote.

b. Submit your assignment in the format specified by your instructor.

2: Viewing Online News with Reading View

Note: This activity requires using Microsoft Edge on a Windows 10 computer.

Reading view in Microsoft Edge can make a webpage less cluttered with ads and other distractions. Perform the following tasks:

a. Create a Word document using the Word Screen Clipping tool to capture the following screenshots.

- Screenshot A—Using Microsoft Edge, open the website **mashable.com**. Open a technology article. Click the Reading view button to display an ad-free page that uses only basic text formatting.
- Screenshot B—Using Microsoft Edge, open the website **bbc.com**. Open any news article. Click the Reading view button to display an ad-free page that uses only basic text formatting.
- Screenshot C—Make three types of annotations (Pen, Highlighter, and Add a typed note) on the BBC article page displayed in Reading view.

b. Submit your assignment in the format specified by your instructor.

3: Inking with Microsoft Edge

Note: This activity requires using Microsoft Edge on a Windows 10 computer.

Microsoft Edge provides many annotation options to record your ideas. Perform the following tasks:

a. Open the website **wolframalpha.com** in the Microsoft Edge browser. Wolfram Alpha is a well-respected academic search engine. Type **US$100 1965 dollars in 2015** in the Wolfram Alpha search text box and press the Enter key.
b. Click the Make a Web Note button to display the Web Note tools. Using the Pen tool, draw a circle around the result on the webpage. Save the page to OneNote.
c. In the Wolfram Alpha search text box, type the name of the city closest to where you live and press the Enter key. Using the Highlighter tool, highlight at least three interesting results. Add a note and then type a sentence about what you learned about this city. Save the page to OneNote. Share your OneNote notebook with your instructor.
d. Submit your assignment link in the format specified by your instructor.

Office 2016 and Windows 10: Essential Concepts and Skills

Objectives

You will have mastered the material in this module when you can:

- Use a touch screen
- Perform basic mouse operations
- Start Windows and sign in to an account
- Identify the objects on the Windows 10 desktop
- Identify the apps in and versions of Microsoft Office 2016
- Run an app
- Identify the components of the Microsoft Office ribbon

- Create folders
- Save files
- Change screen resolution
- Perform basic tasks in Microsoft Office apps
- Manage files
- Use Microsoft Office Help and Windows Help

This introductory module uses Word 2016 to cover features and functions common to Office 2016 apps, as well as the basics of Windows 10.

Roadmap

In this module, you will learn how to perform basic tasks in Windows and Word. The following roadmap identifies general activities you will perform as you progress through this module:

1. SIGN IN to an account.
2. USE WINDOWS.
3. USE features in Word that are common across Office APPS.
4. FILE and folder MANAGEMENT.
5. SWITCH between APPS.
6. SAVE and manage FILES.

7. CHANGE SCREEN RESOLUTION.

8. EXIT APPS.

9. USE ADDITIONAL Office APPS FEATURES.

10. USE Office and Windows HELP.

At the beginning of the step instructions throughout each module, you will see an abbreviated form of this roadmap. The abbreviated roadmap uses colors to indicate module progress: gray means the module is beyond that activity, blue means the task being shown is covered in that activity, and black means that activity is yet to be covered. For example, the following abbreviated roadmap indicates the module would be showing a task in the USE APPS activity.

1 SIGN IN | 2 USE WINDOWS | 3 USE APPS | 4 FILE MANAGEMENT | 5 SWITCH APPS | 6 SAVE FILES

7 CHANGE SCREEN RESOLUTION | 8 EXIT APPS | 9 USE ADDITIONAL APP FEATURES | 10 USE HELP

Use the abbreviated roadmap as a progress guide while you read or step through the instructions in this module.

Introduction to the Windows 10 Operating System

Windows 10 is the newest version of Microsoft Windows, which is a popular and widely used operating system (Figure 1). An **operating system (OS)** is a set of programs that coordinate all the activities among computer or mobile device hardware.

Windows 10 desktop

Figure 1

The Windows operating system simplifies the process of working with documents and apps by organizing the manner in which you interact with the computer. Windows is used to run apps. An application, or **app**, consists of programs designed to make users more productive and/or assist them with personal tasks, such as word processing or browsing the web.

Using a Touch Screen and a Mouse

Windows users who have computers or devices with touch screen capability can interact with the screen using gestures. A **gesture** is a motion you make on a touch screen with the tip of one or more fingers or your hand. Touch screens are convenient because they do not require a separate device for input. Table 1 presents common ways to interact with a touch screen.

If you are using your finger on a touch screen and are having difficulty completing the steps in this module, consider using a stylus. Many people find it easier to be precise with a stylus than with a finger. In addition, with a stylus you see the pointer. If you still are having trouble completing the steps with a stylus, try using a mouse.

Table 1 Touch Screen Gestures

Motion	Description	Common Uses	Equivalent Mouse Operation
Tap	Quickly touch and release one finger one time.	Activate a link (built-in connection). Press a button. Run a program or an app.	Click
Double-tap	Quickly touch and release one finger two times.	Run a program or an app. Zoom in (show a smaller area on the screen, so that contents appear larger) at the location of the double-tap.	Double-click
Press and hold	Press and hold one finger to cause an action to occur, or until an action occurs.	Display a shortcut menu (immediate access to allowable actions). Activate a mode enabling you to move an item with one finger to a new location.	Right-click
Drag, or slide	Press and hold one finger on an object and then move the finger to the new location.	Move an item around the screen. Scroll.	Drag
Swipe	Press and hold one finger and then move the finger horizontally or vertically on the screen.	Select an object. Swipe from edge to display a bar such as the Action Center, Apps bar, and Navigation bar (all discussed later).	Drag
Stretch	Move two fingers apart.	Zoom in (show a smaller area on the screen, so that contents appear larger).	None
Pinch	Move two fingers together.	Zoom out (show a larger area on the screen, so that contents appear smaller).	None

© 2015 Cengage Learning

Will the screen look different if you are using a touch screen?
The Windows and Microsoft Office interface varies slightly if you are using a touch screen. For this reason, you might notice that your Windows or Word screens looks slightly different from the screens in this book.

Windows users who do not have touch screen capabilities typically work with a mouse that has at least two buttons. For a right-handed user, the left button usually is

CONSIDER THIS

the primary mouse button, and the right mouse button is the secondary mouse button. Left-handed people, however, can reverse the function of these buttons.

Table 2 explains how to perform a variety of mouse operations. Some apps also use keys in combination with the mouse to perform certain actions. For example, when you hold down the CTRL key while rolling the mouse wheel, text on the screen may become larger or smaller based on the direction you roll the wheel. The function of the mouse buttons and the wheel varies depending on the app.

Table 2 Mouse Operations

Operation	Mouse Action	Example*	Equivalent Touch Gesture
Point	Move the mouse until the pointer on the desktop is positioned on the item of choice.	Position the pointer on the screen.	None
Click	Press and release the primary mouse button, which usually is the left mouse button.	Select or deselect items on the screen or run an app or app feature.	Tap
Right-click	Press and release the secondary mouse button, which usually is the right mouse button.	Display a shortcut menu.	Press and hold
Double-click	Quickly press and release the primary mouse button twice without moving the mouse.	Run an app or app feature.	Double-tap
Triple-click	Quickly press and release the primary mouse button three times without moving the mouse.	Select a paragraph.	Triple-tap
Drag	Point to an item, hold down the primary mouse button, move the item to the desired location on the screen, and then release the mouse button.	Move an object from one location to another or draw pictures.	Drag or slide
Right-drag	Point to an item, hold down the right mouse button, move the item to the desired location on the screen, and then release the right mouse button.	Display a shortcut menu after moving an object from one location to another.	Press and hold, then drag
Rotate wheel	Roll the wheel forward or backward.	Scroll vertically (up and down).	Swipe
Free-spin wheel	Whirl the wheel forward or backward so that it spins freely on its own.	Scroll through many pages in seconds.	Swipe
Press wheel	Press the wheel button while moving the mouse.	Scroll continuously.	None
Tilt wheel	Press the wheel toward the right or left.	Scroll horizontally (left and right).	None
Press thumb button	Press the button on the side of the mouse with your thumb.	Move forward or backward through webpages and/or control media, games, etc.	None

*Note: The examples presented in this column are discussed as they are demonstrated in this module.

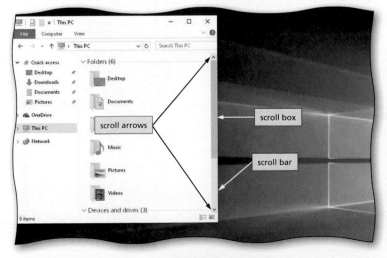

Figure 2

Scrolling

A **scroll bar** is a horizontal or vertical bar that appears when the contents of an area may not be visible completely on the screen (Figure 2). A scroll bar contains **scroll arrows** and a **scroll box** that enable you to view areas that currently cannot be seen on the screen. Clicking the up and down scroll arrows moves the screen content up or down one line. You also can click above or below the scroll box to move up or down a section, or drag the scroll box up or down to move to a specific location.

Keyboard Shortcuts

In many cases, you can use the keyboard instead of the mouse to accomplish a task. To perform tasks using the keyboard, you press one or more keyboard keys, sometimes identified as a **keyboard shortcut**. Some keyboard shortcuts consist of a single key, such as the F1 key. For example, to obtain help in many apps, you can press the F1 key. Other keyboard shortcuts consist of multiple keys, in which case a plus sign separates the key names, such as CTRL+ESC. This notation means to press and hold down the first key listed, press one or more additional keys, and then release all keys. For example, to display the Start menu, press CTRL+ESC, that is, hold down the CTRL key, press the ESC key, and then release both keys.

Starting Windows

It is not unusual for multiple people to use the same computer in a work, educational, recreational, or home setting. Windows enables each user to establish a **user account**, which identifies to Windows the resources, such as apps and storage locations, a user can access when working with the computer.

Each user account has a user name and may have a password and an icon, as well. A **user name** is a unique combination of letters or numbers that identifies a specific user to Windows. A **password** is a private combination of letters, numbers, and special characters associated with the user name that allows access to a user's account resources. An icon is a small image that represents an object; thus, a **user icon** is a picture associated with a user name.

When you turn on a computer, Windows starts and displays a **lock screen** consisting of the time and date (Figure 3). To unlock the screen, click the lock screen. Depending on your computer's settings, Windows may or may not display a sign-in screen that shows the user names and user icons for users who have accounts on the computer. This **sign-in screen** enables you to sign in to your user account and makes the computer available for use. Clicking the user icon begins the process of signing in, also called logging on, to your user account.

BTW
Minimize Wrist Injury
Computer users frequently switch between the keyboard and the mouse during a word processing session; such switching strains the wrist. To help prevent wrist injury, minimize switching. For instance, if your fingers already are on the keyboard, use keyboard keys to scroll. If your hand already is on the mouse, use the mouse to scroll. If your hand is on the touch screen, use touch gestures to scroll.

Figure 3

At the bottom of the sign-in screen is the 'Connect to Internet' button, 'Ease of access' button, and a Shut down button. Clicking the 'Connect to Internet' button displays a list of each network connection and its status. You also can connect to or disconnect from a network. Clicking the 'Ease of access' button displays the Ease of access menu, which provides tools to optimize a computer to accommodate the needs of mobility, hearing, and vision impaired users. Clicking the Shut down button displays a menu containing commands related to putting the computer or mobile device in a low-power state, shutting it down, and restarting the computer or mobile device. The commands available on your computer or mobile device may differ.

- The Sleep command saves your work, turns off the computer fans and hard drive, and places the computer in a lower-power state. To wake the computer from sleep mode, press the power button or lift a laptop's cover, and sign in to your account.
- The Shut down command exits running apps, shuts down Windows, and then turns off the computer.
- The Restart command exits running apps, shuts down Windows, and then restarts Windows.

To Sign In to an Account

1 SIGN IN | 2 USE WINDOWS | 3 USE APPS | 4 FILE MANAGEMENT | 5 SWITCH APPS | 6 SAVE FILES
7 CHANGE SCREEN RESOLUTION | 8 EXIT APPS | 9 USE ADDITIONAL APP FEATURES | 10 USE HELP

The following steps, which use SCSeries as the user name, sign in to an account based on a typical Windows installation. **Why?** *After starting Windows, you might be required to sign in to an account to access the computer or mobile device's resources.* You may need to ask your instructor how to sign in to your account.

- Click the lock screen (shown in Figure 3) to display a sign-in screen.

- Click the user icon (for SCSeries, in this case) on the sign-in screen, which depending on settings, either will display a second sign-in screen that contains a Password text box (Figure 4) or will display the Windows desktop (Figure 5).

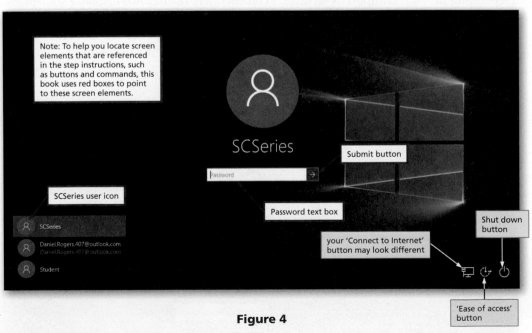

Figure 4

Q&A

Why do I not see a user icon?
Your computer may require you to type a user name instead of clicking an icon.

What is a text box?
A text box is a rectangular box in which you type text.

Why does my screen not show a Password text box?
Your account does not require a password.

- If Windows displays a sign-in screen with a Password text box, type your password in the text box.

2
- Click the Submit button (shown in Figure 4) to sign in to your account and display the Windows desktop (Figure 5).

Q&A Why does my desktop look different from the one in Figure 5?
The Windows desktop is customizable, and your school or employer may have modified the desktop to meet its needs. Also, your screen resolution, which affects the size of the elements on the screen, may differ from the screen resolution used in this book. Later in this module, you learn how to change screen resolution.

How do I type if my tablet has no keyboard?
You can use your fingers to press keys on a keyboard that appears on the screen, called an on-screen keyboard, or you can purchase a separate physical keyboard that attaches to or wirelessly communicates with the tablet.

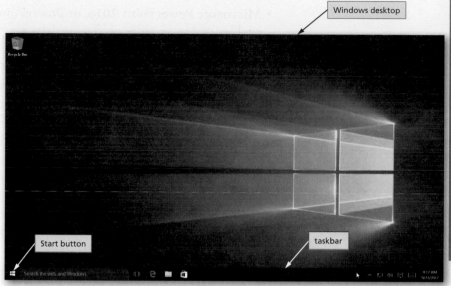

Figure 5

The Windows Desktop

The Windows 10 desktop (shown in Figure 5) and the objects on the desktop emulate a work area in an office. Think of the Windows desktop as an electronic version of the top of your desk. You can perform tasks such as placing objects on the desktop, moving the objects around the desktop, and removing items from the desktop.

When you run an app in Windows 10, it appears on the desktop. Some icons also may be displayed on the desktop. For instance, the icon for the **Recycle Bin**, the location of files that have been deleted, appears on the desktop by default. A **file** is a named unit of storage. Files can contain text, images, audio, and video. You can customize your desktop so that icons representing programs and files you use often appear on your desktop.

Introduction to Microsoft Office 2016

Microsoft Office 2016 is the newest version of Microsoft Office, offering features that provide users with better functionality and easier ways to work with the various files they create. This version of Office also is designed to work more optimally on mobile devices and online.

Microsoft Office 2016 Apps

Microsoft Office 2016 includes a wide variety of apps, such as Word, PowerPoint, Excel, Access, Outlook, Publisher, and OneNote:

- **Microsoft Word 2016**, or Word, is a full-featured word processing app that allows you to create professional-looking documents and revise them easily.

- **Microsoft PowerPoint 2016**, or PowerPoint, is a complete presentation app that enables you to produce professional-looking presentations and then deliver them to an audience.
- **Microsoft Excel 2016**, or Excel, is a powerful spreadsheet app that allows you to organize data, complete calculations, make decisions, graph data, develop professional-looking reports, publish organized data to the web, and access real-time data from websites.
- **Microsoft Access 2016**, or Access, is a database management system that enables you to create a database; add, change, and delete data in the database; ask questions concerning the data in the database; and create forms and reports using the data in the database.
- **Microsoft Outlook 2016**, or Outlook, is a communications and scheduling app that allows you to manage email accounts, calendars, contacts, and access to other Internet content.
- **Microsoft Publisher 2016**, or Publisher, is a desktop publishing app that helps you create professional-quality publications and marketing materials that can be shared easily.
- **Microsoft OneNote 2016**, or OneNote, is a note taking app that allows you to store and share information in notebooks with other people.

Microsoft Office 2016 Suites

A **suite** is a collection of individual apps available together as a unit. Microsoft offers a variety of Office suites, including a stand-alone desktop app, Microsoft Office 365, and Microsoft Office Online. **Microsoft Office 365**, or Office 365, provides plans that allow organizations to use Office in a mobile setting while also being able to communicate and share files, depending upon the type of plan selected by the organization. **Microsoft Office Online** includes apps that allow you to edit and share files on the web using the familiar Office interface.

During the Office 365 installation, you select a plan, and depending on your plan, you receive different apps and services. Office Online apps do not require a local installation and can be accessed through OneDrive and your browser. **OneDrive** is a cloud storage service that provides storage and other services, such as Office Online, to computer and mobile device users.

CONSIDER THIS

How do you sign up for a OneDrive account?

- Use your browser to navigate to onedrive.live.com.
- Create a Microsoft account by clicking the Sign up button and then entering your information to create the account.
- Sign in to OneDrive using your new account or use it in Word to save your files on OneDrive.

Apps in a suite, such as Microsoft Office, typically use a similar interface and share features. Once you are comfortable working with the elements and the interface and performing tasks in one app, the similarity can help you apply the knowledge and skills you have learned to another app(s) in the suite. For example, the process for saving a file in Word is the same in PowerPoint, Excel, and some of the other Office apps. While briefly showing how to use Word, this module illustrates some of the common functions across the Office apps and identifies the characteristics unique to Word.

Running and Using an App

To use an app, you must instruct the operating system to run the app. Windows provides many different ways to run an app, one of which is presented in this section (other ways to run an app are presented throughout this module). After an app is running, you can use it to perform a variety of tasks. The following pages use Word to discuss some elements of the Office interface and to perform tasks that are common to other Office apps.

Word

Word is a full-featured word processing app that allows you to create many types of personal and business documents, including flyers, letters, memos, resumes, reports, fax cover sheets, mailing labels, and newsletters. Word also provides tools that enable you to create webpages and save these webpages directly on a web server. Word has many features designed to simplify the production of documents and add visual appeal. Using Word, you easily can change the shape, size, and color of text. You also can include borders, shading, tables, images, pictures, charts, and web addresses in documents.

To Run an App Using the Start Menu and Create a Blank Document

1 SIGN IN | 2 USE WINDOWS | 3 USE APPS | 4 FILE MANAGEMENT | 5 SWITCH APPS | 6 SAVE FILES
7 CHANGE SCREEN RESOLUTION | 8 EXIT APPS | 9 USE ADDITIONAL APP FEATURES | 10 USE HELP

Across the bottom of the Windows 10 desktop is the taskbar. The taskbar contains the **Start button**, which you use to access apps, files, folders, and settings. A **folder** is a named location on a storage medium that usually contains related documents.

Clicking the Start button displays the Start menu. The **Start menu** allows you to access programs, folders, and files on the computer or mobile device and contains commands that allow you to start programs, store and search for documents, customize the computer or mobile device, and sign out of a user account or shut down the computer or mobile device. A **menu** is a list of related items, including folders, programs, and commands. Each **command** on a menu performs a specific action, such as saving a file or obtaining help. *Why? When you install an app, for example, the app's name will be added to the All apps list on the Start menu.*

The following steps, which assume Windows is running, use the Start menu to run Word and create a blank document based on a typical installation. You may need to ask your instructor how to run Word on your computer. Although the steps illustrate running the Word app, the steps to run any Office app are similar.

- Click the Start button on the Windows 10 taskbar to display the Start menu (Figure 6).

Figure 6

- Click All apps at the bottom of the left pane of the Start menu to display a list of apps installed on the computer or mobile device. If necessary, scroll to display the app you wish to run, Word 2016, in this case (Figure 7).

Figure 7

❸

- If the app you wish to run is located in a folder, click or scroll to and then click the folder in the All apps list to display a list of the folder's contents.

- Click, or scroll to and then click the app name (Word 2016, in this case) in the list to run the selected app (Figure 8).

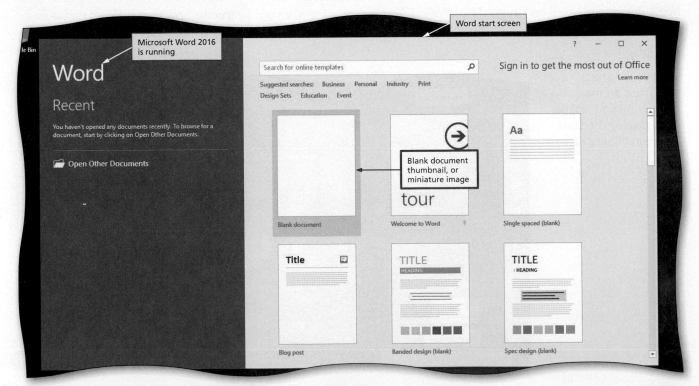

Figure 8

4

- Click the Blank document thumbnail on the Word start screen to create a blank Word document in the Word window (Figure 9).

Q&A

What happens when you run an app?

Some apps provide a means for you to create a blank document, as shown in Figure 8; others immediately display a blank document in an app window, such as the Word window shown in Figure 9. A **window** is a rectangular area that displays data and information. The top of a window has a **title bar**, which is a horizontal space that contains the window's name.

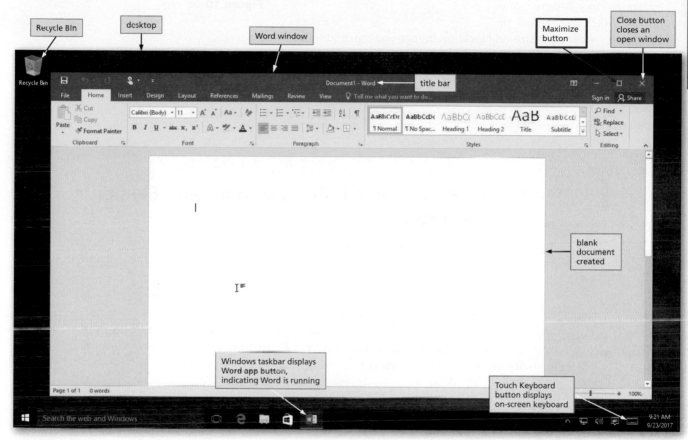

Figure 9

Other Ways
1. Type app name in search box, click app name in results list
2. Double-click file created in app you want to run

To Maximize a Window

1 SIGN IN | 2 USE WINDOWS | 3 USE APPS | 4 FILE MANAGEMENT | 5 SWITCH APPS | 6 SAVE FILES
7 CHANGE SCREEN RESOLUTION | 8 EXIT APPS | 9 USE ADDITIONAL APP FEATURES | 10 USE HELP

Sometimes content is not visible completely in a window. One method of displaying the entire contents of a window is to **maximize** it, or enlarge the window so that it fills the entire screen. The following step maximizes the Word window; however, any Office app's window can be maximized using this step. *Why? A maximized window provides the most space available for using the app.*

- If the Word window is not maximized already, click the Maximize button (shown in Figure 9) next to the Close button on the Word window's title bar to maximize the window (Figure 10).

Q&A

What happened to the Maximize button?

It changed to a Restore Down button, which you can use to return a window to its size and location before you maximized it.

How do I know whether a window is maximized?

A window is maximized if it fills the entire display area and the Restore Down button is displayed on the title bar.

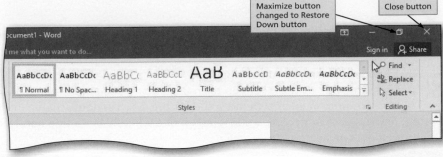

Figure 10

Other Ways

1. Double-click title bar
2. Drag title bar to top of screen

Word Document Window, Ribbon, and Elements Common to Office Apps

The Word window consists of a variety of components to make your work more efficient and documents more professional. These include the document window, ribbon, Tell Me box, mini toolbar, shortcut menus, Quick Access Toolbar, and Microsoft Account area. Most of these components are common to other Microsoft Office apps; others are unique to Word.

You view a portion of a document on the screen through a **document window** (Figure 11). The default (preset) view is **Print Layout view**, which shows the document on a mock sheet of paper in the document window.

Scroll Bars   You use a scroll bar to display different portions of a document in the document window. At the right edge of the document window is a vertical scroll bar. If a document is too wide to fit in the document window, a horizontal scroll bar also appears at the bottom of the document window. On a scroll bar, the position of the scroll box reflects the location of the portion of the document that is displayed in the document window.

BTW

Touch Keyboard
To display the on-screen touch keyboard, click the Touch Keyboard button on the Windows taskbar (shown in Figure 9). When finished using the touch keyboard, click the X button on the touch keyboard to close the keyboard.

Status Bar   The **status bar**, located at the bottom of the document window above the Windows taskbar, presents information about the document, the progress of current tasks, and the status of certain commands and keys; it also provides controls for viewing the document. As you type text or perform certain tasks, various indicators and buttons may appear on the status bar.

The left side of the status bar in Figure 11 shows the current page followed by the total number of pages in the document, the number of words in the document, and an icon to check spelling and grammar. The right side of the status bar includes buttons and controls you can use to change the view of a document and adjust the size of the displayed document.

Ribbon   The ribbon, located near the top of the window below the title bar, is the control center in Word and other Office apps (Figure 12). The ribbon provides easy, central access to the tasks you perform while creating a document. The ribbon consists

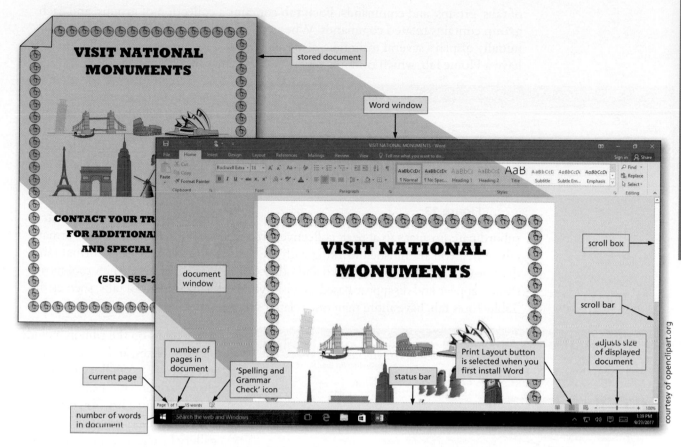

courtesy of openclipart.org

Figure 11

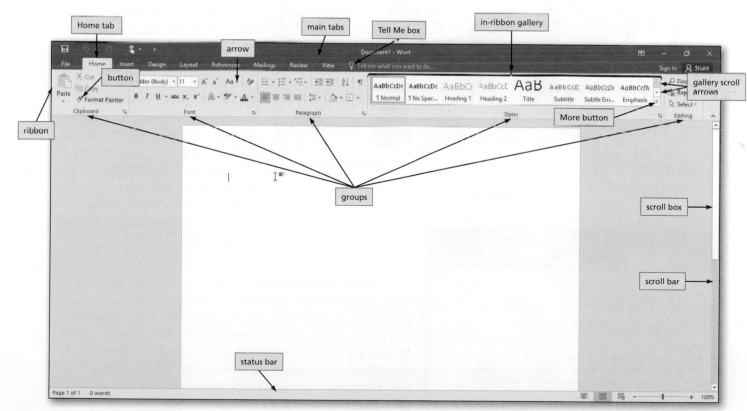

Figure 12

of tabs, groups, and commands. Each **tab** contains a collection of groups, and each **group** contains related commands. When you run an Office app, such as Word, it initially displays several main tabs, also called default or top-level tabs. All Office apps have a Home tab, which contains the more frequently used commands.

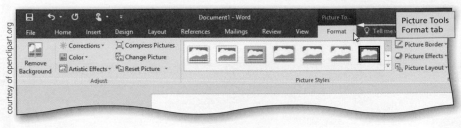

Figure 13

In addition to the main tabs, the Office apps display **tool tabs**, also called contextual tabs (Figure 13), when you perform certain tasks or work with objects such as pictures or tables. If you insert a picture in a Word document, for example, the Picture Tools tab and its related subordinate Format tab appear, collectively referred to as the Picture Tools Format tab. When you are finished working with the picture, the Picture Tools Format tab disappears from the ribbon. Word and other Office apps determine when tool tabs should appear and disappear based on tasks you perform. Some tool tabs, such as the Table Tools tab, have more than one related subordinate tab.

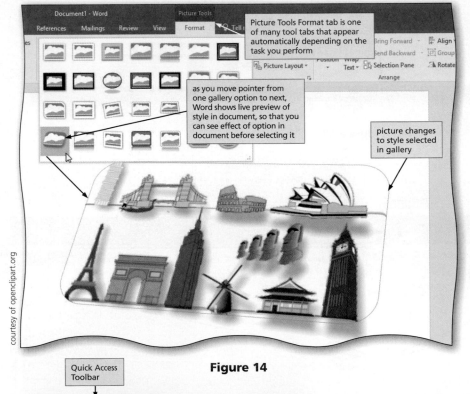

Figure 14

Items on the ribbon include buttons, boxes, and galleries (shown in Figure 12). A **gallery** is a set of choices, often graphical, arranged in a grid or in a list. You can scroll through choices in an in-ribbon gallery by clicking the gallery's scroll arrows. Or, you can click a gallery's More button to view more gallery options on the screen at a time.

Some buttons and boxes have arrows that, when clicked, also display a gallery; others always cause a gallery to be displayed when clicked. Most galleries support **live preview**, which is a feature that allows you to point to a gallery choice and see its effect in the document — without actually selecting the choice (Figure 14). Live preview works only if you are using a mouse; if you are using a touch screen, you will not be able to view live previews.

Some commands on the ribbon display an image to help you remember their function. When you point to a command on the ribbon, all or part of the command glows in a shade of gray, and a ScreenTip appears on the screen. A **ScreenTip** is an on-screen note that provides the name of the command, available keyboard shortcut(s), a description of the command, and sometimes instructions for how to obtain help about the command (Figure 15).

Figure 15

Some groups on the ribbon have a small arrow in the lower-right corner, called a **Dialog Box Launcher**, that when clicked, displays a dialog box or a task pane with additional options for the group (Figure 16). When presented with a dialog box, you make selections and must close the dialog box before returning to the document. A **task pane**, in contrast to a dialog box, is a window that can remain open and visible while you work in the document.

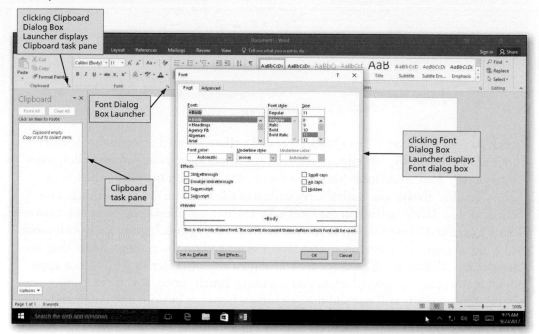

Figure 16

Tell Me Box The **Tell Me box**, which appears to the right of the tabs on the ribbon, is a type of search box that helps you to perform specific tasks in an Office app (Figure 17). As you type in the Tell Me box, the word-wheeling feature displays search results that are refined as you type. For example, if you want to center text in a document, you can type "center" in the Tell Me box and then select the appropriate command. The Tell Me box also lists the last five commands accessed from the box.

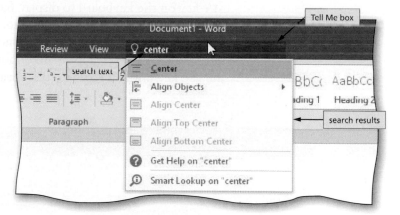

Figure 17

Mini Toolbar The **mini toolbar**, which appears automatically based on tasks you perform, contains commands related to changing the appearance of text in a document (Figure 18). If you do not use the mini toolbar, it disappears from the screen. The buttons, arrows, and boxes on the mini toolbar vary, depending on whether you are using Touch mode versus Mouse mode. If you right-click an item in the document window, Word displays both the mini toolbar and a shortcut menu, which is discussed in a later section in this module.

All commands on the mini toolbar also exist on the ribbon. The purpose of the mini toolbar is to minimize hand or mouse movement.

BTW

Turning Off the Mini Toolbar
If you do not want the mini toolbar to appear, click File on the ribbon to open the Backstage view, click the Options tab in the Backstage view, if necessary, click General (Options dialog box), remove the check mark from the 'Show Mini Toolbar on selection' check box, and then click the OK button.

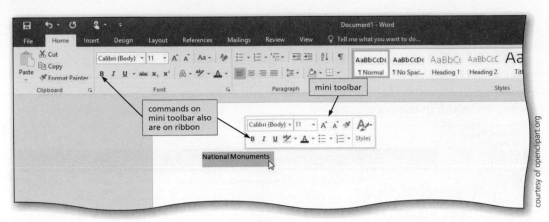

Figure 18

Quick Access Toolbar   The **Quick Access Toolbar**, located initially (by default) above the ribbon at the left edge of the title bar, provides convenient, one-click access to frequently used commands (shown in Figure 15). The commands on the Quick Access Toolbar always are available, regardless of the task you are performing. The Touch/Mouse Mode button on the Quick Access Toolbar allows you to switch between Touch mode and Mouse mode. If you primarily are using touch gestures, Touch mode will add more space between commands on menus and on the ribbon so that they are easier to tap. While touch gestures are convenient ways to interact with Office apps, not all features are supported when you are using Touch mode. If you are using a mouse, Mouse mode will not add the extra space between buttons and commands. The Quick Access Toolbar is discussed in more depth later in the module.

BTW
Touch Mode
The Office and Windows interfaces may vary if you are using Touch mode. For this reason, you might notice that the function or appearance of your touch screen in Word differs slightly from this module's presentation.

KeyTips   If you prefer using the keyboard instead of the mouse, you can press the ALT key on the keyboard to display **KeyTips**, or keyboard code icons, for certain commands (Figure 19). To select a command using the keyboard, press the letter or number displayed in the KeyTip, which may cause additional KeyTips related to the selected command to appear. To remove KeyTips from the screen, press the ALT key or the ESC key until all KeyTips disappear, or click anywhere in the app window.

Figure 19

Microsoft Account Area   In this area, you can use the Sign in link to sign in to your Microsoft account. Once signed in, you will see your account information, as well as a picture if you have included one in your Microsoft account.

To Display a Different Tab on the Ribbon

1 SIGN IN | 2 USE WINDOWS | 3 USE APPS | 4 FILE MANAGEMENT | 5 SWITCH APPS | 6 SAVE FILES
7 CHANGE SCREEN RESOLUTION | 8 EXIT APPS | 9 USE ADDITIONAL APP FEATURES | 10 USE HELP

When you run Word, the ribbon displays nine main tabs: File, Home, Insert, Design, Layout, References, Mailings, Review, and View. The tab currently displayed is called the **active tab**.

The following step displays the Insert tab, that is, makes it the active tab. *Why? When working with an Office app, you may need to switch tabs to access other options for working with a document.*

1

- Click Insert on the ribbon to display the Insert tab (Figure 20).

Experiment

- Click the other tabs on the ribbon to view their contents. When you are finished, click Insert on the ribbon to redisplay the Insert tab.

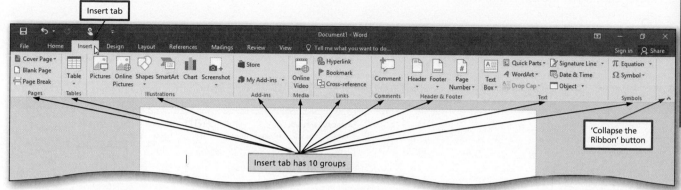

Figure 20

Other Ways

1. Press ALT, press letter corresponding to tab to display   2. Press ALT, press LEFT ARROW or RIGHT ARROW until desired tab is displayed

To Collapse and Expand the Ribbon and Use Full Screen Mode

1 SIGN IN | 2 USE WINDOWS | 3 USE APPS | 4 FILE MANAGEMENT | 5 SWITCH APPS | 6 SAVE FILES
7 CHANGE SCREEN RESOLUTION | 8 EXIT APPS | 9 USE ADDITIONAL APP FEATURES | 10 USE HELP

To display more of a document or other item in the window of an Office app, some users prefer to collapse the ribbon, which hides the groups on the ribbon and displays only the main tabs, or to use **Full Screen mode**, which hides all the commands and just displays the document. Each time you run an Office app, such as Word, the ribbon appears the same way it did the last time you used that Office app. The modules in this book, however, begin with the ribbon appearing as it did at the initial installation of Office or Word.

The following steps collapse, expand, and restore the ribbon in Word and then switch to Full Screen mode. *Why? If you need more space on the screen to work with your document, you may consider collapsing the ribbon or switching to Full Screen mode to gain additional workspace.*

1

- Click the 'Collapse the Ribbon' button on the ribbon (shown in Figure 20) to collapse the ribbon (Figure 21).

Q&A What happened to the 'Collapse the Ribbon' button?
The 'Pin the ribbon' button replaces the 'Collapse the Ribbon' button when the ribbon is collapsed. You will see the 'Pin the ribbon' button only when you expand a ribbon by clicking a tab.

Figure 21

• Click Home on the ribbon to expand the Home tab (Figure 22).

Q&A
Why would I click the Home tab?
If you want to use a command on a collapsed ribbon, click the main tab to display the groups for that tab. After you select a command on the ribbon and resume working in the document, the groups will be collapsed once again. If you decide not to use a command on the ribbon, you can collapse the groups by clicking the same main tab or clicking in the app window.

Experiment

• Click Home on the ribbon to collapse the groups again. Click Home on the ribbon to expand the Home tab.

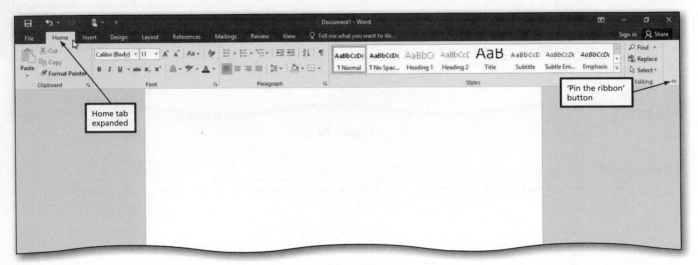

Figure 22

3

• Click the 'Pin the ribbon' button on the expanded Home tab to restore the ribbon.

• Click the 'Ribbon Display Options' button to display the Ribbon Display Options menu (Figure 23).

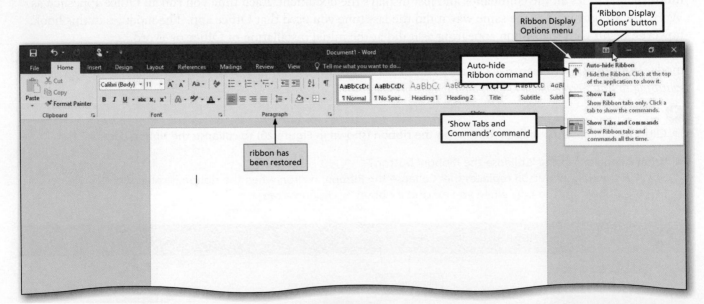

Figure 23

Office 2016 and Windows 10 Module

4
- Click Auto-hide Ribbon to use Full Screen mode, which hides all the commands from the screen (Figure 24).
- Click the ellipsis to display the ribbon temporarily.
- Click the 'Ribbon Display Options' button to display the Ribbon Display Options menu (shown in Figure 23).
- Click 'Show Tabs and Commands' on the Ribbon Display Options menu to exit Full Screen mode.

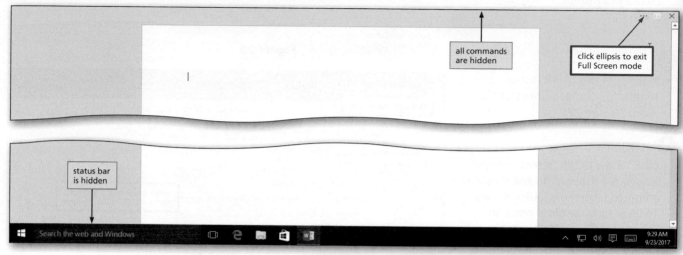

Figure 24

Other Ways

1. Double-click a main tab on the ribbon
2. Press CTRL+F1

To Use a Shortcut Menu to Relocate the Quick Access Toolbar

1 SIGN IN | 2 USE WINDOWS | 3 USE APPS | 4 FILE MANAGEMENT | 5 SWITCH APPS | 6 SAVE FILES
7 CHANGE SCREEN RESOLUTION | 8 EXIT APPS | 9 USE ADDITIONAL APP FEATURES | 10 USE HELP

When you right-click certain areas of the Word and other Office app windows, a shortcut menu will appear. A **shortcut menu** is a list of frequently used commands that relate to an object. *Why? You can use shortcut menus to access common commands quickly.* When you right-click the status bar, for example, a shortcut menu appears with commands related to the status bar. When you right-click the Quick Access Toolbar, a shortcut menu appears with commands related to the Quick Access Toolbar. The following steps use a shortcut menu to move the Quick Access Toolbar, which by default is located on the title bar.

1
- Right-click the Quick Access Toolbar to display a shortcut menu that presents a list of commands related to the Quick Access Toolbar (Figure 25).

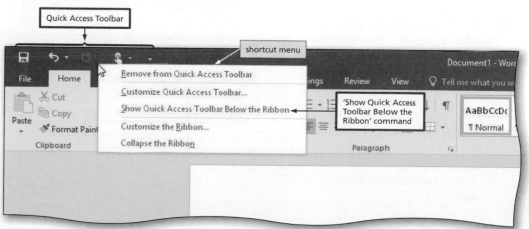

Figure 25

- Click 'Show Quick Access Toolbar Below the Ribbon' on the shortcut menu to display the Quick Access Toolbar below the ribbon (Figure 26).

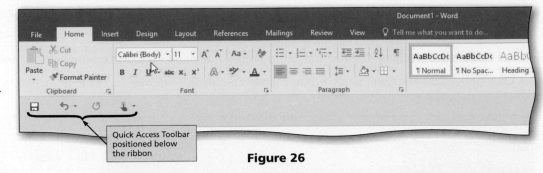

Quick Access Toolbar positioned below the ribbon

Figure 26

- Right-click the Quick Access Toolbar to display a shortcut menu (Figure 27).

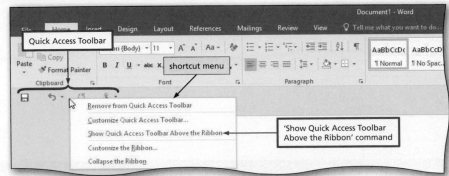

- Click 'Show Quick Access Toolbar Above the Ribbon' on the shortcut menu to return the Quick Access Toolbar to its original position (shown in Figure 25).

Figure 27

Other Ways

1. Click 'Customize Quick Access Toolbar' button on Quick Access Toolbar, click 'Show Below the Ribbon' or 'Show Above the Ribbon'

To Customize the Quick Access Toolbar

1 SIGN IN | 2 USE WINDOWS | 3 USE APPS | 4 FILE MANAGEMENT | 5 SWITCH APPS | 6 SAVE FILES
7 CHANGE SCREEN RESOLUTION | 8 EXIT APPS | 9 USE ADDITIONAL APP FEATURES | 10 USE HELP

The Quick Access Toolbar provides easy access to some of the more frequently used commands in the Office apps. By default, the Quick Access Toolbar contains buttons for the Save, Undo, and Redo commands. If your computer or mobile device has a touch screen, the Quick Access Toolbar also might display the Touch/ Mouse Mode button. You can customize the Quick Access Toolbar by changing its location in the window, as shown in the previous steps, and by adding more buttons to reflect commands you would like to access easily. The following steps add the Quick Print button to the Quick Access Toolbar in the Word window. *Why? Adding the Quick Print button to the Quick Access Toolbar speeds up the process of printing.*

- Click the 'Customize Quick Access Toolbar' button to display the Customize Quick Access Toolbar menu (Figure 28).

Q&A | Which commands are listed on the Customize Quick Access Toolbar menu?
It lists commands that commonly are added to the Quick Access Toolbar.

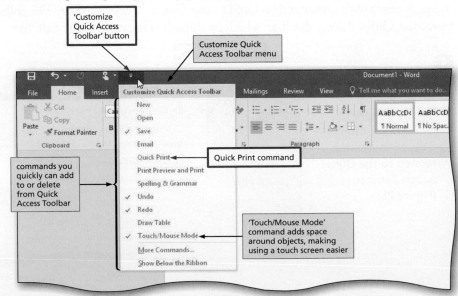

Figure 28

- If it is not selected already, click
Quick Print on the Customize
Quick Access Toolbar menu to
add the Quick Print button to the
Quick Access Toolbar (Figure 29).

Q&A How would I remove a button
from the Quick Access Toolbar?
You would right-click the button
you wish to remove and then
click 'Remove from Quick Access
Toolbar' on the shortcut menu or
click the 'Customize Quick Access
Toolbar' button on the Quick Access
Toolbar and then click the button name in the Customize Quick Access Toolbar menu to remove the check mark.

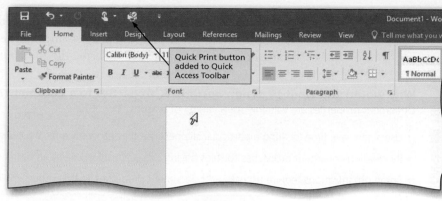

Figure 29

To Enter Text in a Document

1 SIGN IN | 2 USE WINDOWS | 3 USE APPS | 4 FILE MANAGEMENT | 5 SWITCH APPS | 6 SAVE FILES
7 CHANGE SCREEN RESOLUTION | 8 EXIT APPS | 9 USE ADDITIONAL APP FEATURES | 10 USE HELP

The first step in creating a document is to enter its text by typing on the keyboard. By default, Word positions text at the left margin as you type. The following steps type this first line of a flyer. **Why?** *To begin creating a flyer, for example, you type the headline in the document window.*

- Type **VISIT NATIONAL MONUMENTS** as the text (Figure 30).

Q&A What is the blinking vertical bar to the right of the text?
The blinking bar is the insertion point, which indicates where text, graphics, and other items will be inserted in the document. As you type, the insertion point moves to the right, and when you reach the end of a line, it moves down to the beginning of the next line.

What if I make an error while typing?
You can press the BACKSPACE key until you have deleted the text in error and then retype the text correctly.

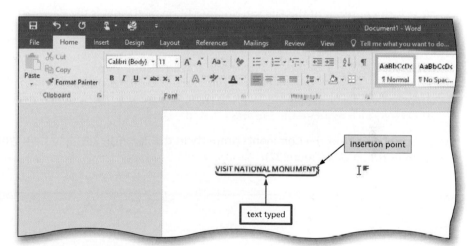

Figure 30

- Press the ENTER key to move the insertion point to the beginning of the next line (Figure 31).

Q&A Why did blank space appear between the entered text and the insertion point?
Each time you press the ENTER key, Word creates a new paragraph and inserts blank space between the two paragraphs. Depending on your settings, Word may or may not insert a blank space between the two paragraphs.

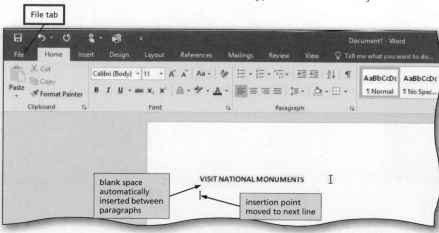

Figure 31

Document Properties

You can organize and identify your files by using **document properties**, which are the details about a file, such as the project author, title, and subject. For example, a class name or document topic can describe the file's purpose or content.

CONSIDER THIS

Why would you want to assign document properties to a document?
Document properties are valuable for a variety of reasons:

- Users can save time locating a particular file because they can view a file's document properties without opening the file.

- By creating consistent properties for files having similar content, users can better organize their files.

- Some organizations require users to add document properties so that other employees can view details about these files.

To Change Document Properties

1 SIGN IN | 2 USE WINDOWS | 3 USE APPS | 4 FILE MANAGEMENT | 5 SWITCH APPS | 6 SAVE FILES
7 CHANGE SCREEN RESOLUTION | 8 EXIT APPS | 9 USE ADDITIONAL APP FEATURES | 10 USE HELP

You can change the document properties while working with the file in an Office app. When you save the file, the Office app (Word, in this case) will save the document properties with the file. The following steps change document properties. *Why? Adding document properties will help you identify characteristics of the file without opening it.*

1

- Click File on the ribbon (shown in Figure 31) to open the Backstage view and then, if necessary, click the Info tab in the Backstage view to display the Info gallery.

Q&A

What is the purpose of the File tab on the ribbon, and what is the Backstage view?
The File tab opens the Backstage view for each Office app, including Word. The **Backstage view** contains a set of commands that enable you to manage documents and provides data about the documents.

What is the purpose of the Info gallery in the Backstage view?
The Info tab, which is selected by default when you click File on the ribbon, displays the Info gallery, where you can protect a document, inspect a document, and manage versions of a document, as well as view all the file properties, such as when the file was created.

- Click to the right of the Comments property in the Properties list and then type   **CIS 101 Assignment**   in the Comments text box (Figure 32).

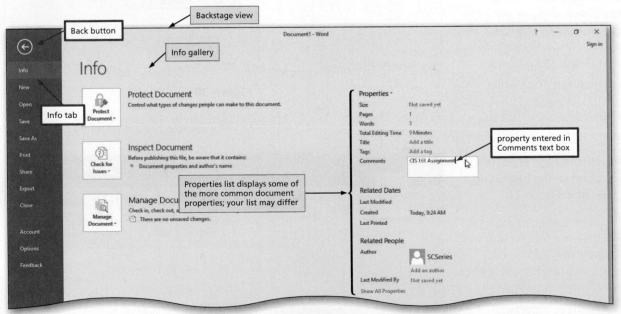

Figure 32

2

- Click the Back button in the upper-left corner of the Backstage view to return to the document window.

Printing, Saving, and Organizing Files

While you are creating a document, the computer or mobile device stores it in memory. When you save a document, the computer or mobile device places it on a storage medium, such as a hard disk, solid state drive (SSD), USB flash drive, or optical disc. The storage medium can be permanent in your computer, may be portable where you remove it from your computer, or may be on a web server you access through a network or the Internet.

A saved document is referred to as a file. A **file name** is the name assigned to a file when it is saved. When saving files, you should organize them so that you easily can find them later. Windows provides tools to help you organize files.

> **BTW**
>
> **File Type**
> Depending on your Windows settings, the file type .docx may be displayed immediately to the right of the file name after you save the file. The file type .docx is a Word 2016 document.

Printing a Document

After creating a document, you may want to print it. Printing a document enables you to distribute it to others in a form that can be read or viewed but typically not edited.

CONSIDER THIS

What is the best method for distributing a document?

The traditional method of distributing a document uses a printer to produce a hard copy. A **hard copy** or **printout** is information that exists on a physical medium, such as paper. Hard copies can be useful for the following reasons:

- Some people prefer proofreading a hard copy of a document rather than viewing it on the screen to check for errors and readability.

- Hard copies can serve as a backup reference if your storage medium is lost or becomes corrupted and you need to recreate the document.

Instead of distributing a hard copy of a document, users can distribute the document as an electronic image that mirrors the original document's appearance. The electronic image of the document can be sent as an email attachment, posted on a website, or copied to a portable storage medium, such as a USB flash drive. Two popular electronic image formats, sometimes called fixed formats, are PDF by Adobe Systems and XPS by Microsoft. In Word, you can create electronic image files through the Save As dialog box and the Export, Share, and Print tabs in the Backstage view. Electronic images of documents, such as PDF and XPS, can be useful for the following reasons:

- Users can view electronic images of documents without the software that created the original document (e.g., Word). For example, to view a PDF file you use a program called Adobe Reader, which can be downloaded free from Adobe's website.

- Sending electronic documents saves paper and printer supplies. Society encourages users to contribute to **green computing**, which involves reducing the electricity consumed and environmental waste generated when using computers, mobile devices, and related technologies.

To Print a Document

1 SIGN IN | 2 USE WINDOWS | 3 USE APPS | 4 FILE MANAGEMENT | 5 SWITCH APPS | 6 SAVE FILES
7 CHANGE SCREEN RESOLUTION | 8 EXIT APPS | 9 USE ADDITIONAL APP FEATURES | 10 USE HELP

With the document opened, you may want to print it. *Why? Because you want to see how the text will appear on paper, you want to print a hard copy on a printer.* The following steps print a hard copy of the contents of the document.

- Click File on the ribbon to open the Backstage view.
- Click the Print tab in the Backstage view to display the Print gallery (Figure 33).

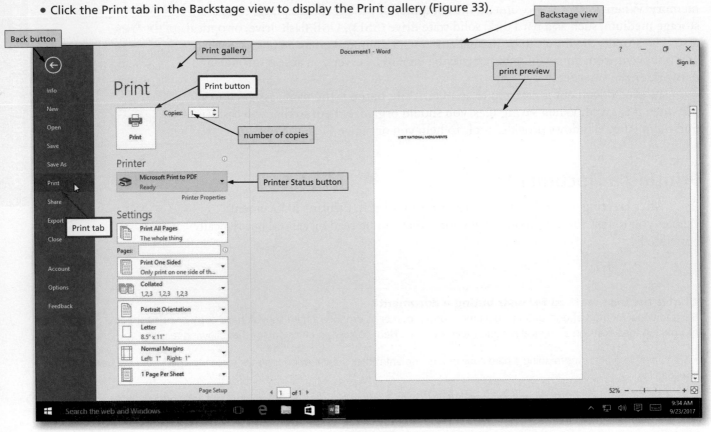

Figure 33

Q&A How can I print multiple copies of my document?
Increase the number in the Copies box in the Print gallery.

What if I decide not to print the document at this time?
Click the Back button in the upper-left corner of the Backstage view to return to the document window.

- Verify that the selected printer will print a hard copy of the document. If necessary, click the Printer Status button to display a list of available printer options and then click the desired printer to change the currently selected printer.

- Click the Print button in the Print gallery to print the document on the currently selected printer.

- When the printer stops, retrieve the hard copy (Figure 34).

Q&A What if I want to print an electronic image of a document instead of a hard copy?
You would click the Printer Status button in the Print gallery and then select the desired electronic image option, such as Microsoft XPS Document Writer, which would create an XPS file.

VISIT NATIONAL MONUMENTS

Figure 34

Other Ways

1. Press CTRL+P

Organizing Files and Folders

A file contains data. This data can range from a research paper to an accounting spreadsheet to an electronic math quiz. You should organize and store files in folders to avoid misplacing a file and to help you find a file quickly.

If you are taking an introductory computer class (CIS 101, for example), you may want to design a series of folders for the different subjects covered in the class. To accomplish this, you can arrange the folders in a hierarchy for the class, as shown in Figure 35. The hierarchy contains three levels. The first level contains the storage medium, such as a hard drive. The second level contains the class folder (CIS 101, in this case), and the third level contains seven folders, one each for a different Office app that will be covered in the class (Word, PowerPoint, Excel, Access, Outlook, Publisher, and OneNote).

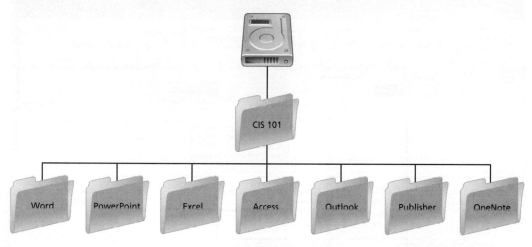

Figure 35

When the hierarchy in Figure 35 is created, the storage medium is said to contain the CIS 101 folder, and the CIS 101 folder is said to contain the separate Office folders (i.e., Word, PowerPoint, Excel, etc.). In addition, this hierarchy easily can be expanded to include folders from other classes taken during additional semesters.

The vertical and horizontal lines in Figure 35 form a pathway that allows you to navigate to a drive or folder on a computer or network. A **path** consists of a drive letter (preceded by a drive name when necessary) and colon, to identify the storage device, and one or more folder names. A hard drive typically has a drive letter of C. Each drive or folder in the hierarchy has a corresponding path.

By default, Windows saves documents in the Documents folder, music in the Music folder, photos in the Pictures folder, videos in the Videos folder, and downloads in the Downloads folder.

The following pages illustrate the steps to organize the folders for this class and save a file in a folder:

1. Create the folder identifying your class.
2. Create the Word folder in the folder identifying your class.
3. Save a file in the Word folder.
4. Verify the location of the saved file.

To Create a Folder

When you create a folder, such as the CIS 101 folder shown in Figure 35, you must name the folder. A folder name should describe the folder and its contents. A folder name can contain spaces and any uppercase or lowercase characters, except a backslash (\), slash (/), colon (:), asterisk (*), question mark (?), quotation marks ("), less than symbol (<), greater than symbol (>), or vertical bar (|). Folder names cannot be CON, AUX, COM1, COM2, COM3, COM4, LPT1, LPT2, LPT3, PRN, or NUL. The same rules for naming folders also apply to naming files.

The following steps create a class folder (CIS 101, in this case) in the Documents folder. *Why? When storing files, you should organize the files so that it will be easier to find them later.*

1
- Click the File Explorer button on the taskbar to run File Explorer.

- If necessary, double-click This PC in the navigation pane to expand the contents of your computer.

- Click the Documents folder in the navigation pane to display the contents of the Documents folder in the file list (Figure 36).

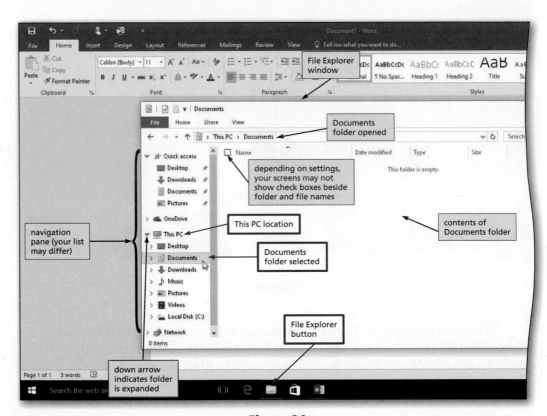

Figure 36

2
- Click the New folder button on the Quick Access Toolbar to create a new folder with the name, New folder, selected in a text box (Figure 37).

Q&A
Why is the folder icon displayed differently on my computer or mobile device?
Windows might be configured to display contents differently on your computer or mobile device.

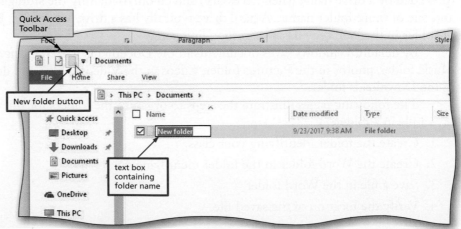

Figure 37

- Type CIS 101 (or your class code) in the text box as the new folder name.

  If requested by your instructor, add your last name to the end of the folder name.

- Press the ENTER key to change the folder name from New folder to a folder name identifying your class (Figure 38).

Q&A | What happens when I press the ENTER key?
| The class folder (CIS 101, in this case) is displayed in the file list, which contains the folder name, date modified, type, and size.

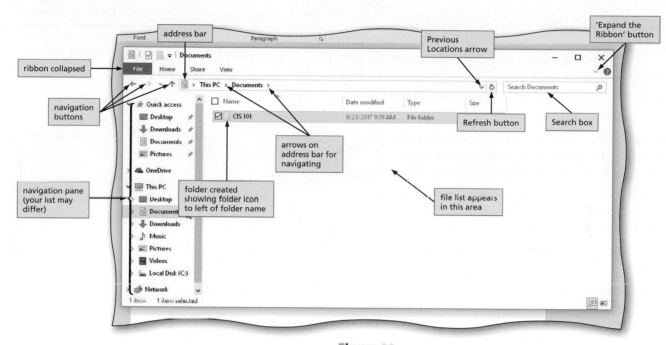

Figure 38

Other Ways

1. Press CTRL+SHIFT+N

2. Click the New folder button (Home tab | New group)

Folder Windows

The File Explorer window (shown in Figure 38) is called a folder window. Recall that a folder is a specific named location on a storage medium that contains related files. Most users rely on **folder windows** for finding, viewing, and managing information on their computers. Folder windows have common design elements, including the following (shown in Figure 38).

- The **address bar** provides quick navigation options. The arrows on the address bar allow you to visit different locations on the computer or mobile device.
- The buttons to the left of the address bar allow you to navigate the contents of the navigation pane and view recent pages.
- The **Previous Locations arrow** displays the locations you have visited.
- The **Refresh button** on the right side of the address bar refreshes the contents of the folder list.
- The **Search box** contains the dimmed words, Search Documents. You can type a term in the search box for a list of files, folders, shortcuts, and elements containing that term within the location you are searching.

- The **ribbon** contains four tabs used to accomplish various tasks on the computer or mobile device related to organizing and managing the contents of the open window. This ribbon works similarly to the ribbon in the Office apps.
- The **navigation pane** on the left contains the Quick access area, the OneDrive area, the This PC area, and the Network area.
- The **Quick access area** shows locations you access frequently. By default, this list contains links only to your Desktop, Downloads, Documents, and Pictures.

To Create a Folder within a Folder

1 SIGN IN | 2 USE WINDOWS | 3 USE APPS | 4 FILE MANAGEMENT | 5 SWITCH APPS | 6 SAVE FILES
7 CHANGE SCREEN RESOLUTION | 8 EXIT APPS | 9 USE ADDITIONAL APP FEATURES | 10 USE HELP

With the class folder created, you can create folders that will store the files you create using Word. The following step creates a Word folder in the CIS 101 folder (or the folder identifying your class). *Why? To be able to organize your files, you should create a folder structure.*

- Double-click the icon or folder name for the CIS 101 folder (or the folder identifying your class) in the file list to open the folder.
- Click the New folder button on the Quick Access Toolbar to create a new folder with the name, New folder, selected in a text box folder.
- Type **Word** in the text box as the new folder name.
- Press the ENTER key to rename the folder (Figure 39).

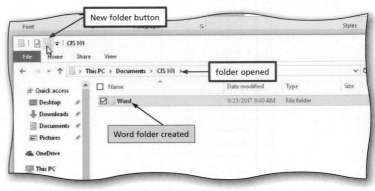

Figure 39

Other Ways

1. Press CTRL+SHIFT+N
2. Click the New folder button (Home tab | New group)

To Expand a Folder, Scroll through Folder Contents, and Collapse a Folder

1 SIGN IN | 2 USE WINDOWS | 3 USE APPS | 4 FILE MANAGEMENT | 5 SWITCH APPS | 6 SAVE FILES
7 CHANGE SCREEN RESOLUTION | 8 EXIT APPS | 9 USE ADDITIONAL APP FEATURES | 10 USE HELP

Folder windows display the hierarchy of items and the contents of drives and folders in the file list. You might want to expand a folder in the navigation pane to view its contents, scroll through its contents, and collapse it when you are finished viewing its contents. *Why? When a folder is expanded, you can see all the folders it contains. By contrast, a collapsed folder hides the folders it contains.* The following steps expand, scroll through, and then collapse the folder identifying your class (CIS 101, in this case).

- Double-click the Documents folder in the This PC area of the navigation pane, which expands the folder to display its contents and displays a black down arrow to the left of the Documents folder icon (Figure 40).

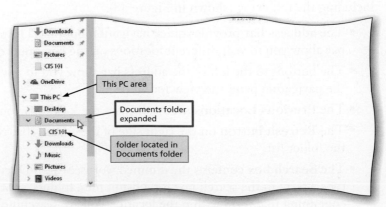

Figure 40

Office 2016 and Windows 10 Module

- Double-click the CIS 101 folder, which expands the folder to display its contents and displays a black down arrow to the left of the folder icon (Figure 41).

Experiment

- Drag the scroll box down or click the down scroll arrow on the vertical scroll bar to display additional folders at the bottom of the navigation pane. Drag the scroll box up or click the scroll bar above the scroll box to move the scroll box to the top of the navigation pane. Drag the scroll box down the scroll bar until the scroll box is halfway down the scroll bar.

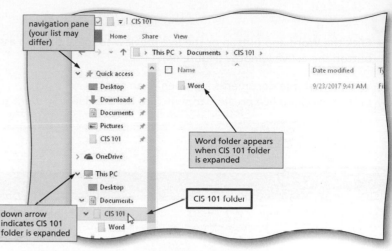

Figure 41

- Double-click the folder identifying your class (CIS 101, in this case) to collapse the folder (Figure 42).

Q&A Why are some folders indented below others?
A folder contains the indented folders below it.

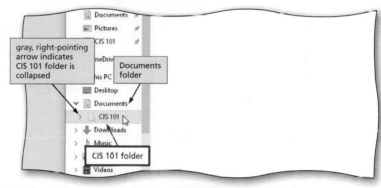

Figure 42

Other Ways

1. Point to display arrows in navigation pane, click arrow to expand or collapse
2. Select folder to expand or collapse using arrow keys, press RIGHT ARROW to expand; press LEFT ARROW to collapse

To Switch from One App to Another

1 SIGN IN | 2 USE WINDOWS | 3 USE APPS | 4 FILE MANAGEMENT | 5 SWITCH APPS | 6 SAVE FILES
7 CHANGE SCREEN RESOLUTION | 8 EXIT APPS | 9 USE ADDITIONAL APP FEATURES | 10 USE HELP

The next step is to save the Word file containing the headline you typed earlier. Word, however, currently is not the active window. You can use the Word app button on the taskbar and live preview to switch to Word and then save the document in the Word document window.

Why? *By clicking the appropriate app button on the taskbar, you can switch to the running app you want to use.* The following steps switch to the Word window; however, the steps are the same for any active Office app currently displayed as a button on the taskbar.

- Point to the Word app button on the taskbar to see a live preview of the open document(s) or the window title(s) of the open document(s), depending on your computer's configuration (Figure 43).

Q&A What if I am using a touch screen?
Live preview will not work if you are using a touch screen. If you are using a touch screen and do not have a mouse, proceed to Step 2.

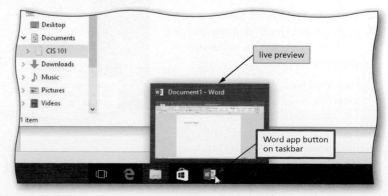

Figure 43

- Click the Word app button or the live preview to make the app associated with the app button the active window (Figure 44).

Q&A What if multiple documents are open in an app?
Click the desired live preview to switch to the window you want to use.

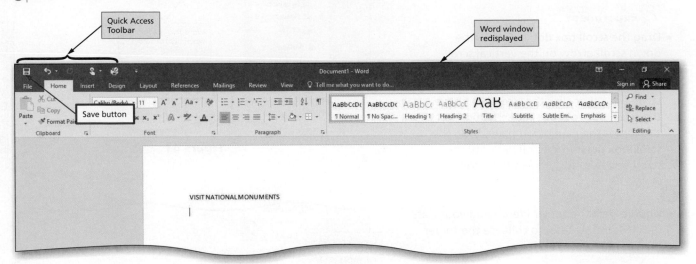

Figure 44

Other Ways

1. Press ALT+TAB until app you wish to display is selected

To Save a File in a Folder

With the Word folder created, you can save the Word document shown in the document window in the Word folder. *Why? Without saving a file, you may lose all the work you have completed and will be unable to reuse or share it with others later.* The following steps save a file in the Word folder contained in your class folder (CIS 101, in this case) using the file name, National Monuments.

- Click the Save button (shown in Figure 44) on the Quick Access Toolbar, which depending on settings, will display either the Save As gallery in the Backstage view (Figure 45) or the Save As dialog box (Figure 46).

Q&A What if the Save As gallery is not displayed in the Backstage view?
Click the Save As tab to display the Save As gallery.

How do I close the Backstage view?
Click the Back button in the upper-left corner of the Backstage view to return to the Word window.

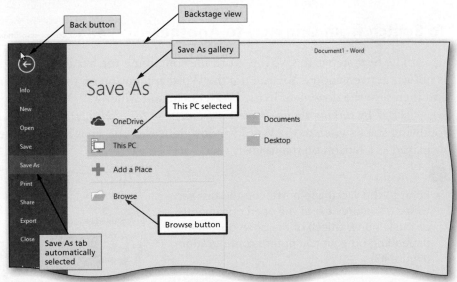

Figure 45

2

- If your screen displays the Backstage view, click This PC, if necessary, to display options in the right pane related to saving on your computer or mobile device; if your screen already displays the Save As dialog box, proceed to Step 3.

Q&A What if I wanted to save on OneDrive instead?
You would click OneDrive. Saving on OneDrive is discussed in a later section in this module.

- Click the Browse button in the left pane to display the Save As dialog box (Figure 46).

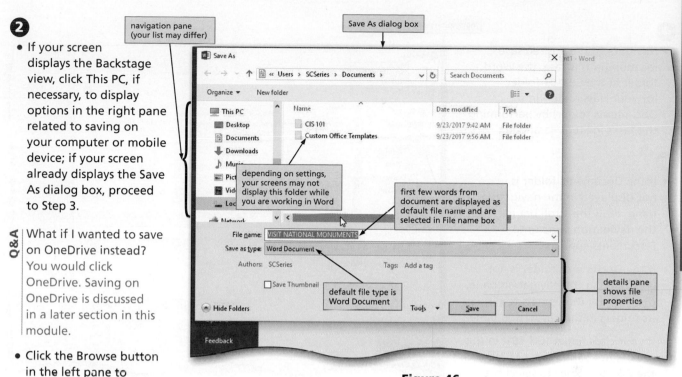

Figure 46

Q&A Why does a file name already appear in the File name box?
Word automatically suggests a file name the first time you save a document. The file name normally consists of the first few words contained in the document. Because the suggested file name is selected, you do not need to delete it; as soon as you begin typing, the new file name replaces the selected text.

3

- Type **National Monuments** in the File name box (Save As dialog box) to change the file name. Do not press the ENTER key after typing the file name because you do not want to close the dialog box at this time (Figure 47).

Q&A What characters can I use in a file name?
The only invalid characters are the backslash (\), slash (/), colon (:), asterisk (*), question mark (?), quotation mark ("), less than symbol (<), greater than symbol (>), and vertical bar (|).

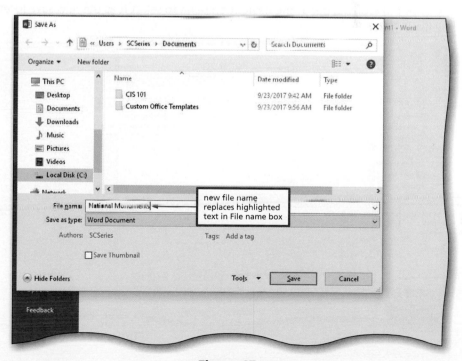

Figure 47

4

- Navigate to the desired save location (in this case, the Word folder in the CIS 101 folder [or your class folder] in the Documents folder) by performing the tasks in Steps 4a and 4b.

- If the Documents folder is not displayed in the navigation pane, drag the scroll bar in the navigation pane until Documents appears.

- If the Documents folder is not expanded in the navigation pane, double-click Documents to display its folders in the navigation pane.

- If your class folder (CIS 101, in this case) is not expanded, double-click the CIS 101 folder to select the folder and display its contents in the navigation pane (Figure 48).

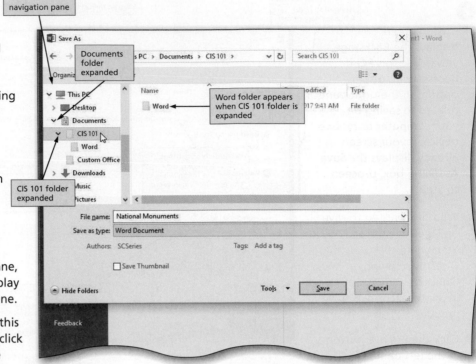

Figure 48

Q&A | What if I do not want to save in a folder?
Although storing files in folders is an effective technique for organizing files, some users prefer not to store files in folders. If you prefer not to save this file in a folder, select the storage device on which you wish to save the file and then proceed to Step 5.

- Click the Word folder in the navigation pane to select it as the new save location and display its contents in the file list (Figure 49).

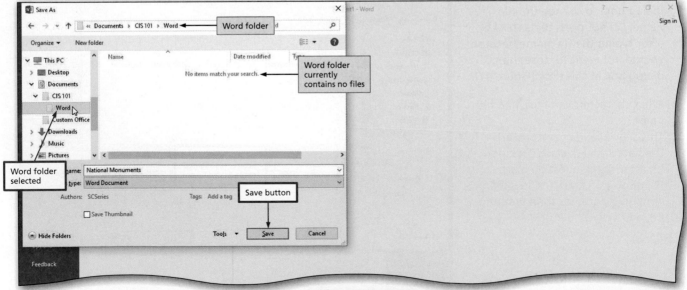

Figure 49

5

- Click the Save button (Save As dialog box) to save the document in the selected folder in the selected location with the entered file name (Figure 50).

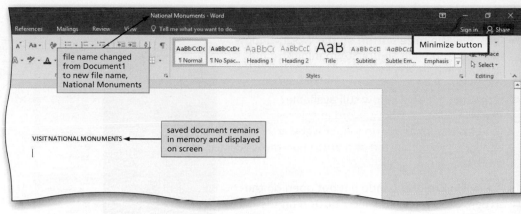

Figure 50

Q&A

How do I know that the file is saved?

While an Office app such as Word is saving a file, it briefly displays a message on the status bar indicating the amount of the file saved. In addition, the file name appears on the title bar.

Other Ways

1. Click File on ribbon, click Save As tab in Backstage view, click This PC, click Browse button, type file name (Save As dialog box), navigate to desired save location, click Save button

2. Press F12, type file name (Save As dialog box), navigate to desired save location, click Save button

---

How often should you save a document?

It is important to save a document frequently for the following reasons:

- The document in memory might be lost if the computer is turned off or you lose electrical power while an app is running.

- If you run out of time before completing a project, you may finish it at a future time without starting over.

CONSIDER THIS

Navigating in Dialog Boxes

Navigating is the process of finding a location on a storage device. While saving the National Monuments file, for example, Steps 4a and 4b navigated to the Word folder located in the CIS 101 folder in the Documents folder. When performing certain functions in Windows apps, such as saving a file, opening a file, or inserting a picture in an existing document, you most likely will have to navigate to the location where you want to save the file or to the folder containing the file you want to open or insert. Most dialog boxes in Windows apps requiring navigation follow a similar procedure; that is, the way you navigate to a folder in one dialog box, such as the Save As dialog box, is similar to how you might navigate in another dialog box, such as the Open dialog box. If you chose to navigate to a specific location in a dialog box, you would follow the instructions in Steps 4a and 4b.

To Minimize and Restore a Window

1 SIGN IN | 2 USE WINDOWS | 3 USE APPS | 4 FILE MANAGEMENT | 5 SWITCH APPS | 6 SAVE FILES
7 CHANGE SCREEN RESOLUTION | 8 EXIT APPS | 9 USE ADDITIONAL APP FEATURES | 10 USE HELP

Before continuing, you can verify that the Word file was saved properly. To do this, you will minimize the Word window and then open the CIS 101 window so that you can verify the file is stored in the CIS 101 folder on the hard drive. A **minimized window** is an open window that is hidden from view but can be displayed quickly by clicking the window's button on the taskbar.

In the following example, Word is used to illustrate minimizing and restoring windows; however, you would follow the same steps regardless of the Office app you are using. *Why? Before closing an app, you should make sure your file saved correctly so that you can find it later.*

The following steps minimize the Word window, verify that the file is saved, and then restore the minimized window.

- Click the Minimize button on the Word window title bar (shown in Figure 50) to minimize the window (Figure 51).

Q&A
Is the minimized window still available?
The minimized window, Word in this case, remains available but no longer is the active window. It is minimized as a button on the taskbar.

- If the File Explorer window is not open on the screen, click the File Explorer button on the taskbar to make the File Explorer window the active window.

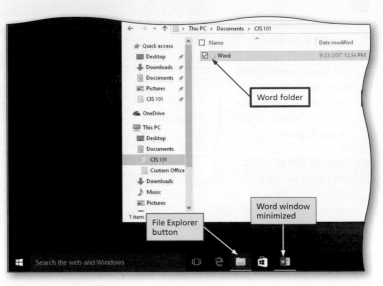

Figure 51

- Double-click the Word folder in the file list to select the folder and display its contents (Figure 52).

Q&A
Why does the File Explorer button on the taskbar change?
A selected app button indicates that the app is active on the screen. When the button is not selected, the app is running but not active.

- After viewing the contents of the selected folder, click the Word app button on the taskbar to restore the minimized window (as shown in Figure 50).

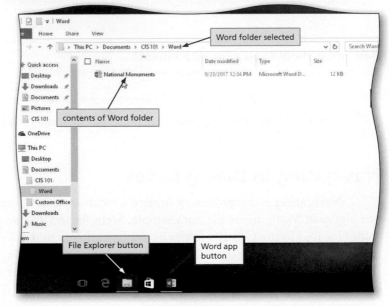

Figure 52

Other Ways

1. Right-click title bar, click Minimize on shortcut menu, click taskbar button in taskbar button area
2. Press WINDOWS+M, press WINDOWS+SHIFT+M
3. Click Word app button on taskbar to minimize window. Click Word app button again to restore window.

1 SIGN IN | 2 USE WINDOWS | 3 USE APPS | 4 FILE MANAGEMENT | 5 SWITCH APPS | 6 SAVE FILES
7 CHANGE SCREEN RESOLUTION | 8 EXIT APPS | 9 USE ADDITIONAL APP FEATURES | 10 USE HELP

To Save a File on OneDrive

One of the features of Office is the capability to save files on OneDrive so that you can use the files on multiple computers or mobile devices without having to use an external storage device, such as a USB flash drive. Storing files on OneDrive also enables you to share files more efficiently with others, such as when using Office Online and Office 365.

In the following example, Word is used to save a file on OneDrive. *Why? Storing files on OneDrive provides more portability options than are available from storing files in the Documents folder.*

You can save files directly on OneDrive from within an Office app. The following steps save the current Word file on OneDrive. These steps require that you have a Microsoft account and an Internet connection.

1

- Click File on the ribbon to open the Backstage view.

- Click the Save As tab in the Backstage view to display the Save As gallery.

- Click OneDrive in the left pane to display OneDrive saving options or a Sign In button, if you are not signed in already to your Microsoft account (Figure 53).

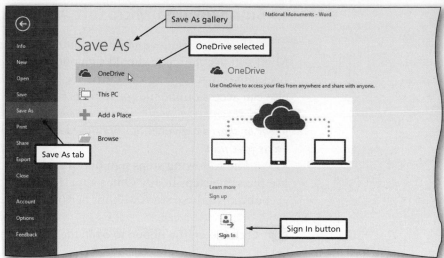

Figure 53

2

- If your screen displays a Sign In button (shown in Figure 53), click it to display the Sign in dialog box (Figure 54).

Q&A
What if the Sign In button does not appear?
If you already are signed into your Microsoft account, the Sign In button will not be displayed. In this case, proceed to Step 3.

- Follow the instructions on the screen to sign in to your Microsoft account.

Figure 54

3

- If necessary, in the Backstage view, click OneDrive in the left pane in the Save As gallery to select OneDrive as the save location.

- Click the Documents, or similar, folder in the right pane to display the Save As dialog box (Figure 55).

Q&A
Why does the path in the OneDrive address bar in the Save As dialog box contain various letters and numbers?
The letters and numbers in the address bar uniquely identify the location of your OneDrive files and folders.

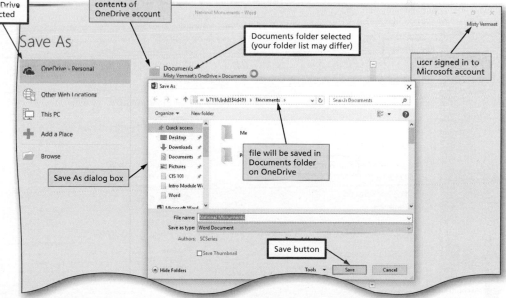

Figure 55

4

- Click the Save button (Save As dialog box) to save the file on OneDrive.

To Sign Out of a Microsoft Account

If you are using a public computer or otherwise wish to sign out of your Microsoft account, you should sign out of the account from the Accounts gallery in the Backstage view. Signing out of the account is the safest way to make sure that nobody else can access online files or settings stored in your Microsoft account. ***Why?*** *For security reasons, you should sign out of your Microsoft account when you are finished using a public or shared computer. Staying signed in to your Microsoft account might enable others to access your files.*

The following steps sign out of a Microsoft account from Word. You would use the same steps in any Office app. If you do not wish to sign out of your Microsoft account, read these steps without performing them.

1 Click File on the ribbon to open the Backstage view.

2 Click the Account tab to display the Account gallery (Figure 56).

3 Click the Sign out link, which displays the Remove Account dialog box. If a Can't remove Windows accounts dialog box appears instead of the Remove Account dialog box, click the OK button and skip the remaining steps.

> **Q&A** Why does a Can't remove Windows accounts dialog box appear?
> If you signed in to Windows using your Microsoft account, then you also must sign out from Windows, rather than signing out from within Word. When you are finished using Windows, be sure to sign out at that time.

4 Click the Yes button (Remove Account dialog box) to sign out of your Microsoft account on this computer or mobile device.

> **Q&A** Should I sign out of Windows after removing my Microsoft account?
> When you are finished using the computer, you should sign out of Windows for maximum security.

5 Click the Back button in the upper-left corner of the Backstage view to return to the document.

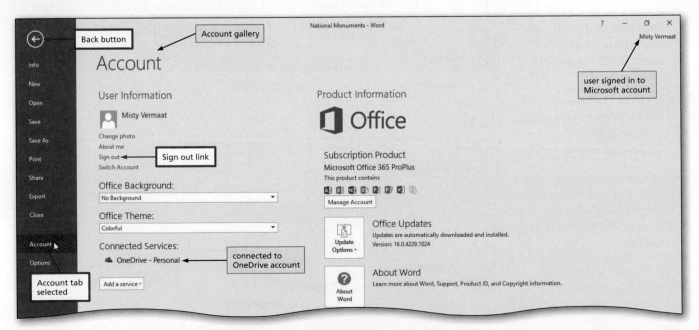

Figure 56

Screen Resolution

Screen resolution indicates the number of pixels (dots) that the computer uses to display the letters, numbers, graphics, and background you see on the screen. When you increase the screen resolution, Windows displays more information on the screen, but the information decreases in size. The reverse also is true: as you decrease the screen resolution, Windows displays less information on the screen, but the information increases in size.

Screen resolution usually is stated as the product of two numbers, such as 1366 × 768 (pronounced "thirteen sixty-six by seven sixty-eight"). A 1366 × 768 screen resolution results in a display of 1366 distinct pixels on each of 768 lines, or about 1,050,624 pixels. Changing the screen resolution affects how the ribbon appears in Office apps and some Windows dialog boxes. Figure 57, for example, shows the Word ribbon at screen resolutions of 1366 × 768 and 1024 × 768. All of the same commands are available regardless of screen resolution. The app (Word, in this case), however, makes changes to the groups and the buttons within the groups to accommodate the various screen resolutions. The result is that certain commands may need to be accessed differently depending on the resolution chosen. A command that is visible on the ribbon and available by clicking a button at one resolution may not be visible and may need to be accessed using its Dialog Box Launcher at a different resolution.

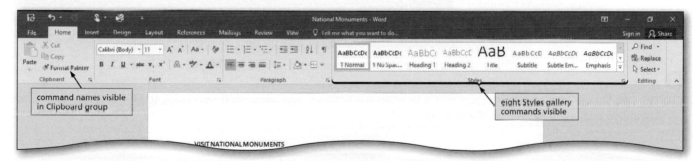

Figure 57 (a) Ribbon at 1366 × 768 Resolution

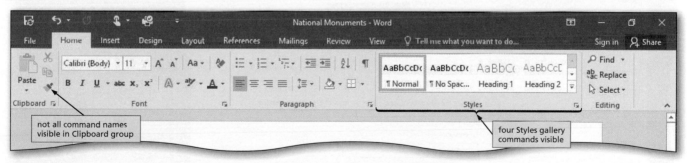

Figure 57 (b) Ribbon at 1024 × 768 Resolution

Comparing the two ribbons in Figure 57, notice the changes in content and layout of the groups and galleries. In some cases, the content of a group is the same in each resolution, but the layout of the group differs. For example, the same gallery and buttons appear in the Styles groups in the two resolutions, but the layouts differ. In other cases, the content and layout are the same across the resolution, but the level of detail differs with the resolution.

To Change the Screen Resolution

If you are using a computer to step through the modules in this book and you want your screen to match the figures, you may need to change your screen's resolution. *Why? The figures in this book use a screen resolution of 1366 × 768.* The following steps change the screen resolution to 1366 × 768. Your computer already may be set to 1366 × 768. Keep in mind that many computer labs prevent users from changing the screen resolution; in that case, read the following steps for illustration purposes.

- Click the Show desktop button, which is located at the far-right edge of the taskbar, to display the Windows desktop.

- Right-click an empty area on the Windows desktop to display a shortcut menu that contains a list of commands related to the desktop (Figure 58).

Q&A Why does my shortcut menu display different commands? Depending on your computer's hardware and configuration, different commands might appear on the shortcut menu.

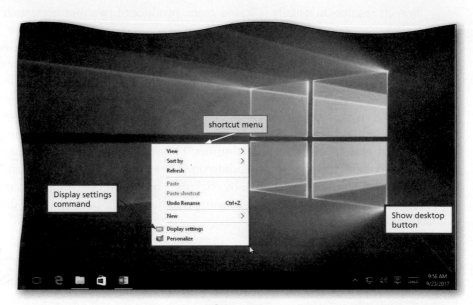

Figure 58

- Click Display settings on the shortcut menu to open the Settings app window. If necessary, scroll to display the 'Advanced display settings' link (Figure 59).

Figure 59

- Click 'Advanced display settings' in the Settings app window to display the advanced display settings.
- If necessary, scroll to display the Resolution box (Figure 60).

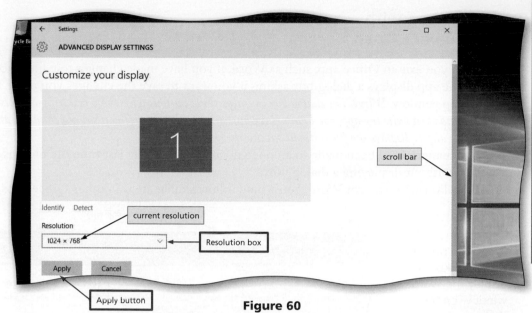

Figure 60

- Click the Resolution box to display a list of available screen resolutions (Figure 61).
- If necessary, scroll to and then click 1366 × 768 to select the screen resolution.

Q&A
What if my computer does not support the 1366 × 768 resolution?
Some computers do not support the 1366 × 768 resolution. In this case, select a resolution that is close to the 1366 × 768 resolution.

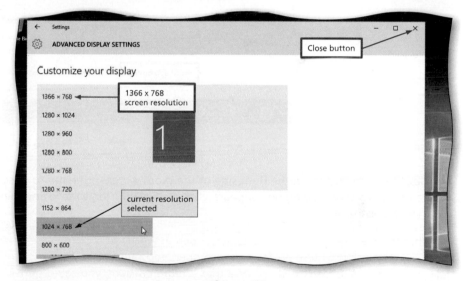

Figure 61

- Click the Apply button (Advanced Display Settings window), shown in Figure 60, to change the screen resolution and a confirmation message (Figure 62).
- Click the Keep changes button to accept the new screen resolution.
- Click the Close button (shown in Figure 61) to close the Settings app window.

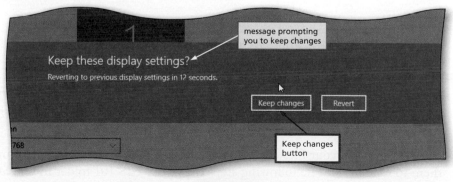

Figure 62

Other Ways

1. Click Start button, click Settings, click System, click Display, click 'Advanced display settings,' select desired resolution in Resolution box, click Apply button, click Keep changes button

2. Type `screen resolution` in search box, click 'Change the screen resolution,' select desired resolution in Resolution box, click Apply button, click Keep changes button

To Exit an App with One Document Open

1 SIGN IN | 2 USE WINDOWS | 3 USE APPS | 4 FILE MANAGEMENT | 5 SWITCH APPS | 6 SAVE FILES
7 CHANGE SCREEN RESOLUTION | 8 EXIT APPS | 9 USE ADDITIONAL APP FEATURES | 10 USE HELP

When you exit an Office app, such as Word, if you have made changes to a file since the last time the file was saved, the app displays a dialog box asking if you want to save the changes you made to the file before it closes the app window. *Why? The dialog box contains three buttons with these resulting actions: the Save button saves the changes and then exits the app, the Don't Save button exits the app without saving changes, and the Cancel button closes the dialog box and redisplays the file without saving the changes.*

If no changes have been made to an open document since the last time the file was saved, the app will close the window without displaying a dialog box.

The following steps exit Word. You would follow similar steps in other Office apps.

1

- If necessary, click the Word app button on the taskbar to display the Word window on the desktop (Figure 63).

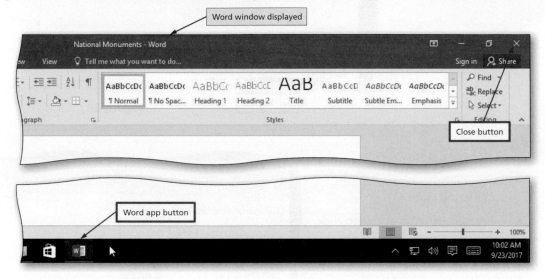

Figure 63

2

- Click the Close button on the right side of the Word window title bar to close the document and exit Word. If a Microsoft Word dialog box appears, click the Save button to save any changes made to the document since the last save.

Q&A What if I have more than one document open in Word?

You could click the Close button for each open document. When you click the last open document's Close button, you also exit Word. As an alternative that is more efficient, you could right-click the Word app button on the taskbar and then click 'Close all windows' on the shortcut menu to close all open documents and exit Word.

Other Ways

1. Right-click the Word app button on Windows taskbar, click 'Close all windows' on shortcut menu
2. Press ALT + F4

To Copy a Folder to OneDrive

1 SIGN IN | 2 USE WINDOWS | 3 USE APPS | **4 FILE MANAGEMENT** | 5 SWITCH APPS | 6 SAVE FILES
7 CHANGE SCREEN RESOLUTION | 8 EXIT APPS | **9 USE ADDITIONAL APP FEATURES** | 10 USE HELP

To back up your files or easily make them available on another computer or mobile device, you can copy them to OneDrive. The following steps copy your CIS 101 folder to OneDrive. If you do not have access to a OneDrive account, read the following steps without performing them. *Why? It often is good practice to have a backup of your files so that they are available in case something happens to your original copies.*

1

- Click the File Explorer button on the taskbar to make the folder window the active window.

- Navigate to the CIS 101 folder (or your class folder) in the Documents folder.

- Click Documents in the This PC area of the navigation pane to display the CIS 101 folder in the file list.

Q&A What if my CIS 101 folder is stored in a different location? Use the navigation pane to navigate to the location of your CIS 101 folder. The CIS 101 folder should be displayed in the file list once you have located it.

- Click the CIS 101 folder in the file list to select it (Figure 64).

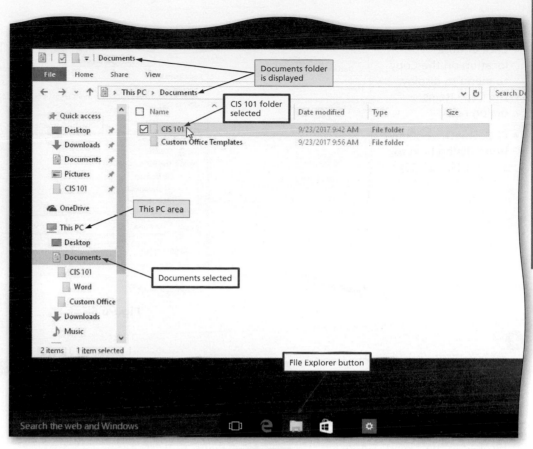

Figure 64

2

- Click Home on the ribbon to display the Home tab.

- Click the Copy to button (Home tab | Organize group) to display the Copy to menu (Figure 65).

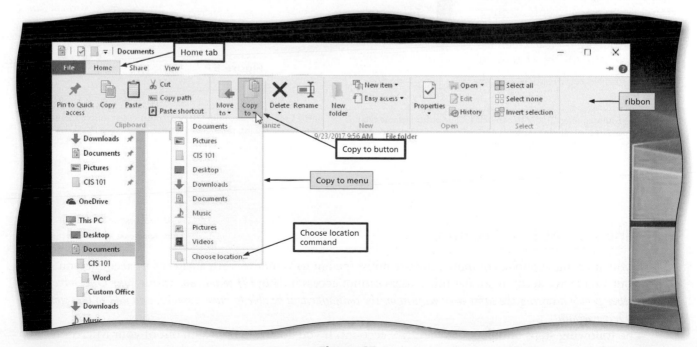

Figure 65

- Click Choose location on the Copy to menu to display the Copy Items dialog box.
- Click OneDrive (Copy Items dialog box) to select it (Figure 66).

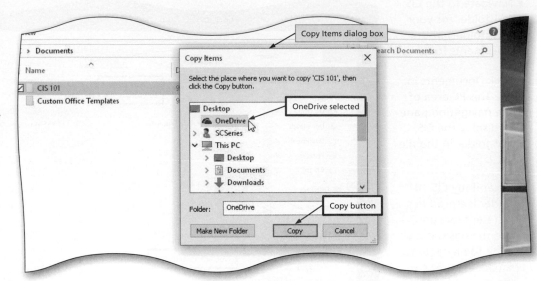

Figure 66

- Click the Copy button (Copy Items dialog box) to copy the selected folder to OneDrive.
- Click OneDrive in the navigation pane to verify the CIS 101 folder displays in the file list (Figure 67).

Q&A

Why does a Microsoft OneDrive dialog box appear when I click OneDrive in the navigation pane?
If you are not currently signed in to Windows using a Microsoft account, you will manually need to sign in to a Microsoft account to save files to OneDrive. Follow the instructions on the screen to sign in to your Microsoft account.

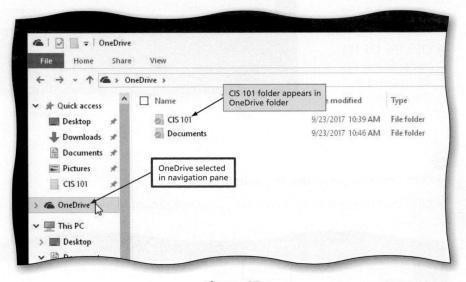

Figure 67

Other Ways

1. In File Explorer, select folder to copy, click Copy button (Home tab | Clipboard group), display contents of OneDrive in file list, click Paste button (Home tab | Clipboard group)

2. In File Explorer, select folder to copy, press CTRL+C, display contents of OneDrive in file list, press CTRL+V

1 SIGN IN | 2 USE WINDOWS | 3 USE APPS | **4 FILE MANAGEMENT** | 5 SWITCH APPS | 6 SAVE FILES
7 CHANGE SCREEN RESOLUTION | 8 EXIT APPS | **9 USE ADDITIONAL APP FEATURES** | 10 USE HELP

To Unlink a OneDrive Account

If you are using a public computer and are not signed in to Windows with a Microsoft account, you should unlink your OneDrive account so that other users cannot access it. *Why? If you do not unlink your OneDrive account, other people accessing the same user account on the computer will be able to view, remove, and add to files stored in your OneDrive account.*

The following steps unlink your OneDrive account. If you do not wish to sign out of your Microsoft account, read these steps without performing them.

- Click the 'Show hidden icons' button on the Windows taskbar to show a menu of hidden icons (Figure 68).

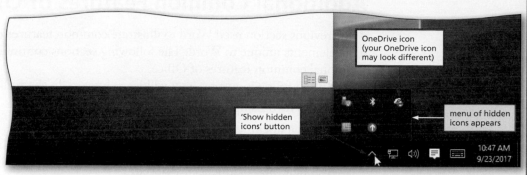

Figure 68

2

- Right click the OneDrive icon (shown in Figure 68) to display a shortcut menu (Figure 69).

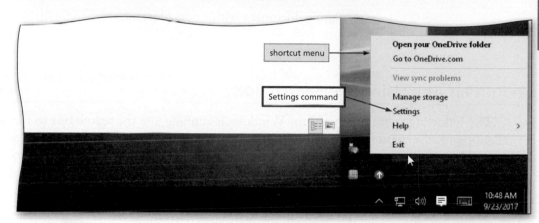

Figure 69

3

- Click Settings on the shortcut menu to display the Microsoft OneDrive dialog box (Figure 70).

- If necessary, click the Settings tab. (Some versions require you click an Account tab instead.)

- Click the Unlink OneDrive button (Microsoft OneDrive dialog box) to unlink the OneDrive account.

- When the Microsoft OneDrive dialog box appears with a Welcome to OneDrive message, click the Close button.

- Minimize the File Explorer window.

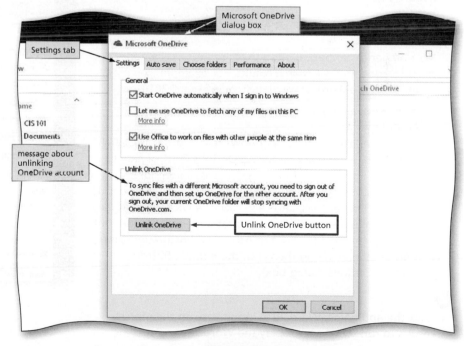

Figure 70

Break Point: If you wish to take a break, this is a good place to do so. To resume at a later time, continue to follow the steps from this location forward.

Additional Common Features of Office Apps

The previous section used Word to illustrate common features of Office and some basic elements unique to Word. The following sections continue to use Word present additional common features of Office.

In the following pages, you will learn how to do the following:

1. Run Word using the search box.
2. Open a document in Word.
3. Close the document.
4. Reopen the document just closed.
5. Create a blank Word document from Windows Explorer and then open the file.
6. Save a document with a new file name.

To Run an App Using the Search Box

1 SIGN IN | **2 USE WINDOWS** | 3 USE APPS | 4 FILE MANAGEMENT | 5 SWITCH APPS | 6 SAVE FILES
7 CHANGE SCREEN RESOLUTION | 8 EXIT APPS | **9 USE ADDITIONAL APP FEATURES** | 10 USE HELP

The following steps, which assume Windows is running, use the search box to run Word based on a typical installation; however, you would follow similar steps to run any app. *Why? Some people prefer to use the search box to locate and run an app, as opposed to searching through a list of all apps on the Start menu.* You may need to ask your instructor how to run Word on your computer.

- Type **Word 2016** as the search text in the search box and watch the search results appear in the search results (Figure 71).

Q&A

Do I need to type the complete app name or use correct capitalization?
No, you need to type just enough characters of the app name for it to appear in the search results. For example, you may be able to type Word or word, instead of Word 2016.

What if the search does not locate the Word app on my computer?
You may need to adjust the Windows search settings. Search for the word, index; click 'Indexing Options Control panel'; click the Modify button (Indexing Options dialog box); expand the Local Disk, if necessary; place a check mark beside all Program Files entries; and then click the OK button. It may take a few minutes for the index to rebuild. If it still does not work, you may need to click the Advanced button (Indexing Options dialog box) and then click the Rebuild button (Advanced Options dialog box).

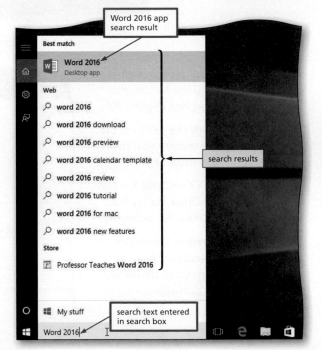

Figure 71

- Click the app name, Word 2016 in this case, in the search results to run Word and display the Word start screen.

- Click the Blank document thumbnail on the Word start screen (shown earlier in this module in Figure 8) to create a blank document and display it in the Word window. If the Word window is not maximized, click the Maximize button on its title bar to maximize the window.

To Open an Existing File

As discussed earlier, the Backstage view contains a set of commands that enable you to manage documents and data about the documents. *Why? From the Backstage view in Word, for example, you can create, open, print, and save documents. You also can share documents, manage versions, set permissions, and modify document properties. In other Office apps, the Backstage view may contain features specific to those apps.* The following steps open a saved file, specifically the National Monuments file, that recently was saved.

1

- Click File on the ribbon to open the Backstage view and then click the Open tab in the Backstage view to display the Open gallery in the Backstage view.

- Click This PC to display recent folders accessed on your computer.

- Click the Browse button to display the Open dialog box.

- If necessary, navigate to the location of the file to open (Word folder in the CIS 101 folder).

- Click the file to open, National Monuments in this case, to select the file (Figure 72).

2

- Click the Open button (Open dialog box) to open the file (shown earlier in the module in Figure 50). If necessary, click the Enable Content button.

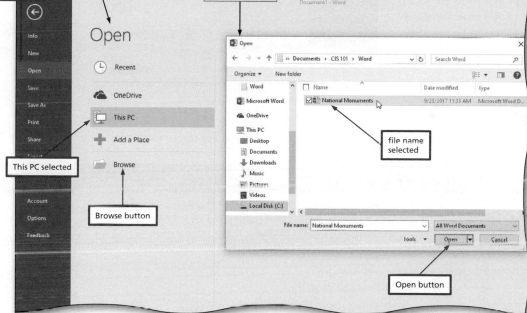

Figure 72

Why did a Security Warning appear?
The Security Warning appears when you open an Office file that might contain harmful content. The files you create in this module are not harmful, but you should be cautious when opening files from other people.

Other Ways

1. Press CTRL+O	2. Navigate to file in File Explorer window, double-click file name

To Create a New Document
from the Backstage View

You can open multiple documents in an Office program, such as Word, so that you can work on the documents at the same time. The following steps create a file, a blank document in this case, from the Backstage view. *Why? You want to create a new document while keeping the current document open.*

1

- Click File on the ribbon to open the Backstage view.

- Click the New tab in the Backstage view to display the New gallery (Figure 73).

Q&A Can I create documents through the Backstage view in other Office apps? Yes. If the Office app has a New tab in the Backstage view, the New gallery displays various options for creating a new file.

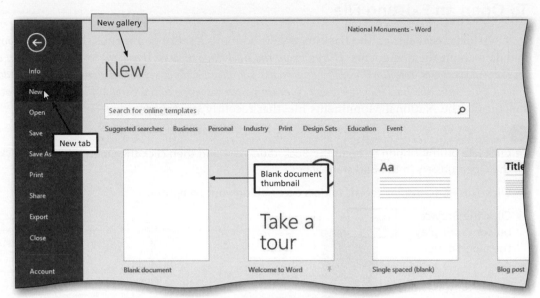

Figure 73

2

- Click the Blank document thumbnail in the New gallery to create a new document (Figure 74).

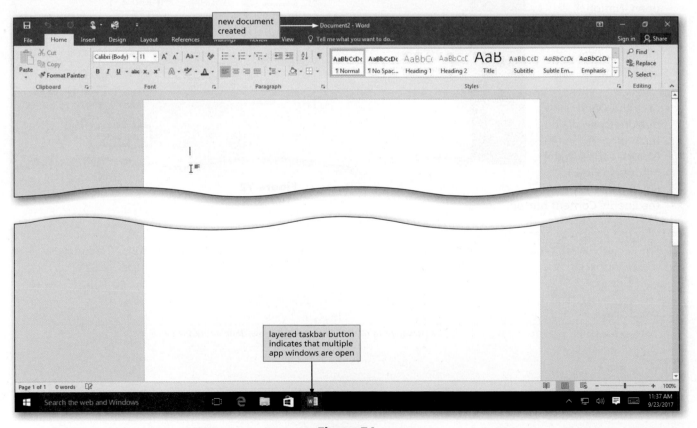

Figure 74

Other Ways

1. Press CTRL+N

To Enter Text in a Document

The following step enters the first line of text in a document.

1 Type `List of Special Rates for National Monuments` and then press the ENTER key (Figure 75).

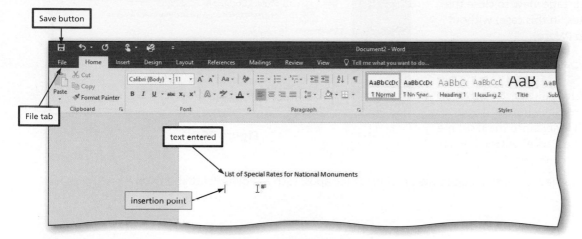

Figure 75

To Save a File in a Folder

The following steps save the second document in the Word folder in the class folder (CIS 101, in this case) in the Documents folder using the file name, Special Rates.

1 Click the Save button on the Quick Access Toolbar, which depending on settings, will display either the Save As gallery in the Backstage view or the Save As dialog box.

2 If your screen displays the Backstage view, click This PC, if necessary, to display options in the right pane related to saving on your computer; if your screen already displays the Save As dialog box, proceed to Step 4.

3 Click the Browse button in the left pane to display the Save As dialog box.

4 If necessary, type `Special Rates` in the File name box (Save As dialog box) to change the file name. Do not press the ENTER key after typing the file name because you do not want to close the dialog box at this time.

5 If necessary, navigate to the desired save location (in this case, the Word folder in the CIS 101 folder [or your class folder] in the Documents folder). For specific instructions, perform the tasks in Steps 4a and 4b in the previous section in this module titled To Save a File in a Folder.

6 Click the Save button (Save As dialog box) to save the document in the selected folder on the selected drive with the entered file name.

To Close a File Using the Backstage View

1 SIGN IN | 2 USE WINDOWS | 3 USE APPS | 4 FILE MANAGEMENT | 5 SWITCH APPS | 6 SAVE FILES
7 CHANGE SCREEN RESOLUTION | 8 EXIT APPS | 9 USE ADDITIONAL APP FEATURES | 10 USE HELP

Sometimes, you may want to close an Office file, such as a Word document, entirely and start over with a new file. You also may want to close a file when you are done working with it. **Why?** *You should close a file when you are done working with it so that you do not make inadvertent changes to it.* The following steps close the current active Word file, that is, the Special Rates document, without exiting Word.

- Click File on the ribbon to open the Backstage view (Figure 76).

- Click Close in the Backstage view to close the open file (Special Rates, in this case) without exiting the active app (Word).

Q&A What if Word displays a dialog box about saving?
Click the Save button if you want to save the changes, click the Don't Save button if you want to ignore the changes since the last time you saved, and click the Cancel button if you do not want to close the document.

Can I use the Backstage view to close an open file in other Office apps, such as PowerPoint and Excel?
Yes.

Figure 76

Other Ways

1. Press CTRL+F4

To Open a Recent File Using the Backstage View

1 SIGN IN | 2 USE WINDOWS | 3 USE APPS | 4 FILE MANAGEMENT | 5 SWITCH APPS | 6 SAVE FILES
7 CHANGE SCREEN RESOLUTION | 8 EXIT APPS | 9 USE ADDITIONAL APP FEATURES | 10 USE HELP

You sometimes need to open a file that you recently modified. **Why?** *You may have more changes to make, such as adding more content or correcting errors.* The Backstage view allows you to access recent files easily. The following steps reopen the Special Rates file just closed.

1

- Click File on the ribbon to open the Backstage view.
- Click the Open tab in the Backstage view to display the Open gallery (Figure 77).

2

- Click the desired file name in the Recent list, Special Rates in this case, to open the file.

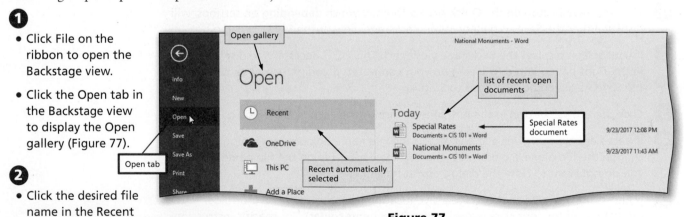

Figure 77

Other Ways

1. Click File on ribbon, click Open tab in Backstage view, click This PC, click Browse button, navigate to file (Open dialog box), click Open button

To Create a New Blank Document from File Explorer

1 SIGN IN | 2 USE WINDOWS | 3 USE APPS | 4 FILE MANAGEMENT | 5 SWITCH APPS | 6 SAVE FILES
7 CHANGE SCREEN RESOLUTION | 8 EXIT APPS | 9 USE ADDITIONAL APP FEATURES | 10 USE HELP

File Explorer provides a means to create a blank Office document without running an Office app. The following steps use File Explorer to create a blank Word document. **Why?** *Sometimes you might need to create a blank document and then return to it later for editing.*

- Click the File Explorer button on the taskbar to make the folder window the active window.

- If necessary, double-click the Documents folder in the navigation pane to expand the Documents folder.

- If necessary, double-click your class folder (CIS 101, in this case) in the navigation pane to expand the folder.

- Click the Word folder in the navigation pane to display its contents in the file list.

- With the Word folder selected, right-click an open area in the file list to display a shortcut menu.

- Point to New on the shortcut menu to display the New submenu (Figure 78).

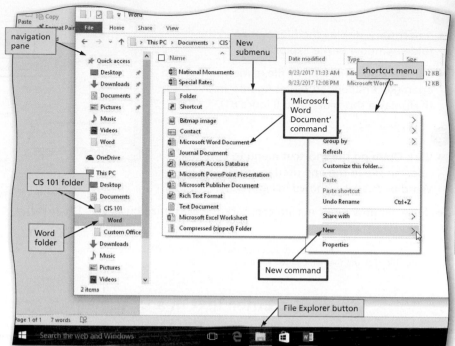

Figure 78

- Click 'Microsoft Word Document' on the New submenu to display an icon and text box for a new file in the current folder window with the file name, New Microsoft Word Document, selected (Figure 79).

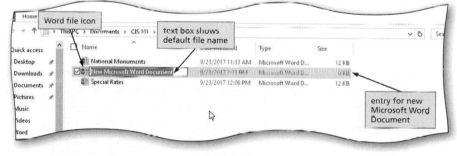

Figure 79

- Type **Recommended Travel Agents** in the text box and then press the ENTER key to assign a new file name to the new file in the current folder (Figure 80).

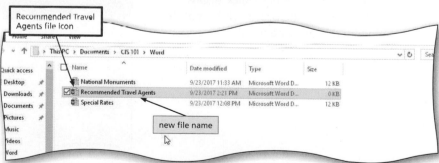

Figure 80

To Run an App from File Explorer and Open a File

1 SIGN IN | 2 USE WINDOWS | 3 USE APPS | 4 FILE MANAGEMENT | 5 SWITCH APPS | 6 SAVE FILES
7 CHANGE SCREEN RESOLUTION | 8 EXIT APPS | **9 USE ADDITIONAL APP FEATURES** | **10 USE HELP**

Previously in this module, you learned how to run Word using the Start menu and the search box. The following steps, which assume Windows is running, use File Explorer to run Word based on a typical installation. **Why?** *When you open an existing file from File Explorer, the app in which the file was created runs and then opens the selected file.* You may need to ask your instructor how to run Word for your computer.

- If necessary, display the file to open in the folder window in File Explorer.

- Right-click the file icon or file name you want to open (Recommended Travel Agents, in this case) to display a shortcut menu (Figure 81).

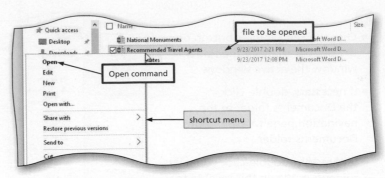

Figure 81

- Click Open on the shortcut menu to open the selected file in the app used to create the file, Word in this case (shown in Figure 82).

- If the window is not maximized, click the Maximize button on the title bar to maximize the window.

Other Ways

1. Double-click the file name in the file list

To Enter Text in a Document

The following step enters a line of text in the blank Word document.

 Type **List of Recommended Travel Agents** and then press the ENTER key (shown in Figure 82).

To Save an Existing Office File with the Same File Name

1 SIGN IN | 2 USE WINDOWS | 3 USE APPS | 4 FILE MANAGEMENT | 5 SWITCH APPS | 6 SAVE FILES
7 CHANGE SCREEN RESOLUTION | 8 EXIT APPS | 9 USE ADDITIONAL APP FEATURES | 10 USE HELP

Saving frequently cannot be overemphasized. *Why? You have made modifications to the file (document) since you created it. Thus, you should save again. You should continue saving files frequently so that you do not lose the changes you have made since the time you last saved the file.* You can use the same file name, such as Recommended Travel Agents, to save the changes made to the document. The following step saves a file again with the same file name.

- Click the Save button on the Quick Access Toolbar to overwrite the previously saved file (Recommended Travel Agents, in this case) in the Word folder (Figure 82).

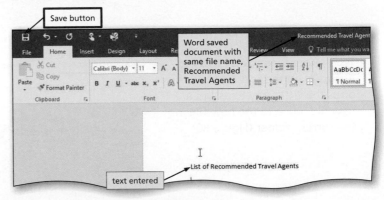

Figure 82

Other Ways

1. Press CTRL+S   2. Press SHIFT+F12

To Save a File with a New File Name

You might want to save a file with a different file name or to a different location. For example, you might start a homework assignment with a data file and then save it with a final file name for submission to your instructor, saving it to a location designated by your instructor. The following steps save a file with a different file name.

① Click the File tab to open the Backstage view. Click the Save As tab to display the Save As gallery.

② If necessary, click This PC to display options in the right pane related to saving on your computer. Click the Browse button in the left pane to display the Save As dialog box.

③ Type **Travel Agents** in the File name box (Save As dialog box) to change the file name. Do not press the ENTER key after typing the file name because you do not want to close the dialog box at this time.

④ If necessary, navigate to the desired save location (in this case, the Word folder in the CIS 101 folder [or your class folder] in the Documents folder). For specific instructions, perform the tasks in Steps 4a and 4b in the previous section titled To Save a File in a Folder.

⑤ Click the Save button (Save As dialog box) to save the document in the selected folder on the selected drive with the entered file name.

To Exit an Office App

You are finished using Word. The following steps exit Word.

① Because you have multiple Word documents open, right-click the Word app button on the taskbar and then click 'Close all windows' on the shortcut menu to close all open documents and exit Word.

② If a dialog box appears, click the Save button to save any changes made to the file since the last save.

Renaming, Moving, and Deleting Files

Earlier in this module, you learned how to organize files in folders, which is part of a process known as **file management**. The following sections cover additional file management topics including renaming, moving, and deleting files.

To Rename a File

1 SIGN IN | 2 USE WINDOWS | 3 USE APPS | **4 FILE MANAGEMENT** | 5 SWITCH APPS | 6 SAVE FILES
7 CHANGE SCREEN RESOLUTION | 8 EXIT APPS | 9 USE ADDITIONAL APP FEATURES | **10 USE HELP**

You may want to change the name of, or rename, a file or a folder. *Why? You may want to distinguish a file in one folder or drive from a copy of a similar file, or you may decide to rename a file to better identify its contents.* The following steps change the name of the National Monuments file in the Word folder to National Monuments Flyer.

①

- If necessary, click the File Explorer button on the taskbar to make the folder window the active window.

- Navigate to the location of the file to be renamed (in this case, the Word folder in the CIS 101 [or your class folder] folder in the Documents folder) to display the file(s) it contains in the file list.

- Click the file to be renamed, the National Monuments icon or file name in the file list in this case, to select it.

- Right-click the selected file to display a shortcut menu that presents a list of commands related to files (Figure 83).

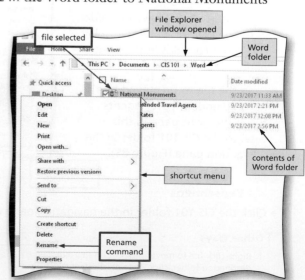

Figure 83

- Click Rename on the shortcut menu to place the current file name in a text box.

- Type **National Monuments Flyer** in the text box and then press the ENTER key (Figure 84).

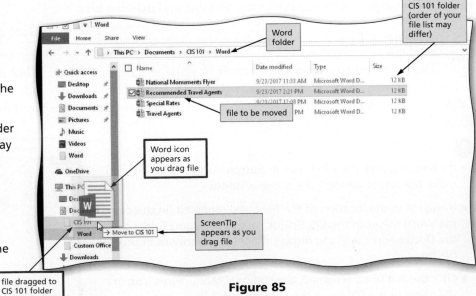

Figure 84

Q&A

Are any risks involved in renaming files that are located on a hard drive?

If you inadvertently rename a file that is associated with certain apps, the apps may not be able to find the file and, therefore, may not run properly. Always use caution when renaming files.

Can I rename a file when it is open?

No, a file must be closed to change the file name.

Other Ways

1. Select file, press F2, type new file name, press ENTER
2. Select file, click Rename (Home tab | Organize group), type new file name, press ENTER

1 SIGN IN | 2 USE WINDOWS | 3 USE APPS | **4 FILE MANAGEMENT** | 5 SWITCH APPS | 6 SAVE FILES
7 CHANGE SCREEN RESOLUTION | 8 EXIT APPS | 9 USE ADDITIONAL APP FEATURES | **10 USE HELP**

To Move a File

Why? *At some time, you may want to move a file from one folder, called the source folder, to another, called the destination folder.* When you move a file, it no longer appears in the original folder. If the destination and the source folders are on the same media, you can move a file by dragging it. If the folders are on different media, you will need to right-drag the file and then click Move here on the shortcut menu. The following step moves the Recommended Travel Agents file from the Word folder to the CIS 101 folder.

- If necessary, in File Explorer, navigate to the location of the file to be moved (in this case, the Word folder in the CIS 101 folder [or your class folder] in the Documents folder).

- If necessary, click the Word folder in the navigation pane to display the files it contains in the right pane.

- Drag the file to be moved, the Recommended Travel Agents file in the right pane in this case, to the CIS 101 folder in the navigation pane (Figure 85).

Figure 85

Experiment

- Click the CIS 101 folder in the navigation pane to verify that the file was moved.

Other Ways

1. Right-click file to move, click Cut on shortcut menu, right-click destination folder, click Paste on shortcut menu
2. Select file to move, press CTRL+X, select destination folder, press CTRL+V

To Delete a File

A final task you may want to perform is to delete a file. Exercise extreme caution when deleting a file or files. When you delete a file from a hard drive, the deleted file is stored in the Recycle Bin where you can recover it until you empty the Recycle Bin. If you delete a file from removable media, such as a USB flash drive, the file is deleted permanently. The next steps delete the Recommended Travel Agents file from the CIS 101 folder. *Why? When a file no longer is needed, you can delete it to conserve space on your storage location.*

- If necessary, in File Explorer, navigate to the location of the file to be deleted (in this case, the CIS 101 folder [or your class folder] in the Documents folder).

- Click the file to be deleted, the Recommended Travel Agents icon or file name in the right pane in this case, to select the file.

- Right-click the selected file to display a shortcut menu (Figure 86).

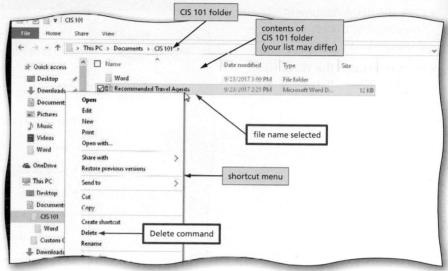

Figure 86

- Click Delete on the shortcut menu to delete the file.

- If a dialog box appears, click the Yes button to delete the file.

Q&A Can I use this same technique to delete a folder?

Yes. Right-click the folder and then click Delete on the shortcut menu. When you delete a folder, all of the files and folders contained in the folder you are deleting, together with any files and folders on lower hierarchical levels, are deleted as well. For example, if you delete the CIS 101 folder, you will delete all folders and files inside the CIS 101 folder.

Other Ways

1. Select file, press DELETE

Microsoft Office and Windows Help

At any time while you are using one of the Office apps, such as Word, you can use Office Help to display information about all topics associated with the app. Help in other Office apps operates in a similar fashion.

In Office, Help is presented in a window that has browser-style navigation buttons. Each Office app has its own Help home page, which is the starting Help page that is displayed in the Help window. If your computer is connected to the Internet, the contents of the Help page reflect both the local help files installed on the computer and material from Microsoft's website.

To Open the Help Window in an Office App

The following step opens the Word Help window. *Why? You might not understand how certain commands or operations work in Word, so you can obtain the necessary information using help.*

- Run Word.

- Click the Blank document thumbnail to display a blank document.

- Press F1 to open the Word Help window (Figure 87).

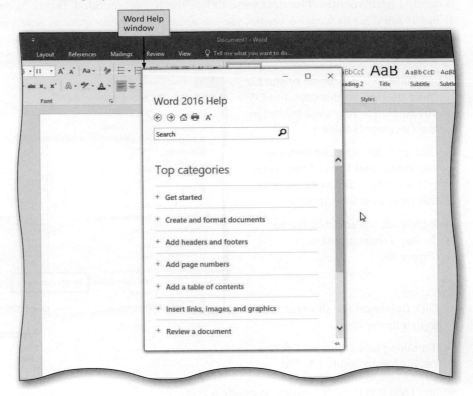

Figure 87

Moving and Resizing Windows

At times, it is useful, or even necessary, to have more than one window open and visible on the screen at the same time. You can resize and move these open windows so that you can view different areas of and elements in the window. In the case of the Help window, for example, it could be covering document text in the Word window that you need to see.

To Move a Window by Dragging

You can move any open window that is not maximized to another location on the desktop by dragging the title bar of the window. *Why? You might want to have a better view of what is behind the window or just want to move the window so that you can see it better.* The following step drags the Word Help window to the upper-left corner of the desktop.

- Drag the window title bar (the Word Help window title bar, in this case) so that the window moves to the upper-left corner of the desktop, as shown in Figure 88.

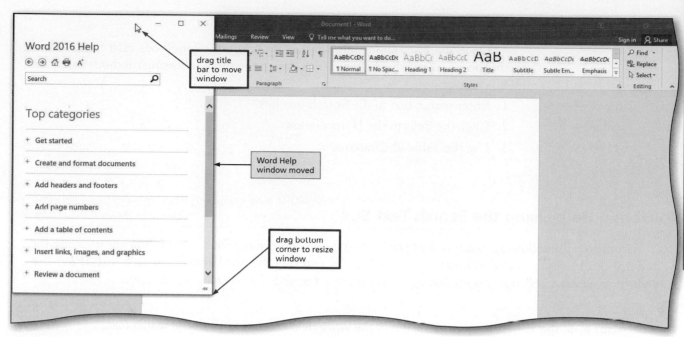

Figure 88

To Resize a Window by Dragging

1 SIGN IN | **2 USE WINDOWS** | 3 USE APPS | 4 FILE MANAGEMENT | 5 SWITCH APPS | 6 SAVE FILES
7 CHANGE SCREEN RESOLUTION | 8 EXIT APPS | 9 USE ADDITIONAL APP FEATURES | 10 USE HELP

A method used to change the size of the window is to drag the window borders. The following step changes the size of the Word Help window by dragging its borders. *Why? Sometimes, information is not visible completely in a window, and you want to increase the size of the window.*

- Point to the lower-right corner of the window (the Word Help window, in this case) until the pointer changes to a two-headed arrow.

- Drag the bottom border downward to display more of the active window (Figure 89).

Q&A
Can I drag other borders on the window to enlarge or shrink the window?
Yes, you can drag the left, right, and top borders and any window corner to resize a window.

Will Windows remember the new size of the window after I close it?
Yes. When you reopen the window, Windows will display it at the same size it was when you closed it.

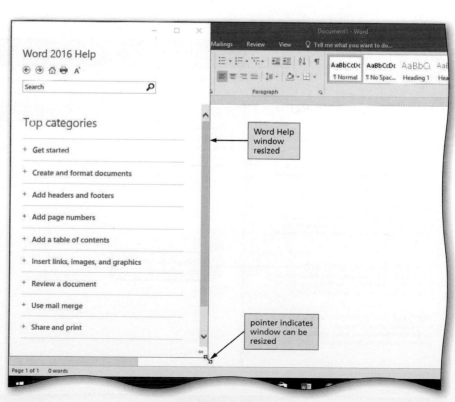

Figure 89

Using Office Help

Once an Office app's Help window is open, several methods exist for navigating Help. You can search for help by using any of the three following methods from the Help window:

1. Enter search text in the Search text box.
2. Click the links in the Help window.
3. Use the Table of Contents.

To Obtain Help Using the Search Text Box

1 SIGN IN | 2 USE WINDOWS | 3 USE APPS | 4 FILE MANAGEMENT | 5 SWITCH APPS | 6 SAVE FILES
7 CHANGE SCREEN RESOLUTION | 8 EXIT APPS | 9 USE ADDITIONAL APP FEATURES | 10 USE HELP

Assume for the following example that you want to know more about fonts. The following steps use the Search text box to obtain useful information about fonts by entering the word, fonts, as search text. *Why? You may not know the exact help topic you are looking to find, so using keywords can help narrow your search.*

- Type **fonts** in the Search text box at the top of the Word Help window to enter the search text.

- Press the ENTER key to display the search results (Figure 90).

Q&A

Why do my search results differ?

If you do not have an Internet connection, your results will reflect only the content of the Help files on your computer. When searching for help online, results also can change as content is added, deleted, and updated on the online Help webpages maintained by Microsoft.

Why were my search results not very helpful?

When initiating a search, be sure to check the spelling of the search text; also, keep your search specific to return the most accurate results.

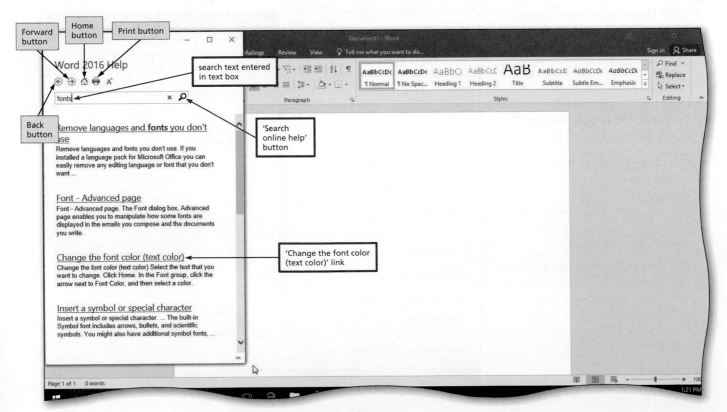

Figure 90

2

- Click the 'Change the font color (text color)', or a similar, link to display the Help information associated with the selected topic (Figure 91).

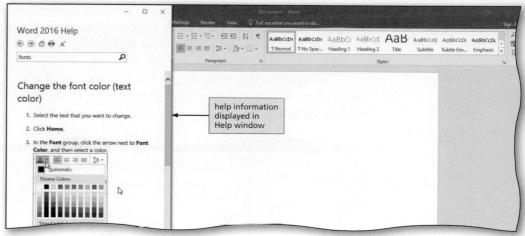

Figure 91

3

- Click the Home button in the Help window to clear the search results and redisplay the Help home page (Figure 92).

- Click the Close button in the Word 2016 Help window to close the window.

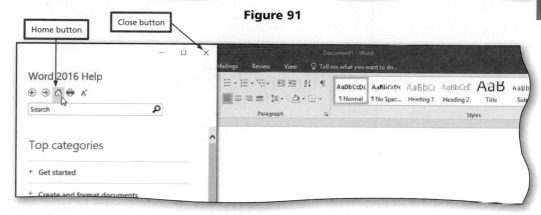

Figure 92

Obtaining Help while Working in an Office App

Help in the Office apps, such as Word, provides you with the ability to obtain help directly, without opening the Help window and initiating a search. For example, you may be unsure about how a particular command works, or you may be presented with a dialog box that you are not sure how to use.

Figure 93 shows one option for obtaining help while working in an Office app. If you want to learn more about a command, point to its button and wait for the ScreenTip to appear. If the Help icon and 'Tell me more' link appear in the ScreenTip, click the 'Tell me more' link or press the F1 key while pointing to the button to open the Help window associated with that command.

BTW
Customizing the Ribbon
In addition to customizing the Quick Access Toolbar, you can add items to and remove items from the ribbon. To customize the ribbon, click File on the ribbon to open the Backstage view, click the Options tab in the Backstage view, and then click Customize Ribbon in the left pane of the Options dialog box. More information about customizing the ribbon is presented in a later module.

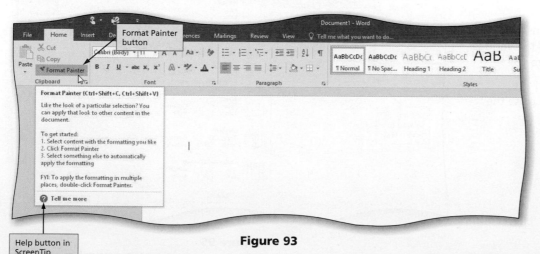

Figure 93

Figure 94 shows a dialog box that contains a Help button. Clicking the Help button or pressing the F1 key while the dialog box is displayed opens a Help window. The Help window contains help about that dialog box, if available. If no help file is available for that particular dialog box, then the main Help window opens.

As mentioned previously, the Tell Me box is available in most Office apps and can perform a variety of functions. One of these functions is to provide easy access to commands by typing a description of the command.

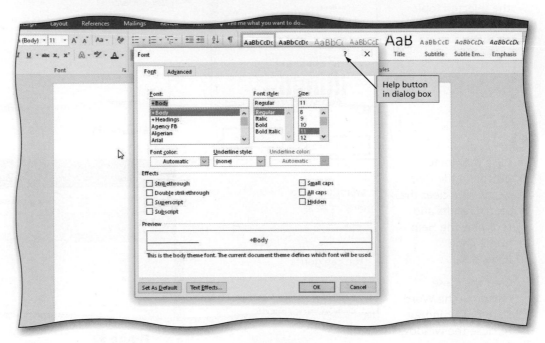

Figure 94

To Obtain Help Using the Tell Me Box

1 SIGN IN | 2 USE WINDOWS | 3 USE APPS | 4 FILE MANAGEMENT | 5 SWITCH APPS | 6 SAVE FILES
7 CHANGE SCREEN RESOLUTION | 8 EXIT APPS | 9 USE ADDITIONAL APP FEATURES | 10 USE HELP

If you are having trouble finding a command in an Office app, you can use the Tell Me box to search for the function you are trying to perform. As you type, the Tell Me box will suggest commands that match the search text you are entering. *Why? You can use the Tell Me box to access commands quickly that you otherwise may be unable to find on the ribbon.* The following steps find information about margins.

- Type **margins** in the Tell Me box and watch the search results appear.

- Point to Adjust Margins to display a submenu displaying the various margin settings (Figure 95).

- Click an empty area of the document window to close the search results.

- Exit Microsoft Word.

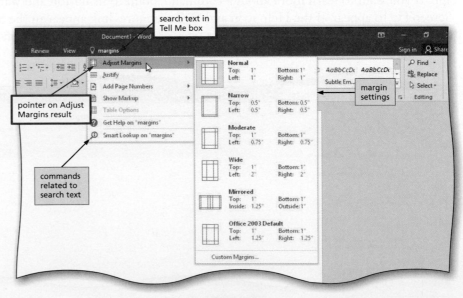

Figure 95

Using the Windows Search Box

One of the more powerful Windows features is the Windows search box. The search box is a central location from where you can type search text and quickly access related Windows commands or web search results. In addition, **Cortana** is a new search tool in Windows that you can access using the search box. It can act as a personal assistant by performing functions such as providing ideas; searching for apps, files, and folders; and setting reminders. In addition to typing search text in the search box, you also can use your computer or mobile device's microphone to give verbal commands.

To Use the Windows Search Box

1 SIGN IN | 2 USE WINDOWS | 3 USE APPS | 4 FILE MANAGEMENT | 5 SWITCH APPS | 6 SAVE FILES
7 CHANGE SCREEN RESOLUTION | 8 EXIT APPS | 9 USE ADDITIONAL APP FEATURES | 10 USE HELP

The following step uses the Windows search box to search for a Windows command. *Why? Using the search box to locate apps, settings, folders, and files can be faster than navigating windows and dialog boxes to search for the desired content.*

- Type **notification** in the search box to display the search results. The search results include related Windows settings, Windows Store apps, and web search results (Figure 96).

- Click an empty area of the desktop to close the search results.

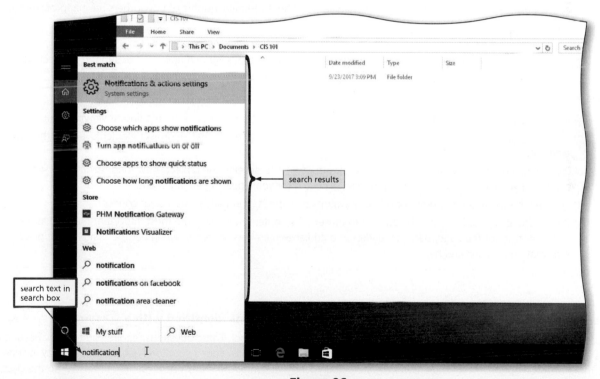

Figure 96

Summary

In this module, you learned how to use the Windows interface, several touch screen and mouse operations, and file and folder management. You also learned some basic features of Word and discovered the common elements that exist among Microsoft Office apps. Topics covered included signing in, using Windows, using apps, file management, switching between apps, saving files, changing screen resolution, exiting apps, using additional app features, and using Help.

What guidelines should you follow to plan your projects?

The process of communicating specific information is a learned, rational skill. Computers and software, especially Microsoft Office 2016, can help you develop ideas and present detailed information to a particular audience and minimize much of the laborious work of drafting and revising projects. No matter what method you use to plan a project, it is beneficial to follow some specific guidelines from the onset to arrive at a final product that is informative, relevant, and effective. Use some aspects of these guidelines every time you undertake a project, and others as needed in specific instances.

1. Determine the project's purpose.

    a) Clearly define why you are undertaking this assignment.

    b) Begin to draft ideas of how best to communicate information by handwriting ideas on paper; composing directly on a laptop, tablet, or mobile device; or developing a strategy that fits your particular thinking and writing style.

2. Analyze your audience.

    a) Learn about the people who will read, analyze, or view your work.

    b) Determine their interests and needs so that you can present the information they need to know and omit the information they already possess.

    c) Form a mental picture of these people or find photos of people who fit this profile so that you can develop a project with the audience in mind.

3. Gather possible content.

    a) Locate existing information that may reside in spreadsheets, databases, or other files.

    b) Conduct a web search to find relevant websites.

    c) Read pamphlets, magazine and newspaper articles, and books to gain insights of how others have approached your topic.

    d) Conduct personal interviews to obtain perspectives not available by any other means.

    e) Consider video and audio clips as potential sources for material that might complement or support the factual data you uncover.

4. Determine what content to present to your audience.

    a) Write three or four major ideas you want an audience member to remember after reading or viewing your project.

    b) Envision your project's endpoint, the key fact you wish to emphasize, so that all project elements lead to this final element.

    c) Determine relevant time factors, such as the length of time to develop the project, how long readers will spend reviewing your project, or the amount of time allocated for your speaking engagement.

    d) Decide whether a graph, photo, or artistic element can express or enhance a particular concept.

    e) Be mindful of the order in which you plan to present the content, and place the most important material at the top or bottom of the page, because readers and audience members generally remember the first and last pieces of information they see and hear.

How should you submit solutions to questions in the assignments identified with a symbol?

Every assignment in this book contains one or more questions with a ✸ symbol. These questions require you to think beyond the assigned file. Present your solutions to the question in the format required by your instructor. Possible formats may include one or more of these options: write the answer; create a document that contains the answer; present your answer to the class; discuss your answer in a group; record the answer as audio or video using a webcam, smartphone, or portable media player; or post answers on a blog, wiki, or website.

Apply Your Knowledge

Reinforce the skills and apply the concepts you learned in this module.

Creating a Folder and a Document

Instructions: You will create a Word Assignments folder and then create a Word document and save it in the folder.

Perform the following tasks:

1. Open the File Explorer window and then double-click to open the Documents folder.

2. Click the New folder button on the Quick Access Toolbar to display a new folder icon and text box for the folder name.

3. Type **Word Assignments** in the text box to name the folder. Press the ENTER key to create the folder in the Documents folder.

4. Run Word and create a new blank document.

5. Type **Contact Information** and then press then ENTER key to enter a line of text (Figure 97).

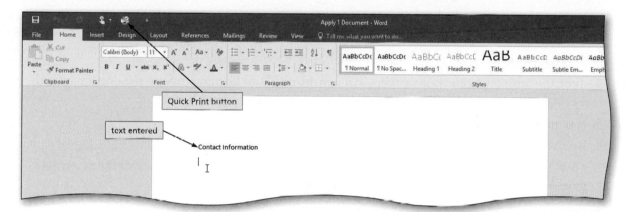

Figure 97

6. If requested by your instructor, enter your name, phone number, and email address in the Word document.

7. Click the Save button on the Quick Access Toolbar. Navigate to the Word Assignments folder in the Documents folder and then save the document using the file name, Apply 1 Document.

8. If your Quick Access Toolbar does not show the Quick Print button, add the Quick Print button to the Quick Access Toolbar. Print the document using the Quick Print button on the Quick Access Toolbar. When you are finished printing, remove the Quick Print button from the Quick Access Toolbar.

9. Submit the printout to your instructor.

10. Exit Word.

11. ✳ What other commands might you find useful to include on the Quick Access Toolbar?

Extend Your Knowledge

Extend the skills you learned in this module and experiment with new skills. You will use Help to complete the assignment.

Continued >

Extend Your Knowledge *continued*

Using Help

Instructions: Use Word Help to perform the following tasks.

Perform the following tasks:

1. Run Word.

2. Press F1 to open the Word Help window (shown in Figure 87).

3. Search Word Help to answer the following questions.

   a. What are three new features of Word 2016?

   b. What type of training is available through Word Help for Word 2016?

   c. What are the steps to customize the ribbon?

   d. What is the purpose of the Office Clipboard?

   e. What is the purpose of Read mode?

   f. Why would you use mail merge?

   g. How do you insert pictures?

   h. How do you change the size of text?

   i. What are the steps to zoom in and out of a document?

   j. What is the purpose of the Insights pane? How do you display it?

4. Type the answers from your searches in a new blank Word document. Save the document with a new file name and then submit it in the format specified by your instructor.

5. If requested by your instructor, enter your name in the Word document.

6. Exit Word.

7. ✳ What search text did you use to perform the searches above? Did it take multiple attempts to search and locate the exact information for which you were searching?

Expand Your World

Create a solution that uses cloud or web technologies by learning and investigating on your own from general guidance.

Creating Folders on OneDrive and Using the Word Online App

Instructions: You will create the folders shown in Figure 98 on OneDrive. Then, you will use the Word Online app to create a small file and save it in a folder on OneDrive.

Perform the following tasks:

1. Sign in to OneDrive in your browser.

2. Use the New button to create the folder structure shown in Figure 98.

Figure 98

3. In the Upcoming Events folder, use the New button to create a Word document with the file name, Expand 1 Task List, that contains the text, Prepare agenda for Tuesday's meeting.

4. If requested by your instructor, add your name to the Word document.

5. Save the document in the Upcoming Events folder and then exit the app.

6. Submit the assignment in the format specified by your instructor.

7. ✹ Based on your current knowledge of OneDrive, do you think you will use it? What about the Word Online app?

In the Labs

Design, create, modify, and/or use files following the guidelines, concepts, and skills presented in this module. Labs 1 and 2, which increase in difficulty, require you to create solutions based on what you learned in the module; Lab 3 requires you to apply your creative thinking and problem-solving skills to design and implement a solution.

Lab 1: **Creating Folders for a Bookstore**

Problem: Your friend works for a local bookstore. He would like to organize his files in relation to the types of books available in the store. He has seven main categories: fiction, biography, children, humor, social science, nonfiction, and medical. You are to create a folder structure similar to Figure 99.

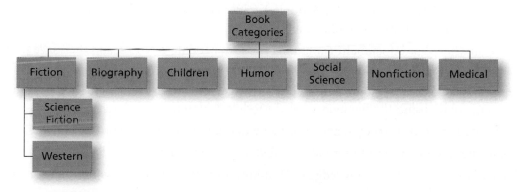

Figure 99

Perform the following tasks:

1. Click the File Explorer button on the taskbar and display the contents of the Documents folder.

2. In the Documents folder, create the main folder and name it Book Categories.

3. Navigate to the Book Categories folder.

4. Within the Book Categories folder, create a folder for each of the following: Fiction, Biography, Children, Humor, Social Science, Nonfiction, and Medical.

5. Within the Fiction folder, create two additional folders, one for Science Fiction and the second for Western.

6. If requested by your instructor, add another folder using your last name as the folder name.

7. Submit the assignment in the format specified by your instructor.

8. ✹ Think about how you use your computer for various tasks (consider personal, professional, and academic reasons). What folders do you think will be required on your computer to store the files you save?

Lab 2: Creating Word Documents and Saving Them in Appropriate Folders

Problem: You are taking a class that requires you to complete three Word modules. You will save the work completed in each module in a different folder (Figure 100).

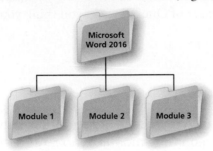

Figure 100

Perform the following tasks:

1. Create the folders shown in Figure 100.

2. Create a Word document containing the text, Module 1 Notes.

3. In the Backstage view, click Save As and then click This PC.

4. Click the Browse button to display the Save As dialog box. Click Documents to open the Documents folder. Navigate to the Module 1 folder and then save the file in the Word folder using the file name, Lab 2 Module 1 Notes.

5. Create another Word document containing the text, Module 2 Notes, and then save it in the Module 2 folder using the file name, Lab 2 Module 2 Notes.

6. Create a third Word document containing the text, Module 3 Notes, and then save it in the Module 3 folder using the file name, Lab 2 Module 3 Notes.

7. If requested by your instructor, add your name to each of the three Word documents.

8. Submit the assignment in the format specified by your instructor.

9. ✹ Based on your current knowledge of Windows and Word, how will you organize folders for assignments in this class? Why?

Lab 3: Consider This: Your Turn

Performing Research about Malware

Problem: You have just installed a new computer with the Windows operating system. Because you want to be sure that it is protected from the threat of malware, you decide to research malware, malware protection, and removing malware.

Perform the following tasks:

Part 1: Research the following three topics: malware, malware protection, and removing malware. Use the concepts and techniques presented in this module to use the search box to find information regarding these topics. Create a Word document that contains steps to safeguard a computer properly from malware, ways to prevent malware, as well as the different ways to remove malware or a virus should your computer become infected. Submit your assignment and the answers to the following critical thinking questions in the format specified by your instructor.

Part 2: ✹ You made several decisions while searching for this assignment. What decisions did you make? What was the rationale behind these decisions? How did you locate the required information about malware?

1 Creating, Formatting, and Editing a Word Document with a Picture

Objectives

You will have mastered the material in this module when you can:

- Enter text in a Word document
- Check spelling as you type
- Format paragraphs
- Format text
- Undo and redo commands or actions
- Change theme colors

- Insert digital pictures in a Word document
- Resize pictures
- Format pictures
- Add a page border
- Adjust spacing
- Correct errors and revise a document

Introduction

To advertise a sale, promote a business, publicize an event, or convey a message to the community, you may want to create a flyer and hand it out in person or post it in a public location. Libraries, schools, community organizations, grocery stores, coffee shops, and other places often provide bulletin boards or windows for flyers. You also see flyers posted on webpages, on social media, or in email messages.

Flyers announce personal items for sale or rent (car, boat, apartment); events, such as garage or block sales; services being offered (animal care, housecleaning, lessons, tours); membership, sponsorship, or donation requests (club, community organization, charity); and other messages, such as a lost or found pet.

Project — Flyer with a Picture

Individuals and businesses create flyers to gain public attention. Flyers, which usually are a single page in length, are an inexpensive means of reaching the community. Many flyers, however, go unnoticed because they are designed poorly.

The project in this module follows general guidelines and uses Word to create the flyer shown in Figure 1–1. This colorful, eye-catching flyer announces surfing lessons. The picture of the surfer riding a wave, taken with a digital camera, entices passersby or viewers to stop and look at the flyer. The headline on the flyer is large and colorful to draw attention into the text. The body copy below the picture briefly describes what is included in the lessons, along with a bulleted list that concisely highlights important information. The signature line of the flyer calls attention to the contact phone number. The word, expert, and the signature line are in a different color so that they stand apart from the rest of the text on the flyer. Finally, the graphical page border nicely frames and complements the contents of the flyer.

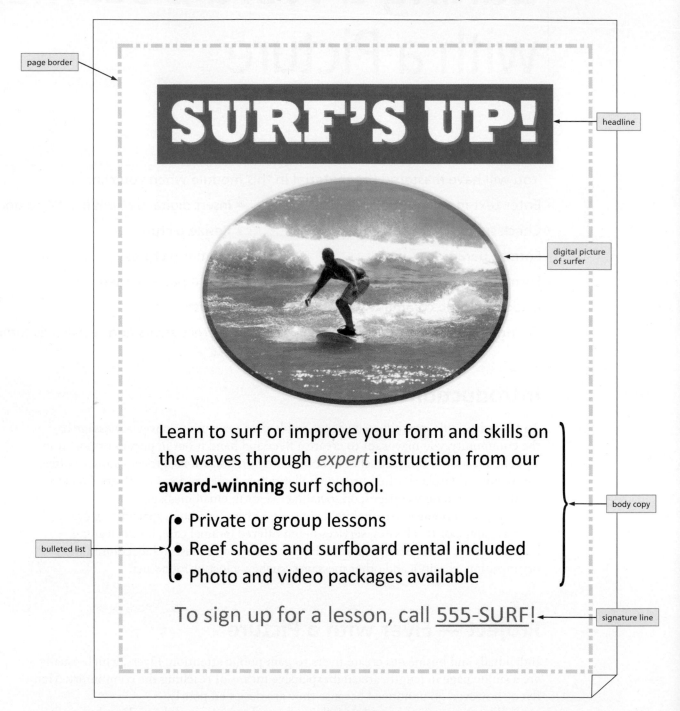

Figure 1–1

In this module, you will learn how to create the flyer shown in Figure 1–1. The following roadmap identifies general activities you will perform as you progress through this module:

1. ENTER TEXT in a new document.
2. FORMAT the TEXT in the flyer.
3. INSERT a PICTURE, called Surfer, in the flyer.
4. FORMAT the PICTURE in the flyer.
5. ENHANCE the PAGE with a border and spacing.
6. CORRECT errors AND REVISE text in the flyer.

To Run Word and Specify Settings

If you are using a computer to step through the project in this module and you want your screens to match the figures in this book, you should change your screen's resolution to 1366 × 768. For information about how to change a computer's resolution, refer to the Office and Windows module at the beginning of this book.

1 Run Word and create a blank document in the Word window.

2 If the Word window is not maximized, click the Maximize button on its title bar to maximize the window.

3 If the Print Layout button on the status bar is not selected (shown in Figure 1–2), click it so that your screen is in Print Layout view.

Q&A What is Print Layout view?
The default (preset) view in Word is **Print Layout view**, which shows the document on a mock sheet of paper in the document window.

4 If Normal (Home tab | Styles group) is not selected in the Styles gallery (shown in Figure 1–2), click it so that your document uses the Normal style.

Q&A What is the Normal style?
When you create a document, Word formats the text using a particular style. The default style in Word is called the **Normal style**, which is discussed later in this book.

What if rulers appear on my screen?
Click View on the ribbon to display the View tab and then remove the check mark from the View Ruler check box (View tab | Show group).

Entering Text

The first step in creating a document is to enter its text. With the projects in this book, you enter text by typing on the keyboard. By default, Word positions text you type at the left margin. In a later section of this module, you will learn how to format, or change the appearance of, the entered text.

For an introduction to Office and instructions about how to perform basic tasks in Office apps, read the Office and Windows module at the beginning of this book, where you can learn how to run an application, use the ribbon, save a file, open a file, print a file, exit an application, use Help, and much more.

For an introduction to Windows and instructions about how to perform basic Windows tasks, read the Office and Windows module at the beginning of this book, where you can learn how to resize windows, change screen resolution, create folders, move and rename files, use Windows Help, and much more.

BTW
The Word Window
The modules in this book begin with the Word window appearing as it did at the initial installation of the software. Your Word window may look different depending on your screen resolution and other Word settings.

To Type Text

To begin creating the flyer in this module, type the headline in the document window. ***Why?*** *The headline is the first line of text in the Surf Flyer.* The following steps type the first line of text in the document.

- Type **Surf's Up!** as the headline (Figure 1–2).

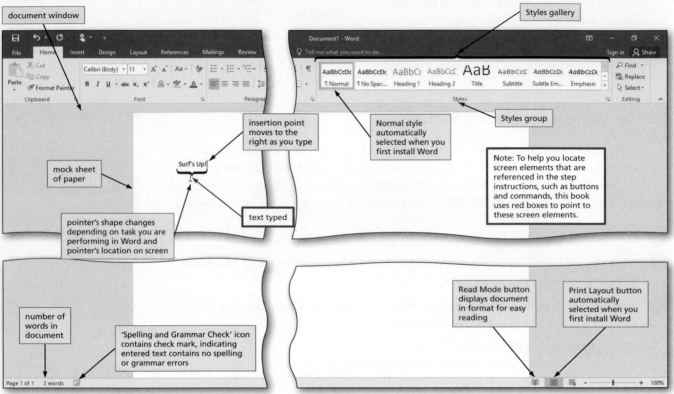

Figure 1–2

 What if I make an error while typing?
You can press the BACKSPACE key until you have deleted the text in error and then retype the text correctly.

What is the purpose of the 'Spelling and Grammar Check' icon on the status bar?
The **'Spelling and Grammar Check' icon** displays either a check mark to indicate the entered text contains no spelling or grammar errors, or an X to indicate that it found potential errors. Word flags potential errors in the document with a red, green, or blue wavy underline. Later in this module, you will learn how to fix flagged errors.

2

- Press the ENTER key to move the insertion point to the beginning of the next line (Figure 1–3).

Why did blank space appear between the headline and the insertion point?
Each time you press the ENTER key, Word creates a new paragraph and inserts blank space between the two paragraphs. Later in this module, you will learn how to increase and decrease the spacing between paragraphs.

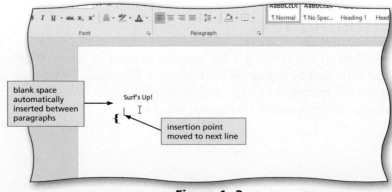

Figure 1–3

How do you use the touch keyboard with a touch screen?
To display the on-screen touch keyboard, tap the Touch Keyboard button on the Windows taskbar as shown in the Office and Windows module at the beginning of this book. When finished using the touch keyboard, tap the X button on the touch keyboard to close the keyboard.

To Display Formatting Marks

1 ENTER TEXT | 2 FORMAT TEXT | 3 INSERT PICTURE
4 FORMAT PICTURE | 5 ENHANCE PAGE | 6 CORRECT & REVISE

You may find it helpful to display formatting marks while working in a document. *Why? Formatting marks indicate where in a document you pressed the* ENTER *key,* SPACEBAR, *and other nonprinting characters.* A **formatting mark** is a character that Word displays on the screen but is not visible on a printed document. For example, the paragraph mark (¶) is a formatting mark that indicates where you pressed the ENTER key. A raised dot (·) shows where you pressed the SPACEBAR. Formatting marks are discussed as they appear on the screen.

Depending on settings made during previous Word sessions, your Word screen already may display formatting marks (Figure 1–4). The following step displays formatting marks, if they do not show already on the screen.

- If the Home tab is not the active tab, click Home on the ribbon to display the Home tab.
- If it is not selected already, click the 'Show/Hide ¶' button (Home tab | Paragraph group) to display formatting marks on the screen (Figure 1–4).

Q&A What if I do not want formatting marks to show on the screen?
You can hide them by clicking the 'Show/Hide ¶' button (Home tab | Paragraph group) again. It is recommended that you display formatting marks so that you visually can identify when you press the ENTER key, SPACEBAR, and other keys associated with nonprinting characters. Most of the document windows presented in this book, therefore, show formatting marks.

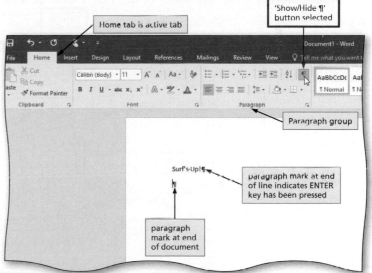

'Show/Hide ¶' button selected

Home tab is active tab

Surf's-Up¶

paragraph mark at end of line indicates ENTER key has been pressed

paragraph mark at end of document

Paragraph group

Figure 1–4

Other Ways

1. Press CTRL+SHIFT+*

To Insert a Blank Line

1 ENTER TEXT | 2 FORMAT TEXT | 3 INSERT PICTURE
4 FORMAT PICTURE | 5 ENHANCE PAGE | 6 CORRECT & REVISE

In the flyer, the digital picture of the surfer appears between the headline and body copy. You will not insert this picture, however, until after you enter and format all text. *Why? Although you can format text and insert pictures in any order, for illustration purposes, this module formats all text first before inserting the picture. Thus, you leave a blank line in the document as a placeholder for the picture.*

To enter a blank line in a document, press the ENTER key without typing any text on the line. The following step inserts one blank line below the headline.

* Press the ENTER key to insert a blank line in the document (Figure 1–5).

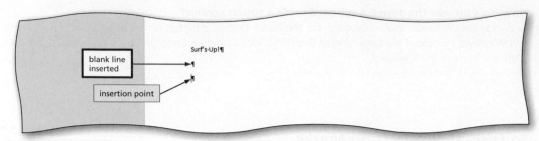

Figure 1–5

To Zoom Page Width

The next step in creating this flyer is to enlarge the contents that appear on the screen. **Why?** *You would like the text on the screen to be larger so that it is easier to read.* The document currently displays at 100% (shown in Figure 1–6). With Word, you can zoom page width, which zooms (enlarges or shrinks) the mock sheet of paper on the screen so that it is the width of the Word window. The following steps zoom page width.

* Click View on the ribbon to display the View tab (Figure 1–6).

Q&A Why did the groups on the ribbon change?
When you switch from one tab to another on the ribbon, the groups on the ribbon change to show commands related to the selected tab.

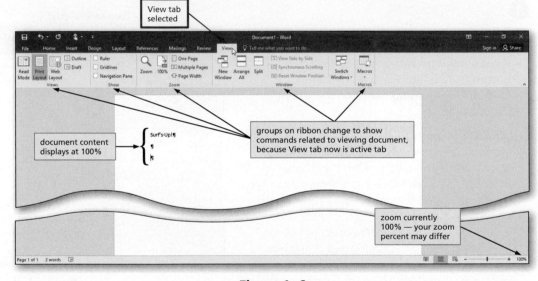

Figure 1–6

* Click the Page Width button (View tab | Zoom group) to display the page the same width as the document window (Figure 1–7).

Q&A If I change the zoom, will the document print differently?
Changing the zoom has no effect on the printed document.

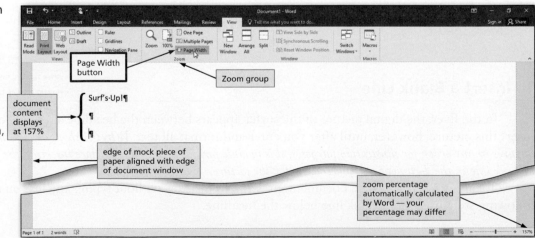

Figure 1–7

Q&A What are the other predefined zoom options?

Through the View tab | Zoom group or the Zoom dialog box (Zoom button in Zoom group), you can zoom to one page (an entire single page appears in the document window), many pages (multiple pages appear at once in the document window), page width, text width, and a variety of set percentages. Whereas page width zoom places the edges of the page at the edges of the document window, text width zoom places the document contents at the edges of the document window.

Other Ways

1. Click Zoom button (View tab | Zoom group), click Page width (Zoom dialog box), click OK button

Wordwrap

Wordwrap allows you to type words in a paragraph continually without pressing the ENTER key at the end of each line. As you type, if a word extends beyond the right margin, Word also automatically positions that word on the next line along with the insertion point.

Word creates a new paragraph each time you press the ENTER key. Thus, as you type text in the document window, do not press the ENTER key when the insertion point reaches the right margin. Instead, press the ENTER key only in these circumstances:

1. To insert a blank line(s) in a document (as shown in previous steps)
2. To begin a new paragraph
3. To terminate a short line of text and advance to the next line
4. To respond to questions or prompts in Word dialog boxes, task panes, and other on-screen objects

BTW

Zooming

If text is too small for you to read on the screen, you can zoom the document by dragging the Zoom slider on the status bar or by clicking the Zoom Out or Zoom In buttons on the status bar. Changing the zoom has no effect on the printed document.

1 ENTER TEXT | 2 FORMAT TEXT | 3 INSERT PICTURE
4 FORMAT PICTURE | 5 ENHANCE PAGE | 6 CORRECT & REVISE

To Wordwrap Text as You Type

The next step in creating the flyer is to type the body copy. *Why? In many flyers, the body copy text appears below the headline.* The following steps illustrate how the body copy text wordwraps as you enter it in the document, which means you will not have to press the ENTER key at the end of the line.

❶

• Type the first sentence of the body copy: **Learn to surf or improve your form and skills on the waves through expert instruction from our award-winning surf school.**

Q&A Why does my document wrap on different words?

The printer connected to a computer is one factor that can control where wordwrap occurs for each line in a document. Thus, it is possible that the same document could wordwrap differently if printed on different printers.

❷

• Press the ENTER key to position the insertion point on the next line in the document (Figure 1–8).

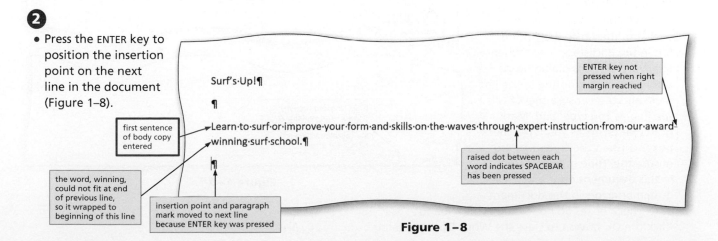

Surf's·Up¶

¶

first sentence of body copy entered

Learn·to·surf·or·improve·your·form·and·skills·on·the·waves·through·expert·instruction·from·our·award-winning·surf·school.¶

¶

ENTER key not pressed when right margin reached

raised dot between each word indicates SPACEBAR has been pressed

the word, winning, could not fit at end of previous line, so it wrapped to beginning of this line

insertion point and paragraph mark moved to next line because ENTER key was pressed

Figure 1–8

Spelling and Grammar Check

As you type text in a document, Word checks your typing for possible spelling and grammar errors. If all of the words you have typed are in Word's dictionary and your grammar is correct, as mentioned earlier, the Spelling and Grammar Check icon on the status bar displays a check mark. Otherwise, the icon shows an X. In this case, Word flags the potential error(s) in the document window with a red, green, or blue wavy underline.

- A red wavy underline means the flagged text is not in Word's dictionary (because it is a proper name or misspelled).
- A green wavy underline indicates the text may be incorrect grammatically.
- A blue wavy underline indicates the text may contain a contextual spelling error, such as the misuse of homophones (words that are pronounced the same but that have different spellings or meanings, such as one and won).

Although you can check the entire document for spelling and grammar errors at once, you also can check flagged errors as they appear on the screen.

A flagged word is not necessarily misspelled. For example, many names, abbreviations, and specialized terms are not in Word's main dictionary. In these cases, you can instruct Word to ignore the flagged word. As you type, Word also detects duplicate words while checking for spelling errors. For example, if your document contains the phrase, to the the store, Word places a red wavy underline below the second occurrence of the word, the.

BTW

Automatic Spelling Correction

As you type, Word automatically corrects some misspelled words. For example, if you type recieve, Word automatically corrects the misspelling and displays the word, receive, when you press the SPACEBAR or type a punctuation mark. To see a complete list of automatically corrected words, click File on the ribbon to open the Backstage view, click the Options tab in the Backstage view, click Proofing in the left pane (Word Options dialog box), click the AutoCorrect Options button, and then scroll through the list near the bottom of the dialog box.

To Check Spelling and Grammar as You Type

1 ENTER TEXT | 2 FORMAT TEXT | 3 INSERT PICTURE
4 FORMAT PICTURE | 5 ENHANCE PAGE | 6 CORRECT & REVISE

In the following steps, the word, group, has been misspelled intentionally as goup. *Why? These steps illustrate Word's check spelling as you type feature. If you are completing this project on a computer, your flyer may contain different or no misspelled words, depending on the accuracy of your typing.*

- Type **Private or goup** and then press the SPACEBAR, so that a red wavy line appears below the misspelled word (Figure 1–9).

Q&A What if Word does not flag my spelling and grammar errors with wavy underlines?
To verify that the check spelling and grammar as you type features are enabled, click File on the ribbon to open the Backstage view and then click the Options tab in the Backstage view. When the Word Options dialog box is displayed, click Proofing in the left pane and then ensure the 'Check spelling as you type' and 'Mark grammar errors as you type' check boxes contain check marks. Also ensure the 'Hide spelling errors in this document only' and 'Hide grammar errors in this document only' check boxes do not contain check marks. Click the OK button to close the Word Options dialog box.

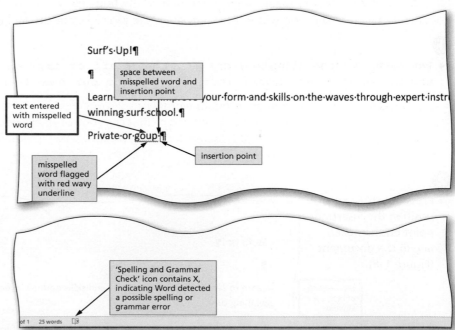

Figure 1–9

- Right-click the flagged word (goup, in this case) to display a shortcut menu that presents a list of suggested spelling corrections for the flagged word (Figure 1–10).

What if, when I right-click the misspelled word, my desired correction is not in the list on the shortcut menu?
You can click outside the shortcut menu to close the shortcut menu and then retype the correct word.

What if a flagged word actually is, for example, a proper name and spelled correctly?
Right-click it and then click Ignore All on the shortcut menu to instruct Word not to flag future occurrences of the same word in this document.

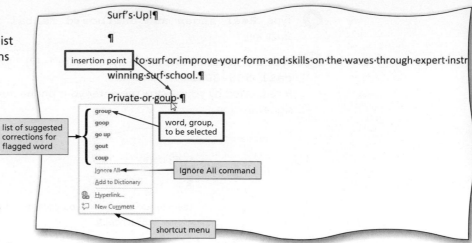

Figure 1–10

- Click group on the shortcut menu to replace the misspelled word in the document with a correctly spelled word (Figure 1–11).

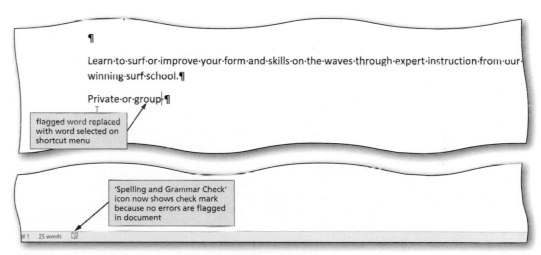

Figure 1–11

Other Ways

1. Click 'Spelling and Grammar Check' icon on status bar, click desired word in Spelling pane, click Change button, click OK button

To Enter More Text

In the flyer, the text yet to be entered includes the remainder of the body copy, which will be formatted as a bulleted list, and the signature line. The following steps enter the remainder of text in the flyer.

1 Press the END key to move the insertion point to the end of the current line.

2 Type **lessons** and then press the ENTER key.

③ Type `Photo and video packages available` and then press the ENTER key.

④ Type `Reef shoes and surfboard rental included` and then press the ENTER key.

⑤ Type the signature line in the flyer (Figure 1–12): `To sign up for a lesson, call 555-SURF!`
If requested by your instructor, enter your phone number instead of 555-SURF in the signature line.

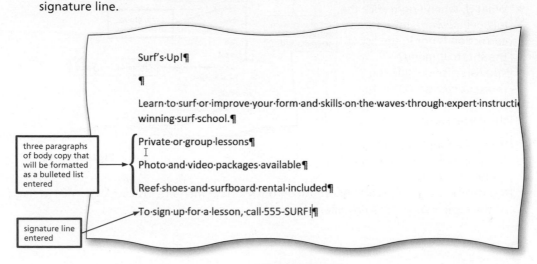

Figure 1–12

BTW

Organizing Files and Folders

You should organize and store files in folders so that you easily can find the files later. For example, if you are taking an introductory technology class called CIS 101, a good practice would be to save all Word files in a Word folder in a CIS 101 folder. For a discussion of folders and detailed examples of creating folders, refer to the Office and Windows module at the beginning of this book.

⑥ Save the flyer on your hard drive, OneDrive, or other storage location using Surf Flyer as the file name.

Q&A Why should I save the flyer at this time?
You have performed many tasks while creating this flyer and do not want to risk losing work completed thus far. For information about how to save, refer to the Office and Windows module at the beginning of this book.

CONSIDER THIS

How should you organize text in a flyer?
The text in a flyer typically is organized into three areas: headline, body copy, and signature line.

- The **headline** is the first line of text on the flyer. It conveys the product or service being offered (such as a car for sale, lessons, or sightseeing tours) or the benefit that will be gained (such as a convenience, better performance, greater security, higher earnings, or more comfort), or it can contain a message (such as a lost or found pet).

- The **body copy** consists of text between the headline and the signature line. This text highlights the key points of the message in as few words as possible. It should be easy to read and follow. While emphasizing the positive, the body copy must be realistic, truthful, and believable.

- The **signature line**, which is the last line of text on the flyer, contains contact information or identifies a call to action.

Navigating a Document

You view only a portion of a document on the screen through the document window. At some point when you type text or insert graphics, Word probably will **scroll** the top or bottom portion of the document off the screen. Although you cannot see the text and graphics once they scroll off the screen, they remain in the document.

You can use touch gestures, the keyboard, or a mouse to scroll to a different location in a document and/or move the insertion point around a document. If you are using a touch screen, simply use your finger to slide the document up or down to display a different location in the document and then tap to move the insertion point to a new location. When you use the keyboard, the insertion point automatically moves when you press the desired keys. For example, the previous steps used the END key to move the insertion point to the end of the current line. Table 1–1 outlines various techniques to navigate a document using the keyboard.

Table 1–1 Moving the Insertion Point with the Keyboard

Insertion Point Direction	Key(s) to Press	Insertion Point Direction	Key(s) to Press
Left one character	LEFT ARROW	Up one paragraph	CTRL+UP ARROW
Right one character	RIGHT ARROW	Down one paragraph	CTRL+DOWN ARROW
Left one word	CTRL+LEFT ARROW	Up one screen	PAGE UP
Right one word	CTRL+RIGHT ARROW	Down one screen	PAGE DOWN
Up one line	UP ARROW	To top of document window	ALT+CTRL+PAGE UP
Down one line	DOWN ARROW	To bottom of document window	ALT+CTRL+PAGE DOWN
To end of line	END	To beginning of document	CTRL+HOME
To beginning of line	HOME	To end of document	CTRL+END

© 2015 Cengage Learning

With the mouse, you can use the scroll arrows or the scroll box on the scroll bar to display a different portion of the document in the document window and then click the mouse to move the insertion point to that location. Table 1–2 explains various techniques for using the scroll bar to scroll vertically with the mouse.

Table 1–2 Using the Scroll Bar to Scroll Vertically with the Mouse

Scroll Direction	Mouse Action	Scroll Direction	Mouse Action
Up	Drag the scroll box upward.	Down one screen	Click anywhere below the scroll box on the vertical scroll bar.
Down	Drag the scroll box downward.	Up one line	Click the scroll arrow at the top of the vertical scroll bar.
Up one screen	Click anywhere above the scroll box on the vertical scroll bar.	Down one line	Click the scroll arrow at the bottom of the vertical scroll bar.

© 2015 Cengage Learning

Formatting Paragraphs and Characters

With the text for the flyer entered, the next step is to **format,** or change the appearance of, its text. A paragraph encompasses the text from the first character in the paragraph up to and including its paragraph mark (¶). **Paragraph formatting** is the process of changing the appearance of a paragraph. For example, you can center or add bullets to a paragraph. Characters include letters, numbers, punctuation marks, and symbols. **Character formatting** is the process of changing the way characters appear on the screen and in print. You use character formatting to emphasize certain words and improve readability of a document. For example, you can color, italicize, or underline characters. Often, you apply both paragraph and character formatting to the same text. For example, you may center a paragraph (paragraph formatting) and underline some of the characters in the same paragraph (character formatting).

Although you can format paragraphs and characters before you type, many Word users enter text first and then format the existing text. Figure 1–13a shows the flyer in this module before formatting its paragraphs and characters. Figure 1–13b shows the flyer after formatting. As you can see from the two figures, a document that is formatted is easier to read and looks more professional. The following sections discuss how to format the flyer so that it looks like Figure 1–13b.

BTW
Minimize Wrist Injury
Computer users frequently switch among the keyboard, the mouse, and touch gestures during a word processing session; such switching strains the wrist. To help prevent wrist injury, minimize switching. For instance, if your hand already is on the mouse, use the mouse to scroll. If your fingers already are on the keyboard, use keyboard keys to scroll. If your fingertips already are on the screen, use your finger to slide the document to a new location.

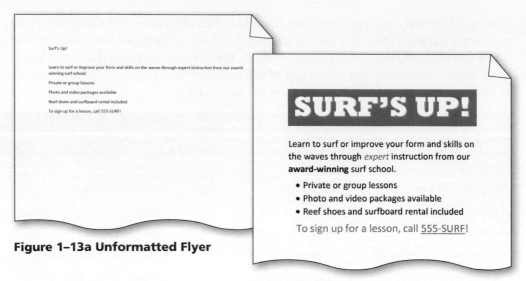

Figure 1–13a Unformatted Flyer

Figure 1–13b Formatted Flyer

Figure 1–13

BTW
Character Widths
Many word processing documents use variable character fonts, where some characters are wider than others; for example, the letter w is wider than the letter i.

Font, Font Sizes, and Themes

Characters that appear on the screen are a specific shape and size. The **font**, or typeface, defines the appearance and shape of the letters, numbers, and special characters. In Word, the default font usually is Calibri (shown in Figure 1–14). You can leave characters in the default font or change them to a different font. **Font size** specifies the size of the characters and is determined by a measurement system called points. A single **point** is about 1/72 of one inch in height. The default font size in Word typically is 11 (Figure 1–14). Thus, a character with a font size of 11 is about 11/72 or a little less than 1/6 of one inch in height. You can increase or decrease the font size of characters in a document.

A document **theme** is a set of unified formats for fonts, colors, and graphics. Word includes a variety of document themes to assist you with coordinating these visual elements in a document. The default theme fonts are Calibri Light for headings and Calibri for body text. By changing the document theme, you quickly can give your document a new look. You also can define your own document themes.

CONSIDER THIS

How do I know which formats to use in a flyer?

In a flyer, consider the following formatting suggestions.

- **Increase the font size of characters.** Flyers usually are posted on a bulletin board or in a window. Thus, the font size should be as large as possible so that passersby easily can read the flyer. To give the headline more impact, its font size should be larger than the font size of the text in the body copy. If possible, make the font size of the signature line larger than the body copy but smaller than the headline.

- **Change the font of characters.** Use fonts that are easy to read. Try to use only two different fonts in a flyer; for example, use one for the headline and the other for all other text. Too many fonts can make the flyer visually confusing.

- **Change the paragraph alignment.** The default alignment for paragraphs in a document is **left-aligned**, that is, flush at the left margin of the document with uneven right edges. Consider changing the alignment of some of the paragraphs to add interest and variety to the flyer.

- **Highlight key paragraphs with bullets.** A bulleted paragraph is a paragraph that begins with a dot or other symbol. Use bulleted paragraphs to highlight important points in a flyer.

- **Emphasize important words.** To call attention to certain words or lines, you can underline them, italicize them, or bold them. Use these formats sparingly, however, because overuse will minimize their effect and make the flyer look too busy.

- **Use color.** Use colors that complement each other and convey the meaning of the flyer. Vary colors in terms of hue and brightness. Headline colors, for example, can be bold and bright. Signature lines should stand out more than body copy but less than headlines. Keep in mind that too many colors can detract from the flyer and make it difficult to read.

To Center a Paragraph

The headline in the flyer currently is left-aligned (shown in Figure 1–14). *Why? Word, by default, left-aligns text, unless you specifically change the alignment.* You want the headline to be **centered**, that is, positioned horizontally between the left and right margins on the page. Recall that Word considers a single short line of text, such as the one-word headline, a paragraph. Thus, you will center the paragraph containing the headline. The following steps center a paragraph.

1

- Click Home on the ribbon to display the Home tab.
- Click somewhere in the paragraph to be centered (in this case, the headline) to position the insertion point in the paragraph to be centered (Figure 1–14).

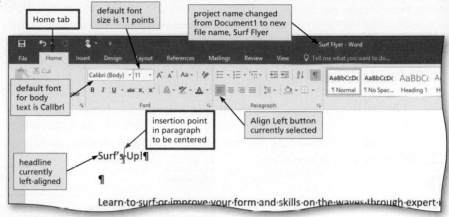

Figure 1–14

2

- Click the Center button (Home tab | Paragraph group) to center the paragraph containing the insertion point (Figure 1–15).

Q&A What if I want to return the paragraph to left-aligned?
You would click the Center button again or click the Align Left button (Home tab | Paragraph group).

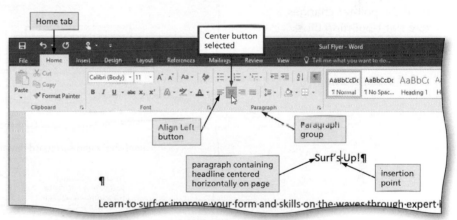

Figure 1–15

Other Ways

1. Right-click paragraph (or if using touch, tap 'Show Context Menu' button on mini toolbar), click Paragraph on shortcut menu, click Indents and Spacing tab (Paragraph dialog box), click Alignment arrow, click Centered, click OK button

2. Click Paragraph Settings Dialog Box Launcher (Home tab or Layout tab | Paragraph group), click Indents and Spacing tab (Paragraph dialog box), click Alignment arrow, click Centered, click OK button

3. Press CTRL+E

To Center Another Paragraph

In the flyer, the signature line is to be centered to match the paragraph alignment of the headline. The following steps center the signature line.

1 Click somewhere in the paragraph to be centered (in this case, the signature line) to position the insertion point in the paragraph to be formatted.

2 Click the Center button (Home tab | Paragraph group) to center the paragraph containing the insertion point (shown in Figure 1–16).

BTW
File Type
Depending on your Windows settings, the file type .docx may be displayed on the title bar immediately to the right of the file name after you save the file. The file type .docx identifies a Word 2016 document.

BTW
The Ribbon and Screen Resolution
Word may change how the groups and buttons within the groups appear on the ribbon, depending on the computer or mobile device's screen resolution. Thus, your ribbon may look different from the ones in this book if you are using a screen resolution other than 1366 × 768.

Formatting Single versus Multiple Paragraphs and Characters

As shown in the previous sections, to format a single paragraph, simply position the insertion point in the paragraph to make it the current paragraph and then format the paragraph. Similarly, to format a single word, position the insertion point in the word to make it the current word, and then format the word.

To format multiple paragraphs or words, however, you first must select the paragraphs or words you want to format and then format the selection.

1 ENTER TEXT | 2 FORMAT TEXT | **3 INSERT PICTURE**
4 FORMAT PICTURE | 5 ENHANCE PAGE | 6 CORRECT & REVISE

To Select a Line

The default font size of 11 point is too small for a headline in a flyer. To increase the font size of the characters in the headline, you first must select the line of text containing the headline. ***Why?*** *If you increase the font size of text without selecting any text, Word will increase the font size only of the word containing the insertion point.* The following step selects a line.

• Move the pointer to the left of the line to be selected (in this case, the headline) until the pointer changes to a right-pointing block arrow (Figure 1–16).

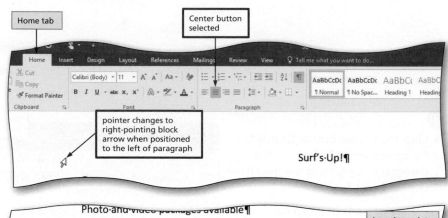

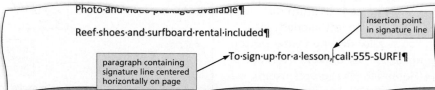

Figure 1–16

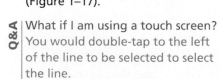

• While the pointer is a right-pointing block arrow, click the mouse button to select the entire line to the right of the pointer (Figure 1–17).

Q&A

What if I am using a touch screen?
You would double-tap to the left of the line to be selected to select the line.

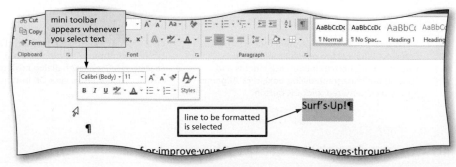

Figure 1–17

Why is the selected text shaded gray?
If your screen normally displays dark letters on a light background, which is the default setting in Word, then selected text is displayed with a light shading color, such as gray, on the dark letters. Note that the selection that appears on the text does not print.

Other Ways

1. Drag pointer through line   2. With insertion point at beginning of desired line, press CRTL+SHIFT+DOWN ARROW

To Change the Font Size of Selected Text

The next step is to increase the font size of the characters in the selected headline. *Why? You would like the headline to be as large as possible and still fit on a single line, which in this case is 72 point.* The following steps increase the font size of the headline from 11 to 72 point.

1

- With the text selected, click the Font Size arrow (Home tab | Font group) to display the Font Size gallery (Figure 1–18).

Q&A

What is the Font Size arrow?
The Font Size arrow is the arrow to the right of the Font Size box, which is the text box that displays the current font size.

Why are the font sizes in my Font Size gallery different from those in Figure 1–18?
Font sizes may vary depending on the current font and your printer driver.

What happened to the mini toolbar?
The mini toolbar disappears if you do not use it. These steps use the Font Size arrow on the Home tab instead of the Font Size arrow on the mini toolbar.

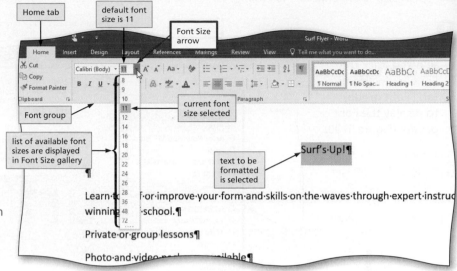

Figure 1–18

2

- Point to 72 in the Font Size gallery to display a live preview of the selected text at the selected point size (Figure 1–19).

Q&A

What is live preview?
Recall from the Office and Windows module at the beginning of this book that live preview is a feature that allows you to point to a gallery choice and see its effect in the document — without actually selecting the choice.

Can I use live preview on a touch screen?
Live preview is not available on a touch screen.

Figure 1–19

Experiment

- Point to various font sizes in the Font Size gallery and watch the font size of the selected text change in the document window.

3

- Click 72 in the Font Size gallery to increase the font size of the selected text.

Other Ways			
1. Click Font Size arrow on mini toolbar, click desired font size in Font Size gallery	2. Right-click selected text (or, if using touch, tap 'Show Context Menu' button on mini toolbar), click Font on shortcut menu, click Font tab (Font dialog box), select desired font size in Size list, click OK button	3. Click Font Dialog Box Launcher, (Home tab | Font group) click Font tab (Font dialog box), select desired font size in Size list, click OK button	4. Press CTRL+D, click Font tab (Font dialog box), select desired font size in Size list, click OK button

To Change the Font of Selected Text

The default theme font for headings is Calibri Light and for all other text, called body text in Word, is Calibri. Many other fonts are available, however, so that you can add variety to documents.

The following steps change the font of the headline from Calibri to Rockwell Extra Bold. *Why? To draw more attention to the headline, you change its font so that it differs from the font of other text in the flyer.*

1

• With the text selected, click the Font arrow (Home tab | Font group) to display the Font gallery (Figure 1–20).

Q&A
Will the fonts in my Font gallery be the same as those in Figure 1–20?
Your list of available fonts may differ, depending on the type of printer you are using and other settings.

What if the text no longer is selected?
Follow the steps described earlier to select a line.

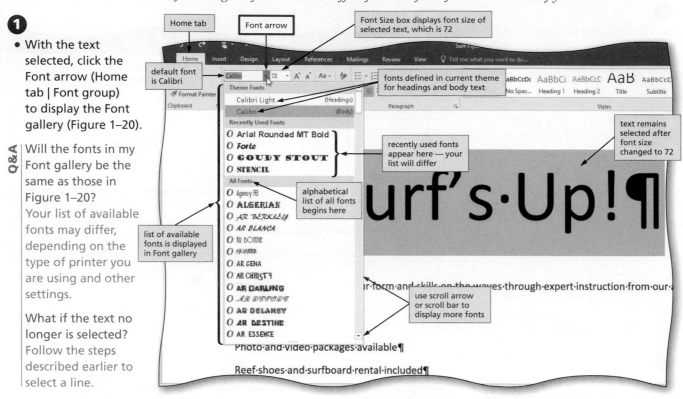

Figure 1–20

2

• If necessary, scroll through the Font gallery to display Rockwell Extra Bold (or a similar font).

• Point to 'Rockwell Extra Bold' (or a similar font) to display a live preview of the selected text in the selected font (Figure 1–21).

 Experiment

• Point to various fonts in the Font gallery and watch the font of the selected text change in the document window.

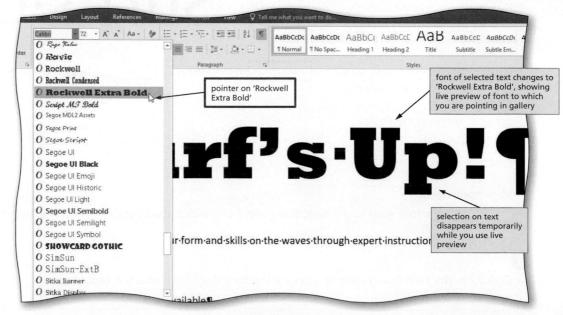

Figure 1–21

• Click 'Rockwell Extra Bold' (or a similar font) in the Font gallery to change the font of the selected text.

Q&A
If the font I want to use appears in the Recently Used Fonts list in the Font gallery, could I click it there instead?
Yes.

Other Ways

1. Click Font arrow on mini toolbar, click desired font in Font gallery	2. Right-click selected text (or, if using touch, tap 'Show Context Menu' button on mini toolbar), click Font on shortcut menu, click Font tab (Font dialog box), select desired font in Font list, click OK button	3. Click Font Dialog Box Launcher (Home tab | Font group), click Font tab (Font dialog box), select desired font in Font list, click OK button	4. Press CTRL+D, click Font tab (Font dialog box), select desired font in Font list, click OK button

To Change the Case of Selected Text

1 ENTER TEXT | 2 FORMAT TEXT | 3 INSERT PICTURE
4 FORMAT PICTURE | 5 ENHANCE PAGE | 6 CORRECT & REVISE

The headline currently shows the first letter in each word capitalized, which sometimes is referred to as initial cap. The following steps change the headline to uppercase. *Why? To draw more attention to the headline, you would like the entire line of text to be capitalized, or in uppercase letters.*

• With the text selected, click the Change Case button (Home tab | Font group) to display the Change Case gallery (Figure 1–22).

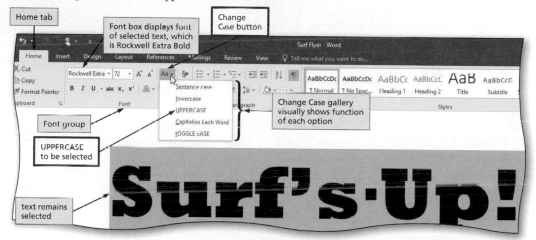

Figure 1–22

2

• Click UPPERCASE in the Change Case gallery to change the case of the selected text (Figure 1–23).

Q&A
What if a ruler appears on the screen or the pointer shape changes?
If you are using a mouse, depending on the position of your pointer and locations you click on the screen, a ruler may appear automatically or the pointer's shape may change. Simply move the mouse and the ruler should disappear and/or the pointer shape will change.

Figure 1–23

Other Ways

1. Right-click selected text (or, if using touch, tap 'Show Context Menu' button on mini toolbar), click Font on shortcut menu, click Font tab (Font dialog box), select All caps in Effects area, click OK button	2. Click Font Dialog Box Launcher (Home tab | Font group), click Font tab (Font dialog box), select All caps in Effects area, click OK button	3. Press SHIFT+F3 repeatedly until text is desired case

To Apply a Text Effect to Selected Text

Word provides many text effects to add interest and variety to text. The following steps apply a text effect to the headline. *Why? You would like the text in the headline to be even more noticeable.*

1

- With the text selected, click the 'Text Effects and Typography' button (Home tab | Font group) to display the Text Effects and Typography gallery (Figure 1–24).

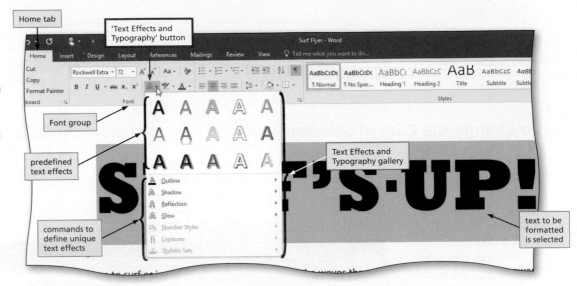

Figure 1–24

2

- Point to 'Fill - White, Outline - Accent 2, Hard Shadow - Accent 2' (fourth text effect in third row) to display a live preview of the selected text with the selected text effect (Figure 1–25).

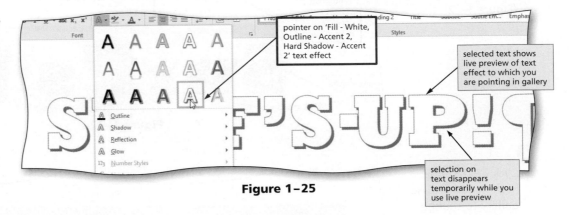

Figure 1–25

Experiment

- Point to various text effects in the Text Effects and Typography gallery and watch the text effects of the selected text change in the document window.

3

- Click 'Fill - White, Outline - Accent 2, Hard Shadow - Accent 2' to change the text effect of the selected text.

4

- Click anywhere in the document window to remove the selection from the selected text.

Other Ways

1. Right-click selected text (or, if using touch, tap 'Show Context Menu' button on mini toolbar), click Font on shortcut menu, click Font tab (Font dialog box), click Text Effects button, expand Text Fill or Text Outline section and then select the desired text effect(s) (Format Text Effects dialog box), click OK button, click OK button

2. Click Font Dialog Box Launcher (Home tab | Font group), click Font tab (Font dialog box), click Text Effects button, expand Text Fill or Text Outline section and then select desired text effect (Format Text Effects dialog box), click OK button, click OK button

To Shade a Paragraph

When you **shade** text, Word colors the rectangular area behind any text or graphics. If the text to shade is a paragraph, Word shades the area from the left margin to the right margin of the current paragraph. To shade a paragraph, place the insertion point in the paragraph. To shade any other text, you must first select the text to be shaded.

This flyer uses a shading color for the headline. **Why?** *To make the headline of the flyer more eye-catching, you shade it.* The following steps shade a paragraph.

1

- Click somewhere in the paragraph to be shaded (in this case, the headline) to position the insertion point in the paragraph to be formatted.

- Click the Shading arrow (Home tab | Paragraph group) to display the Shading gallery (Figure 1–26).

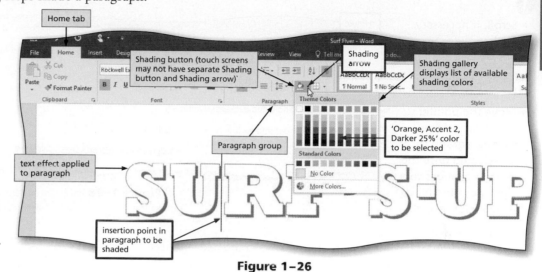

Figure 1–26

Q&A What if I click the Shading button by mistake?

Click the Shading arrow and proceed with Step 2. Note that if you are using a touch screen, you may not have a separate Shading button.

Why does my Shading gallery display different colors?

Your color scheme setting may display colors in a different order or may be different from Office, which is the default color scheme. To change the color scheme, click Design on the ribbon, click the Theme Colors button (Design tab | Document Formatting group), and then click Office in the Theme Colors gallery.

Experiment

- Point to various colors in the Shading gallery and watch the shading color of the current paragraph change.

2

- Click 'Orange, Accent 2, Darker 25%' (sixth color in fifth row) to shade the current paragraph (Figure 1–27).

Figure 1–27

Q&A What if I apply a dark shading color to dark text?

When the font color of text is Automatic, the color usually is black. If you select a dark shading color, Word automatically may change the text color to white so that the shaded text is easier to read.

Other Ways

1. Click Borders arrow (Home tab | Paragraph group), click Borders and Shading, click Shading tab (Borders and Shading dialog box), click Fill arrow, select desired color, click OK button

To Select Multiple Lines

The next formatting step for the flyer is to increase the font size of the characters between the headline and the signature line. *Why? You want this text to be easier to read from a distance.*

To change the font size of the characters in multiple lines, you first must select all the lines to be formatted. The following steps select multiple lines.

- Scroll, if necessary, so that all text below the headline is displayed on the screen.

- Move the pointer to the left of the first paragraph to be selected until the pointer changes to a right-pointing block arrow (Figure 1–28).

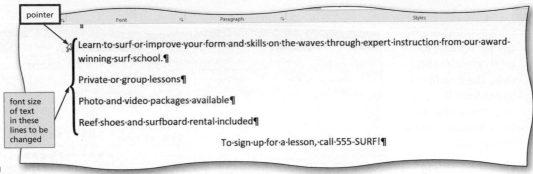

Figure 1–28

Q&A What if I am using a touch screen?
You would tap to position the insertion point in the text to select.

- While the pointer is a right-pointing block arrow, drag downward to select all lines that will be formatted (Figure 1–29).

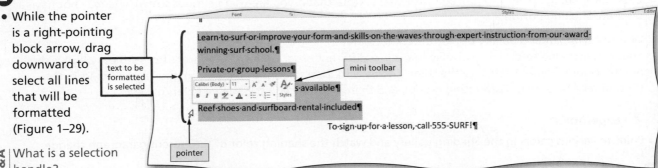

Figure 1–29

Q&A What is a selection handle?
When working on a touch screen, a **selection handle** (small circle) appears below the insertion point. Using a fingertip, you drag a selection handle to select text.

Other Ways

1. With insertion point at beginning of desired line, press SHIFT+DOWN ARROW repeatedly until all lines are selected

---

BTW
Formatting Marks
With some fonts, the formatting marks will not be displayed properly on the screen. For example, the raised dot that signifies a blank space between words may be displayed behind a character instead of in the blank space, causing the characters to look incorrect.

To Change the Font Size of Selected Text

The characters between the headline and the signature line in the flyer currently are 11 point. To make them easier to read from a distance, this flyer uses a 24-point font size for these characters. The following steps change the font size of the selected text.

1 With the text selected, click the Font Size arrow (Home tab | Font group) to display the Font Size gallery.

2 Click 24 in the Font Size gallery to increase the font size of the selected text.

③ Click anywhere in the document window to remove the selection from the text.

④ If necessary, scroll so that you can see all the resized text on the screen (Figure 1–30).

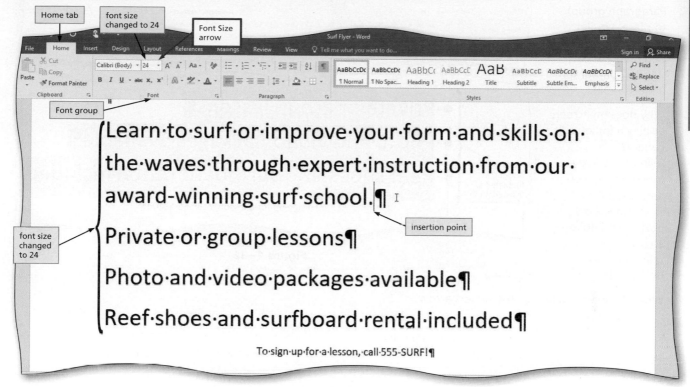

Figure 1–30

To Bullet a List of Paragraphs

1 ENTER TEXT | 2 FORMAT TEXT | 3 INSERT PICTURE
4 FORMAT PICTURE | 5 ENHANCE PAGE | 6 CORRECT & REVISE

A **bulleted list** is a series of paragraphs, each beginning with a bullet character. The next step is to format the three paragraphs about the lessons that are above the signature line in the flyer as a bulleted list.

To format a list of paragraphs with bullets, you first must select all the lines in the paragraphs. *Why? If you do not select all paragraphs, Word will place a bullet only in the paragraph containing the insertion point.* The following steps bullet a list of paragraphs.

①

- Move the pointer to the left of the first paragraph to be selected until the pointer changes to a right-pointing block arrow.

- Drag downward until all paragraphs that will be

formatted with a bullet character are selected (Figure 1–31).

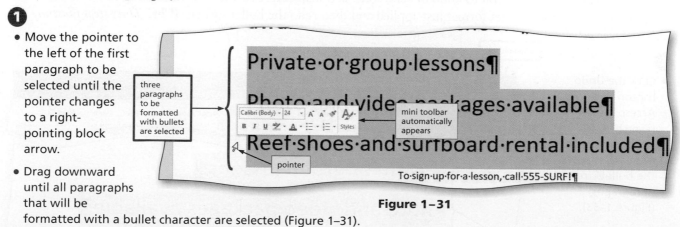

Figure 1–31

Q&A What if I am using a touch screen?
Tap to position the insertion point in the text to select and then drag the selection handle(s) as necessary to select the text that will be formatted.

②

- Click the Bullets button (Home tab | Paragraph group) to place a bullet character at the beginning of each selected paragraph (Figure 1–32).

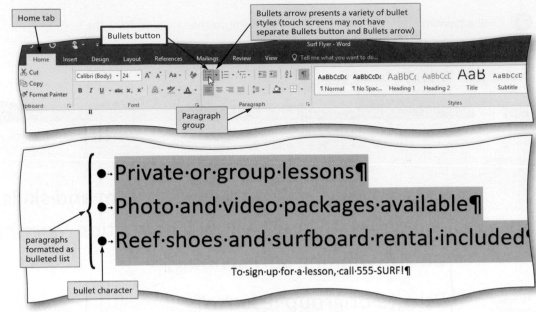

Figure 1–32

Q&A Why does my screen display a Bullets gallery?
If you are using a touch screen, you may not have a separate Bullets button and Bullets arrow. In this case, select the desired bullet style in the Bullets gallery.

What if I accidentally click the Bullets arrow?
Press the ESCAPE key to remove the Bullets gallery from the screen and then repeat Step 2.

How do I remove bullets from a list or paragraph?
Select the list or paragraph and then click the Bullets button again, or click the Bullets arrow and then click None in the Bullet Library.

Other Ways

1. Right-click selected paragraphs, click Bullets button on mini toolbar

To Undo and Redo an Action

1 ENTER TEXT | 2 FORMAT TEXT | 3 INSERT PICTURE
4 FORMAT PICTURE | 5 ENHANCE PAGE | 6 CORRECT & REVISE

Word provides a means of canceling your recent command(s) or action(s). For example, if you format text incorrectly, you can undo the format and try it again. When you point to the Undo button, Word displays the action you can undo as part of a ScreenTip.

If, after you undo an action, you decide you did not want to perform the undo, you can redo the undone action. Word does not allow you to undo or redo some actions, such as saving or printing a document. The following steps undo the bullet format just applied and then redo the bullet format. *Why? These steps illustrate the undo and redo actions.*

①

- Click the Undo button on the Quick Access Toolbar to reverse your most recent action (in this case, remove the bullets from the paragraphs) (Figure 1–33).

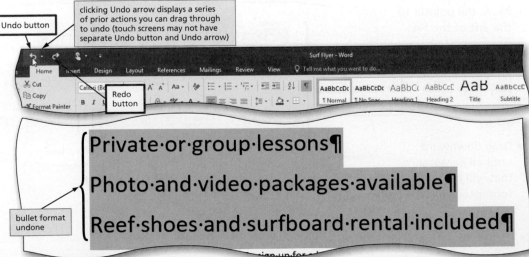

Figure 1–33

- Click the Redo button on the Quick Access Toolbar to reverse your most recent undo (in this case, place a bullet character on the paragraphs again) (shown in Figure 1–32).

Other Ways

1. Press CTRL+Z to undo; press CTRL+Y to redo

To Italicize Text

Italic text has a slanted appearance. The next step is to italicize the word, expert, in the flyer to further emphasize it. As with a single paragraph, if you want to format a single word, you do not need to select it. *Why? To format a single word, you simply position the insertion point somewhere in the word and apply the desired format.* The following step italicizes a word.

- Click somewhere in the word to be italicized (expert, in this case) to position the insertion point in the word to be formatted.

- Click the Italic button (Home tab | Font group) to italicize the word containing the insertion point (Figure 1–34).

Q&A

How would I remove an italic format?
You would click the Italic button a second time, or you immediately could click the Undo button on the Quick Access Toolbar or press CTRL+Z.

Figure 1–34

How can I tell what formatting has been applied to text?
The selected buttons and boxes on the Home tab show formatting characteristics of the location of the insertion point. With the insertion point in the word, expert, the Home tab shows these formats: 24-point Calibri italic font.

Why did the appearance of the Redo button change?
It changed to a Repeat button. When it is a Repeat button, you can click it to repeat your last action. For example, you can select different text and then click the Repeat button to apply (repeat) the italic format to the selected text.

Other Ways

1. Click Italic button on mini toolbar

2. Right-click selected text (or, if using touch, tap 'Show Context Menu' button on mini toolbar), click Font on shortcut menu, click Font tab (Font dialog box), click Italic in Font style list, click OK button

3. Click Font Dialog Box Launcher (Home tab | Font group), click Font tab (Font dialog box), click Italic in Font style list, click OK button

4. Press CTRL+I

To Color Text

The following steps change the color of the word, expert. *Why? To emphasize the word even more, you change its color.*

- With the insertion point in the word to format, click the Font Color arrow (Home tab | Font group) to display the Font Color gallery (Figure 1–35).

Q&A What if I click the Font Color button by mistake?
Click the Font Color arrow and then proceed with Step 2. Note that you may not have a separate Font Color button if you are using a touch screen.

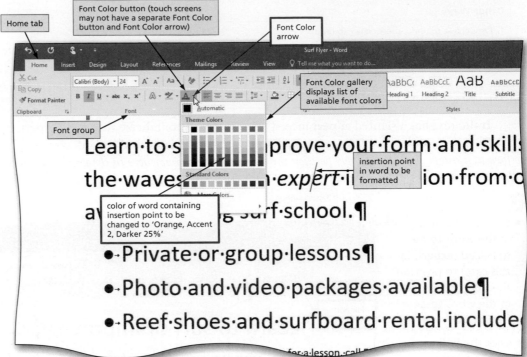

Figure 1–35

 Experiment

- If you are using a mouse, point to various colors in the Font Color gallery and watch the color of the current word change.

2

- Click 'Orange, Accent 2, Darker 25%' (sixth color in fifth row) to change the color of the text (Figure 1–36).

Q&A How would I change the text color back to black?
You would position the insertion point in the word or select the text, click the Font Color arrow (Home tab | Font group) again, and then click Automatic in the Font Color gallery.

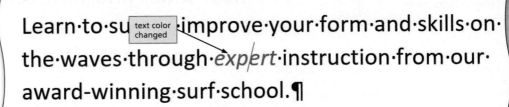

Figure 1–36

Other Ways

1. Click Font Color arrow on mini toolbar, click desired color
2. Right-click selected text (or, if using touch, tap 'Show Context Menu' button on mini toolbar), click Font on shortcut menu, click Font tab (Font dialog box), click Font color arrow, click desired color, click OK button
3. Click Font Dialog Box Launcher (Home tab | Font group), click Font tab (Font dialog box), click Font color arrow, click desired color, click OK button

To Use the Mini Toolbar to Format Text

Recall from the Office and Windows module at the beginning of this book that the mini toolbar automatically appears based on certain tasks you perform. *Why? Word places commonly used buttons and boxes on the mini toolbar for your convenience. If you do not use the mini toolbar, it disappears from the screen.* All commands on the mini toolbar also exist on the ribbon.

The following steps use the mini toolbar to change the color and font size of text in the signature line of the flyer.

1
- Move the pointer to the left of the line to be selected until the pointer changes to a right-pointing block arrow and then click to select the line and display the mini toolbar (Figure 1–37).

Q&A What if I am using a touch screen?
Double-tap to the left of the line to be selected to select the line and then tap the selection to display the mini toolbar. If you are using a touch screen, the buttons and boxes on the mini toolbar differ. For example, it contains a 'Show Context Menu' button at the far-right edge, which you tap to display a shortcut menu.

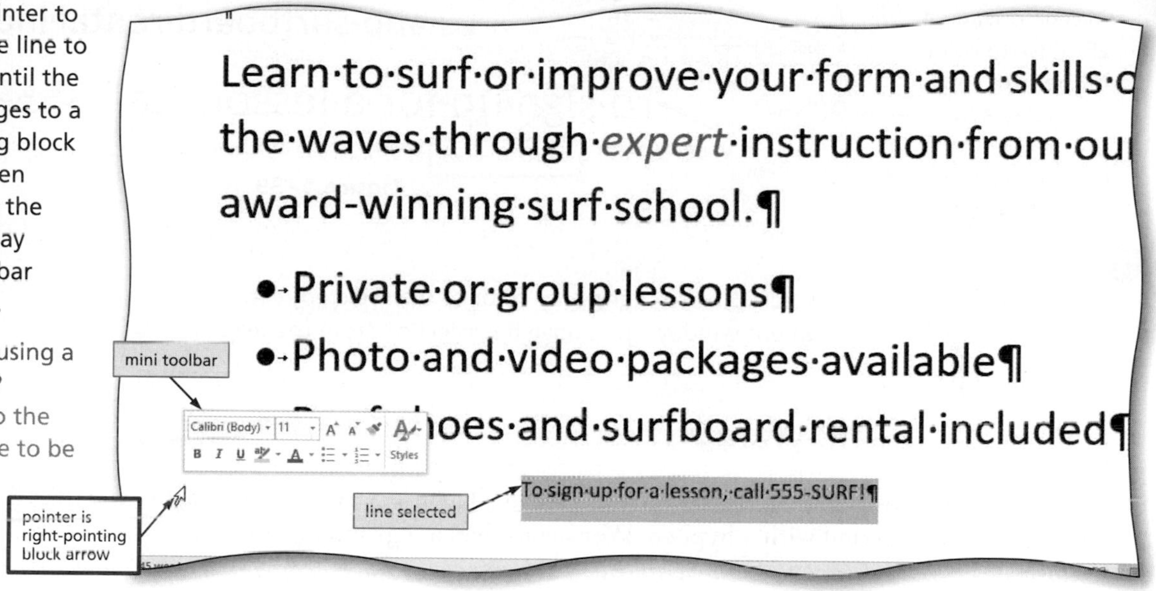

Figure 1–37

2
- Click the Font Size arrow on the mini toolbar to display the Font Size gallery.
- Point to 28 in the Font Size gallery to display a live preview of the selected font size (Figure 1–38).

3
- Click 28 in the Font Size gallery to increase the font size of the selected text.

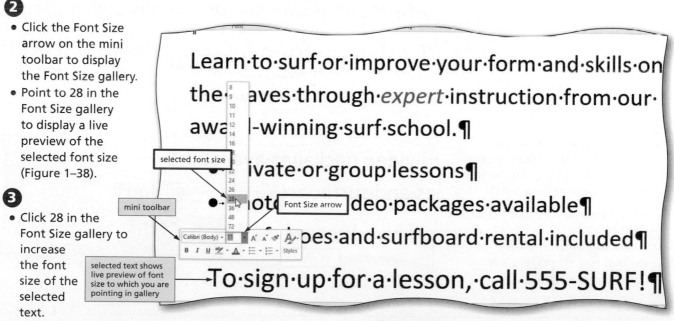

Figure 1–38

- With the text still selected and the mini toolbar still displayed, click the Font Color arrow on the mini toolbar to display the Font Color gallery.
- Point to 'Orange, Accent 2, Darker 25%' (sixth color in the fifth row) to display a live preview of the selected font color (Figure 1–39).

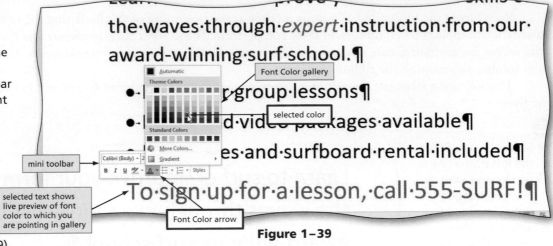

Figure 1–39

- Click 'Orange, Accent 2, Darker 25%' to change the color of the selected text.
- Click anywhere in the document window to remove the selection from the text.

---

1 ENTER TEXT | 2 FORMAT TEXT | 3 INSERT PICTURE

4 FORMAT PICTURE | 5 ENHANCE PAGE | 6 CORRECT & REVISE

To Select a Group of Words

To emphasize the contact phone number (555-SURF), this text is underlined in the flyer. Because the phone number is separated with a hyphen, Word considers it a group of words. To format a group of words, you first must select them. ***Why?*** *If you underline text without selecting any text first, Word will underline only the word containing the insertion point.* The following steps select a group of words.

- Position the pointer immediately to the left of the first character of the text to be selected, in this case, the 5 in 555 (Figure 1–40).

Q&A Why did the shape of the pointer change?
The pointer's shape is an I-beam when positioned in unselected text in the document window.

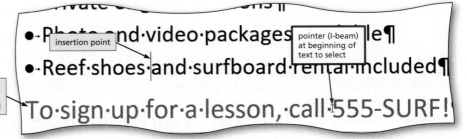

Figure 1–40

- Drag the pointer through the last character of the text to be selected, in this case, the F in the phone number (Figure 1–41).

Q&A Why did the pointer shape change again?
When the pointer is positioned in selected text, its shape is a left-pointing block arrow.

Figure 1–41

Other Ways

1. With insertion point at beginning of first word in group, press CTRL+SHIFT+RIGHT ARROW repeatedly until all words are selected

To Underline Text

Underlined text prints with an underscore (_) below each character. In the flyer, the contact phone number, 555-SURF, in the signature line is underlined. **Why?** *Underlines are used to emphasize or draw attention to specific text.* The following step formats selected text with an underline.

1

- With the text selected, click the Underline button (Home tab | Font group) to underline the selected text (Figure 1–42).

Q&A What if my screen displays an Underline gallery?
If you are using a touch screen, you may not have a separate Underline button and Underline arrow. In this case, select the desired underline style in the Underline gallery.

If a button exists on the mini toolbar, can I click that instead of using the ribbon?
Yes.

How would I remove an underline?
You would click the Underline button a second time, or you immediately could click the Undo button on the Quick Access Toolbar.

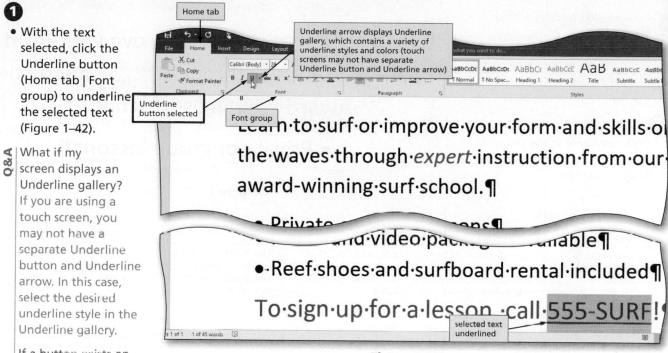

Figure 1–42

Other Ways

1. Click Underline button on mini toolbar	2. Right click text (or, if using touch, tap 'Show Context Menu' button on mini toolbar), click Font on shortcut menu, click Font tab (Font dialog box), click Underline style box arrow, click desired underline style, click OK button	3. Click Font Dialog Box Launcher (Home tab | Font group), click Font tab (Font dialog box), click Underline style arrow, click desired underline style, click OK button	4. Press CTRL+U

To Bold Text

Bold characters appear somewhat thicker and darker than those that are not bold. The following steps format the text, award-winning, in bold characters. **Why?** *To further emphasize this text, it is bold in the flyer.* Recall that if you want to format a single word, you simply position the insertion point in the word and then format the word. To format text that consists of more than one word, as you have learned previously, you select the text first.

1

- Select the text to be formatted (the text, award-winning, in this case); that is, position the pointer immediately to the left of the first character of the text to be selected and then drag the pointer through the last character of the text to be selected.

Q&A What if I am using a touch screen?
Tap to position the insertion point in the text you want to select and then drag the selection handle(s) to select the text to be formatted.

- With the text selected, click the Bold button (Home tab | Font group) to bold the selected text (Figure 1–43).

Q&A

How would I remove a bold format?

You would click the Bold button a second time, or you immediately could click the Undo button on the Quick Access Toolbar.

- Click anywhere in the document window to remove the selection from the screen.

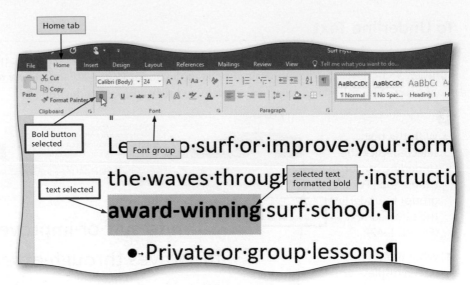

Figure 1–43

Other Ways

1. Click Bold button on mini toolbar

2. Right-click selected text (or, if using touch, tap 'Show Context Menu' button on mini toolbar), click Font on shortcut menu, click Font tab (Font dialog box), click Bold in Font style list, click OK button

3. Click Font Dialog Box Launcher (Home tab | Font group), click Font tab (Font dialog box), click Bold in Font style list, click OK button

4. Press CTRL+B

---

1 ENTER TEXT | 2 FORMAT TEXT | 3 INSERT PICTURE
4 FORMAT PICTURE | 5 ENHANCE PAGE | 6 CORRECT & REVISE

To Zoom One Page

Earlier in this module, you changed the zoom to page width so that the text on the screen was larger and easier to read. In the next set of steps, you want to see the entire page (as a mock sheet of paper) on the screen at once. *Why? You want be able to see the effect of adjusting colors in the document as a whole.* The next step displays a single page in its entirety in the document window as large as possible.

1

- Click View on the ribbon to display the View tab.
- Click the One Page button (View tab | Zoom group) to display the entire page in the document window as large as possible (Figure 1–44).

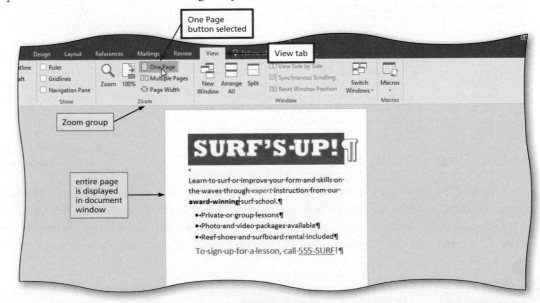

Figure 1–44

Other Ways

1. Click Zoom button (View tab | Zoom group), click Whole page (Zoom dialog box), click OK button

What colors should I choose when creating documents?

When choosing color, associate the meaning of the color with your message:

- Red expresses danger, power, or energy and often is associated with sports or physical exertion.

- Brown represents simplicity, honesty, and dependability.

- Orange denotes success, victory, creativity, and enthusiasm.

- Yellow suggests sunshine, happiness, hope, liveliness, and intelligence.

- Green symbolizes growth, healthiness, harmony, and healing and often is associated with safety or money.

- Blue indicates integrity, trust, importance, confidence, and stability.

- Purple represents wealth, power, comfort, extravagance, magic, mystery, and spirituality.

- White stands for purity, goodness, cleanliness, precision, and perfection.

- Black suggests authority, strength, elegance, power, and prestige.

- Gray conveys neutrality and, thus, often is found in backgrounds and other effects.

To Change Theme Colors

1 ENTER TEXT | 2 FORMAT TEXT | 3 INSERT PICTURE
4 FORMAT PICTURE | 5 ENHANCE PAGE | 6 CORRECT & REVISE

A **color scheme** in Word is a document theme that identifies complementary colors for text, background, accents, and links in a document. With more than 20 predefined color schemes, Word provides a simple way to coordinate colors in a document.

The default color scheme is called Office. In the flyer, you will change the color scheme. *Why? You want the colors in the flyer to represent integrity, trust, confidence, stability, healthiness, harmony, blooming, and safety, which are conveyed by shades of blues and greens. In Word, the Blue color scheme uses these colors.* The following steps change theme colors.

- Click Design on the ribbon to display the Design tab.

- Click the Theme Colors button (Design tab | Document Formatting group) to display the Theme Colors gallery.

- Point to Blue in the Theme Colors gallery to display a live preview of the selected theme color (Figure 1–45).

Experiment

- Point to various color schemes in the Theme Colors gallery and watch the colors change in the document.

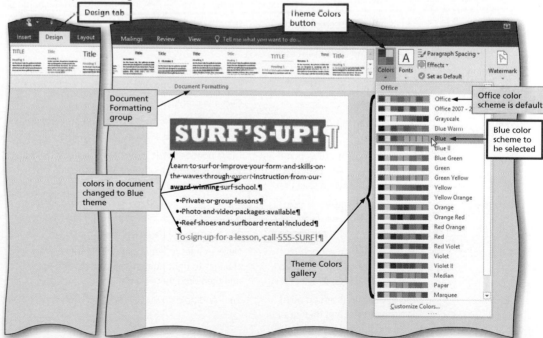

Figure 1–45

- Click Blue in the Theme Colors gallery to change the document theme colors.

What if I want to return to the original color scheme?

You would click the Theme Colors button again and then click Office in the Theme Colors gallery.

To Zoom Page Width

Because the document contents are small when displayed on one page, the next steps zoom page width again.

1 Click View on the ribbon to display the View tab.

2 Click the Page Width button (View tab | Zoom group) to display the page the same width as the document window (shown earlier in the module in Figure 1–7).

3 Save the flyer again on the same storage location with the same file name.

Q&A Why should I save the flyer again?
You have made several modifications to the flyer since you last saved it; thus, you should save it again.

Selecting Text

In many of the previous steps, you have selected text. Table 1–3 summarizes the techniques used to select various items.

Table 1–3 Techniques for Selecting Text

Item to Select	Touch	Mouse	Keyboard (where applicable)
Block of text	Tap to position insertion point in text to select and then drag selection handle(s) to select text.	Click at beginning of selection, scroll to end of selection, position pointer at end of selection, hold down SHIFT key, and then click; or drag through the text.	
Character(s)	Tap to position insertion point in text to select and then drag selection handle(s) to select text.	Drag through character(s).	SHIFT+RIGHT ARROW or SHIFT+LEFT ARROW
Document		Move pointer to left of text until pointer changes to right-pointing block arrow and then triple-click.	CTRL+A
Graphic	Tap the graphic.	Click the graphic.	
Line	Double-tap to left of line to be selected.	Move pointer to left of line until pointer changes to right-pointing block arrow and then click.	HOME, then SHIFT+END or END, then SHIFT+HOME
Lines	Tap to position insertion point in text to select and then drag selection handle(s) to select text.	Move pointer to left of first line until pointer changes to right-pointing block arrow and then drag up or down.	HOME, then SHIFT+DOWN ARROW or END, then SHIFT+UP ARROW
Paragraph	Tap to position insertion point in text to select and then drag selection handle(s) to select text.	Triple-click paragraph; or move pointer to left of paragraph until pointer changes to right-pointing block arrow and then double-click.	CTRL+SHIFT+DOWN ARROW or CTRL+SHIFT+UP ARROW
Paragraphs	Tap to position insertion point in text to select and then drag selection handle(s) to select text.	Move pointer to left of paragraph until pointer changes to right-pointing block arrow, double-click, and then drag up or down.	CTRL+SHIFT+DOWN ARROW or CTRL+SHIFT+UP ARROW repeatedly
Sentence	Tap to position insertion point in text to select and then drag selection handle(s) to select text.	Press and hold down CTRL key and then click sentence.	
Word	Double-tap word.	Double-click word.	CTRL+SHIFT+RIGHT ARROW or CTRL+SHIFT+LEFT ARROW
Words	Tap to position insertion point in text to select and then drag selection handle(s) to select text.	Drag through words.	CTRL+SHIFT+RIGHT ARROW or CTRL+SHIFT+LEFT ARROW repeatedly

Break Point: If you wish to take a break, this is a good place to do so. You can exit Word now. To resume at a later time, run Word, open the file called Surf Flyer, and continue following the steps from this location forward. For a detailed example of exiting Word, running Word, and opening a file, refer to the Office and Windows module at the beginning of the book.

Inserting and Formatting a Picture in a Word Document

With the text formatted in the flyer, the next step is to insert a digital picture in the flyer and format the picture. Flyers usually contain a graphical image(s), such as a picture, to attract the attention of passersby. In the following sections, you will perform these tasks:

1. Insert a digital picture into the flyer.
2. Reduce the size of the picture.
3. Change the look of the picture.

How do I locate a graphic file to use in a document?

To use a graphic in a Word document, the image must be stored digitally in a file. Files containing graphics are available from a variety of sources:

• The web has images available, some of which are free, while others require a fee.

• You can take a picture with a digital camera or smartphone and **download** it, which is the process of copying the digital picture from the camera or phone to your computer.

• With a scanner, you can convert a printed picture, drawing, or diagram to a digital file.

If you receive a picture from a source other than yourself, do not use the file until you are certain it does not contain a virus. A **virus** is a computer program that can damage files and programs on your computer. Use an antivirus program to verify that any files you use are virus free.

To Center Another Paragraph

In the flyer, the digital picture of a surfer should be centered on the blank line below the headline. The blank paragraph below the headline currently is left-aligned. The following steps center this paragraph.

1 Click Home on the ribbon to display the Home tab.

2 Click somewhere in the paragraph to be centered (in this case, the blank line below the headline) to position the insertion point in the paragraph to be formatted.

3 Click the Center button (Home tab | Paragraph group) to center the paragraph containing the insertion point (shown in Figure 1–46).

To Insert a Picture

1 ENTER TEXT | 2 FORMAT TEXT | **3 INSERT PICTURE**
4 FORMAT PICTURE | 5 ENHANCE PAGE | 6 CORRECT & REVISE

The next step in creating the flyer is to insert a digital picture of a surfer in the flyer on the blank line below the headline. The picture, which was taken with a digital camera, is available on the Data Files. Please contact your instructor for information about accessing Data Files.

The following steps insert a picture, which, in this example, is located in the Module 01 folder in the Data Files folder. **Why?** *It is good practice to organize and store files in folders so that you easily can find the files at a later date.*

1

- If necessary, position the insertion point at the location where you want to insert the picture (in this case, on the centered blank paragraph below the headline).

- Click Insert on the ribbon to display the Insert tab (Figure 1–46).

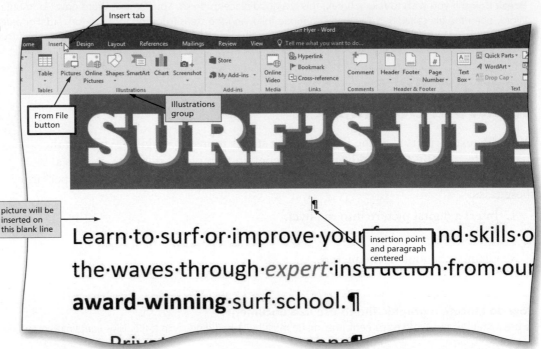

Figure 1–46

2

- Click the From File button (Insert tab | Illustrations group) (shown in Figure 1–46) to display the Insert Picture dialog box (shown in Figure 1–47).

3

- Navigate to the desired picture location (in this case, the Module 01 folder in the Data Files folder). For a detailed example of this procedure, refer to Steps 4a and 4b in the To Save a File in a Folder section in the Office and Windows module at the beginning of this book.

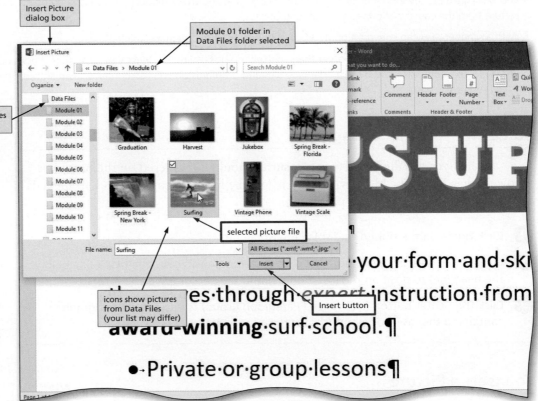

- Click Surfing to select the file (Figure 1–47).

Figure 1–47

4

- Click the Insert button (Insert Picture dialog box) to insert the picture at the location of the insertion point in the document (Figure 1–48).

Q&A

What are the symbols around the picture?

A selected graphic appears surrounded by a **selection rectangle**, which has small squares and circles, called **sizing handles**, at each corner and middle location.

What is the purpose of the Layout Options button?

When you click the Layout Options button, Word provides options for changing how the graphic is positioned with text in the document.

Figure 1–48

How do you know where to position a graphic on a flyer?

The content, size, shape, position, and format of a graphic should capture the interest of passersby, enticing them to stop and read the flyer. Often, the graphic is the center of attention and visually the largest element on a flyer. If you use colors in the graphical image, be sure they are part of the document's color scheme.

CONSIDER THIS

1 ENTER TEXT | 2 FORMAT TEXT | **3 INSERT PICTURE**

4 FORMAT PICTURE | 5 ENHANCE PAGE | 6 CORRECT & REVISE

To Zoom the Document

In the steps in the following sections, you will work with the picture just inserted. The next task is to adjust the zoom percentage. *Why? Currently, you can see only a small amount of text with the picture. Seeing more of the document at once helps you determine the appropriate size for the picture.* The following step zooms the document.

1

 Experiment

- Repeatedly click the Zoom Out and Zoom In buttons on the status bar and watch the size of the document change in the document window.

What if I am using a touch screen?

Repeatedly pinch (move two fingers together on the screen) and stretch (move two fingers apart on the screen) and watch the size of the document change in the document window.

- Click the Zoom Out or Zoom In button as many times as necessary until the Zoom button on the status bar displays 40% on its face (Figure 1–49).

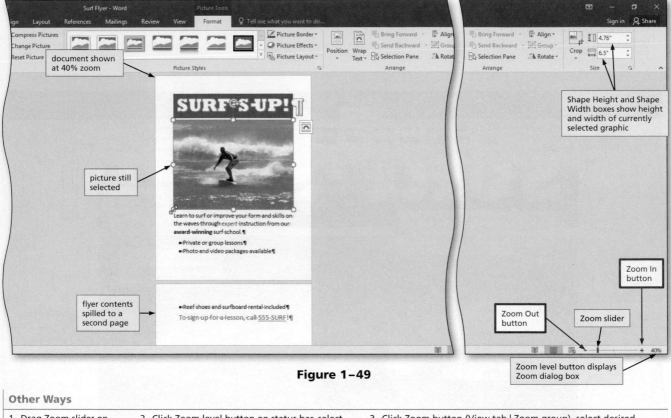

Figure 1–49

Other Ways

1. Drag Zoom slider on status bar	2. Click Zoom level button on status bar, select desired zoom percent or type (Zoom dialog box), click OK button	3. Click Zoom button (View tab | Zoom group), select desired zoom percent or type (Zoom dialog box), click OK button

1 ENTER TEXT | 2 FORMAT TEXT | 3 INSERT PICTURE
4 FORMAT PICTURE | 5 ENHANCE PAGE | 6 CORRECT & REVISE

To Resize a Graphic

Resizing includes both increasing and reducing the size of a graphic. The next step is to resize the picture so that it is smaller in the flyer. *Why? You want the graphic and all the text on the flyer to fit on a single sheet of paper.* The following steps resize a selected graphic.

1

- Be sure the graphic still is selected.

What if my graphic (picture) is not selected?

To select a graphic, click it.

- Point to the lower-left corner sizing handle on the picture so that the pointer shape changes to a two-headed arrow (Figure 1–50).

Figure 1–50

- Drag the sizing handle diagonally inward until the lower-left corner of the picture is positioned approximately as shown in Figure 1–51. Do not release the mouse button at this point.

Q&A

What if I am using a touch screen?
Drag a corner of the graphic, without lifting your finger, until the graphic is the desired size.

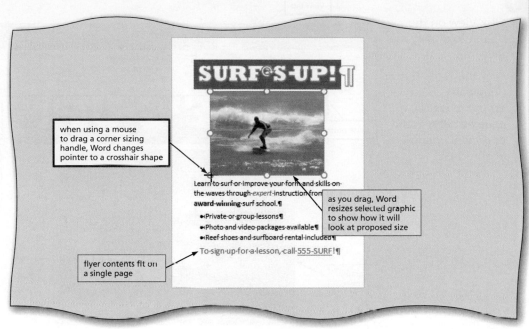

when using a mouse to drag a corner sizing handle, Word changes pointer to a crosshair shape

as you drag, Word resizes selected graphic to show how it will look at proposed size

flyer contents fit on a single page

Figure 1–51

- Release the mouse button to resize the graphic, which, in this case, should have a height of about 3.7" and a width of about 5.06".

Q&A

How can I see the height and width measurements?
Look in the Size group on the Picture Tools Format tab to see the height and width measurements of the currently selected graphic (shown in Figure 1–49).

What if the graphic is the wrong size?
Repeat Steps 1, 2, and 3, or enter the desired height and width values in the Shape Height and Shape Width boxes (Picture Tools Format tab | Size group).

What if I want to return a graphic to its original size and start again?
With the graphic selected, click the Size Dialog Box Launcher (Picture Tools Format tab | Size group), click the Size tab (Layout dialog box), click the Reset button, and then click the OK button.

Other Ways

1. Enter height and width of graphic in Shape Height and Shape Width boxes (Picture Tools Format tab | Size group)

2. Click Advanced Layout: Size Dialog Box Launcher (Picture Tools Format tab | Size group), click Size tab (Layout dialog box), enter desired height and width values in boxes, click OK button

To Zoom 100%

1 ENTER TEXT | 2 FORMAT TEXT | 3 INSERT PICTURE
4 FORMAT PICTURE | 5 ENHANCE PAGE | 6 CORRECT & REVISE

In the next series of steps, you will format the picture. Earlier in this module, you changed the zoom to 40% so that you could see more of the page while resizing the graphic. The following step zooms the screen to 100%. **Why?** *You want the contents of the image to be enlarged a bit, while still seeing some of the text in the document.*

1

- Click View on the ribbon to display the View tab.

- Click the 100% button (View tab | Zoom group) to display the page at 100% in the document window (Figure 1–52).

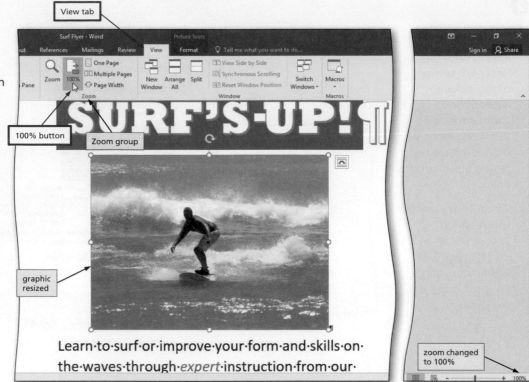

Figure 1–52

Other Ways

1. Click Zoom button (View tab | Zoom group), click 100% (Zoom dialog box), click OK button

To Apply a Picture Style

1 ENTER TEXT | 2 FORMAT TEXT | 3 INSERT PICTURE
4 FORMAT PICTURE | 5 ENHANCE PAGE | 6 CORRECT & REVISE

A **style** is a named group of formatting characteristics. Word provides more than 25 picture styles. *Why? Picture styles enable you easily to change a picture's look to a more visually appealing style, including a variety of shapes, angles, borders, and reflections.* The flyer in this module uses a style that applies an oval shape to the picture. The following steps apply a picture style to a picture.

1

- Ensure the graphic still is selected and then click Picture Tools Format on the ribbon to display the Picture Tools Format tab (Figure 1–53).

Q&A
What if my graphic (picture) is not selected?
To select a graphic, click it.

What is the white circle attached to top of the selected graphic?
It is called a rotate handle. When you drag a graphic's **rotate handle,** the graphic moves in either a clockwise or counterclockwise direction.

Figure 1–53

- Click the More button in the Picture Styles gallery (Picture Tools Format tab | Picture Styles group) (shown in Figure 1–53) to expand the gallery.

- Point to 'Soft Edge Oval' in the Picture Styles gallery to display a live preview of that style applied to the picture in the document (Figure 1–54).

 Experiment

- Point to various picture styles in the Picture Styles gallery and watch the style of the picture change in the document window.

❸

- Click 'Soft Edge Oval' in the Picture Styles gallery (sixth style in third row) to apply the style to the selected picture.

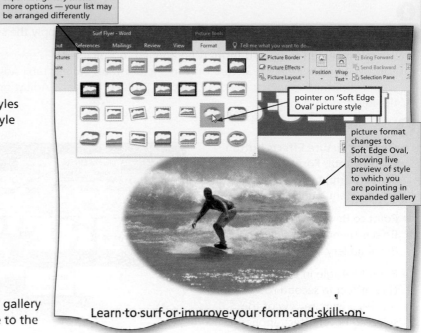

Figure 1–54

Other Ways

1. Right-click picture, click 'Picture Styles' on mini toolbar, select desired style

To Apply Picture Effects

1 ENTER TEXT | 2 FORMAT TEXT | 3 INSERT PICTURE
4 FORMAT PICTURE | 5 ENHANCE PAGE | 6 CORRECT & REVISE

Word provides a variety of picture effects, such as shadows, reflections, glow, soft edges, bevel, and 3-D rotation. The difference between the effects and the styles is that each effect has several options, providing you with more control over the exact look of the image.

In this flyer, the picture has a slight lime green glow effect and beveled edges. The following steps apply picture effects to the selected picture. *Why? Picture effects enable you to further customize a picture.*

❶

- With the picture still selected, click the Picture Effects button (Picture Tools Format tab | Picture Styles group) to display the Picture Effects menu.

- Point to Glow on the Picture Effects menu to display the Glow gallery.

- Point to 'Lime, 5 pt glow, Accent color 6' in the Glow Variations area (rightmost glow in first row) to display a live preview of the selected glow effect applied to the picture in the document window (Figure 1–55).

 Experiment

- If you are using a mouse, point to various glow effects in the Glow gallery and watch the picture change in the document window.

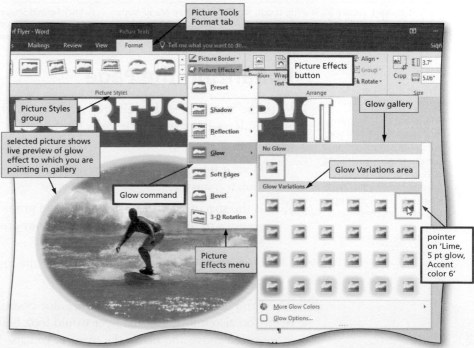

Figure 1–55

- Click 'Lime, 5 pt glow, Accent color 6' in the Glow gallery to apply the selected picture effect.

Q&A
What if I wanted to discard formatting applied to a picture?
You would click the Reset Picture button (Picture Tools Format tab | Adjust group). To reset formatting and size, you would click the Reset Picture arrow (Picture Tools Format tab | Adjust group) and then click 'Reset Picture & Size' on the Reset Picture menu.

- Click the Picture Effects button (Picture Tools Format tab | Picture Styles group) to display the Picture Effects menu again.

- Point to Bevel on the Picture Effects menu to display the Bevel gallery.

- Point to Angle in the Bevel area (first effect in second row) to display a live preview of the selected bevel effect applied to the picture in the document window (Figure 1–56).

🔎 **Experiment**

- If you are using a mouse, point to various bevel effects in the Bevel gallery and watch the picture change in the document window.

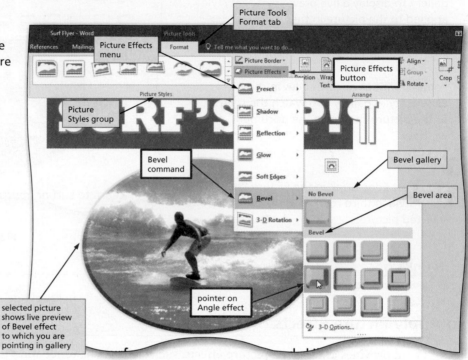

Figure 1–56

- Click Angle in the Bevel gallery to apply the selected picture effect.

Other Ways

1. Right-click picture (or, if using touch, tap 'Show Context Menu' button on mini toolbar), click Format Object or Format Picture on shortcut menu, click Effects button (Format Picture task pane), select desired options, click Close button

2. Click Format Shape Dialog Box Launcher (Picture Tools Format tab | Picture Styles group), click Effects button (Format Picture task pane), select desired options, click Close button

---

BTW

Touch Screen Differences

The Office and Windows interfaces may vary if you are using a touch screen. For this reason, you might notice that the function or appearance of your touch screen differs slightly from this module's presentation.

Enhancing the Page

With the text and graphics entered and formatted, the next step is to look at the page as a whole and determine if it looks finished in its current state. As you review the page, answer these questions:

- Does it need a page border to frame its contents, or would a page border make it look too busy?

- Is the spacing between paragraphs and graphics on the page adequate? Do any sections of text or graphics look as if they are positioned too closely to the items above or below them?

- Does the flyer have too much space at the top or bottom? Should the contents be centered vertically?

You determine that a graphical, color-coordinated border would enhance the flyer. You also notice that the flyer would look better proportioned if it had a little more space above and below the picture. You also want to ensure that the contents are centered vertically. The following sections make these enhancements to the flyer.

To Add a Page Border

In Word, you can add a border around the perimeter of an entire page. The flyer in this module has a lime border. **Why?** *This border color complements the color of the flyer contents.* The following steps add a page border.

- Click Design on the ribbon to display the Design tab.

- Click the 'Borders and Shading' button (Design tab | Page Background group) to display the Borders and Shading dialog box (Figure 1–57).

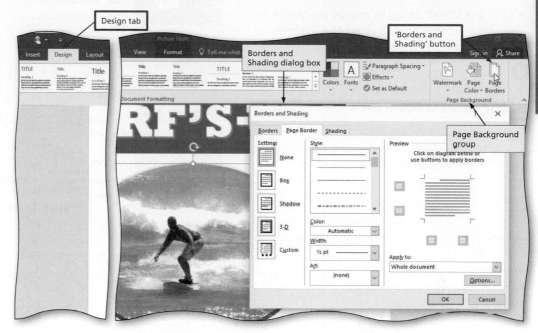

Figure 1–57

- Scroll to, if necessary, and then click the sixth border style in the Style list (Borders and Shading dialog box) to select the style.

- Click the Color arrow to display a Color palette (Figure 1–58).

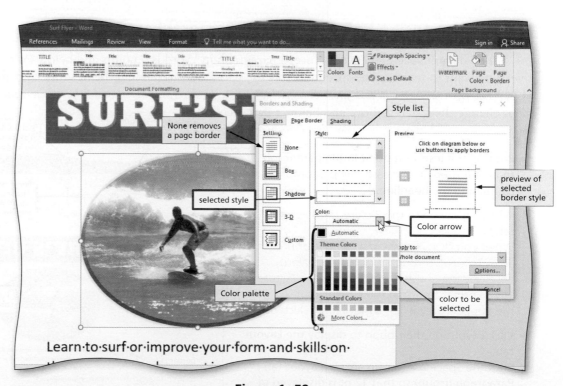

Figure 1–58

- Click 'Lime, Accent 6, Lighter 40%' (rightmost color in fourth row) in the Color palette to select the color for the page border.
- Click the Width arrow to display the Width list and then click 4 ½ pt to select the thickness of the page border (Figure 1–59).

- Click the OK button to add the border to the page (shown in Figure 1–60).

Q&A What if I wanted to remove the border?
You would click None in the Setting list in the Borders and Shading dialog box.

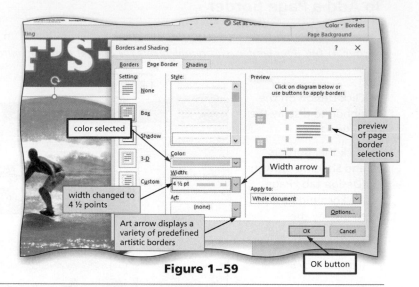

Figure 1–59

To Zoom One Page

The next steps zoom one page so that you can see the entire page on the screen at once.

1 Click View on the ribbon to display the View tab.

2 Click the One Page button (View tab | Zoom group) to display the entire page in the document window as large as possible.

To Change Spacing before and after Paragraphs

1 ENTER TEXT | 2 FORMAT TEXT | 3 INSERT PICTURE
4 FORMAT PICTURE | 5 ENHANCE PAGE | 6 CORRECT & REVISE

The default spacing above (before) a paragraph in Word is 0 points and below (after) is 8 points. In the flyer, you want to increase the spacing below the paragraph containing the headline and above the signature line. *Why? The flyer spacing will look more balanced with spacing increased above and below these paragraphs.* The following steps change the spacing above and below a paragraph.

- Position the insertion point in the paragraph to be adjusted, in this case, the paragraph containing the headline.

Q&A What happened to the Picture Tools Format tab?
When you click outside of a graphic or press a key to scroll through a document, Word deselects the graphic and removes the Picture Tools Format tab from the screen. That is, this tab appears only when a graphic is selected.

- Click Layout on the ribbon to display the Layout tab.
- Click the Spacing After up arrow (Layout tab | Paragraph group) so that 12 pt is displayed in the Spacing After box to increase the space below the current paragraph (Figure 1–60).

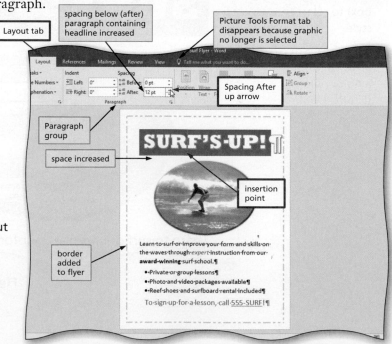

Figure 1–60

- Position the insertion point in the paragraph to be adjusted, in this case, the paragraph containing the signature line.

- Click the Spacing Before up arrow (Layout tab | Paragraph group) as many times as necessary so that 12 pt is displayed in the Spacing Before box to increase the space above the current paragraph (Figure 1–61).

- If the text flows to two pages, reduce the spacing above and below paragraphs as necessary.

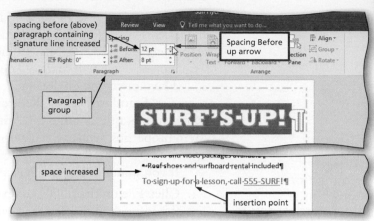

Figure 1–61

Other Ways

1. Right-click paragraph (or, if using touch, tap 'Show Context Menu' button on mini toolbar), click Paragraph on shortcut menu, click Indents and Spacing tab (Paragraph dialog box), enter spacing before and after values, click OK button

2. Click Paragraph Settings Dialog Box Launcher (Home tab or Layout tab | Paragraph group), click Indents and Spacing tab (Paragraph dialog box), enter spacing before and after values, click OK button

To Center Page Contents Vertically

1 ENTER TEXT | 2 FORMAT TEXT | 3 INSERT PICTURE
4 FORMAT PICTURE | 5 ENHANCE PAGE | 6 CORRECT & REVISE

In Word, you can center the page contents vertically. *Why? This places the same amount of space at the top and bottom of the page.* The following steps center page contents vertically.

- If necessary, click Layout on the ribbon to display the Layout tab.

- Click the Page Setup Dialog Box Launcher (Layout tab | Page Setup group) to display the Page Setup dialog box.

- Click the Layout tab (Page Setup dialog box) to display the Layout sheet (Figure 1–62).

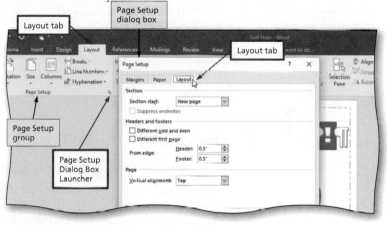

Figure 1–62

- Click the Vertical alignment arrow (Page Setup dialog box) to display the list of alignment options and then click Center in the list (Figure 1–63).

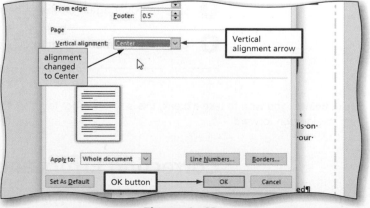

- Click the OK button to center the page contents vertically on the screen (shown in Figure 1–1 at the beginning of this module).

Q&A What if I wanted to change the alignment back?

You would select the Top vertical alignment from the Vertical alignment list in the Layout sheet (Page Setup dialog box).

Figure 1–63

To Change Document Properties

Word helps you organize and identify your files by using **document properties**, which, as discussed in the Office and Windows module at the beginning of this book, are the details about a file, such as the project author, title, and subject. For example, a class name or document topic can describe the file's purpose or content.

The more common document properties are standard and automatically updated properties. **Standard properties** are associated with all Microsoft Office files and include author, title, and subject. **Automatically updated properties** include file system properties, such as the date you create or change a file, and statistics, such as the file size.

If you wanted to change document properties, you would follow these steps.

BTW
Printing Document Properties
To print document properties, click File on the ribbon to open the Backstage view, click the Print tab in the Backstage view to display the Print gallery, click the first button in the Settings area to display a list of options specifying what you can print, click Document Info in the list to specify you want to print the document properties instead of the actual document, and then click the Print button in the Print gallery to print the document properties on the currently selected printer.

1. Click File on the ribbon to open the Backstage view and then, if necessary, click the Info tab in the Backstage view to display the Info gallery.

2. If the property you wish to change is displayed in the Properties list in the right pane of the Info gallery, try to click to the right of the property. If a text box appears to the right of the property, type the text for the property in the text box and then click the Back button in the upper-left corner of the Backstage view to return to the Word window. Skip the remaining steps.

3. If the property you wish to change is not displayed in the Properties list in the right pane of the Info gallery or you cannot change it in the Info gallery, click the Properties button in the right pane to display the Properties menu and then click Advanced Properties on the Properties menu to display the Properties dialog box. If necessary, click the Summary tab (Properties dialog box) to display the Summary sheet, fill in the appropriate text boxes, and then click the OK button.

Q&A Why are some of the document properties in the dialog box already filled in?
The person who installed Office 2016 on your computer or network may have set or customized the properties.

To Save the Document and Exit Word

Although you still need to make some edits to this document, you want to exit Word and resume working on the project at a later time. Thus, the following steps save the document and exit Word. For a detailed example of the procedure summarized below, refer to the Office and Windows module at the beginning of this book.

1 Save the flyer again on the same storage location with the same file name.

2 Close the open document and exit Word.

Break Point: If you wish to take a break, this is a good place to do so. To resume at a later time, continue following the steps from this location forward.

Correcting Errors and Revising a Document

After creating a document, you may need to change it. For example, the document may contain an error, or new circumstances may require you to add text to the document.

Types of Changes Made to Documents

The types of changes made to documents normally fall into one of the three following categories: additions, deletions, or modifications.

Additions Additional words, sentences, or paragraphs may be required in a document. Additions occur when you omit text from a document and want to insert it later. For example, you may want to add your email address to the flyer.

Deletions Sometimes, text in a document is incorrect or no longer is needed. For example, you may discover that the lessons no longer include reef shoes. In this case, you would delete the words, reef shoes, from the flyer.

Modifications If an error is made in a document or changes take place that affect the document, you might have to revise a word(s) in the text. For example, the phone number may change.

To Run Word, Open a Document, and Specify Settings

Once you have created and saved a document, you may need to retrieve it from storage. For example, you might want to revise the document or distribute it. Earlier in this module you saved the flyer using the file name, Surf Flyer. The following steps run Word, open this document, and specify settings. For a detailed example of the procedures summarized below for running Word or opening a document, refer to the Office and Windows module.

1 Run Word.

2 Open the document named Surf Flyer from the Recent list or use the Open dialog box to navigate to the location of the file and then open it in the Word window.

3 If the Word window is not maximized, click the Maximize button on its title bar to maximize the window.

4 Click View on the ribbon to display the View tab and then click the 100% button (View tab | Zoom group) to display the page at 100% in the document window.

> **BTW**
> **Word Help**
> At any time while using Word, you can find answers to questions and display information about various topics through Word Help. Used properly, this form of assistance can increase your productivity and reduce your frustrations by minimizing the time you spend learning how to use Word. For instructions about Word Help and exercises that will help you gain confidence in using it, read the Office and Windows module at the beginning of this book.

To Insert Text in an Existing Document

1 ENTER TEXT | 2 FORMAT TEXT | 3 INSERT PICTURE
4 FORMAT PICTURE | 5 ENHANCE PAGE | 6 CORRECT & REVISE

Word inserts text to the left of the insertion point. The text to the right of the insertion point moves to the right and downward to fit the new text. The following steps insert the word, today, to the left of the word, or, in the flyer. *Why? These steps illustrate the process of inserting text.*

1

• Scroll through the document and then click to the left of the location of text to be inserted (in this case, the o in or) to position the insertion point where text should be inserted (Figure 1–64).

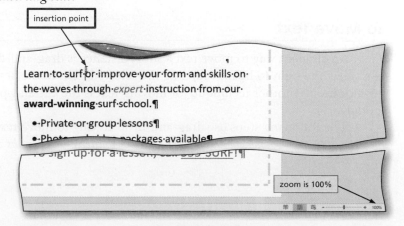

Figure 1–64

- Type **today** and then press the SPACEBAR to insert the word to the left of the insertion point (Figure 1–65).

Q&A Why did the text move to the right as I typed?

In Word, the default typing mode is **insert mode**, which means as you type a character, Word moves all the characters to the right of the typed character one position to the right.

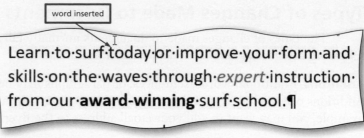

word inserted

Learn·to·surf·today·or·improve·your·form·and· skills·on·the·waves·through·*expert*·instruction· from·our·**award-winning**·surf·school.¶

Figure 1–65

To Delete Text

1 ENTER TEXT | 2 FORMAT TEXT | 3 INSERT PICTURE
4 FORMAT PICTURE | 5 ENHANCE PAGE | **6 CORRECT & REVISE**

It is not unusual to type incorrect characters or words in a document. As discussed earlier in this module, you can click the Undo button on the Quick Access Toolbar to undo a command or action immediately — this includes typing. Word also provides other methods of correcting typing errors.

To delete an incorrect character in a document, simply click next to the incorrect character and then press the BACKSPACE key to erase to the left of the insertion point, or press the DELETE key to erase to the right of the insertion point.

To delete a word or phrase, you first must select the word or phrase. The following steps select the word, today, which was just added in the previous steps, and then delete the selection. ***Why?*** *These steps illustrate the process of selecting a word and then deleting selected text.*

- Double-click the word to be selected (in this case, today) to select the word (Figure 1–66).

- Press the DELETE key to delete the selected text.

Q&A What if I am using a touch screen?

Tap the selected text to display the mini toolbar and then tap the Cut button on the mini toolbar to delete the selected text.

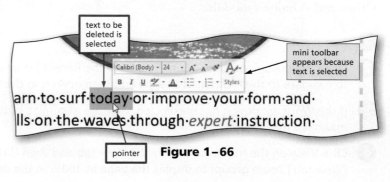

text to be deleted is selected

mini toolbar appears because text is selected

Calibri (Body) 24

B I U

arn·to·surf·today·or·improve·your·form·and· lls·on·the·waves·through·*expert*·instruction·

pointer   **Figure 1–66**

Other Ways

1. Right-click selected item, click Cut on shortcut menu	2. Select item, press BACKSPACE to delete to left of insertion point or press DELETE to delete to right of insertion point	3. Select item, press CTRL+X

To Move Text

1 ENTER TEXT | 2 FORMAT TEXT | 3 INSERT PICTURE
4 FORMAT PICTURE | 5 ENHANCE PAGE | **6 CORRECT & REVISE**

An efficient way to move text a short distance is drag-and-drop editing. With **drag-and-drop editing**, you select the item to be moved, drag the selected item to the new location, and then drop, or insert, it in the new location. Another technique for moving text is the cut-and-paste technique, which is discussed in the next module.

The following steps use drag-and-drop editing to move text. ***Why?*** *While proofreading the flyer, you realize that the body copy would read better if the last two bulleted paragraphs were reversed.*

- Position the pointer in the paragraph to be moved (in this case, the last bulleted item) and then triple-click to select the paragraph.

- With the pointer in the selected text, press and hold down the mouse button, which displays a small dotted box with the pointer (Figure 1–67).

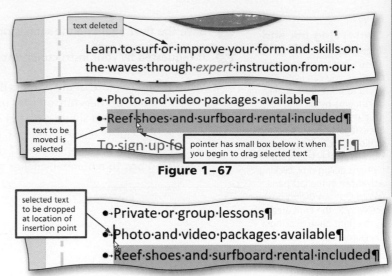

Figure 1–67

- Drag the insertion point to the location where the selected text is to be moved, as shown in Figure 1–68.

Figure 1–68

- Release the mouse button to move the selected text to the location of the dotted insertion point (Figure 1–69).

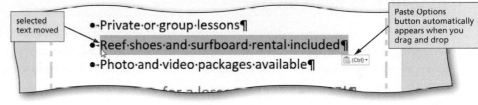

Figure 1–69

Q&A What if I accidentally drag text to the wrong location?
Click the Undo button on the Quick Access Toolbar and try again.

Can I use drag-and-drop editing to move any selected item?
Yes, you can select words, sentences, phrases, and graphics and then use drag-and-drop editing to move them.

What is the purpose of the Paste Options button?
If you click the Paste Options button, a menu appears that allows you to change the format of the item that was moved. The next module discusses the Paste Options menu.

- Click anywhere in the document window to remove the selection from the bulleted item.

Q&A What if I am using a touch screen?
If you have a stylus, you can follow Steps 1 through 3 using the stylus. If you are using your finger, you will need to use the cut-and-paste technique: tap to position the insertion point in the text to be moved and then drag the selection handles as necessary to select the text that you want to move; tap the selection to display the mini toolbar and then tap the Cut button on the mini toolbar to remove the text; tap to position the insertion point at the location where you want to move the text; display the Home tab and then tap the Paste button on the Home tab to place the text at the location of the insertion point. The next module discusses this procedure in more depth.

Other Ways

1. Click Cut button (Home tab | Clipboard group), click where text or object is to be pasted, click Paste button (Home tab | Clipboard group)

2. Right-click selected text, click Cut on mini toolbar or shortcut menu, right-click where text or object is to be pasted, click Paste on mini toolbar or 'Keep Source Formatting' on shortcut menu

3. Press CTRL+X, position insertion point where text or object is to be pasted, press CTRL+V

To Save and Print the Document

It is a good practice to save a document before printing it, in the event you experience difficulties printing. The following steps save and print the document. For a detailed example of the procedure summarized next for saving and printing a document, refer to the Office and Windows module at the beginning of this book.

BTW

Conserving Ink and Toner
If you want to conserve ink or toner, you can instruct Word to print draft quality documents by clicking File on the ribbon to open the Backstage view, clicking the Options tab in the Backstage view to display the Word Options dialog box, clicking Advanced in the left pane (Word Options dialog box), scrolling to the Print area in the right pane, placing a check mark in the 'Use draft quality' check box, and then clicking the OK button. Then, use the Backstage view to print the document as usual.

1 Save the flyer again on the same storage location with the same file name.

2 If requested by your instructor, print the flyer.

Q&A What if one or more of my borders do not print?

Click the Page Borders button (Design tab | Page Background group), click the Options button (Borders and Shading dialog box), click the Measure from arrow and click Text, change the four text boxes to 15 pt, and then click the OK button in each dialog box. Try printing the document again. If the borders still do not print, adjust the boxes in the dialog box to a number smaller than 15 point.

To Switch to Read Mode

1 ENTER TEXT | 2 FORMAT TEXT | 3 INSERT PICTURE
4 FORMAT PICTURE | 5 ENHANCE PAGE | **6 CORRECT & REVISE**

Some users prefer reading a document on-screen instead of on paper. *Why? If you are not composing a document, you can switch to **Read mode**, which hides the ribbon and other writing tools so that more content fits on the screen. Read mode is intended to make it easier to read a document.* The following step switches from Print Layout view to Read mode.

- Click the Read Mode button on the status bar to switch to Read mode (Figure 1–70).

 **Experiment**

- Click the arrows to advance forward and then move backward through the document.

Q&A Besides reading, what can I do in Read mode?

You can zoom, copy text, highlight text, search, add comments, and more.

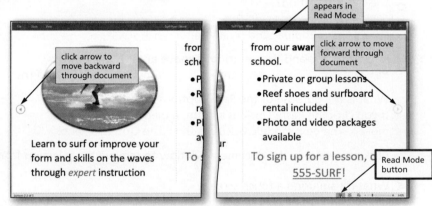

Figure 1–70

Other Ways

1. Click Read Mode button (View tab | Views group)

BTW

Distributing a Document
Instead of printing and distributing a hard copy of a document, you can distribute the document electronically. Options include sending the document via email; posting it on cloud storage (such as OneDrive) and sharing the file with others; posting it on social media, a blog, or other website; and sharing a link associated with an online location of the document. You also can create and share a PDF or XPS image of the document, so that users can view the file in Acrobat Reader or XPS Viewer instead of in Word.

To Switch to Print Layout View

1 ENTER TEXT | 2 FORMAT TEXT | 3 INSERT PICTURE
4 FORMAT PICTURE | 5 ENHANCE PAGE | **6 CORRECT & REVISE**

The next steps switch back to Print Layout view. *Why? If you want to show the document on a mock sheet of paper in the document window, along with the ribbon and other writing tools, you should switch to Print Layout view.* The following step switches to Print Layout view.

1

- Click the Print Layout button on the status bar to switch to Print Layout view (Figure 1–71).

- Because the project now is complete, you can exit Word.

Figure 1–71

Other Ways

1. Click Print Layout button (View tab | Views group)   2. Click View on the ribbon, click Edit Document

Summary

In this module, you have learned how to enter text in a document, correct spelling errors as you type, format paragraphs and characters, insert and format a picture, add a page border, adjust paragraph and page spacing, and correct errors and revise a document.

What decisions will you need to make when creating your next flyer?

Use these guidelines as you complete the assignments in this module and create your own flyers outside of this class.

1. Choose the text for the headline, body copy, and signature line — using as few words as possible to make a point.

2. Format various elements of the text.

    a) Select appropriate font sizes for text in the headline, body copy, and signature line.

    b) Select appropriate fonts for text in the headline, body copy, and signature line.

    c) Adjust paragraph alignment, as appropriate.

    d) Highlight key paragraphs with bullets.

    e) Emphasize important words.

    f) Use color to convey meaning and add appeal.

3. Find an eye-catching graphic(s) that conveys the overall message and meaning of the flyer.

4. Establish where to position and how to format the graphical image(s) so that the image grabs the attention of passersby and draws them into reading the flyer.

5. Determine whether the flyer needs enhancements, such as a graphical, color-coordinated border, or spacing adjustments to improve readability or overall appearance.

6. Correct errors and revise the document as necessary.

    a) Post the flyer on a wall and make sure all text and images are legible from a distance.

    b) Ask someone else to read the flyer and give you suggestions for improvements.

7. Determine the best method for distributing the document, such as printing, sending via email, or posting on the web or social media.

CONSIDER THIS: PLAN AHEAD

Apply Your Knowledge

Reinforce the skills and apply the concepts you learned in this module.

Modifying Text and Formatting a Document

Note: To complete this assignment, you will be required to use the Data Files. Please contact your instructor for information about accessing the Data Files.

Instructions: Run Word. Open the document, Apply 1–1 Graduation Flyer Unformatted, which is located in the Data Files. The flyer you open contains an unformatted flyer. You are to modify text, format paragraphs and characters, and insert a picture in the flyer to create the flyer shown in Figure 1–72.

Figure 1–72

Perform the following tasks:

1. Correct each spelling (red wavy underline) and grammar (green and blue wavy underlines) error by right-clicking the flagged text and then clicking the appropriate correction on the shortcut menu.

2. Delete the word, degree, in the sentence below the headline.

3. Insert the word, need, between the words, or directions (so that it reads: Questions or need directions?), in the second to last line of the flyer.

4. Change the word, on, to the word, by, in the last line so that the text reads: Please RSVP by May 18.

5. If requested by your instructor, change the phone number in the flyer to your phone number.

6. Center the headline and the last two paragraphs of the flyer.

7. Select the third, fourth, and fifth paragraphs of text in the flyer and add bullets to the selected paragraphs.

8. Change the theme colors to the Blue II color scheme.

9. Change the font and font size of the headline to 48-point Arial Rounded MT Bold, or a similar font. Change the case of the word, Celebrate, in the headline to uppercase letters. Apply the text effect called Fill - Dark Green, Accent 1, Outline - Background 1, Hard Shadow - Accent 1 to the entire headline. Change the font color of the headline text to Dark Green, Accent 5, Darker 25%.

10. Change the font size of the sentence below the headline, the bulleted list, and the last line of flyer to 26 point.

11. Use the mini toolbar to change the font size of the sentence below the bulleted list to 18 point.

12. Switch the last two bulleted paragraphs. That is, select the '125 Park Court in Condor' bullet and move it so that it is the second bulleted paragraph.

13. Select the words, open house, in the paragraph below the headline and italicize these words. Undo this change and then redo the change.

14. Select the text, Saturday, May 27, in the first bulleted paragraph and bold this text. Change the font color of this same text to Dark Red.

15. Underline the word, and, in the third bulleted paragraph.

16. Bold the text, Please RSVP by May 18., in the last line of the flyer. Shade this same text Dark Green, Accent 5, Darker 50%. If the font color does not automatically change to a lighter color, change its color to White, Background 1.

17. Change the zoom so that the entire page is visible in the document window.

18. Insert the picture of the graduate centered on the blank line below the headline. The picture is called Graduation and is available on the Data Files. Resize the picture so that it is approximately 2.9" × 2.89". Apply the Simple Frame, Black picture style to the inserted picture.

19. Change the spacing before the first bulleted paragraph to 12 points and the spacing after the last bulleted paragraph to 24 points.

20. The entire flyer should fit on a single page. If it flows to two pages, resize the picture or decrease spacing before and after paragraphs until the entire flyer text fits on a single page.

21. Change the zoom to text width, then page width, then 100% and notice the differences.

22. If requested by your instructor, enter the text, Graduation Open House, as the keywords in the document properties. Change the other document properties, as specified by your instructor.

23. Click File on the ribbon and then click Save As. Save the document using the file name, Apply 1–1 Graduation Flyer Formatted.

24. Print the document. Switch to Read Mode and browse pages through the document. Switch to Print Layout view.

25. Submit the revised document, shown in Figure 1–72, in the format specified by your instructor.

26. Exit Word.

27. ✸ If this flyer were announcing a victory parade instead of a graduation, which color scheme would you apply and why?

Extend Your Knowledge

Extend the skills you learned in this module and experiment with new skills. You may need to use Help to complete the assignment.

Modifying Text and Picture Formats and Adding Page Borders

Note: To complete this assignment, you will be required to use the Data Files. Please contact your instructor for information about accessing the Data Files.

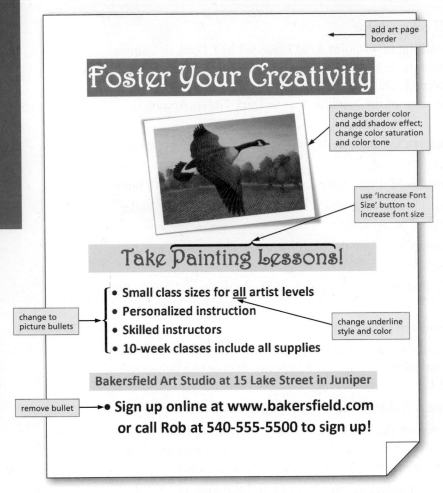

add art page border

change border color and add shadow effect; change color saturation and color tone

use 'Increase Font Size' button to increase font size

change to picture bullets

change underline style and color

remove bullet

Figure 1–73

Instructions: Run Word. Open the document, Extend 1–1 Painting Lessons Flyer Draft, from the Data Files. You will enhance the look of the flyer shown in Figure 1–73. *Hint:* Remember, if you make a mistake while formatting the picture, you can reset it by using the Reset Picture button or Reset Picture arrow (Picture Tools Format tab | Adjust group).

Perform the following tasks:

1. Use Help to learn about the following: remove bullets, grow font, shrink font, art page borders, decorative underline(s), picture bullets, picture border shading, picture border color, shadow picture effects, and color saturation and tone.

2. Remove the bullet from the last paragraph of the flyer.

3. Select the text, Painting Lessons, and use the 'Increase Font Size' button (Home tab | Font group) to increase its font size.

4. Add an art page border to the flyer. If the border is not in color, add color to it if the border supports color.

5. Change the solid underline below the word, all, to a decorative underline. Change the color of the underline.

6. Change the style of the bullets to picture bullet(s). Adjust the hanging indent, if necessary, to align the text in the bulleted list.

7. Change the color of the picture border. Add a shadow picture effect to the picture.

8. Change the color saturation and color tone of the picture.

9. If requested by your instructor, change the name of the art studio (Bakersfield) to your last name.

10. Save the revised document with the file name, Extend 1–1 Painting Lessons Flyer Final, and then submit it in the format specified by your instructor.

11. ✷ In this assignment, you changed the bullets to picture bullets. Which bullet character did you select and why?

Expand Your World

Create a solution that uses cloud or web technologies by learning and investigating on your own from general guidance.

Using Word Online to Create a Flyer with a Picture

Note: To complete this assignment, you will be required to use the Data Files. Please contact your instructor for information about accessing the Data Files.

Instructions: You will use Word Online to prepare a flyer. The text for the unformatted flyer is shown in Figure 1–74. You will enter the text in Word Online and then use its tools to enhance the look of the flyer.

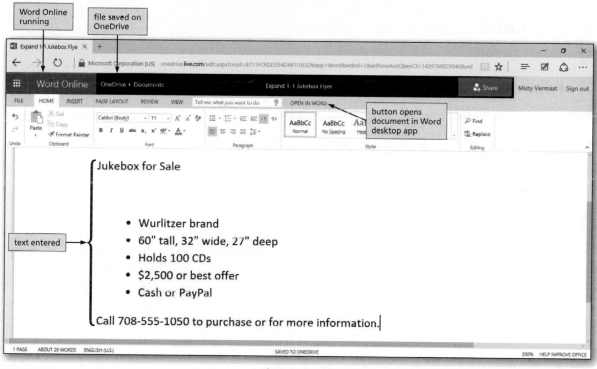

Figure 1–74

Perform the following tasks:

1. Run a browser. Search for the text, Word Online, using a search engine. Visit several websites to learn about Word Online. Navigate to the Office Online website. You will need to sign in to your OneDrive account.

2. Create a new blank Word document using Word Online. Name the document Expand 1–1 Jukebox Flyer.

3. Notice the differences between Word Online and the Word desktop app you used to create the project in this module.

4. Enter the text in the flyer, shown in Figure 1–74, checking spelling as you type.

5. Insert the picture called Jukebox, which is located in the Data Files.

Continued >

Expand Your World *continued*

6. Use the features available in Word Online, along with the concepts and techniques presented in this module, to format this flyer. Be sure to change the font and font size of text, center a paragraph(s), italicize text, color text, underline text, and apply a picture style. Resize the picture. Adjust spacing above and below paragraphs as necessary. The flyer should fit on a single page.

7. If requested by your instructor, replace the phone number in the flyer with your phone number.

8. Save the document again. Click the button to open the document in the Word desktop app. If necessary, sign in to your Microsoft account when prompted. Notice how the document appears in the Word desktop app.

9. Using either Word Online or the Word desktop app, submit the document in the format requested by your instructor. Exit Word Online. If necessary, sign out of your OneDrive account and your Microsoft account in Word.

10. ✳ What is Word Online? Which features that are covered in this module are not available in Word Online? Do you prefer using Word Online or the Word desktop app? Why?

In the Labs

Design, create, modify, and/or use a document following the guidelines, concepts, and skills presented in this module. Labs 1 and 2, which increase in difficulty, require you to create solutions based on what you learned in the module; Lab 3 requires you to apply your creative thinking and problem-solving skills to design and implement a solution.

Lab 1: Creating a Flyer with a Picture

Note: To complete this assignment, you will be required to use the Data Files. Please contact your instructor for information about accessing the Data Files.

Problem: Your boss asked you to prepare a flyer that advertises the company's commodity trading seminars. First, you prepare the unformatted flyer shown in Figure 1–75a, and then you format it so that it looks like Figure 1–75b. *Hint:* Remember, if you make a mistake while formatting the flyer, you can use the Undo button on the Quick Access Toolbar to undo your last action.

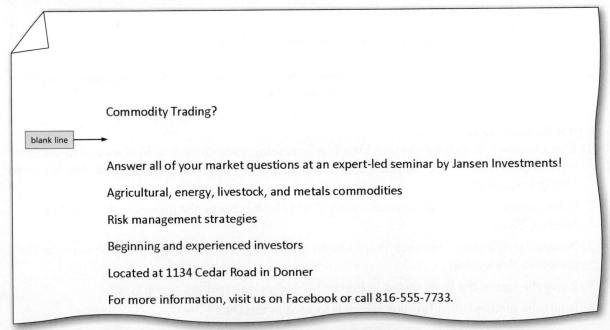

Commodity Trading?

blank line →

Answer all of your market questions at an expert-led seminar by Jansen Investments!

Agricultural, energy, livestock, and metals commodities

Risk management strategies

Beginning and experienced investors

Located at 1134 Cedar Road in Donner

For more information, visit us on Facebook or call 816-555-7733.

Figure 1–75a Unformatted Text

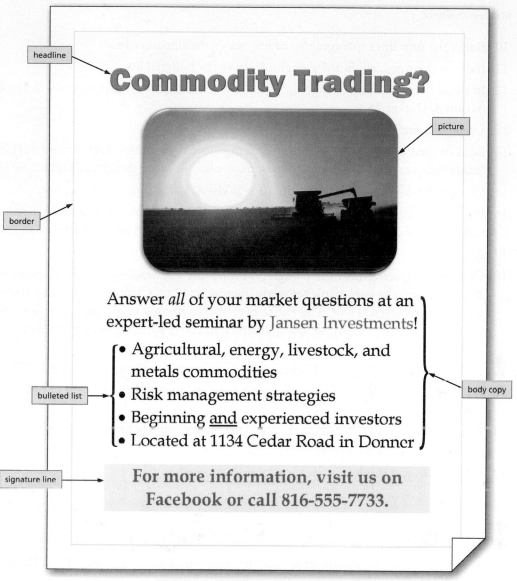

Figure 1–75b Formatted Document

Perform the following tasks:

1. Run Word. Display formatting marks on the screen.
2. Type the flyer text, unformatted, as shown in Figure 1–75a, inserting a blank line between the headline and the body copy. If Word flags any misspelled words as you type, check their spelling and correct them.
3. Save the document using the file name, Lab 1–1 Commodity Trading Flyer.
4. Center the headline and the signature line.
5. Change the theme colors to Green.
6. Change the font size of the headline to 48 point and the font to Franklin Gothic Heavy or a similar font. Apply the text effect called Fill - Dark Teal, Accent 4, Soft Bevel.
7. Change the font size of body copy between the headline and the signature line to 24 point.
8. Change the font size of the signature line to 26 point.
9. Change the font of the body copy and signature line to Book Antiqua.

Continued >

In the Labs *continued*

10. Bullet the four lines (paragraphs) of text above the signature line.

11. Italicize the word, all, in the paragraph above the bulleted list.

12. In the same paragraph, change the color of the words, Jansen Investments, to Dark Teal, Accent 4, Darker 25%.

13. Underline the word, and, in the third bulleted paragraph.

14. Bold the text in the signature line and change its color to Dark Teal, Accent 4, Darker 25%. Shade the paragraph containing the signature line in Lime, Accent 2, Lighter 80%.

15. Change the zoom so that the entire page is visible in the document window.

16. Insert the picture centered on a blank line below the headline. The picture is called Harvest, which is on the Data Files. Reduce the size of the picture to approximately 3.29" × 5.11".

17. Apply the Bevel Rectangle picture style to the inserted picture.

18. Change the spacing after the paragraph containing the headline to 0 pt. Change the spacing above (before) the paragraph below the picture to 12 pt. Change the spacing above (before) the signature line to 18 pt. The entire flyer should fit on a single page. If it flows to two pages, resize the picture or decrease spacing before and after paragraphs until the entire flyer text fits on a single page.

19. Add a ½-pt Lime, Accent 3, Lighter 40% page border, as shown in Figure 1–75b.

20. If requested by your instructor, change the street address in the flyer to your home street address.

21. Save the flyer again with the same file name. Submit the document, shown in Figure 1–75b, in the format specified by your instructor.

22. ✹ Why do you think this flyer used shades of green?

Lab 2: **Creating a Flyer with Multiple Pictures**

Note: To complete this assignment, you will be required to use the Data Files. Please contact your instructor for information about accessing the Data Files.

Problem: Your boss at Gingham Travel has asked you to prepare a flyer that promotes its business. You prepare the flyer shown in Figure 1–76. *Hint:* Remember, if you make a mistake while formatting the flyer, you can use the Undo button on the Quick Access Toolbar to undo your last action.

Perform the following tasks:

1. Run Word. Type the flyer text, unformatted. If Word flags any misspelled words as you type, check their spelling and correct them.

2. Save the document using the file name, Lab 1–2 Spring Break Flyer.

3. Change the theme colors to the Aspect color scheme.

4. Add bullets to the four paragraphs shown in the figure. Center all paragraphs, except the paragraphs containing the bulleted list.

5. Change the font size of both lines in the headline to 48 point. Change the font of the first line in the headline to Ravie, or a similar font, and the second line in the headline to Arial Rounded MT Bold, or a similar font. Apply this text effect to the first line in the headline: Fill - Dark Purple, Accent 1, Outline - Background 1, Hard Shadow - Accent 1. Shade the second line of the headline to the Dark Green, Accent 4 color, and change the font color to White, Background 1.

Figure 1–76

6. Change the font of all text below the headline to Arial Rounded MT Bold. Change the font size of the company name to 28 point, the company address to 24 point, and the bulleted list and signature line to 22 point.

7. Change the color of the company name and address to Dark Green, Accent 4, Darker 25%. Underline the company name.

8. Italicize the word, and, in the first bulleted paragraph.

9. Bold the word, Discounted, in the second bulleted paragraph. Change the color of this same word to Dark Purple, Accent 5.

10. Shade the signature line to the Dark Green, Accent 4 color, and change the font color to White, Background 1.

11. Change the zoom so that the entire page is visible in the document window.

12. Insert two pictures on the same blank line below the headline. The pictures are called Spring Break - Florida and Spring Break - New York, which are both in the Data Files.

Continued >

In the Labs *continued*

13. Resize the top picture so that it is approximately 2.4" × 3". Apply the Simple Frame, White picture style to both pictures. Apply the Perspective Right 3-D Rotation picture effect to the picture on the left and the Perspective Left 3-D Rotation to the picture on the right. Resize the pictures, if necessary, so that they fit on the same line. Add space as necessary between the two pictures.

14. Change the spacing before and after the paragraph containing the company name to 0 pt, the spacing after the company address to 12 pt, and the spacing before the signature line to 12 pt. The entire flyer should fit on a single page. If it flows to two pages, resize the pictures or decrease spacing before and after paragraphs until the entire flyer text fits on a single page.

15. Add the 6-point page border shown in Figure 1–76, using the color Dark Purple, Accent 5.

16. Center the page contents vertically.

17. If requested by your instructor, change the company name to your last name.

18. Save the flyer again with the same file name. Submit the document, shown in Figure 1–76, in the format specified by your instructor.

19. ✸ Why do you think this flyer used shades of purple and green?

Lab 3: **Consider This: Your Turn**

Design and Create an Antique Store Flyer

Note: To complete this assignment, you will be required to use the Data Files. Please contact your instructor for information about accessing the Data Files.

Problem: Your boss at Antiques Galore has asked you to prepare a flyer that promotes its business.

Perform the following tasks:

Part 1: The flyer should contain two digital pictures appropriately resized; the Data Files contains two pictures called Vintage Phone and Vintage Scale, or you can use your own digital pictures if they are appropriate for the topic of the flyer. The flyer should contain the headline, Antiques Galore, and this signature line: Questions? Call 312-555-2000 or find us on Facebook. The body copy consists of the following text, in any order: We sell all types of vintage items and also buy items individually or as an entire estate. Bring your items in for a free appraisal!; 1,200 square foot shop; Collectibles, costume jewelry, furniture, paintings, pottery, toys, and more!; Affordable items with new inventory daily; Located at 229 Center Street in Snow Hill; Open from 9:00 a.m. to 8:00 p.m. daily.

Use the concepts and techniques presented in this module to create and format this flyer. Be sure to check spelling and grammar. Submit your assignment and answers to the Part 2 critical thinking questions in the format specified by your instructor.

Part 2: ✸ You made several decisions while creating the flyer in this assignment: where to place text, how to format the text (i.e., font, font size, paragraph alignment, bulleted paragraphs, underlines, italics, bold, color, etc.), which graphics to use, where to position the graphics, how to format the graphics, and which page enhancements to add (i.e., borders and spacing). What was the rationale behind each of these decisions? When you proofread the document, what further revisions did you make and why? How would you recommend distributing this flyer?

2 | Creating a Research Paper with References and Sources

Objectives

You will have mastered the material in this module when you can:

- Describe the MLA documentation style for research papers
- Modify a style
- Change line and paragraph spacing in a document
- Use a header to number pages of a document
- Apply formatting using keyboard shortcuts
- Modify paragraph indentation
- Insert and edit citations and their sources
- Add a footnote to a document
- Insert a manual page break
- Create a bibliographical list of sources
- Cut, copy, and paste text
- Find text and replace text
- Find a synonym
- Check spelling and grammar at once
- Look up information

Introduction

In both academic and business environments, you will be asked to write reports. Business reports range from proposals to cost justifications to five-year plans to research findings. Academic reports focus mostly on research findings.

A **research paper** is a document you can use to communicate the results of research findings. To write a research paper, you learn about a particular topic from a variety of sources (research), organize your ideas from the research results, and then present relevant facts and/or opinions that support the topic. Your final research paper combines properly credited outside information along with personal insights. Thus, no two research papers — even if they are about the same topic — will or should be the same.

Project — Research Paper

When preparing a research paper, you should follow a standard documentation style that defines the rules for creating the paper and crediting sources. A variety of documentation styles exists, depending on the nature of the research paper. Each style requires the same basic information; the differences in styles relate to requirements for presenting the information. For example, one documentation style uses the term, bibliography, for the list of sources, whereas another uses the term, references, and yet a third prefers the term, works cited. Two popular documentation styles for research papers are the **Modern Language Association of America** (**MLA**) and **American Psychological Association** (**APA**) styles. This module uses the MLA documentation style because it is used in a wide range of disciplines.

The project in this module follows research paper guidelines and uses Word to create the short research paper shown in Figure 2–1. This paper, which discusses using headphones and earbuds safely, follows the MLA documentation style. Each page contains a page number. The first two pages present the name and course information (student name, instructor name, course name, and paper due date), paper title, an introduction with a thesis statement, details that support the thesis, and a conclusion. This section of the paper also includes references to research sources and a footnote. The third page contains a detailed, alphabetical list of the sources referenced in the research paper. All pages include a header at the upper-right edge of the page.

In this module, you will learn how to create the research paper shown in Figure 2–1. The following roadmap identifies general activities you will perform as you progress through this module:

1. CHANGE the DOCUMENT SETTINGS.
2. CREATE the HEADER for each page of the research paper.
3. TYPE the RESEARCH PAPER text WITH CITATIONS.
4. CREATE an ALPHABETICAL WORKS CITED page.
5. PROOFREAD AND REVISE the RESEARCH PAPER.

MLA Documentation Style

The research paper in this project follows the guidelines presented by the MLA. To follow the MLA documentation style, use a 12-point Times New Roman or similar font. Double-space text on all pages of the paper using one-inch top, bottom, left, and right margins. Indent the first word of each paragraph one-half inch from the left margin. At the right margin of each page, place a page number one-half inch from the top margin. On each page, precede the page number with your last name.

The MLA documentation style does not require a title page. Instead, place your name and course information in a block at the left margin beginning one inch from the top of the page. Center the title one double-spaced line below your name and course information.

In the text of the paper, place author references in parentheses with the page number(s) of the referenced information. The MLA documentation style uses in-text **parenthetical references** instead of noting each source at the bottom of the page or at the end of the paper. In the MLA documentation style, notes are used only for optional content or bibliographic notes.

If used, content notes elaborate on points discussed in the paper, and bibliographic notes direct the reader to evaluations of statements in a source or provide a means for identifying multiple sources. Use a superscript (raised number) both to signal that a note exists and to sequence the notes (shown in Figure 2–1). Position notes at the bottom of the page as footnotes or at the end of the paper as endnotes. Indent the first line of each note one-half inch from the left margin. Place one space following the superscripted number before beginning the note text. Double-space the note text (shown in Figure 2–1).

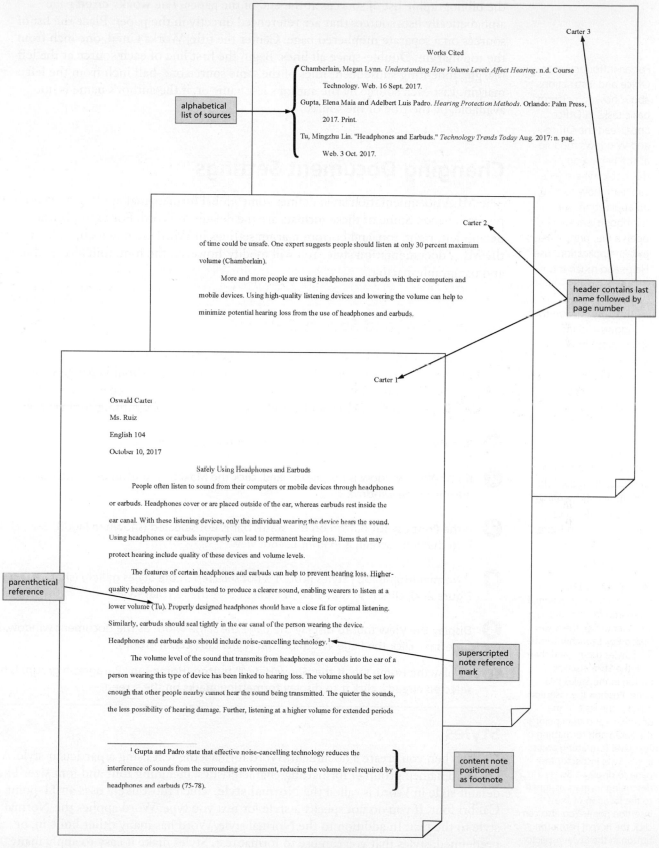

alphabetical list of sources

Carter 3

Works Cited

Chamberlain, Megan Lynn. *Understanding How Volume Levels Affect Hearing*. n.d. Course Technology. Web. 16 Sept. 2017.

Gupta, Elena Maia and Adelbert Luis Padro. *Hearing Protection Methods*. Orlando: Palm Press, 2017. Print.

Tu, Mingzhu Lin. "Headphones and Earbuds." *Technology Trends Today* Aug. 2017: n. pag. Web. 3 Oct. 2017.

header contains last name followed by page number

Carter 2

of time could be unsafe. One expert suggests people should listen at only 30 percent maximum volume (Chamberlain).

More and more people are using headphones and earbuds with their computers and mobile devices. Using high-quality listening devices and lowering the volume can help to minimize potential hearing loss from the use of headphones and earbuds.

Carter 1

Oswald Carter

Ms. Ruiz

English 104

October 10, 2017

Safely Using Headphones and Earbuds

People often listen to sound from their computers or mobile devices through headphones or earbuds. Headphones cover or are placed outside of the ear, whereas earbuds rest inside the ear canal. With these listening devices, only the individual wearing the device hears the sound. Using headphones or earbuds improperly can lead to permanent hearing loss. Items that may protect hearing include quality of these devices and volume levels.

The features of certain headphones and earbuds can help to prevent hearing loss. Higher-quality headphones and earbuds tend to produce a clearer sound, enabling wearers to listen at a lower volume (Tu). Properly designed headphones should have a close fit for optimal listening. Similarly, earbuds should seal tightly in the ear canal of the person wearing the device. Headphones and earbuds also should include noise-cancelling technology.[1]

The volume level of the sound that transmits from headphones or earbuds into the ear of a person wearing this type of device has been linked to hearing loss. The volume should be set low enough that other people nearby cannot hear the sound being transmitted. The quieter the sounds, the less possibility of hearing damage. Further, listening at a higher volume for extended periods

parenthetical reference

superscripted note reference mark

[1] Gupta and Padro state that effective noise-cancelling technology reduces the interference of sounds from the surrounding environment, reducing the volume level required by headphones and earbuds (75-78).

content note positioned as footnote

Figure 2–1

The MLA documentation style uses the term, works cited, to refer to the bibliographic list of sources at the end of the paper. The **works cited** page alphabetically lists sources that are referenced directly in the paper. Place the list of sources on a separate numbered page. Center the title, Works Cited, one inch from the top margin. Double-space all lines. Begin the first line of each source at the left margin, indenting subsequent lines of the same source one-half inch from the left margin. List each source by the author's last name or, if the author's name is not available, by the title of the source.

Changing Document Settings

The MLA documentation style defines some global formats that apply to the entire research paper. Some of these formats are the default in Word. For example, the default left, right, top, and bottom margin settings in Word are one inch, which meets the MLA documentation style. You will modify, however, the font, font size, and line and paragraph spacing.

To Run Word and Specify Settings

If you are using a computer to step through the project in this module and you want your screens to match the figures in this book, you should change your screen's resolution to 1366 × 768. For information about how to change a computer's resolution, refer to the Office and Windows module at the beginning of this book.

1 Run Word and create a blank document in the Word window.

2 If the Word window is not maximized, click the Maximize button on its title bar to maximize the window.

3 If the Print Layout button on the status bar is not selected (shown in Figure 2–2), click it so that your screen is in Print Layout view.

4 If Normal (Home tab | Styles group) is not selected in the Styles gallery (shown in Figure 2–2), click it so that your document uses the Normal style.

5 Display the View tab. To display the page the same width as the document window, if necessary, click the Page Width button (View tab | Zoom group).

6 Display the Home tab. If the 'Show/Hide ¶' button (Home tab | Paragraph group) is not selected already, click it to display formatting marks on the screen.

Styles

When you create a document, Word formats the text using a particular style. A **style** is a named group of formatting characteristics, including font and font size. The default style in Word is called the **Normal style**, which most likely uses an 11-point Calibri font. If you do not specify a style for text you type, Word applies the Normal style to the text. In addition to the Normal style, Word has many other built-in, or predefined, styles that you can use to format text. Styles make it easy to apply many formats at once to text. You can modify existing styles and create your own styles. Styles are discussed as they are used in this book.

For an introduction to Office and instructions about how to perform basic tasks in Office apps, read the Office and Windows module at the beginning of this book, where you can learn how to run an application, use the ribbon, save a file, open a file, print a file, exit an application, use Help, and much more.

For an introduction to Windows and instructions about how to perform basic Windows tasks, read the Office and Windows module at the beginning of this book, where you can learn how to resize windows, change screen resolution, create folders, move and rename files, use Windows Help, and much more.

BTW
Style Formats
To see the formats assigned to a particular style in a document, click the Styles Dialog Box Launcher (Home tab | Styles group) and then click the Style Inspector button in the Styles task pane. Position the insertion point in the style in the document and then point to the Paragraph formatting or Text level formatting areas in the Style Inspector task pane to display a ScreenTip describing formats assigned to the location of the insertion point. You also can click the Reveal Formatting button in the Style Inspector task pane or press SHIFT+F1 to display the Reveal Formatting task pane.

To Modify a Style

The MLA documentation style requires that all text in the research paper use a 12-point Times New Roman or similar font. If you change the font and font size using buttons on the ribbon, you will need to make the change many times during the course of creating the paper. ***Why?*** *Word formats various areas of a document based on the Normal style, which uses an 11-point Calibri font. For example, body text, headers, and bibliographies all display text based on the Normal style.*

Thus, instead of changing the font and font size for various document elements, a more efficient technique is to change the Normal style for this document to use a 12-point Times New Roman font. ***Why?*** *By changing the Normal style, you ensure that all text in the document will use the format required by the MLA.* The following steps change the Normal style.

1
- Right-click Normal in the Styles gallery (Home tab | Styles group) to display a shortcut menu related to styles (Figure 2–2).

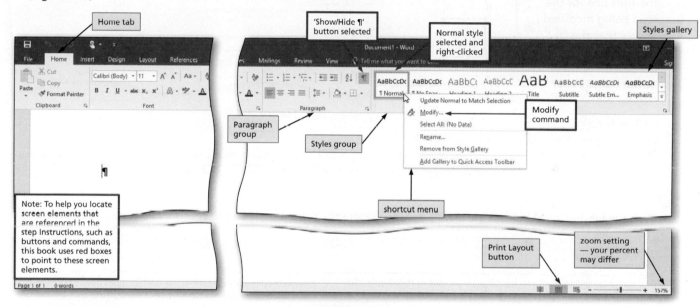

Figure 2–2

2
- Click Modify on the shortcut menu to display the Modify Style dialog box (Figure 2–3).

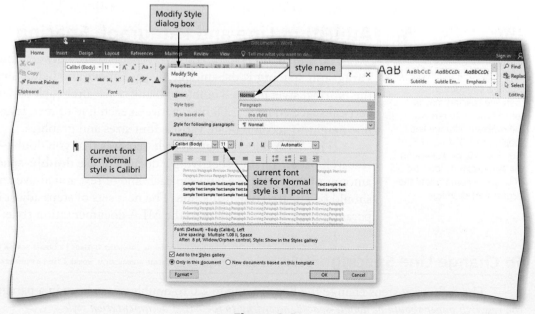

Figure 2–3

3

- Click the Font arrow (Modify Style dialog box) to display the Font list. Scroll to and then click Times New Roman in the list to change the font for the style being modified.
- Click the Font Size arrow (Modify Style dialog box) and then click 12 in the Font Size list to change the font size for the style being modified.
- Ensure that the 'Only in this document' option button is selected (Figure 2–4).

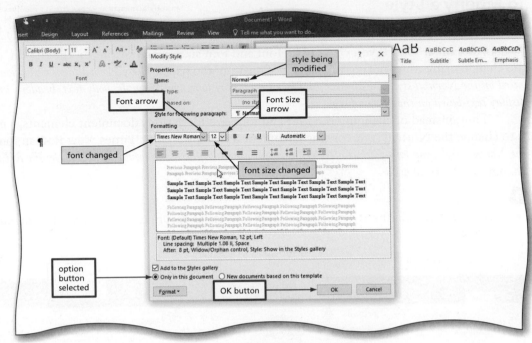

Figure 2–4

Q&A
Will all future documents use the new font and font size?
No, because the 'Only in this document' option button is selected. If you wanted all future documents to use a new setting, you would select the 'New documents based on this template' option button.

4

- Click the OK button (Modify Style dialog box) to update the Normal style to the specified settings.

Other Ways

1. Click Styles Dialog Box Launcher, click arrow next to style name, click Modify on menu, change settings (Modify Style dialog box), click OK button

2. Press ALT+CTRL+SHIFT+S, click arrow next to style name, click Modify on menu, change settings (Modify Style dialog box), click OK button

---

BTW

Line Spacing
If the top of a set of characters or a graphical image is chopped off, then line spacing may be set to Exactly. To remedy the problem, change line spacing to 1.0, 1.15, 1.5, 2.0, 2.5, 3.0, or At least (in the Paragraph dialog box), all of which accommodate the largest font or image.

Adjusting Line and Paragraph Spacing

Line spacing is the amount of vertical space between lines of text in a paragraph. **Paragraph spacing** is the amount of space above and below a paragraph. By default, the Normal style places 8 points of blank space after each paragraph and inserts a vertical space equal to 1.08 lines between each line of text. It also automatically adjusts line height to accommodate various font sizes and graphics.

The MLA documentation style requires that you double-space the entire research paper. That is, specifying a document use **double-space** means that the amount of vertical space between each line of text and above and below paragraphs should be equal to one blank line. The next sets of steps adjust line spacing and paragraph spacing according to the MLA documentation style.

1 CHANGE DOCUMENT SETTINGS | 2 CREATE HEADER | 3 TYPE RESEARCH PAPER WITH CITATIONS
4 CREATE ALPHABETICAL WORKS CITED | 5 PROOFREAD & REVISE RESEARCH PAPER

To Change Line Spacing

The following steps change the line spacing to 2.0 to double-space lines in a paragraph. *Why? The lines of the research paper should be double-spaced, according to the MLA documentation style.*

1
- Click the 'Line and Paragraph Spacing' button (Home tab | Paragraph group) to display the Line and Paragraph Spacing gallery (Figure 2–5).

Q&A What do the numbers in the Line and Paragraph Spacing gallery represent?

The options 1.0, 2.0, and 3.0 set line spacing to single, double, and triple, respectively. Similarly, the 1.15, 1.5, and 2.5 options set line spacing to 1.15, 1.5, and 2.5 lines. All of these options adjust line spacing automatically to accommodate the largest font or graphic on a line.

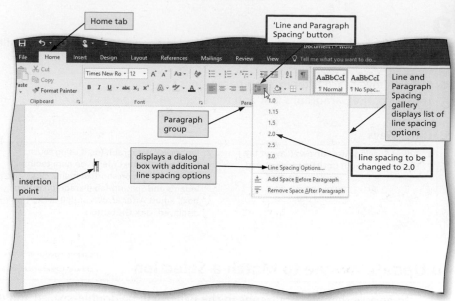

Figure 2–5

2
- Click 2.0 in the Line and Paragraph Spacing gallery to change the line spacing at the location of the insertion point.

Q&A Can I change the line spacing of existing text?

Yes. Select the text first and then change the line spacing as described in these steps.

Other Ways

1. Right-click paragraph (or, if using touch, tap 'Show Context Menu' on mini toolbar), click Paragraph on shortcut menu, or click Indents and Spacing tab (Paragraph dialog box), click Line spacing arrow, select desired spacing, click OK button

2. Click Paragraph Settings Dialog Box Launcher (Home tab or Layout tab | Paragraph group), click Indents and Spacing tab (Paragraph dialog box), click Line spacing arrow, select desired spacing, click OK button

3. Press CTRL+2 for double-spacing

To Remove Space after a Paragraph

1 CHANGE DOCUMENT SETTINGS | 2 CREATE HEADER | 3 TYPE RESEARCH PAPER WITH CITATIONS
4 CREATE ALPHABETICAL WORKS CITED | 5 PROOFREAD & REVISE RESEARCH PAPER

The following steps remove space after a paragraph. *Why? The research paper should not have additional blank space after each paragraph, according to the MLA documentation style.*

1
- Click the 'Line and Paragraph Spacing' button (Home tab | Paragraph group) to display the Line and Paragraph Spacing gallery (Figure 2–6).

Q&A Why does a check mark appear to the left of 2.0 in the gallery?

The check mark indicates the currently selected line spacing.

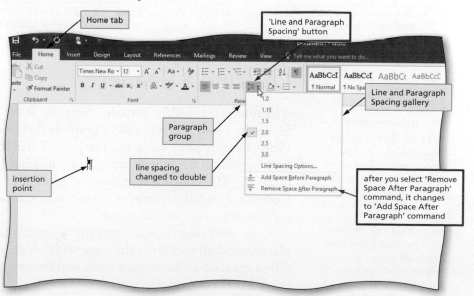

Figure 2–6

2

- Click 'Remove Space After Paragraph' in the Line and Paragraph Spacing gallery so that no blank space appears after paragraphs.

Q&A Can I remove space after existing paragraphs?

Yes. Select the paragraphs first and then remove the space as described in these steps.

Other Ways

1. Adjust Spacing After arrows (Layout tab | Paragraph group) until 0 pt is displayed

2. Right-click paragraph (or, if using touch, tap 'Show Context Menu' on mini toolbar), click Paragraph on shortcut menu, click Indents and Spacing tab (Paragraph dialog box), adjust After arrows until 0 pt is displayed, click OK button

3. Click Paragraph Settings Dialog Box Launcher (Home tab or Layout tab | Paragraph group), click Indents and Spacing tab (Paragraph dialog box), adjust After arrows until 0 pt is displayed, click OK button

To Update a Style to Match a Selection

1 CHANGE DOCUMENT SETTINGS | 2 CREATE HEADER | 3 TYPE RESEARCH PAPER WITH CITATIONS
4 CREATE ALPHABETICAL WORKS CITED | 5 PROOFREAD & REVISE RESEARCH PAPER

To ensure that all paragraphs in the paper will be double-spaced and do not have space after the paragraphs, you want the Normal style to include the line and paragraph spacing changes made in the previous two sets of steps. The following steps update the Normal style. *Why? You can update a style to reflect the settings of the location of the insertion point or selected text. Because no text has been typed in the research paper yet, you do not need to select text prior to updating the Normal style.*

- Right-click Normal in the Styles gallery (Home tab | Styles group) to display a shortcut menu (Figure 2–7).

- Click 'Update Normal to Match Selection' on the shortcut menu to update the selected (or current) style to reflect the settings at the location of the insertion point.

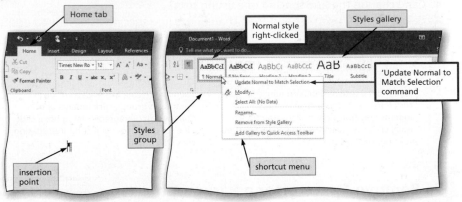

Figure 2–7

Other Ways

1. Click Styles Dialog Box Launcher, click arrow next to style name, click 'Update Normal to Match Selection'

2. Press ALT+CTRL+SHIFT+S, click arrow next to style name in Styles pane, click 'Update Normal to Match Selection'

Creating a Header

BTW

The Ribbon and Screen Resolution
Word may change how the groups and buttons within the groups appear on the ribbon, depending on the computer or mobile device's screen resolution. Thus, your ribbon may look different from the ones in this book if you are using a screen resolution other than 1366 x 768.

A **header** is text and/or graphics that print at the top of each page in a document. Similarly, a **footer** is text and/or graphics that print at the bottom of every page. In Word, headers print in the top margin one-half inch from the top of every page, and footers print in the bottom margin one-half inch from the bottom of each page, which meets the MLA documentation style. In addition to text and graphics, headers and footers can include document information, such as the page number, current date, current time, and author's name.

In this research paper, you are to precede the page number with your last name placed one-half inch from the upper-right edge of each page. The procedures in the following sections enter your name and the page number in the header, as specified by the MLA documentation style.

To Switch to the Header

The following steps switch from editing the document text to editing the header. *Why? To enter text in the header, you instruct Word to edit the header.*

- Click Insert on the ribbon to display the Insert tab.
- Click the 'Add a Header' button (Insert tab | Header & Footer group) to display the Add a Header gallery (Figure 2–8)

Experiment

- Click the down scroll arrow in the Add a Header gallery to see the available built-in headers.

Q&A

Can I use a built-in header for this research paper?
None of the built-in headers adheres to the MLA documentation style; thus, you should enter your own header content instead of using a built-in header for this research paper.

How would I remove a header from a document?
You would click Remove Header in the Add a Header gallery. Similarly, to remove a footer, you would click Remove Footer in the Add a Footer gallery.

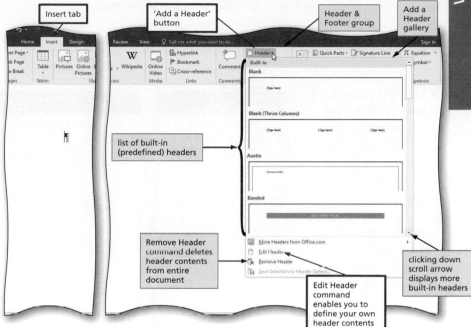

Figure 2–8

- Click Edit Header in the Add a Header gallery to switch from the document text to the header, which allows you to edit the contents of the header (Figure 2–9).

Q&A

How do I remove the Header & Footer Tools Design tab from the ribbon?
When you are finished editing the header, you will close it, which removes the Header & Footer Tools Design tab.

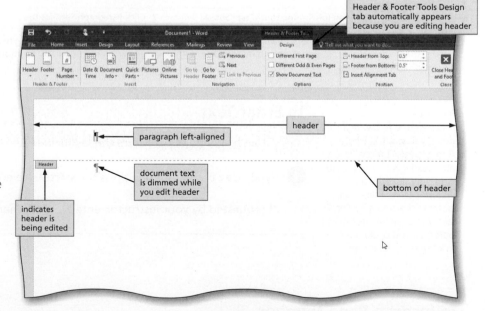

Figure 2–9

Other Ways

1. Double-click dimmed header
2. Right-click header in document, click Edit Header button that appears

To Right-Align a Paragraph

The paragraph in the header currently is left-aligned (shown in Figure 2–9). The following steps right-align this paragraph. **Why?** *Your last name and the page number should print* **right-aligned**; *that is, they should print at the right margin, according to the MLA documentation style.*

• Click Home on the ribbon to display the Home tab.

• Click the Align Right button (Home tab | Paragraph group) to right-align the current paragraph (Figure 2–10).

Q&A What if I wanted to return the paragraph to left-aligned? You would click the Align Right button again, or click the Align Left button (Home tab | Paragraph group).

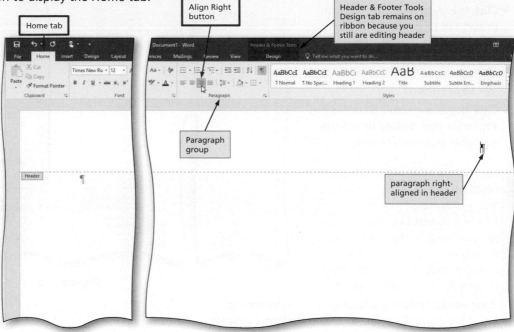

Figure 2–10

Other Ways

1. Right-click paragraph (or, if using touch, tap 'Show Context Menu' button on mini toolbar), click Paragraph on shortcut menu, click Indents and Spacing tab (Paragraph dialog box), click Alignment arrow, click Right, click OK button

2. Click Paragraph Settings Dialog Box Launcher (Home tab or Layout tab | Paragraph group), click Indents and Spacing tab (Paragraph dialog box), click Alignment arrow, click Right, click OK button

3. Press CTRL+R

BTW
Footers
If you wanted to create a footer, you would click the 'Add a Footer' button (Insert tab | Header & Footer group) and then select the desired built-in footer or click Edit Footer in the Add a Footer gallery to create a customized footer; or, you could double-click the dimmed footer.

To Enter Text

The following step enters the last name right-aligned in the header area.

 Type **Carter** and then press the SPACEBAR to enter the last name in the header.

If requested by your instructor, enter your last name instead of Carter in the header.

To Insert a Page Number

The following steps insert a page number at the location of the insertion point. **Why?** *The MLA documentation style requires a page number following the last name in the header.*

1

- Click Header & Footer Tools Design on the ribbon to display the Header & Footer Tools Design tab.
- Click the 'Add Page Numbers' button (Header & Footer Tools Design tab | Header & Footer group) to display the Add Page Numbers menu.

Q&A Why does the button name in the step differ from the name on the face of the button in the figure?
The text that appears on the face of the button may vary, depending on screen resolution. The name that appears in the ScreenTip (when you point to the button), however, never changes. For this reason, this book uses the name that appears in the ScreenTip to identify buttons, boxes, and other on-screen elements.

- Point to Current Position on the Add Page Numbers menu to display the Current Position gallery (Figure 2–11).

 Experiment

- Click the down scroll arrow in the Current Position gallery to see the available page number formats.

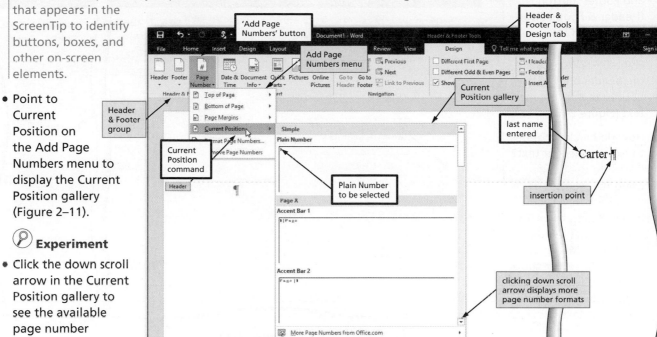

Figure 2–11

2

- If necessary, scroll to the top of the Current Position gallery.
- Click Plain Number in the Current Position gallery to insert an unformatted page number at the location of the insertion point (Figure 2–12).

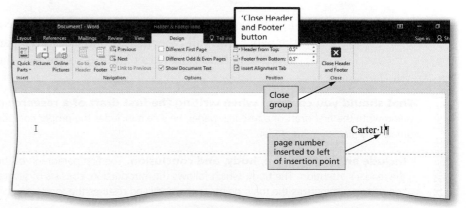

Figure 2–12

Other Ways

1. Click 'Add Page Numbers' button (Insert tab | Header & Footer group)

2. Click 'Explore Quick Parts' button (Insert tab | Text group or Header & Footer Tools Design tab | Insert group), click Field on Explore Quick Parts menu, select Page in Field names list (Field dialog box), select desired format in Format list, click OK button

To Close the Header

The next task is to switch back to the document text. *Why? You are finished entering text in the header.* The following step closes the header.

• Click the 'Close Header and Footer' button (Header & Footer Tools Design tab | Close group) (shown in Figure 2–12) to close the header and switch back to the document text (Figure 2–13).

Q&A

How do I make changes to existing header text? Switch to the header using the steps described previously in the section titled To Switch to the Header, edit the header as you would edit text in the document window, and then switch back to the document text.

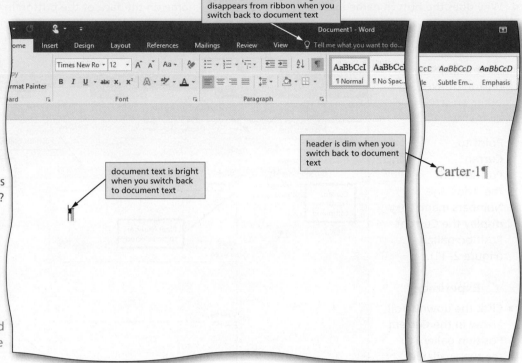

Figure 2–13

Other Ways

1. Double-click dimmed document text

Typing the Research Paper Text

The text of the research paper in this module encompasses the first two pages of the paper. You will type the text of the research paper and then modify it later in the module, so that it matches Figure 2–1 shown at the beginning of this module.

CONSIDER THIS

What should you consider when writing the first draft of a research paper?
As you write the first draft of a research paper, be sure it includes the proper components, uses credible sources, and does not contain any plagiarized material.

• **Include an introduction, body, and conclusion.** The first paragraph of the paper introduces the topic and captures the reader's attention. The body, which follows the introduction, consists of several paragraphs that support the topic. The conclusion summarizes the main points in the body and restates the topic.

• **Evaluate sources for authority, currency, and accuracy.** Be especially wary of information obtained on the web. Any person, company, or organization can publish a webpage on the Internet. When considering the source, consider the following:

  • Authority: Does a reputable institution or group support the source? Is the information presented without bias? Are the author's credentials listed and verifiable?

  • Currency: Is the information up to date? Are dates of sources listed? What is the last date revised or updated?

  • Accuracy: Is the information free of errors? Is it verifiable? Are the sources clearly identified?

• **Acknowledge all sources of information; do not plagiarize.** Sources of research include books, magazines, newspapers, and the Internet. As you record facts and ideas, list details about the source: title, author, place of publication, publisher, date of publication, etc. When taking notes, be careful not to **plagiarize**. That is, do not use someone else's work and claim it to be your own. If you copy information directly, place it in quotation marks and identify its source. Not only is plagiarism unethical, but it is considered an academic crime that can have severe punishments, such as failing a course or being expelled from school.

When you summarize, paraphrase (rewrite information in your own words), present facts, give statistics, quote exact words, or show a map, chart, or other graphic, you must acknowledge the source. Information that commonly is known or accessible to the audience constitutes common knowledge and does not need to be acknowledged. If, however, you question whether certain information is common knowledge, you should document it — just to be safe.

To Enter Name and Course Information

As discussed earlier in this module, the MLA documentation style does not require a separate title page for research papers. Instead, place your name and course information in a block at the top of the page, below the header, at the left margin. The following steps enter the name and course information in the research paper.

BTW
Date Formats
The MLA style prefers the day-month-year (10 October 2017) or month-day-year (October 10, 2017) format.

1 Type `Oswald Carter` as the student name and then press the ENTER key.

2 Type `Ms. Ruiz` as the instructor name and then press the ENTER key.

3 Type `English 104` as the course name and then press the ENTER key.

4 Type `October 10, 2017` as the paper's due date and then press the ENTER key (Figure 2–14).

If requested by your instructor, enter your name and course information instead of the information shown above.

Q&A Why did the word, October, appear on the screen as I began typing the month name? Word has an AutoComplete feature, where it predicts some words or phrases as you are typing and displays its prediction in a ScreenTip. If the AutoComplete prediction is correct, you can press the ENTER key (or, if using touch, tap the ScreenTip) to instruct Word to finish your typing with the word or phrase that appears in the ScreenTip.

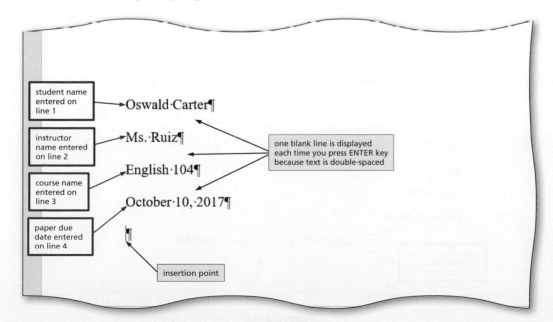

student name entered on line 1 → Oswald·Carter¶

instructor name entered on line 2 → Ms.·Ruiz¶

one blank line is displayed each time you press ENTER key because text is double-spaced

course name entered on line 3 → English·104¶

paper due date entered on line 4 → October·10,·2017¶

¶

insertion point

Figure 2–14

To Click and Type

The next task is to enter the title of the research paper centered between the page margins. In Module 1, you used the Center button (Home tab | Paragraph group) to center text and graphics. As an alternative, if you are using a mouse, you can use Word's Click and Type feature to format and enter text, graphics, and other items. *Why? With **Click and Type**, you can double-click a blank area of the document window and Word automatically formats the item you type or insert according to the location where you double-clicked.* The following steps use Click and Type to center and then type the title of the research paper.

1

 Experiment

- Move the pointer around the document below the entered name and course information and observe the various icons that appear with the I-beam.

- Position the pointer in the center of the document at the approximate location for the research paper title until a center icon appears below the I-beam (Figure 2–15).

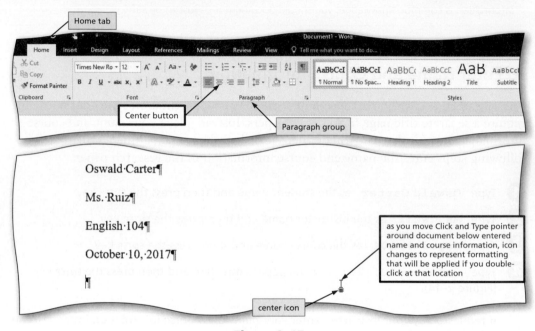

Figure 2–15

What are the other icons that appear in the Click and Type pointer?
A left-align icon appears to the right of the I-beam when the Click and Type pointer is in certain locations on the left side of the document window. A right-align icon appears to the left of the I-beam when the Click and Type pointer is in certain locations on the right side of the document window.

What if I am using a touch screen?
Tap the Center button (Home tab | Paragraph group) and then proceed to Step 3 because the Click and Type feature does not work with a touch screen.

2

- Double-click to center the paragraph mark and insertion point between the left and right margins.

3

- Type **Safely Using Headphones and Earbuds** as the paper title and then press the ENTER key to position the insertion point on the next line (Figure 2–16).

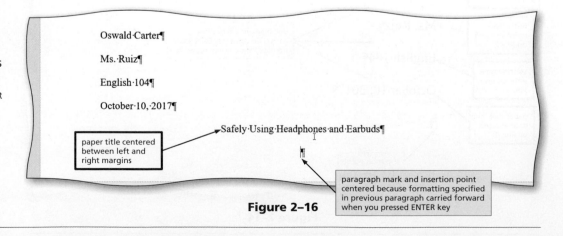

Figure 2–16

Keyboard Shortcuts

Word has many **keyboard shortcuts**, sometimes called shortcut keys or keyboard key combinations, for your convenience while typing. Table 2–1 lists the common keyboard shortcuts for formatting characters. Table 2–2 lists common keyboard shortcuts for formatting paragraphs.

Table 2–1 Keyboard Shortcuts for Formatting Characters

Character Formatting Task	Keyboard Shortcut	Character Formatting Task	Keyboard Shortcut
All capital letters	CTRL+SHIFT+A	Italic	CTRL+I
Bold	CTRL+B	Remove character formatting (plain text)	CTRL+SPACEBAR
Case of letters	SHIFT+F3	Small uppercase letters	CTRL+SHIFT+K
Decrease font size	CTRL+SHIFT+<	Subscript	CTRL+EQUAL SIGN
Decrease font size 1 point	CTRL+[	Superscript	CTRL+SHIFT+PLUS SIGN
Double-underline	CTRL+SHIFT+D	Underline	CTRL+U
Increase font size	CTRL+SHIFT+>	Underline words, not spaces	CTRL+SHIFT+W
Increase font size 1 point	CTRL+]		

© 2015 Cengage Learning

Table 2–2 Keyboard Shortcuts for Formatting Paragraphs

Paragraph Formatting	Keyboard Shortcut	Paragraph Formatting	Keyboard Shortcut
1.5 line spacing	CTRL+5	Justify paragraph	CTRL+J
Add/remove one line above paragraph	CTRL+0 (ZERO)	Left-align paragraph	CTRL+L
Center paragraph	CTRL+E	Remove hanging indent	CTRL+SHIFT+T
Decrease paragraph indent	CTRL+SHIFT+M	Remove paragraph formatting	CTRL+Q
Double-space lines	CTRL+2	Right-align paragraph	CTRL+R
Hanging indent	CTRL+T	Single-space lines	CTRL+1
Increase paragraph indent	CTRL+M		

© 2015 Cengage Learning

To Format Text Using a Keyboard Shortcut

The paragraphs below the paper title should be left-aligned, instead of centered. Thus, the next step is to left-align the paragraph below the paper title. When your fingers already are on the keyboard, you may prefer using keyboard shortcuts to format text as you type it.

The following step left-aligns a paragraph using the keyboard shortcut CTRL+L. (Recall from Module 1 that a notation such as CTRL+L means to press the letter L on the keyboard while holding down the CTRL key.)

1 Press CTRL+L to left-align the current paragraph, that is, the paragraph containing the insertion point (shown in Figure 2–17).

Q&A Why would I use a keyboard shortcut instead of the ribbon to format text?
Switching between the mouse and the keyboard takes time. If your hands are already on the keyboard, use a keyboard shortcut. If your hand is on the mouse, use the ribbon.

2 Save the research paper on your hard drive, OneDrive, or other storage location using the file name, Headphones and Earbuds Paper.

Q&A Why should I save the research paper at this time?
You have performed many tasks while creating this flyer and do not want to risk losing work completed thus far.

To Display the Rulers

According to the MLA documentation style, the first line of each paragraph in the research paper is to be indented one-half inch from the left margin. Although you can use a dialog box to indent paragraphs, Word provides a quicker way through the **horizontal ruler**. This ruler is displayed at the top edge of the document window just below the ribbon. Word also provides a **vertical ruler** that is displayed along the left edge of the Word window. The following step displays the rulers. *Why? You want to use the horizontal ruler to indent paragraphs.*

- If necessary, scroll the document so that the research paper title is at the top of the document window.
- Click View on the ribbon to display the View tab.
- If the rulers are not displayed, click the View Ruler check box (View tab | Show group) to place a check mark in the check box and display the horizontal and vertical rulers on the screen (Figure 2–17).

Q&A What tasks can I accomplish using the rulers?
You can use the rulers to indent paragraphs, set tab stops, change page margins, and adjust column widths.

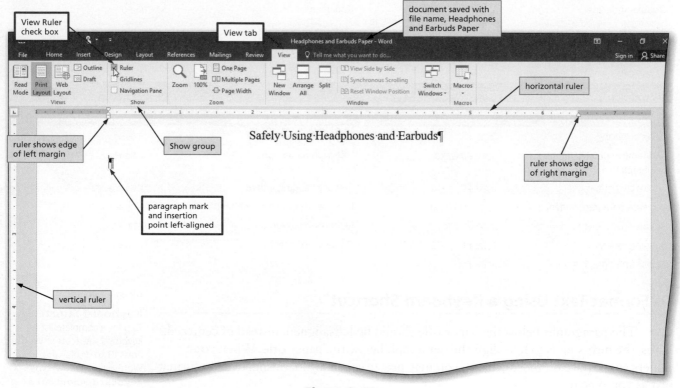

Figure 2–17

To First-Line Indent Paragraphs

If you are using a mouse, you can use the horizontal ruler, usually simply called the **ruler**, to indent just the first line of a paragraph, which is called a **first-line indent**. The left margin on the ruler contains two triangles above a square. The '**First Line Indent' marker** is the top triangle at the 0" mark on the ruler (shown in Figure 2–18). The bottom triangle is discussed later in this module. The small square at the 0" mark is the Left Indent marker. The **Left Indent marker** allows you to change the entire left margin, whereas the 'First Line Indent' marker indents only the first line of the paragraph.

The following steps first-line indent paragraphs in the research paper. *Why? The first line of each paragraph in the research paper is to be indented one-half inch from the left margin, according to the MLA documentation style.*

1

- With the insertion point on the paragraph mark below the research paper title, point to the 'First Line Indent' marker on the ruler (Figure 2–18).

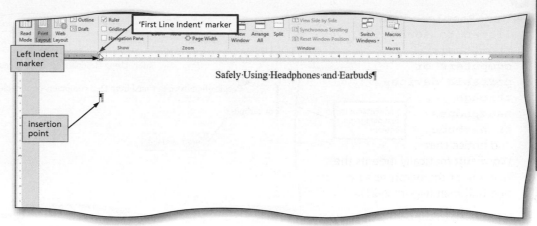

Figure 2–18

2

- Drag the 'First Line Indent' marker to the .5" mark on the ruler to display a vertical dotted line in the document window, which indicates the proposed indent location of the first line of the paragraph (Figure 2–19).

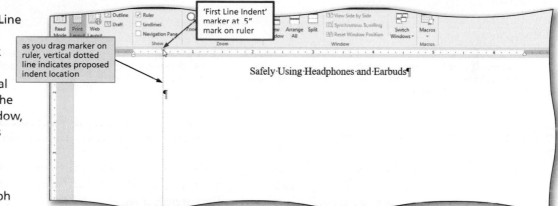

Figure 2–19

3

- Release the mouse button to place the 'First Line Indent' marker at the .5" mark on the ruler, or one-half inch from the left margin (Figure 2–20).

Q&A

What if I am using a touch screen?

If you are using a touch screen, you cannot drag the 'First Line Indent' marker and must follow these steps instead: tap the

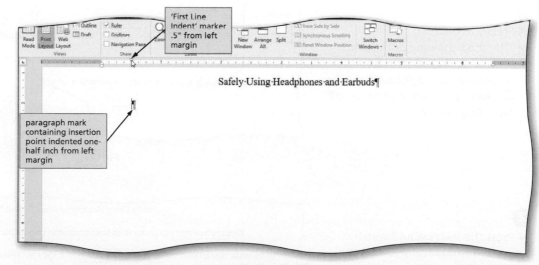

Figure 2–20

Paragraph Settings Dialog Box Launcher (Home tab or Layout tab | Paragraph group) to display the Paragraph dialog box, tap the Indents and Spacing tab (Paragraph dialog box), tap the Special arrow, tap First line, and then tap the OK button.

4

- Type `People often listen to sound from their computers or portable devices through headphones or earbuds.` and notice that Word automatically indents the first line of the paragraph by one-half inch (Figure 2–21).

Q&A

Will I have to set a first-line indent for each paragraph in the paper?

No. Each time you press the ENTER key, paragraph formatting in the previous paragraph carries forward to the next paragraph. Thus, once you set the first-line indent, its format carries forward automatically to each subsequent paragraph you type.

Figure 2–21

Other Ways

1. Right-click paragraph (or, if using touch, tap 'Show Context Menu' button on mini toolbar), click Paragraph on shortcut menu, click Indents and Spacing tab (Paragraph dialog box), click Special arrow, click First line, click OK button

2. Click Paragraph Settings Dialog Box Launcher (Home tab or Layout tab | Paragraph group), click Indents and Spacing tab (Paragraph dialog box), click Special arrow, click First line, click OK button

---

To AutoCorrect as You Type

1 CHANGE DOCUMENT SETTINGS | 2 CREATE HEADER | 3 TYPE RESEARCH PAPER WITH CITATIONS
4 CREATE ALPHABETICAL WORKS CITED | 5 PROOFREAD & REVISE RESEARCH PAPER

Word has predefined many commonly misspelled words, which it automatically corrects for you. ***Why?*** *As you type, you may make typing, spelling, capitalization, or grammar errors. Word's **AutoCorrect** feature automatically corrects these kinds of errors as you type them in the document. For example, if you type the characters, ahve, Word automatically changes it to the correct spelling, have, when you press the SPACEBAR or a punctuation mark key, such as a period or comma.*

The following steps intentionally misspell the word, the, as teh to illustrate the AutoCorrect feature.

1

- Press the SPACEBAR.
- Type the beginning of the next sentence, misspelling the word, the, as follows: `Headphones cover or are placed outside of teh` (Figure 2–22).

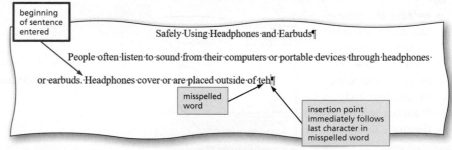

Figure 2–22

2

- Press the SPACEBAR and watch Word automatically correct the misspelled word.
- Type the rest of the sentence (Figure 2–23): `ear, whereas earbuds rest inside the ear canal.`

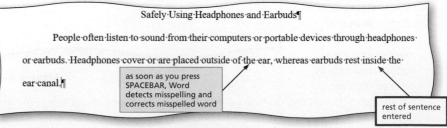

Figure 2–23

To Use the AutoCorrect Options Button

The following steps illustrate the AutoCorrect Options button and menu. *Why? If you are using a mouse, when you position the pointer on text that Word automatically corrected, a small blue box appears below the text. If you point to the small blue box, Word displays the AutoCorrect Options button. When you click the **AutoCorrect Options button**, Word displays a menu that allows you to undo a correction or change how Word handles future automatic corrections of this type.*

- Position the pointer in the text automatically corrected by Word (the word, the, in this case) to display a small blue box below the automatically corrected word (Figure 2–24).

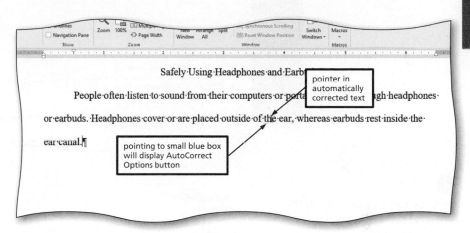

Figure 2–24

- Point to the small blue box to display the AutoCorrect Options button.
- Click the AutoCorrect Options button to display the AutoCorrect Options menu (Figure 2–25).
- Press the ESC key to remove the AutoCorrect Options menu from the screen.

Q&A

Do I need to remove the AutoCorrect Options button from the screen?
No. When you move the pointer, the AutoCorrect Options button will disappear from the screen. If, for some reason, you wanted to remove the AutoCorrect Options button from the screen, you could press the ESC key a second time.

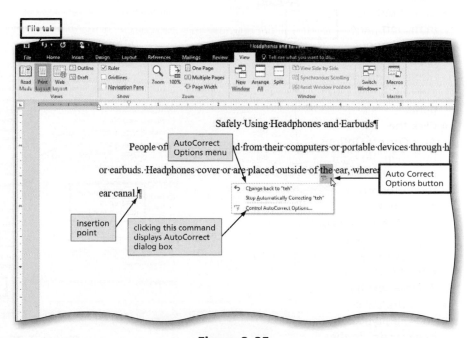

Figure 2–25

To Create an AutoCorrect Entry

The next steps create an AutoCorrect entry. *Why? In addition to the predefined list of AutoCorrect spelling, capitalization, and grammar errors, you can create your own AutoCorrect entries to add to the list. For example, if you tend to mistype the word computer as comptuer, you should create an AutoCorrect entry for it.*

1

- Click File on the ribbon (shown in Figure 2–25) to open the Backstage view (Figure 2–26).

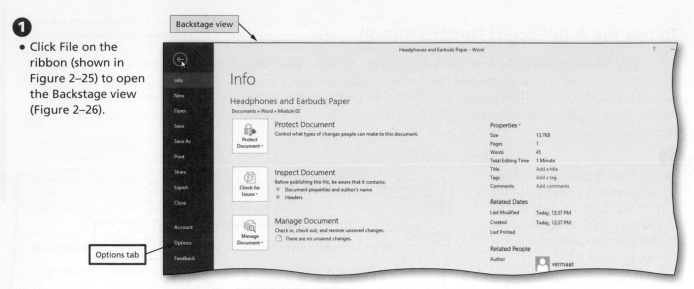

Figure 2–26

2

- Click the Options tab in the Backstage view to display the Word Options dialog box.
- Click Proofing in the left pane (Word Options dialog box) to display proofing options in the right pane.
- Click the AutoCorrect Options button in the right pane to display the AutoCorrect dialog box.
- When Word displays the AutoCorrect dialog box, type **comptuer** in the Replace text box.
- Press the TAB key and then type **computer** in the With text box (Figure 2–27).

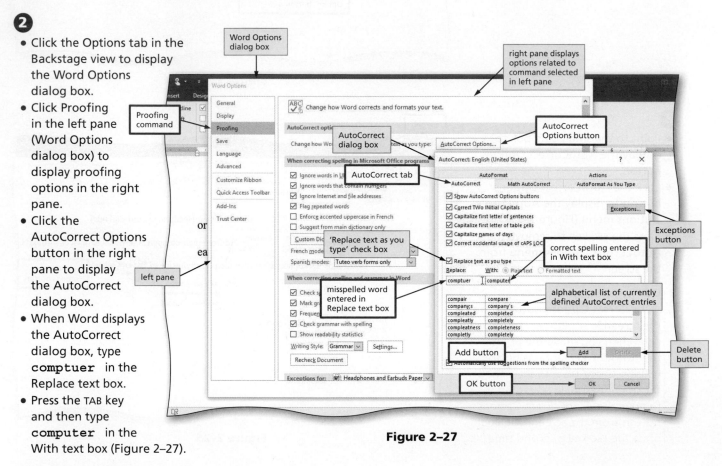

Figure 2–27

Q&A How would I delete an existing AutoCorrect entry?
You would select the entry to be deleted in the list of defined entries in the AutoCorrect dialog box and then click the Delete button (AutoCorrect dialog box).

3

- Click the Add button (AutoCorrect dialog box) to add the entry alphabetically to the list of words to correct automatically as you type. (If your dialog box displays a Replace button instead, click it and then click the Yes button in the Microsoft Word dialog box to replace the previously defined entry.)
- Click the OK button (AutoCorrect dialog box) to close the dialog box.
- Click the OK button (Word Options dialog box) to close the dialog box.

The AutoCorrect Dialog Box

In addition to creating AutoCorrect entries for words you commonly misspell or mistype, you can create entries for abbreviations, codes, and so on. For example, you could create an AutoCorrect entry for asap, indicating that Word should replace this text with the phrase, as soon as possible.

If, for some reason, you do not want Word to correct automatically as you type, you can turn off the Replace text as you type feature by clicking the Options tab in the Backstage view, clicking Proofing in the left pane (Word Options dialog box), clicking the AutoCorrect Options button in the right pane (shown in Figure 2–27), removing the check mark from the 'Replace text as you type' check box, and then clicking the OK button in each open dialog box.

The AutoCorrect sheet in the AutoCorrect dialog box (Figure 2–27) contains other check boxes that correct capitalization errors if the check boxes are selected:

- If you type two capital letters in a row, such as TH, Word makes the second letter lowercase, Th.
- If you begin a sentence with a lowercase letter, Word capitalizes the first letter of the sentence.
- If you type the name of a day in lowercase letters, such as tuesday, Word capitalizes the first letter in the name of the day, Tuesday.
- If you leave the CAPS LOCK key on and begin a new sentence, such as after, Word corrects the typing, After, and turns off the CAPS LOCK key.

If you do not want Word to perform any of these corrections automatically, simply remove the check mark from the appropriate check box in the AutoCorrect dialog box.

Sometimes, you do not want Word to AutoCorrect a particular word or phrase. For example, you may use the code, WD., in your documents. Because Word automatically capitalizes the first letter of a sentence, the character you enter following the period will be capitalized (in the previous sentence, it would capitalize the letter i in the word, in). To allow the code, WD., to be entered into a document and still leave the AutoCorrect feature turned on, you would set an exception. To set an exception to an AutoCorrect rule, click the Options tab in the Backstage view, click Proofing in the left pane (Word Options dialog box), click the AutoCorrect Options button in the right pane, click the Exceptions button (Figure 2–27), click the appropriate tab in the AutoCorrect Exceptions dialog box, type the exception entry in the text box, click the Add button, click the Close button (AutoCorrect Exceptions dialog box), and then click the OK button in each of the remaining dialog boxes.

To Enter More Text

The next task is to continue typing text in the research paper up to the location of the in-text parenthetical reference. The following steps enter this text.

1 With the insertion point positioned at the end of the first paragraph in the paper, as shown in Figure 2–25, press the SPACEBAR and then type these three sentences, intentionally misspelling the word sound as sould: `With these listening devices, only the individual wearing the device hears the sould. Using headphones or earbuds improperly can lead to permanent hearing loss. Items that may protect hearing include quality of these devices and volume levels.`

Q&A Why is the word, sound, misspelled?
Later in this module, you will use Word's check spelling and grammar at once feature to check the entire document for errors.

BTW
Automatic Corrections
If you do not want to keep a change made automatically by Word and you immediately notice the automatic correction, you can undo the change by clicking the Undo button on the Quick Access Toolbar or pressing CTRL+Z. You also can undo a correction through the AutoCorrect Options button (Word Options dialog box) (shown in Figure 2–27).

BTW
Spacing after Punctuation
Because word processing documents use variable character fonts, it often is difficult to determine in a printed document how many times someone has pressed the SPACEBAR between sentences. Thus, the rule is to press the SPACEBAR only once after periods, colons, and other punctuation marks.

2 Press the ENTER key to start a new paragraph.

3 Type **The features of certain headphones and earbuds can help to prevent hearing loss. Higher-quality headphones and earbuds tend to produce a clearer sound, enabling wearers to listen at a lower volume** and then press the SPACEBAR (Figure 2–28).

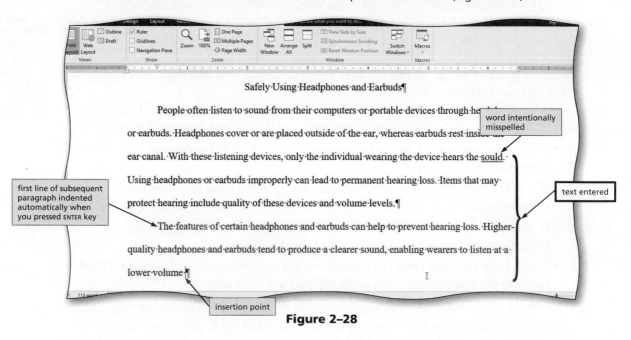

Figure 2–28

BTW
Word Help
At any time while using Word, you can find answers to questions and display information about various topics through Word Help. Used properly, this form of assistance can increase your productivity and reduce your frustrations by minimizing the time you spend learning how to use Word. For instructions about Word Help and exercises that will help you gain confidence in using it, read the Office and Windows module at the beginning of this book.

Citations

Both the MLA and APA guidelines suggest the use of in-text parenthetical references (placed at the end of a sentence), instead of footnoting each source of material in a paper. These parenthetical references, called citations in Word, guide the reader to the end of the paper for complete information about the source.

Word provides tools to assist you with inserting citations in a paper and later generating a list of sources from the citations. With a documentation style selected, Word automatically formats the citations and list of sources according to that style. The process for adding citations in Word is as follows:

1. Modify the documentation style, if necessary.
2. Insert a citation placeholder.
3. Enter the source information for the citation.

You can combine Steps 2 and 3, where you insert the citation placeholder and enter the source information at once. Or, you can insert the citation placeholder as you write and then enter the source information for the citation at a later time. While creating the research paper in this module, you will use both methods.

To Change the Bibliography Style

1 CHANGE DOCUMENT SETTINGS | 2 CREATE HEADER | 3 TYPE RESEARCH PAPER WITH CITATIONS
4 CREATE ALPHABETICAL WORKS CITED | 5 PROOFREAD & REVISE RESEARCH PAPER

The first step in inserting a citation is to be sure the citations and sources will be formatted using the correct documentation style, called the bibliography style in Word. **Why?** *You want to ensure that Word is using the MLA documentation style for this paper.* The following steps change the specified documentation style.

1

- Click References on the ribbon to display the References tab.
- Click the Bibliography Style arrow (References tab | Citations & Bibliography group) to display the Bibliography Style gallery, which lists predefined documentation styles (Figure 2–29).

2
- Click 'MLA Seventh Edition' in the Bibliography Style gallery to change the documentation style to MLA.

Q&A
What if I am using a different edition of a documentation style shown in the Bibliography Style gallery?
Select the closest one and then, if necessary, perform necessary edits before submitting the paper.

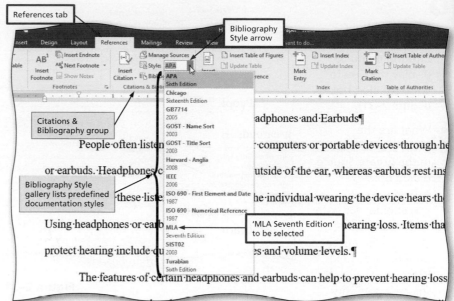

Figure 2–29

What details are required for sources?

During your research, be sure to record essential publication information about each of your sources. Following is a sample list of types of required information for the MLA documentation style.

- Book: full name of author(s), complete title of book, edition (if available), volume (if available), publication city, publisher name, publication year, and publication medium

- Magazine: full name of author(s), complete title of article, magazine title, issue number (if available), date of magazine, page numbers of article, publication medium, and date viewed (if medium is a website)

- Website: full name of author(s), title of website, website publisher or sponsor (if none, write N.p.), publication date (if none, write n.d.), publication medium, and date viewed

CONSIDER THIS

To Insert a Citation and Create Its Source

1 CHANGE DOCUMENT SETTINGS | 2 CREATE HEADER | **3 TYPE RESEARCH PAPER WITH CITATIONS**
4 CREATE ALPHABETICAL WORKS CITED | 5 PROOFREAD & REVISE RESEARCH PAPER

With the documentation style selected, the next task is to insert a citation at the location of the insertion point and enter the source information for the citation. You can accomplish these steps at once by instructing Word to add a new source. The following steps add a new source for a magazine (periodical) article on the web. **Why?** *The material preceding the insertion point was summarized from an online magazine article.*

1

- With the insertion point at the location for the citation (as shown in Figure 2–28), click the Insert Citation button (References tab | Citations & Bibliography group) to display the Insert Citation menu (Figure 2–30).

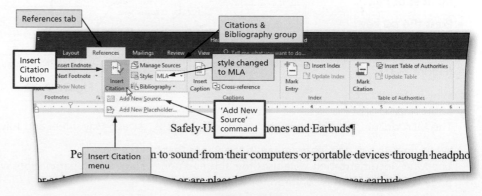

Figure 2–30

2

- Click 'Add New Source' on the Insert Citation menu to display the Create Source dialog box (Figure 2–31).

Q&A

What are the Bibliography Fields in the Create Source dialog box?

A **field** is a placeholder for data whose contents can change. You enter data in some fields; Word supplies data for others. In this case, you enter the contents of the fields for a particular source, for example, the author name in the Author field.

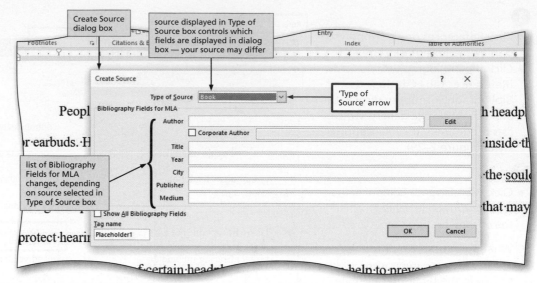

Figure 2–31

Experiment

- Click the 'Type of Source' arrow and then click one of the source types in the list, so that you can see how the list of fields changes to reflect the type of source you selected.

3

- If necessary, click the 'Type of Source' arrow (Create Source dialog box) and then click 'Article in a Periodical', so that the list shows fields required for a magazine (periodical).

- Click the Author text box. Type **Tu, Mingzhu Lin** as the author.

- Click the Title text box. Type **Headphones and Earbuds** as the article title.

- Press the TAB key and then type **Technology and Trends Today** as the periodical title.

- Press the TAB key and then type **2017** as the year.

- Press the TAB key and then type **Aug.** as the month.

- Press the TAB key twice and then type **n. pag.** as the number of pages.

- Press the TAB key and then type **Web** as the medium (Figure 2–32).

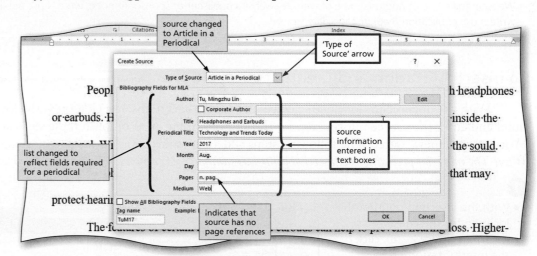

Figure 2–32

Q&A

Why is the month abbreviated?

The MLA documentation style abbreviates all months, except May, June, and July, when they appear in a source.

What does the n. pag. entry mean in the Pages text box?

The MLA documentation style uses the abbreviation n. pag. for no pagination, which indicates the source has no page references. This is common for web sources.

- Place a check mark in the 'Show All Bibliography Fields' check box so that Word displays all fields available for the selected source, including the date viewed (accessed) fields.

- If necessary, scroll to the bottom of the Bibliography Fields list to display the date viewed (accessed) fields.

- Click the Year Accessed text box. Type 2017 as the year.

- Press the TAB key and then type Oct. as the month accessed.

- Press the TAB key and then type 3 as the day accessed (Figure 2–33).

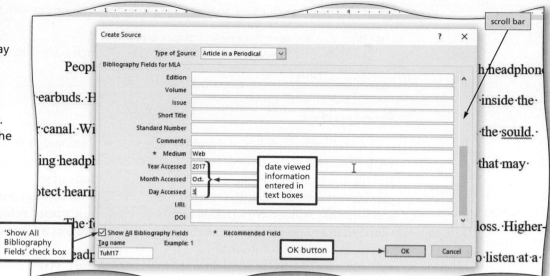

Figure 2–33

What if some of the text boxes disappear as I enter the fields?
With the 'Show All Bibliography Fields' check box selected, the dialog box may not be able to display all fields at the same time. In this case, some may scroll up off the screen.

- Click the OK button to close the dialog box, create the source, and insert the citation in the document at the location of the insertion point.
- Press the END key to move the insertion point to the end of the line, if necessary, which also deselects the citation.
- Press the PERIOD key to end the sentence (Figure 2–34).

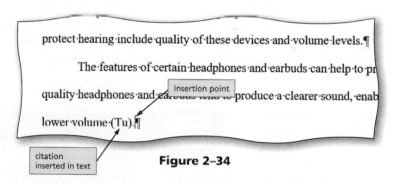

Figure 2–34

To Enter More Text

The next task is to continue typing text in the research paper up to the location of the footnote. The following steps enter this text.

1 Press the SPACEBAR.

2 Type the next sentences (Figure 2–35): **Properly designed headphones**

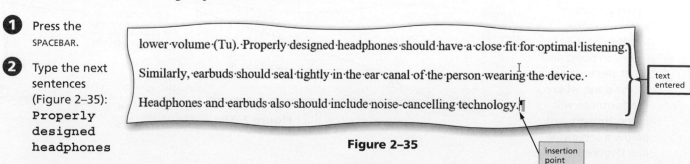

Figure 2–35

> should have a close fit for optimal listening. Similarly, earbuds should seal tightly in the ear canal of the person wearing the device. Headphones and earbuds also should include noise-cancelling technology.

3 Save the research paper again on the same storage location with the same file name.

Q&A Why should I save the research paper again?
You have made several modifications to the research paper since you last saved it; thus, you should save it again.

Footnotes

BTW
Touch Screen Differences
The Office and Windows interfaces may vary if you are using a touch screen. For this reason, you might notice that the function or appearance of your touch screen differs slightly from this module's presentation.

As discussed earlier in this module, notes are optional in the MLA documentation style. If used, content notes elaborate on points discussed in the paper, and bibliographic notes direct the reader to evaluations of statements in a source or provide a means for identifying multiple sources. The MLA documentation style specifies that a superscript (raised number) be used for a **note reference mark** to signal that a note exists either at the bottom of the page as a **footnote** or at the end of the document as an **endnote**.

In Word, **note text** can be any length and format. Word automatically numbers notes sequentially by placing a note reference mark both in the body of the document and to the left of the note text. If you insert, rearrange, or remove notes, Word renumbers any subsequent note reference marks according to their new sequence in the document.

To Insert a Footnote Reference Mark

1 CHANGE DOCUMENT SETTINGS | 2 CREATE HEADER | 3 TYPE RESEARCH PAPER WITH CITATIONS
4 CREATE ALPHABETICAL WORKS CITED | 5 PROOFREAD & REVISE RESEARCH PAPER

The following step inserts a footnote reference mark in the document at the location of the insertion point and at the location where the footnote text will be typed. *Why? You will insert a content note elaborating on noise-cancelling technology, which you want to position as a footnote.*

1

- With the insertion point positioned as shown in Figure 2–35, click the Insert Footnote button (References tab | Footnotes group) to display a note reference mark (a superscripted 1) in two places: (1) in the document window at the location of the insertion point and (2) at the bottom of the page where the footnote will be positioned, just below a separator line (Figure 2–36).

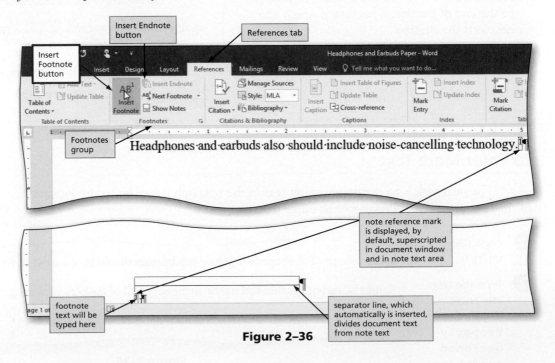

Figure 2–36

Q&A | What if I wanted notes to be positioned as endnotes instead of as footnotes?
You would click the Insert Endnote button (References tab | Footnotes group), which places the separator line and the endnote text at the end of the document, instead of the bottom of the page containing the reference.

Other Ways

1. Press ALT+CTRL+F

To Enter Footnote Text

The following step types the footnote text to the right of the note reference mark below the separator line.

1 Type the footnote text up to the citation (shown in Figure 2–37): `Gupta and Padro state that effective noise-cancelling technology reduces the interference of sounds from the surrounding environment, reducing the volume level required by headphones and earbuds` and then press the SPACEBAR.

To Insert a Citation Placeholder

1 CHANGE DOCUMENT SETTINGS | 2 CREATE HEADER | 3 TYPE RESEARCH PAPER WITH CITATIONS
4 CREATE ALPHABETICAL WORKS CITED | 5 PROOFREAD & REVISE RESEARCH PAPER

Earlier in this module, you inserted a citation and its source at once. In Word, you also can insert a citation without entering the source information. *Why? Sometimes, you may not have the source information readily available and would prefer to enter it at a later time.*

The following steps insert a citation placeholder in the footnote, so that you can enter the source information later.

1

- With the insertion point positioned as shown in Figure 2–37, click the Insert Citation button (References tab | Citations & Bibliography group) to display the Insert Citation menu (Figure 2–37).

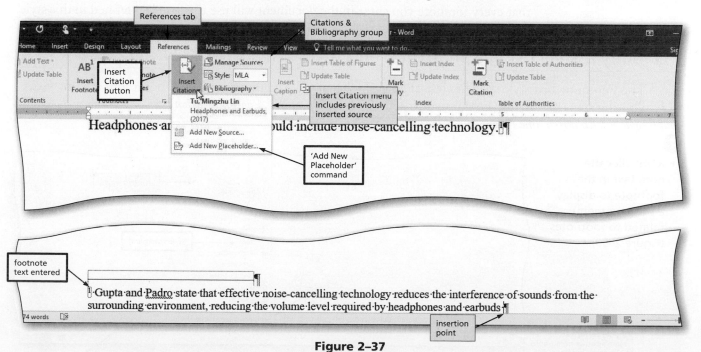

Figure 2–37

2

- Click 'Add New Placeholder' on the Insert Citation menu to display the Placeholder Name dialog box.
- Type `Gupta` as the tag name for the source (Figure 2–38).

Q&A What is a tag name?
A tag name is an identifier that links a citation to a source. Word automatically creates a tag name when you enter a source. When you create a citation placeholder, enter a meaningful tag name, which will appear in the citation placeholder until you edit the source.

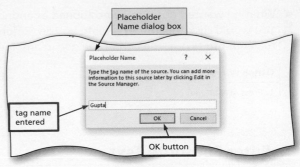

Figure 2–38

3

- Click the OK button (Placeholder Name dialog box) to close the dialog box and insert the entered tag name in the citation placeholder in the document (shown in Figure 2–39).
- Press the PERIOD key to end the sentence.

Q&A What if the citation is in the wrong location?
Click the citation to select it and then drag the citation tab (on the upper-left corner of the selected citation) to any location in the document.

Footnote Text Style

When you insert a footnote, Word formats it using the Footnote Text style, which does not adhere to the MLA documentation style. For example, notice in Figure 2–37 that the footnote text is single-spaced, left-aligned, and a smaller font size than the text in the research paper. According to the MLA documentation style, notes should be formatted like all other paragraphs in the paper.

You could change the paragraph formatting of the footnote text to first-line indent and double-spacing and then change the font size from 10 to 12 point. If you use this technique, however, you will need to change the format of the footnote text for each footnote you enter into the document.

A more efficient technique is to modify the format of the Footnote Text style so that every footnote you enter in the document will use the formats defined in this style.

1 CHANGE DOCUMENT SETTINGS | 2 CREATE HEADER | **3 TYPE RESEARCH PAPER WITH CITATIONS**

To Modify a Style Using a Shortcut Menu
4 CREATE ALPHABETICAL WORKS CITED | 5 PROOFREAD & REVISE RESEARCH PAPER

The Footnote Text style specifies left-aligned single-spaced paragraphs with a 10-point font size for text. The following steps modify the Footnote Text style. *Why? To meet MLA documentation style, the footnotes should be double-spaced with a first-line indent and a 12-point font size for text.*

1

- Right-click the note text in the footnote to display a shortcut menu related to footnotes (Figure 2–39).

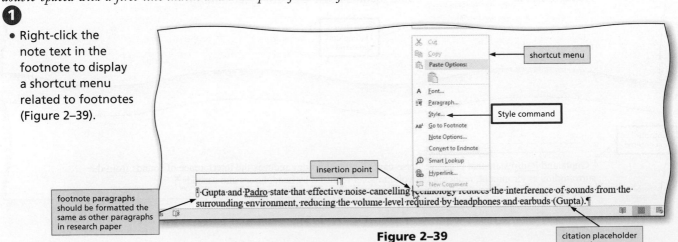

Figure 2–39

- Click Style on the shortcut menu to display the Style dialog box. If necessary, click the Category arrow, click All styles in the Category list, and then click Footnote Text in the Styles list to select the style to modify.

- Click the Modify button (Style dialog box) to display the Modify Style dialog box.

- Click the Font Size arrow (Modify Style dialog box) to display the Font Size list and then click 12 in the Font Size list to change the font size.

- Click the Double Space button to change the line spacing.

- Click the Format button to display the Format menu (Figure 2–40).

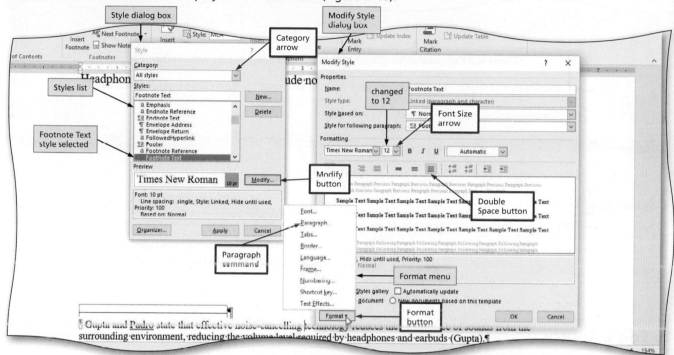

Figure 2–40

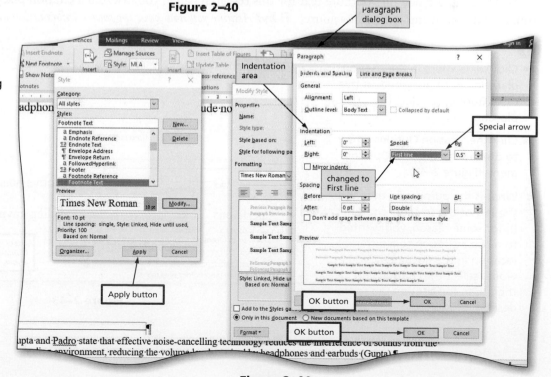

- Click Paragraph on the Format menu (Modify Style dialog box) to display the Paragraph dialog box.

- Click the Special arrow in the Indentation area (Paragraph dialog box) and then click First line (Figure 2–41).

Figure 2–41

4
- Click the OK button (Paragraph dialog box) to close the dialog box.
- Click the OK button (Modify Style dialog box) to close the dialog box.
- Click the Apply button (Style dialog box) to apply the style changes to the footnote text (Figure 2–42).

Q&A
Will all footnotes use this modified style?
Yes. Any future footnotes entered in the document will use a 12-point font with the paragraphs first-line indented and double-spaced.

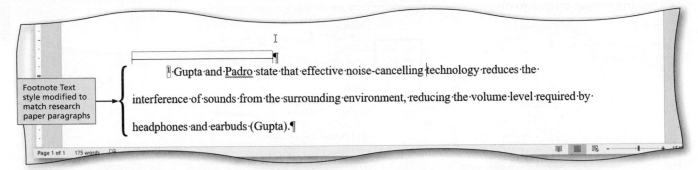

Footnote Text style modified to match research paper paragraphs

¹·Gupta·and·Padro·state·that·effective·noise-cancelling·technology·reduces·the·
interference·of·sounds·from·the·surrounding·environment,·reducing·the·volume·level·required·by·
headphones·and·earbuds·(Gupta).¶

Page 1 of 1   175 words

Figure 2–42

Other Ways

1. Click Styles Dialog Box Launcher (Home tab | Styles group), point to style name in list, click style name arrow, click Modify, change settings (Modify Style dialog box), click OK button

2. Click Styles Dialog Box Launcher (Home tab | Styles group), click Manage Styles button in task pane, select style name in list, click Modify button (Manage Styles dialog box), change settings (Modify Style dialog box), click OK button in each dialog box

1 CHANGE DOCUMENT SETTINGS | 2 CREATE HEADER | **3 TYPE RESEARCH PAPER WITH CITATIONS**
4 CREATE ALPHABETICAL WORKS CITED | **5 PROOFREAD & REVISE RESEARCH PAPER**

To Edit a Source

When you typed the footnote text for this research paper, you inserted a citation placeholder for the source. The following steps edit a source. ***Why?*** *Assume you now have the source information and are ready to enter it.*

1
- Click somewhere in the citation placeholder to be edited, in this case (Gupta), to select the citation placeholder.
- Click the Citation Options arrow to display the Citation Options menu (Figure 2–43).

Q&A
What is the purpose of the tab to the left of the selected citation?
If, for some reason, you wanted to move a citation to a different location in the document, you would select the citation and then drag the citation tab to the desired location.

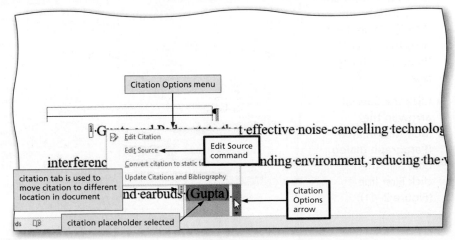

Citation Options menu

Edit Citation
Edit Source
Edit Source command
Convert citation to static text
Update Citations and Bibliography

citation tab is used to move citation to different location in document

¹·Gupta·and·Padro·state·that·effective·noise-cancelling·technolog
interference·of·sounds·from·the·surrounding·environment,·reducing·the·v
nd·earbuds·(Gupta).

Citation Options arrow

citation placeholder selected

Figure 2–43

2

- Click Edit Source on the Citation Options menu to display the Edit Source dialog box.

- If necessary, click the 'Type of Source' arrow (Edit Source dialog box) and then click Book, so that the list shows fields required for a book.

- Because this source has two authors, click the Edit button to display the Edit Name dialog box, which assists you with entering multiple author names.

- Type **Gupta** as the first author's last name; press the TAB key and then type **Elena** as the first name; press the TAB key and then type **Maia** as the middle name (Figure 2–44).

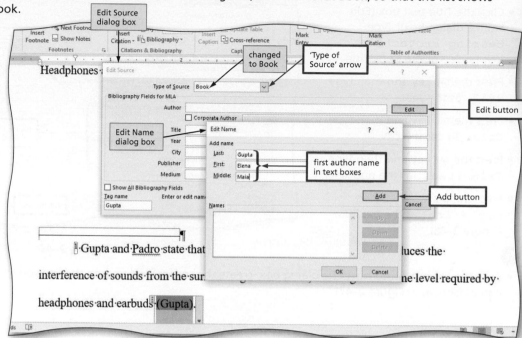

Figure 2–44

Q&A What if I already know how to punctuate the author entry properly?
You can enter the name directly in the Author box.

3

- Click the Add button (Edit Name dialog box) to add the first author name to the Names list.

- Type **Padro** as the second author's last name; press the TAB key and then type **Adelbert** as the first name; press the TAB key and then type **Luis** as the middle name.

- Click the Add button (Edit Name dialog box) to add the second author name to the Names list (Figure 2–45).

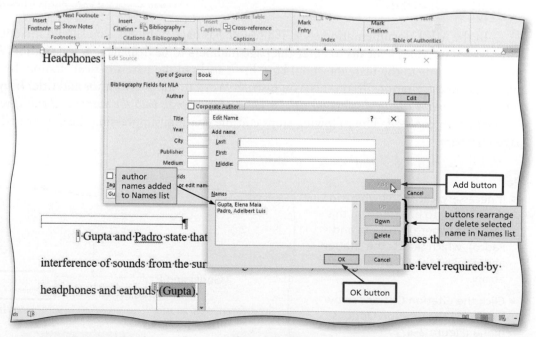

Figure 2–45

- Click the OK button (Edit Name dialog box) to add the author names that appear in the Names list to the Author box in the Edit Source dialog box.

- Click the Title text box (Edit Source dialog box). Type **Hearing Protection Methods** as the book title.

- Press the TAB key and then type **2017** as the year.

- Press the TAB key and then type **Orlando** as the city.

- Press the TAB key and then type **Palm Press** as the publisher.

- Press the TAB key and then type **Print** as the medium (Figure 2–46).

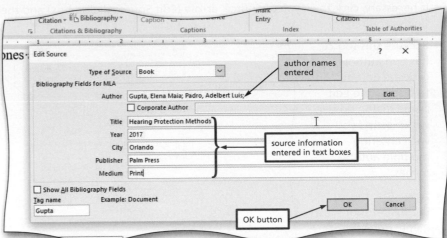

Figure 2–46

- Click the OK button to close the dialog box, create the source, and update the citation to display both author last names (shown in Figure 2–47).

Other Ways

1. Click Manage Sources button (References tab | Citations & Bibliography group), click placeholder source in Current List, click Edit button (Source Manager dialog box)

To Edit a Citation

1 CHANGE DOCUMENT SETTINGS | 2 CREATE HEADER | 3 TYPE RESEARCH PAPER WITH CITATIONS
4 CREATE ALPHABETICAL WORKS CITED | 5 PROOFREAD & REVISE RESEARCH PAPER

In the MLA documentation style, if a source has page numbers, you should include them in the citation. Thus, Word provides a means to enter the page numbers to be displayed in the citation. Also, if you reference the author's name in the text, you should not list it again in the parenthetical citation. Instead, just list the page number(s) in the citation. To do this, you instruct Word to suppress author and title. *Why? If you suppress the author, Word automatically displays the title, so you need to suppress both the author and title if you want just the page number(s) to be displayed.* The following steps edit the citation, suppressing the author and title but displaying the page numbers.

①

- If necessary, click somewhere in the citation to be edited, in this case somewhere in (Gupta and Padro), which selects the citation and displays the Citation Options arrow.

- Click the Citation Options arrow to display the Citation Options menu (Figure 2–47).

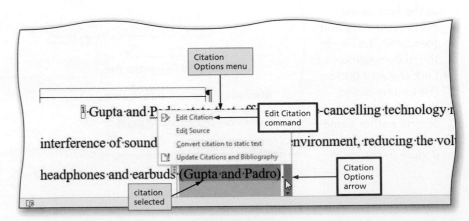

Figure 2–47

- Click Edit Citation on the Citation Options menu to display the Edit Citation dialog box.

- Type **75-78** in the Pages text box (Edit Citation dialog box).

- Click the Author check box to place a check mark in it.

- Click the Title check box to place a check mark in it (Figure 2–48).

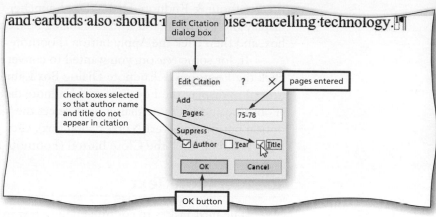

Figure 2–48

- Click the OK button to close the dialog box, remove the author names from the citation in the footnote, suppress the title from showing, and add page numbers to the citation.

- Press the END key to move the insertion point to the end of the line, which also deselects the citation (Figure 2–49).

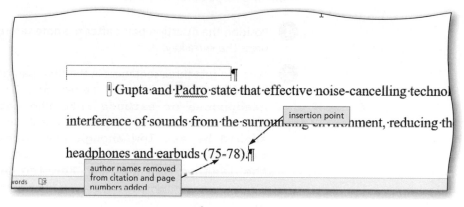

Figure 2–49

Working with Footnotes and Endnotes

You edit footnote text just as you edit any other text in the document. To delete or move a note reference mark, however, the insertion point must be in the document text (not in the footnote text).

To delete a note, select the note reference mark in the document text (not in the footnote text) by dragging through the note reference mark and then click the Cut button (Home tab | Clipboard group). Or, click immediately to the right of the note reference mark in the document text and then press the BACKSPACE key twice, or click immediately to the left of the note reference mark in the document text and then press the DELETE key twice.

To move a note to a different location in a document, select the note reference mark in the document text (not in the footnote text), click the Cut button (Home tab | Clipboard group), click the location where you want to move the note, and then click the Paste button (Home tab | Clipboard group). When you move or delete notes, Word automatically renumbers any remaining notes in the correct sequence.

If you are using a mouse and position the pointer on the note reference mark in the document text, the note text is displayed above the note reference mark as a ScreenTip. To remove the ScreenTip, move the pointer.

If, for some reason, you wanted to change the format of note reference marks in footnotes or endnotes (i.e., from 1, 2, 3 to A, B, C), you would click the Footnote & Endnote Dialog Box Launcher (References tab | Footnotes group) to display the Footnote and Endnote dialog box, click the Number format arrow (Footnote and Endnote dialog box), click the desired number format in the list, and then click the Apply button.

BTW

Footnote and Endnote Location
You can change the location of footnotes from the bottom of the page to the end of the text by clicking the Footnote & Endnote Dialog Box Launcher (References tab | Footnotes group), clicking the Footnotes arrow (Footnote and Endnote dialog box), and then clicking Below text. Similarly, clicking the Endnotes arrow (Footnote and Endnote dialog box) enables you to change the location of endnotes from the end of the document to the end of a section.

If, for some reason, you wanted to change a footnote number, you would click the Footnote & Endnote Dialog Box Launcher (References tab | Footnotes group) to display the Footnote and Endnote dialog box, enter the desired number in the Start at box, and then click the Apply button (Footnote and Endnote dialog box).

If, for some reason, you wanted to convert footnotes to endnotes, you would click the Footnote & Endnote Dialog Box Launcher (References tab | Footnotes group) to display the Footnote and Endnote dialog box, click the Convert button (Footnote and Endnote dialog box), select the 'Convert all footnotes to endnotes' option button (Convert Notes dialog box), click the OK button (Convert Notes dialog box), and then click the Close button (Footnote and Endnote dialog box).

To Enter More Text

The next task is to continue typing text in the body of the research paper. The following steps enter this text.

1 Position the insertion point after the note reference mark in the document and then press the ENTER key.

2 Type the first three sentences in the third paragraph of the research paper (shown in Figure 2–50): `The volume level of the sound that transmits from headphones or earbuds into the ear of a person wearing this type of device has been linked to hearing loss. The volume should be set low enough that other people nearby cannot hear the sound being transmitted. The quieter the sounds, the less possibility of hearing damage.`

To Count Words

1 CHANGE DOCUMENT SETTINGS | 2 CREATE HEADER | 3 TYPE RESEARCH PAPER WITH CITATIONS
4 CREATE ALPHABETICAL WORKS CITED | 5 PROOFREAD & REVISE RESEARCH PAPER

Often when you write papers, you are required to compose the papers with a minimum number of words. The minimum requirement for the research paper in this module is 275 words. You can look on the status bar and see the total number of words thus far in a document. For example, Figure 2–50 shows the research paper has 231 words, but you are not sure if that count includes the words in your footnote. The following steps display the Word Count dialog box. ***Why?*** *You want to verify that the footnote text is included in the count.*

1

- Click the Word Count indicator on the status bar to display the Word Count dialog box.

- If necessary, place a check mark in the 'Include textboxes, footnotes and endnotes' check box (Word Count dialog box) (Figure 2–50).

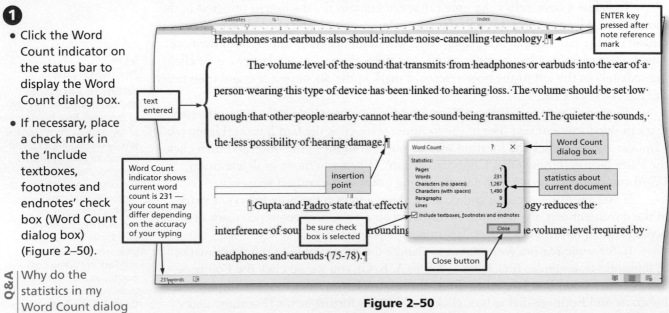

Figure 2–50

Q&A Why do the statistics in my Word Count dialog box differ from those in Figure 2–50?
Depending on the accuracy of your typing, your statistics may differ.

- Click the Close button (Word Count dialog box) to close the dialog box.

Q&A Can I display statistics for just a section of the document?
Yes. Select the section and then click the Word Count indicator on the status bar to display statistics about the selected text.

Other Ways

1. Click Word Count button (Review tab | Proofing group)   2. Press CTRL+SHIFT+G

Automatic Page Breaks

As you type documents that exceed one page, Word automatically inserts page breaks, called **automatic page breaks** or **soft page breaks**, when it determines the text has filled one page according to paper size, margin settings, line spacing, and other settings. If you add text, delete text, or modify text on a page, Word recalculates the location of automatic page breaks and adjusts them accordingly.

Word performs page recalculation between the keystrokes, that is, in between the pauses in your typing. Thus, Word refers to the automatic page break task as **background repagination**. An automatic page break will occur in the next set of steps.

To Enter More Text and Insert a Citation Placeholder

The next task is to type the remainder of the third paragraph in the body of the research paper. The following steps enter this text and a citation placeholder at the end of the paragraph.

1 With the insertion point positioned at the end of the third sentence in the third paragraph, as shown in Figure 2–50, press the SPACEBAR.

2 Type the rest of the third paragraph: `Further, listening at a higher volume for extended periods of time could be unsafe. One expert suggests people should listen at only 30 percent maximum` and then press the SPACEBAR.

Q&A Why does the text move from the second page to the first page as I am typing?
Word, by default, will not allow the first line of a paragraph to be by itself at the bottom of a page (an **orphan**) or the last line of a paragraph to be by itself at the top of a page (a **widow**). As you type, Word adjusts the placement of the paragraph to avoid orphans and widows.

3 Click the Insert Citation button (References tab | Citations & Bibliography group) to display the Insert Citation menu. Click 'Add New Placeholder' on the Insert Citation menu to display the Placeholder Name dialog box.

4 Type `Chamberlain` as the tag name for the source.

5 Click the OK button (Placeholder Name dialog box) to close the dialog box and insert the tag name in the citation placeholder (shown in Figure 2–51).

6 Press the PERIOD key to end the sentence.

BTW
Page Break Locations
As you type, your page break may occur at different locations depending on Word settings and the type of printer connected to the computer.

To Hide and Show White Space

With the page break and header, it is difficult to see the entire third paragraph at once on the screen. With the screen in Print Layout view, you can hide white space, which is the space that is displayed at the top and bottom of pages (including headers and footers) and also the space between pages. The following steps hide white space, if your screen displays it, and then shows white space. *Why? You want to see as much of the third paragraph as possible at once, which spans the bottom of the first page and the top of the second page.*

1

- Position the pointer in the document window in the space between pages so that the pointer changes to a 'Hide White Space' button (Figure 2–51).

Q&A What if I am using a touch screen?
Proceed to step 2.

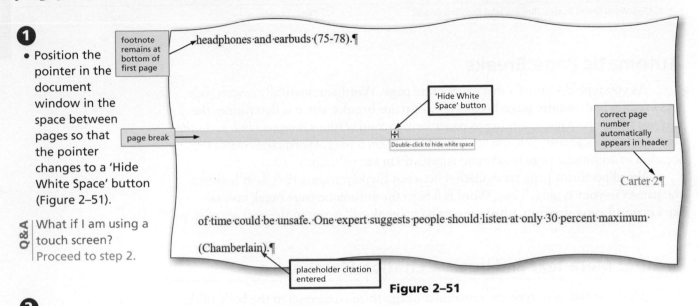

Figure 2–51

2

- Double-click while the pointer is a 'Hide White Space' button to hide white space.

Q&A What if I am using a touch screen?
Double-tap in the space between pages.

Does hiding white space have any effect on the printed document?
No.

3

- Position the pointer in the document window on the page break between pages so that the pointer changes to a 'Show White Space' button (Figure 2–52).

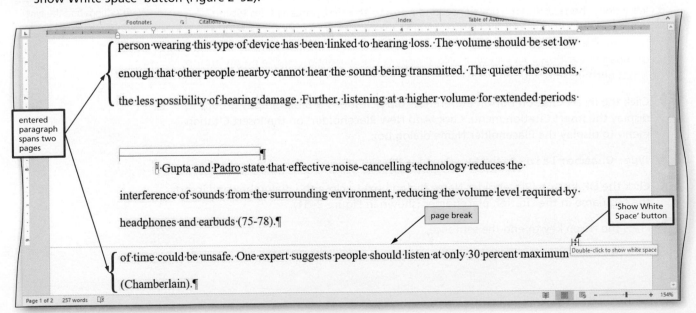

Figure 2–52

4

- Double-click while the pointer is a 'Show White Space' button to show white space.

Q&A What if I am using a touch screen?
Double-tap the page break.

Other Ways

1. Click File on ribbon, click Options tab in Backstage view, click Display in left pane (Word Options dialog box), remove or select check mark from 'Show white space between pages in Print Layout view' check box, click OK button

To Edit a Source

When you typed the third paragraph of the research paper, you inserted a citation placeholder, Chamberlain, for the source. You now have the source information, which is for a website, and are ready to enter it. The following steps edit the source for the Chamberlain citation placeholder.

1 Click somewhere in the citation placeholder to be edited, in this case (Chamberlain), to select the citation placeholder.

2 Click the Citation Options arrow to display the Citation Options menu.

3 Click Edit Source on the Citation Options menu to display the Edit Source dialog box.

4 If necessary, click the 'Type of Source' arrow (Edit Source dialog box); scroll to and then click Web site, so that the list shows fields required for a Web site.

5 Place a check mark in the 'Show All Bibliography Fields' check box to display more fields related to Web sites.

6 Click the Author text box. Type **Chamberlain, Megan Lynn** as the author.

7 Click the 'Name of Web Page' text box. Type **Understanding How Volume Levels Affect Hearing** as the webpage name.

8 Click the Production Company text box. Type **Course Technology** as the production company.

9 Click the Year Accessed text box. Type **2017** as the year accessed (Figure 2–53).

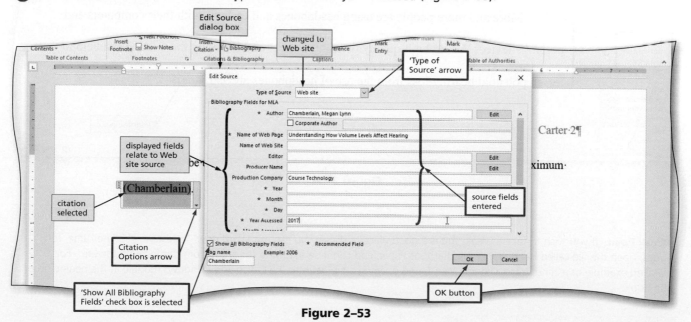

Figure 2–53

10 Press the TAB key and then type `Sept.` as the month accessed.

11 Press the TAB key and then type `16` as the day accessed.

12 Press the TAB key as many times as necessary to move the insertion point to the Medium text box and then type `Web` as the Medium.

Q&A Do I need to enter a web address (URL)?
The latest MLA documentation style update does not require the web address in the source.

13 Click the OK button to close the dialog box and create the source.

BTW
Organizing Files and Folders
You should organize and store files in folders so that you easily can find the files later. For example, if you are taking an introductory technology class called CIS 101, a good practice would be to save all Word files in a Word folder in a CIS 101 folder. For a discussion of folders and detailed examples of creating folders, refer to the Office and Windows module at the beginning of this book.

To Enter More Text

The next task is to type the last paragraph of text in the research paper. The following steps enter this text.

1 Press the END key to position the insertion point at the end of the third paragraph and then press the ENTER key.

2 Type the last paragraph of the research paper (Figure 2–54): `More and more people are using headphones and earbuds with their computers and portable devices. Using high-quality listening devices and lowering the volume can help to lessen potential hearing loss from the use of headphones and earbuds.`

3 Save the research paper again on the same storage location with the same file name.

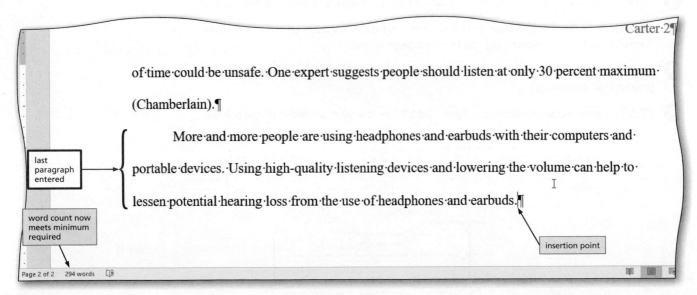

Figure 2–54

Break Point: If you wish to take a break, this is a good place to do so. You can exit Word now. To resume at a later time, run Word, open the file called Headphones and Earbuds Paper, and continue following the steps from this location forward. For a detailed example of exiting Word, running Word, and opening a file, refer to the Office and Windows module at the beginning of the book.

Creating an Alphabetical Works Cited Page

According to the MLA documentation style, the **works cited page** is a list of sources that are referenced directly in a research paper. You place the list on a separate numbered page with the title, Works Cited, centered one inch from the top margin. The works are to be alphabetized by the author's last name or, if the work has no author, by the work's title. The first line of each entry begins at the left margin. Indent subsequent lines of the same entry one-half inch from the left margin.

What is a bibliography?

A **bibliography** is an alphabetical list of sources referenced in a paper. Whereas the text of the research paper contains brief references to the source (the citations), the bibliography lists all publication information about the source. Documentation styles differ significantly in their guidelines for preparing a bibliography. Each style identifies formats for various sources, including books, magazines, pamphlets, newspapers, websites, television programs, paintings, maps, advertisements, letters, memos, and much more. You can find information about various styles and their guidelines in printed style guides and on the web.

To Page Break Manually

1 CHANGE DOCUMENT SETTINGS | 2 CREATE HEADER | 3 TYPE RESEARCH PAPER WITH CITATIONS
4 CREATE ALPHABETICAL WORKS CITED | 5 PROOFREAD & REVISE RESEARCH PAPER

The next step is to insert a manual page break following the body of the research paper. *Why? According to the MLA documentation style, the works cited are to be displayed on a separate numbered page.*

A **manual page break**, or **hard page break**, is one that you force into the document at a specific location. Word never moves or adjusts manual page breaks. Word, however, does adjust any automatic page breaks that follow a manual page break. Word inserts manual page breaks immediately above or to the left of the location of the insertion point. The following step inserts a manual page break after the text of the research paper.

1

- Verify that the insertion point is positioned at the end of the text of the research paper, as shown in Figure 2–54.

- Click Insert on the ribbon to display the Insert tab.

- Click the 'Insert a Page Break' button (Insert tab | Pages group) to insert a manual page break immediately to the left of the insertion point and position the insertion point immediately below the manual page break (Figure 2–55).

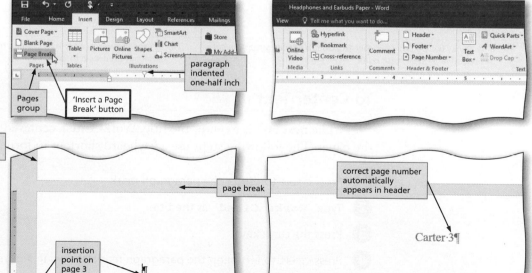

Figure 2–55

Other Ways

1. Press CTRL+ENTER

To Apply a Style

The works cited title is to be centered between the margins of the paper. If you simply issue the Center command, the title will not be centered properly. *Why? It will be to the right of the center point because earlier you set the first-line indent for paragraphs to one-half inch.*

To properly center the title of the works cited page, you could drag the 'First Line Indent' marker back to the left margin before centering the paragraph, or you could apply the Normal style to the location of the insertion point. Recall that you modified the Normal style for this document to 12-point Times New Roman with double-spaced, left-aligned paragraphs that have no space after the paragraphs.

To apply a style to a paragraph, first position the insertion point in the paragraph and then apply the style. The following step applies the modified Normal style to the location of the insertion point.

- Click Home on the ribbon to display the Home tab.

- With the insertion point on the paragraph mark at the top of page 3 (as shown in Figure 2–55) even if Normal is selected, click Normal in the Styles gallery (Home tab | Styles group) to apply the Normal style to the paragraph containing the insertion point (Figure 2–56).

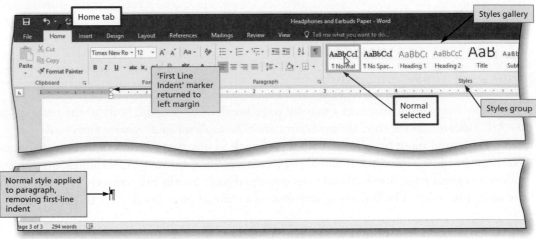

Figure 2–56

Other Ways

1. Click Styles Dialog Box Launcher (Home tab | Styles group), select desired style in Styles task pane
2. Press CTRL+SHIFT+S, click Style Name arrow in Apply Styles task pane, select desired style in list

To Center Text

The next task is to enter the title, Works Cited, centered between the margins of the paper. The following steps use a keyboard shortcut to format the title.

1 Press CTRL+E to center the paragraph mark.

2 Type **Works Cited** as the title.

3 Press the ENTER key.

4 Press CTRL+L to left-align the paragraph mark (shown in Figure 2–57).

To Create a Bibliographical List

While typing the research paper, you created several citations and their sources. The next task is to use Word to format the list of sources and alphabetize them in a **bibliographical list**. *Why? Word can create a bibliographical list with each element of the source placed in its correct position with proper punctuation, according to the specified style, saving you time looking up style guidelines. For example, in this research paper, the book source will list, in* *this order, the author name(s), book title, publisher city, publishing company name, and publication year with the correct punctuation between each element according to the MLA documentation style.* The following steps create an MLA-styled bibliographical list from the sources previously entered.

①

- Click References on the ribbon to display the References tab.

- With the insertion point positioned as shown in Figure 2–57, click the Bibliography button (References tab | Citations & Bibliography group) to display the Bibliography gallery (Figure 2–57).

Q&A Will I select the Works Cited option from the Bibliography gallery? No. The title it inserts is not formatted according to the MLA documentation style. Thus, you will use the Insert Bibliography command instead.

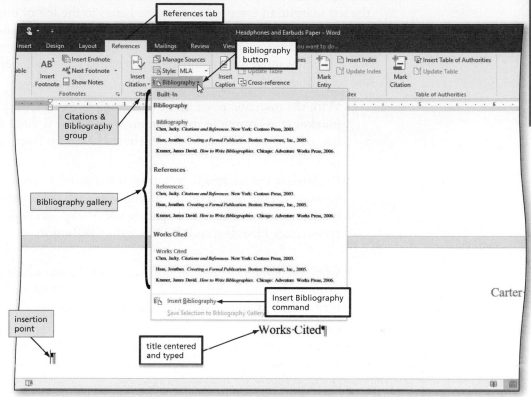

Figure 2–57

②

- Click Insert Bibliography in the Bibliography gallery to insert a list of sources at the location of the insertion point.

- If necessary, scroll to display the entire list of sources in the document window (Figure 2–58).

Q&A What is the n.d. in the first work? The MLA documentation style uses the abbreviation n.d. for no date (for example, no date appears on the webpage).

Carter 3

Works Cited

Chamberlain, Megan Lynn. *Understanding How Volume Levels Affect Hearing.* n.d. Course Technology. Web. 16 Sept. 2017.

Gupta, Elena Maia and Adelbert Luis Padro. *Hearing Protection Methods.* Orlando: Palm Press, 2017. Print.

Tu, Mingzhu Lin. "Headphones and Earbuds." *Technology and Trends Today* Aug. 2017: n. pag. Web. 3 Oct. 2017.

stands for no date

second line in paragraphs indented one-half inch from left margin, called a hanging indent

Hanging Indent marker

alphabetical list of sources automatically generated by Word

Figure 2–58

- Save the research paper again on the same storage location with the same file name.

TO FORMAT PARAGRAPHS WITH A HANGING INDENT

Notice in Figure 2–58 that the first line of each source entry begins at the left margin, and subsequent lines in the same paragraph are indented one-half inch from the left margin. In essence, the first line hangs to the left of the rest of the paragraph; thus, this type of paragraph formatting is called a **hanging indent**. The Bibliography style in Word automatically formats the works cited paragraphs with a hanging indent.

If you wanted to format paragraphs with a hanging indent, you would use one of the following techniques.

- With the insertion point in the paragraph to format, drag the **Hanging Indent marker** (the bottom triangle) on the ruler to the desired mark on the ruler (i.e., .5") to set the hanging indent at that location from the left margin.

  or

- Right-click the paragraph to format (or, if using a touch screen, tap the 'Show Context Menu' button on the mini toolbar), click Paragraph on the shortcut menu, click the Indents and Spacing tab (Paragraph dialog box), click the Special arrow, click Hanging, and then click the OK button.

  or

- Click the Paragraph Dialog Box Launcher (Home tab or Layout tab | Paragraph group), click the Indents and Spacing tab (Paragraph dialog box), click the Special arrow, click Hanging, and then click the OK button.

  or

- With the insertion point in the paragraph to format, press CTRL+T.

Proofreading and Revising the Research Paper

As discussed in Module 1, once you complete a document, you might find it necessary to make changes to it. Before submitting a paper to be graded, you should proofread it. While **proofreading**, ensure all the source information is correct and look for grammatical, typographical, and spelling errors. Also ensure that transitions between sentences flow smoothly and the sentences themselves make sense.

To assist you with the proofreading effort, Word provides several tools. You can go to a page, copy text, find text, replace text, insert a synonym, check spelling and grammar, and look up information. The following pages discuss these tools.

CONSIDER THIS

What should you consider when proofreading and revising a paper?

As you proofread the paper, look for ways to improve it. Check all grammar, spelling, and punctuation. Be sure the text is logical and transitions are smooth. Where necessary, add text, delete text, reword text, and move text to different locations. Ask yourself these questions:

- Does the title suggest the topic?
- Is the thesis clear?
- Is the purpose of the paper clear?
- Does the paper have an introduction, body, and conclusion?
- Does each paragraph in the body relate to the thesis?
- Is the conclusion effective?
- Are sources acknowledged correctly?

To Modify a Source

1 CHANGE DOCUMENT SETTINGS | 2 CREATE HEADER | 3 TYPE RESEARCH PAPER WITH CITATIONS
4 CREATE ALPHABETICAL WORKS CITED | 5 PROOFREAD & REVISE RESEARCH PAPER

While proofreading the paper, you notice an error in the magazine title; specifically, the word, and, should be removed. If you modify the contents of any source, the list of sources automatically updates. **Why?** *Word automatically updates the contents of fields, and the bibliography is a field.* The following steps delete a word from the title of the magazine article.

- Click the Manage Sources button (References tab | Citations & Bibliography group) to display the Source Manager dialog box.
- Click the source you wish to edit in the Current List, in this case the article by Tu, to select the source.
- Click the Edit button (Source Manager dialog box) to display the Edit Source dialog box.
- In the Periodical Title text box, delete the word, and, from the title (Figure 2–59).

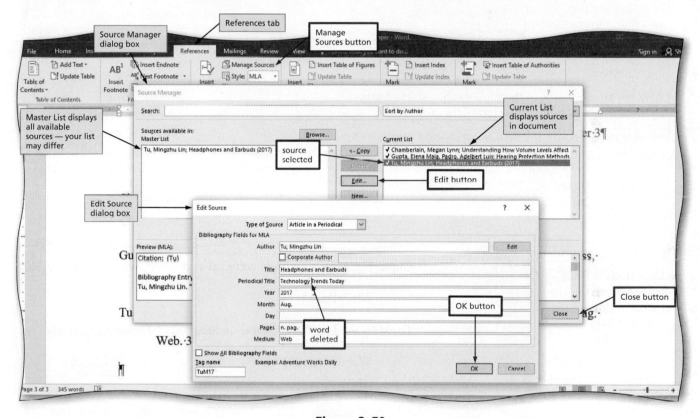

Figure 2–59

- Click the OK button (Edit Source dialog box) to close the dialog box.
- If a Microsoft Word dialog box appears, click its Yes button to update all occurrences of the source.
- Click the Close button (Source Manager dialog box) to update the list of sources and close the dialog box.

To Update a Field

1 CHANGE DOCUMENT SETTINGS | 2 CREATE HEADER | 3 TYPE RESEARCH PAPER WITH CITATIONS
4 CREATE ALPHABETICAL WORKS CITED | 5 PROOFREAD & REVISE RESEARCH PAPER

Depending on settings, the bibliography field may not automatically reflect the edited magazine title. Thus, the following steps update the bibliography field. **Why?** *Because the bibliography is a field, you may need to instruct Word to update its contents.*

1

- Right-click anywhere in the bibliography text to display a shortcut menu related to fields (Figure 2–60).

Q&A

What if I am using a touch screen?

Press and hold anywhere in the bibliography text and then tap the 'Show Context Menu' button on the mini toolbar.

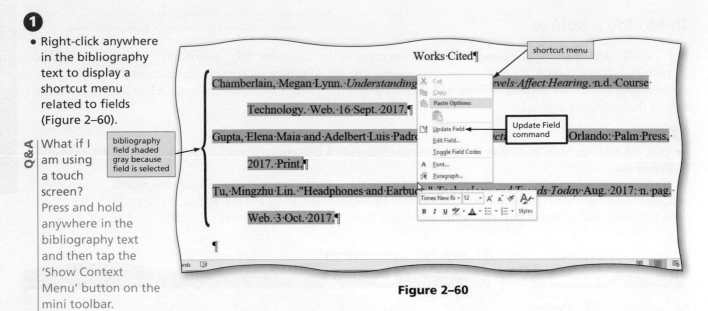

Figure 2–60

Why are all the words in the bibliography shaded gray?
By default, Word shades selected fields gray.

What if the bibliography field is not shaded gray?
Click File on the ribbon to open the Backstage view, click the Options tab in the Backstage view, click Advanced in the left pane (Word Options dialog box), scroll to the 'Show document content' area, click the Field shading arrow, click When selected, and then click the OK button.

2

- Click Update Field on the shortcut menu to update the selected field (Figure 2–61).

Q&A

Can I update all fields in a document at once?
Yes. Select the entire document and then follow these steps.

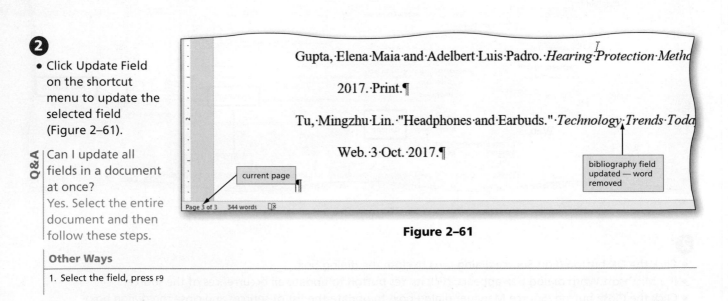

Figure 2–61

Other Ways

1. Select the field, press F9

TO CONVERT A FIELD TO REGULAR TEXT

If, for some reason, you wanted to convert a field, such as the bibliography field, to regular text, you would perform the following steps. Keep in mind, though, once you convert the field to regular text, it no longer is a field that can be updated.

1. Click somewhere in the field to select it, in this case, somewhere in the bibliography.
2. Press CTRL+SHIFT+F9 to convert the selected field to regular text.

To Go to a Page

The next task in revising the paper is to modify text on the second page of the document. *Why? You want to copy text from one location to another on the second page.* You could scroll to the desired location in the document, or you can use the Navigation Pane to browse through pages in a document. The following steps display the top of the second page in the document window and position the insertion point at the beginning of that page.

1

- Click View on the ribbon to display the View tab.

- Place a check mark in the 'Open the Navigation Pane' check box (View tab | Show group) to open the Navigation Pane on the left side of the Word window.

- If necessary, click the Pages tab in the Navigation Pane to display thumbnails of the pages in the document.

- Scroll to, if necessary, and then click the thumbnail of the second page to display the top of the selected page in the top of the document window (Figure 2–62).

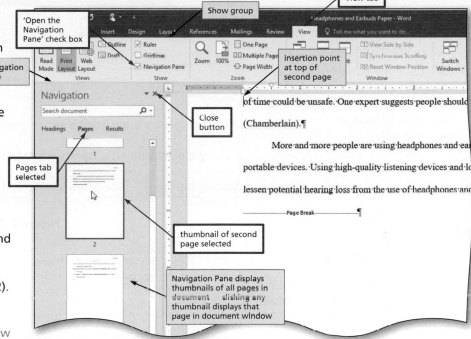

Q&A What is the Navigation Pane?
The Navigation Pane is a window that enables you to browse through headings in a document, browse through pages in a document, or search for text in a document.

Figure 2–62

2

- Click the Close button in the Navigation Pane to close the pane.

Other Ways

1. Click Find arrow (Home tab | Editing group), click Go To on Find menu, click Go To tab (Find and Replace dialog box), enter page number, click Go To button

2. Click Page Number indicator on status bar, click Pages tab in Navigation Pane, click thumbnail of desired page (Navigation Pane)

3. Press CTRL+G, enter page number (Find and Replace dialog box), click Go To button

Copying, Cutting, and Pasting

While proofreading the research paper, you decide it would read better if the word, volume, in the second sentence of the last paragraph also appeared after the word, maximum, in the last sentence of the previous paragraph. You could type the word at the desired location, but you decide to use the Office Clipboard. The **Office Clipboard** is a temporary storage area that holds up to 24 items (text or graphics) copied from any Office program. The Office Clipboard works with the copy, cut, and paste commands:

- **Copying** is the process of placing items on the Office Clipboard, leaving the item in the document.

- **Cutting** removes the item from the document before placing it on the Office Clipboard.

- **Pasting** is the process of copying an item from the Office Clipboard into the document at the location of the insertion point.

To Copy and Paste

In the research paper, you copy a word from one location to another. **Why?** *The sentence reads better with the word, volume, inserted after the word, maximum.* The following steps copy and paste a word.

 1

- Select the item to be copied (the word, volume, in this case).
- Click Home on the ribbon to display the Home tab.
- Click the Copy button (Home tab | Clipboard group) to copy the selected item in the document to the Office Clipboard (Figure 2–63).

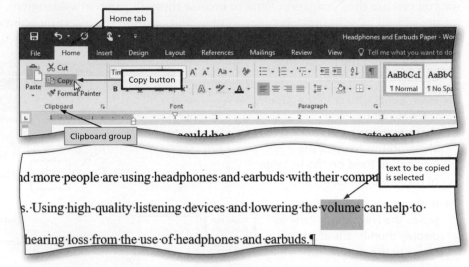

Figure 2–63

2

- Position the insertion point at the location where the item should be pasted (immediately following the space to the right of the word, maximum, in this case) (Figure 2–64).

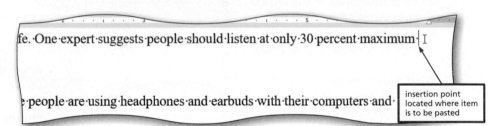

Figure 2–64

3

- Click the Paste button (Home tab | Clipboard group) to paste the copied item in the document at the location of the insertion point (Figure 2–65).

Q&A What if I click the Paste arrow by mistake?
Click the Paste arrow again to remove the Paste menu and repeat Step 3.

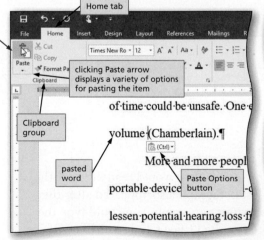 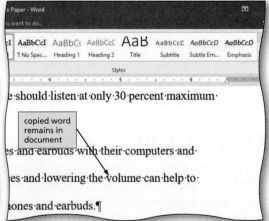

Figure 2–65

Other Ways

1. Click Copy on shortcut menu (or, if using touch, tap Copy on mini toolbar), right-click where item is to be pasted, click 'Keep Source Formatting' in Paste Options area on shortcut menu (or, if using touch, tap Paste on mini toolbar)

2. Select item, press CTRL+C, position insertion point at paste location, press CTRL+V

To Display the Paste Options Menu

When you paste an item or move an item using drag-and-drop editing, which was discussed in the previous module, Word automatically displays a Paste Options button near the pasted or moved text (shown in Figure 2–65). *Why? The Paste Options button allows you to change the format of a pasted item. For example, you can instruct Word to format the pasted item the same way as where it was copied (the source) or format it the same way as where it is being pasted (the destination).* The following steps display the Paste Options menu.

1

- Click the Paste Options button to display the Paste Options menu (Figure 2–66).

Q&A What are the functions of the buttons on the Paste Options menu?

In general, the left button indicates the pasted item should look the same as it did in its original location (the source). The second button formats the pasted text to match the rest of the item where it was pasted (the destination). The third button removes all formatting from the pasted item. The 'Set Default Paste' command displays the Word Options dialog box. Keep in mind that the buttons shown on a Paste Options menu will vary, depending on the item being pasted.

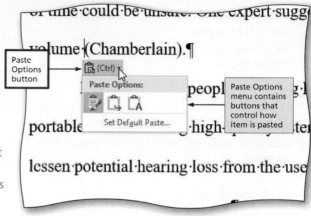

Figure 2–66

2

- Click anywhere to remove the Paste Options menu from the window.

Other Ways

1. CTRL or ESC (to remove the Paste Options menu)

To Find Text

While proofreading the paper, you would like to locate all occurrences of the word, portable. *Why? You are contemplating changing occurrences of this word to the word, mobile.* The following steps find all occurrences of specific text in a document.

1

- Click the Find button (Home tab | Editing group) to display the Navigation Pane.

Q&A What if I am using a touch screen?

Tap the Find button (Home tab | Editing group) and then tap Find on the menu.

- If necessary, click the Results tab in the Navigation Pane, which displays a Search box where you can type text for which you want to search (Figure 2–67).

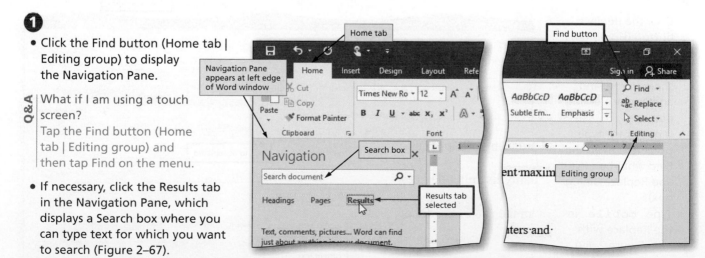

Figure 2–67

- Type **portable** in the Navigation Pane Search box to display all occurrences of the typed text, called the search text, in the Navigation Pane and to highlight the occurrences of the search text in the document window (Figure 2–68).

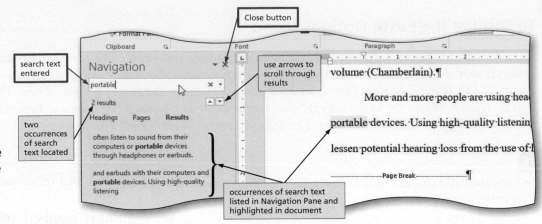

Figure 2–68

🔎 Experiment

- Click both occurrences in the Navigation Pane and watch Word display the associated text in the document window.

🔎 Experiment

- Type various search text in the Navigation Pane Search box, and watch Word both list matches in the Navigation Pane and highlight matches in the document window.

- Click the Close button in the Navigation Pane to close the pane.

Other Ways

1. Click Find arrow (Home tab | Editing group), click Find on Find menu, enter search text in Navigation Pane
2. Click Page Number indicator on status bar, enter search text in Navigation Pane
3. Press CTRL+F, enter search text in Navigation Pane

To Replace Text

1 CHANGE DOCUMENT SETTINGS | 2 CREATE HEADER | 3 TYPE RESEARCH PAPER WITH CITATIONS
4 CREATE ALPHABETICAL WORKS CITED | 5 PROOFREAD & REVISE RESEARCH PAPER

You decide to change all occurrences of the word, portable, to the word, mobile. *Why? The term, mobile devices, is more commonly used than portable devices.* Word's find and replace feature locates each occurrence of a word or phrase and then replaces it with text you specify. The following steps find and replace text.

- Click the Replace button (Home tab | Editing group) to display the Replace sheet in the Find and Replace dialog box.
- If necessary, type **portable** in the Find what box (Find and Replace dialog box).
- Type **mobile** in the Replace with box (Figure 2–69).

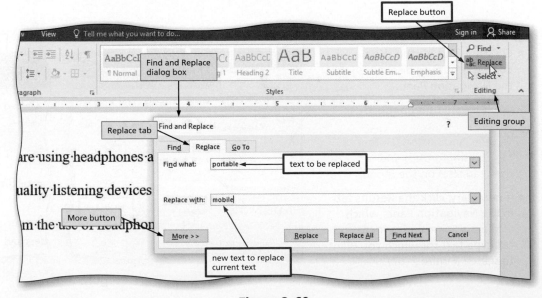

Figure 2–69

2

- Click the Replace All button to instruct Word to replace all occurrences of the Find what text with the Replace with text (Figure 2–70). If Word displays a dialog box asking if you want to continue searching from the beginning of the document, click the Yes button.

volume·(Chamberlain).¶

More·and·more·people·are | phones·a

mobile·devices.·Using·high-quali | devices·a

potential·hearing·loss·from·the·u | hones·and

———— Page Break ————¶

portable changed to mobile

dialog box indicates 2 replacements were made

Microsoft Word ×

All done. We made 2 replacements.

OK

Find and Replace

Find Replace Go To

Find what: portable

Replace with: mobile

OK button

More >> Replace Replace All Find Next Cancel

Replace All button

Find Next button

after clicking OK button (Microsoft Word dialog box), Cancel button changes to Close button

Figure 2–70

Q&A
Does Word search the entire document?

If the insertion point is at the beginning of the document, Word searches the entire document; otherwise, Word may search from the location of the insertion point to the end of the document and then display a dialog box asking if you want to continue searching from the beginning. You also can search a section of text by selecting the text before clicking the Replace or Replace All button.

3

- Click the OK button (Microsoft Word dialog box) to close the dialog box.
- Click the Close button (Find and Replace dialog box) to close the dialog box.

Other Ways

1. Press CTRL+H

Find and Replace Dialog Box

The Replace All button (Find and Replace dialog box) replaces all occurrences of the Find what text with the Replace with text. In some cases, you may want to replace only certain occurrences of a word or phrase, not all of them. To instruct Word to confirm each change, click the Find Next button (Find and Replace dialog box) (shown in Figure 2–70), instead of the Replace All button. When Word locates an occurrence of the text, it pauses and waits for you to click either the Replace button or the Find Next button. Clicking the Replace button changes the text; clicking the Find Next button instructs Word to disregard the replacement and look for the next occurrence of the Find what text.

If you accidentally replace the wrong text, you can undo a replacement by clicking the Undo button on the Quick Access Toolbar. If you used the Replace All button, Word undoes all replacements. If you used the Replace button, Word undoes only the most recent replacement.

BTW

Finding Formatting
To search for formatting or a special character, click the More button in the Find and Replace dialog box (shown in Figure 2–69). To find formatting, use the Format button in the Find dialog box. To find a special character, use the Special button.

To Find and Insert a Synonym

1 CHANGE DOCUMENT SETTINGS | 2 CREATE HEADER | 3 TYPE RESEARCH PAPER WITH CITATIONS
4 CREATE ALPHABETICAL WORKS CITED | 5 PROOFREAD & REVISE RESEARCH PAPER

In this project, you would like a synonym for the word, lessen, in the last paragraph of the research paper. *Why? When writing, you may discover that you used the same word in multiple locations or that a word you used was not quite appropriate, which is the case here.* In these instances, you will want to look up a **synonym**, or a word similar in meaning, to the duplicate or inappropriate word. A **thesaurus** is a book of synonyms. Word provides synonyms and a thesaurus for your convenience. The following steps find a suitable synonym.

- Right-click the word for which you want to find a synonym (in this case, lessen) to display a shortcut menu.
- Point to Synonyms on the shortcut menu to display a list of synonyms for the word you right-clicked (Figure 2–71).

Q&A What if I am using a touch screen? Press and hold the word for which you want a synonym, tap the 'Show Context Menu' button on the mini toolbar, and then tap Synonyms on the shortcut menu.

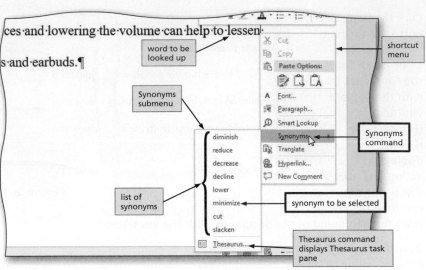

Figure 2–71

- Click the synonym you want (in this case, minimize) on the Synonyms submenu to replace the selected word in the document with the selected synonym (Figure 2–72).

Q&A What if the synonyms list on the shortcut menu does not display a suitable word?
You can display the thesaurus in the Thesaurus task pane by clicking Thesaurus on the Synonyms submenu. The Thesaurus task pane displays a complete thesaurus, in which you can look up synonyms for various meanings of a word. You also can look up an antonym, or word with an opposite meaning.

More·and·more·people·are·using·headphones·and·earbuds·with·the mobile·devices.·Using·high-quality·listening·devices·and·lowering·the·vol minimize·potential·hearing·loss·from·the·use·of·headphones·and·earbuds.¶

word, lessen, changed to minimize

Figure 2–72

Other Ways

1. Click Thesaurus button (Review tab | Proofing group)
2. Press SHIFT+F7

To Check Spelling and Grammar at Once

1 CHANGE DOCUMENT SETTINGS | 2 CREATE HEADER | 3 TYPE RESEARCH PAPER WITH CITATIONS
4 CREATE ALPHABETICAL WORKS CITED | 5 PROOFREAD & REVISE RESEARCH PAPER

As discussed in Module 1, Word checks spelling and grammar as you type and places a wavy underline below possible spelling or grammar errors. Module 1 illustrated how to check these flagged words immediately. The next steps check spelling and grammar at once. *Why? Some users prefer to wait and check their entire document for spelling and grammar errors at once.*

Note: In the following steps, the word, sound, has been misspelled intentionally as sould to illustrate the use of Word's check spelling and grammar at once feature. If you are completing this project on a computer or mobile device, your research paper may contain different misspelled words, depending on the accuracy of your typing.

- Press CTRL+HOME because you want the spelling and grammar check to begin from the top of the document.
- Click Review on the ribbon to display the Review tab.

- Click the 'Spelling & Grammar' button (Review tab | Proofing group) to begin the spelling and grammar check at the location of the insertion point, which, in this case, is at the beginning of the document.
- Click the desired word in the list of suggestions in the Spelling task pane (sound, in this case) (Figure 2–73).

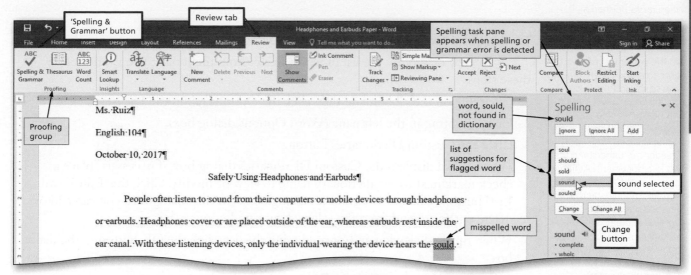

Figure 2–73

- With the word, sound, selected in the list of suggestions, click the Change button (Spelling task pane) to change the flagged word to the selected suggestion and then continue the spelling and grammar check until the next error is identified or the end of the document is reached (Figure 2–74).

- Because the flagged word is a proper noun and spelled correctly, click the Ignore All button (Spelling task pane) to ignore this and future occurrences of the flagged proper noun and then continue the spelling and grammar check until the next error is identified or the end of the document is reached.

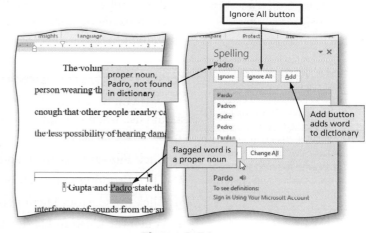

Figure 2–74

- When the spelling and grammar check is finished and Word displays a dialog box, click its OK button.

Q&A Can I check spelling of just a section of a document?
Yes, select the text before starting the spelling and grammar check.

Other Ways

1. Click 'Spelling and Grammar Check' icon on status bar   2. Press F7

The Main and Custom Dictionaries

As shown in the previous steps, Word may flag a proper noun as an error because the proper noun is not in its main dictionary. You may want to add some proper nouns that you use repeatedly, such as a company name or employee names, to Word's dictionary. To prevent Word from flagging proper nouns as errors, you can add the proper nouns to the custom dictionary. To add a correctly spelled word to the custom dictionary, click the Add button (Spelling task pane) or right-click the flagged word (or, if using touch, press and hold and then tap 'Show Context Menu' button on the mini toolbar) and then click 'Add to Dictionary' on the shortcut menu. Once you have added a word to the custom dictionary, Word no longer will flag it as an error.

TO VIEW OR MODIFY ENTRIES IN A CUSTOM DICTIONARY

To view or modify the list of words in a custom dictionary, you would follow these steps.

1. Click File on the ribbon and then click the Options tab in the Backstage view.
2. Click Proofing in the left pane (Word Options dialog box).
3. Click the Custom Dictionaries button.
4. When Word displays the Custom Dictionaries dialog box, if necessary, place a check mark next to the dictionary name to view or modify. Click the 'Edit Word List' button (Custom Dictionaries dialog box). (In this dialog box, you can add or delete entries to and from the selected custom dictionary.)
5. When finished viewing and/or modifying the list, click the OK button in the dialog box.
6. Click the OK button (Custom Dictionaries dialog box).
7. If the 'Suggest from main dictionary only' check box is selected in the Word Options dialog box, remove the check mark. Click the OK button (Word Options dialog box).

TO SET THE DEFAULT CUSTOM DICTIONARY

If you have multiple custom dictionaries, you can specify which one Word should use when checking spelling. To set the default custom dictionary, you would follow these steps.

1. Click File on the ribbon and then click the Options tab in the Backstage view.
2. Click Proofing in the left pane (Word Options dialog box).
3. Click the Custom Dictionaries button.
4. When the Custom Dictionaries dialog box is displayed, place a check mark next to the desired dictionary name. Click the Change Default button (Custom Dictionaries dialog box).
5. Click the OK button (Custom Dictionaries dialog box).
6. If the 'Suggest from main dictionary only' check box is selected in the Word Options dialog box, remove the check mark. Click the OK button (Word Options dialog box).

To Look Up Information

1 CHANGE DOCUMENT SETTINGS | 2 CREATE HEADER | 3 TYPE RESEARCH PAPER WITH CITATIONS
4 CREATE ALPHABETICAL WORKS CITED | 5 PROOFREAD & REVISE RESEARCH PAPER

If you are connected to the Internet, you can use the Insights task pane to search through various forms of reference information, including images, on the web and/or look up a definition of a word. The following steps use the Insights task pane to look up a definition of a word. *Why? Assume you want to see some images and know more about the word, headphones.*

- Position the insertion point in the word you want to look up (in this case, headphones).
- Click the Smart Lookup button (Review tab | Insights group) to open the Insights task pane (Figure 2–75).

Q&A Why does my Insights task pane look different? Depending on your settings, your Insights task pane may appear different from the figure shown here.

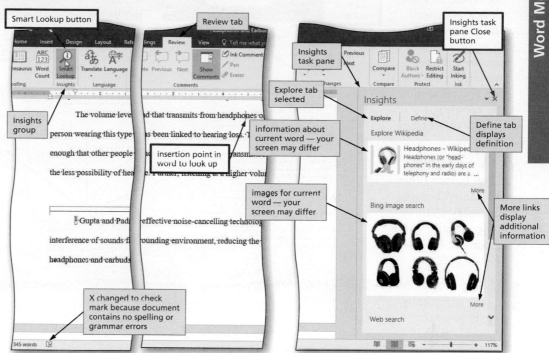

Figure 2–75

Experiment

- With the Explore tab selected in the Insights task pane, scroll through the information and images that appear in the Insights task pane. Click the Define tab in the Insights task pane to see a definition of the current word. Click the Explore tab to redisplay information from the web and images of the current word. Click one of the More links in the Insights task pane to view additional information. Click the Back button at the top of the Insights task pane to return to the previous display.

Q&A Can I copy information from the Insights task pane into my document?
Yes, you can use the Copy and Paste commands. When using Word to insert material from the Insights task pane or any other online reference, however, be careful not to plagiarize.

❷

- Click the Close button in the Insights task pane.

Q&A Is the Research task pane from previous Word editions still available?
Yes. While holding down the ALT key, you can click the word you want to look up (such as headphones) to open the Research task pane and display a dictionary entry for the ALT+clicked word.

To Zoom Multiple Pages

1 CHANGE DOCUMENT SETTINGS | 2 CREATE HEADER | 3 TYPE RESEARCH PAPER WITH CITATIONS
4 CREATE ALPHABETICAL WORKS CITED | 5 PROOFREAD & REVISE RESEARCH PAPER

The next steps display multiple pages in the document window at once. *Why? You want to be able to see all pages in the research paper on the screen at the same time. You also hide formatting marks and the rulers so that the display is easier to view.*

❶

- Click Home on the ribbon to display the Home tab.
- If the 'Show/Hide ¶' button (Home tab | Paragraph group) is selected, click it to hide formatting marks.
- Click View on the ribbon to display the View tab.

• If the rulers are displayed, click the View Ruler check box (View tab | Show group) to remove the check mark from the check box and remove the horizontal and vertical rulers from the screen.

• Click the Multiple Pages button (View tab | Zoom group) to display all three pages at once in the document window (Figure 2–76).

 Q&A Why do the pages appear differently on my screen?

Depending on settings, Word may display all the pages as shown in Figure 2–76 or may show the pages differently.

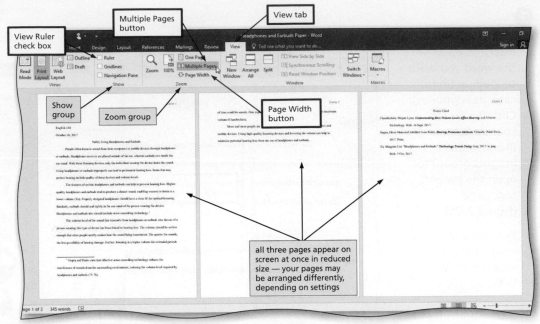

Figure 2–76

❷

• When finished, click the Page Width button (View tab | Zoom group) to return to the page width zoom.

To Change Read Mode Color

1 CHANGE DOCUMENT SETTINGS | 2 CREATE HEADER | 3 TYPE RESEARCH PAPER WITH CITATIONS
4 CREATE ALPHABETICAL WORKS CITED | 5 PROOFREAD & REVISE RESEARCH PAPER

You would like to read the entire research paper using Read mode but would like to change the background color of the Read mode screen. *Why? You prefer a different background color for reading on the screen.* The following steps change the color of the screen in Read mode.

❶

• Click the Read Mode button on the status bar to switch to Read mode.

• Click the View tab to display the View menu.

• Point to Page Color on the View menu to display the Page Color submenu (Figure 2–77).

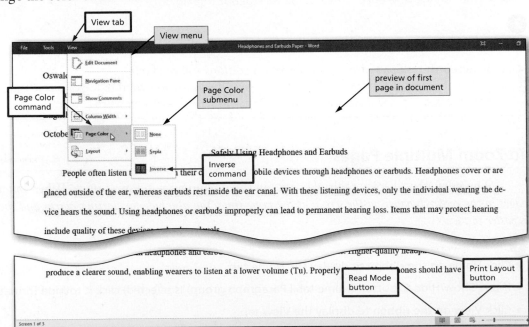

Figure 2–77

• Click Inverse on the Page Color submenu to change the color of the Read mode screen to inverse (Figure 2–78).

• When finished, click the Print Layout button (shown in Figure 2–77) on the status bar to return to Print Layout view.

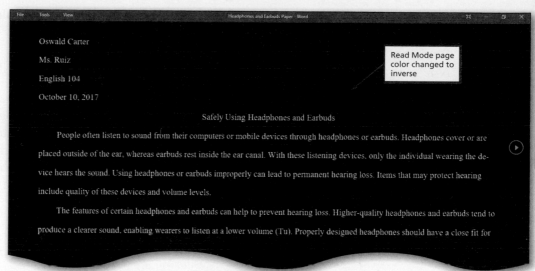

Figure 2–78

To Save and Print the Document and Exit Word

The following steps save and print the document and then exit Word. For a detailed example of the procedure summarized below, refer to the Office and Windows module at the beginning of this book.

1 Save the research paper again on the same storage location with the same file name.

2 If requested by your instructor, print the research paper.

3 Exit Word.

Summary

In this module, you have learned how to modify styles, adjust line and paragraph spacing, use headers to number pages, insert and edit citations and their sources, add footnotes, create a bibliographical list of sources, update a field, go to a page, copy and paste text, find and replace text, check spelling and grammar, and look up information.

What decisions will you need to make when creating your next research paper?

Use these guidelines as you complete the assignments in this module and create your own research papers outside of this class.

1. Select a topic.
   a) Spend time brainstorming ideas for a topic.
   b) Choose a topic you find interesting.
   c) For shorter papers, narrow the scope of the topic; for longer papers, broaden the scope.
   d) Identify a tentative thesis statement, which is a sentence describing the paper's subject matter.

2. Research the topic and take notes, being careful not to plagiarize.

3. Organize your notes into related concepts, identifying all main ideas and supporting details in an outline.

4. Write the first draft from the outline, referencing all sources of information and following the guidelines identified in the required documentation style.

5. Create the list of sources, using the formats specified in the required documentation style.

6. Proofread and revise the paper.

CONSIDER THIS: PLAN AHEAD

Apply Your Knowledge

Reinforce the skills and apply the concepts you learned in this module.

Revising Text and Paragraphs in a Document

Note: To complete this assignment, you will be required to use the Data Files. Please contact your instructor for information about accessing the Data Files.

Instructions: Run Word. Open the document, Apply 2-1 3-D Printers Paragraph Draft, which is located in the Data Files. The document you open contains a paragraph of text. You are to revise the document as follows: move a word, move another word and change the format of the moved word, change paragraph indentation, change line spacing, find all occurrences of a word, replace all occurrences of a word with another word, locate a synonym, and edit the header. The modified paragraph is shown in Figure 2–79.

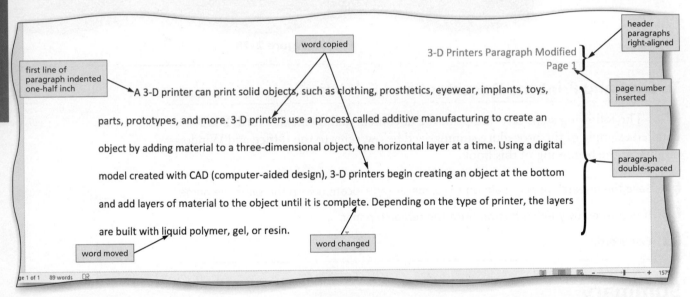

Figure 2–79

Perform the following tasks:

1. Copy the text, printers, from the second sentence and paste it in the third sentence after the underlined word, liquid.

2. Select the underlined word, liquid, in the third sentence. Use drag-and-drop editing to move the selected word, liquid, so that it is before the word, polymer, in the last sentence. (If you are using a touch screen, use the cut and paste commands to move the word.) Click the Paste Options button that displays to the right of the moved word, liquid. Remove the underline format from the moved word by clicking 'Keep Text Only' on the Paste Options menu.

3. Display the ruler, if necessary. Use the ruler to indent the first line of the paragraph one-half inch. (If you are using a touch screen, use the Paragraph dialog box.)

4. Change the line spacing of the paragraph to double.

5. Use the Navigation Pane to find all occurrences of the word, printer. How many are there?

6. Use the Find and Replace dialog box to replace all occurrences of the word, 3D, with the word, 3-D. How many replacements were made?

7. Use the Navigation Pane to find the word, finished. Use Word's thesaurus to change the word, finished, to the word, complete. What other words are in the list of synonyms?

8. Switch to the header so that you can edit it. In the first line of the header, change the word, Draft, to the word, Modified, so that it reads: 3-D Printers Paragraph Modified.

9. In the second line of the header, insert a page number (a plain number with no formatting) one space after the word, Page.

10. Change the alignment of both lines of text in the header from left-aligned to right-aligned. Switch back to the document text.

11. If requested by your instructor, enter your first and last name on a separate line below the page number in the header.

12. Click File on the ribbon and then click Save As. Save the document using the file name, Apply 2-1 3-D Printers Paragraph Modified.

13. Submit the modified document, shown in Figure 2–79, in the format specified by your instructor.

14. Use the Insights task pane to look up the word prosthetics. Click the Explore tab in the Insights task pane. Which web articles appeared? What images appeared? Click the Define tab in the Insights task pane. Which dictionary was used?

15. ✸ Answer the questions posed in #5, #6, #7, and #14. How would you find and replace a special character, such as a paragraph mark?

Extend Your Knowledge

Extend the skills you learned in this module and experiment with new skills. You may need to use Help to complete the assignment.

Working with References and Proofing Tools

Note: To complete this assignment, you will be required to use the Data Files. Please contact your instructor for information about accessing the Data Files.

Instructions: Run Word. Open the document, Extend 2-1 Databases Paper Draft, from the Data Files. You will add another footnote to the paper, convert the footnotes to endnotes, modify the Endnote Text style, change the format of the note reference marks, use Word's readability statistics, translate the document to another language (Figure 2–80), and convert the document from MLA to APA documentation style.

Perform the following tasks:

1. Use Help to learn more about footers, footnotes and endnotes, readability statistics, bibliography styles, AutoCorrect, and Word's translation features.

2. Delete the footer from the document.

3. Insert a second footnote at an appropriate place in the research paper. Use the following footnote text: A data warehouse is a huge database that stores and manages the data required to analyze past and current transactions.

4. Change the location of the footnotes from bottom of page to below text. How did the placement of the footnotes change?

5. Convert the footnotes to endnotes. Where are the endnotes positioned?

6. Modify the Endnote Text style to 12-point Times New Roman font, double-spaced text with a hanging-line indent.

7. Change the format of the note reference marks to capital letters (A, B, etc.).

Continued >

Extend Your Knowledge *continued*

8. Add an AutoCorrect entry that replaces the word, buziness, with the word, business. Type the following sentence as the first sentence in the last paragraph of the paper, misspelling the word, business, as buziness to test the AutoCorrect entry: `Organizations often use a database to manage buziness or other functions.` Delete the AutoCorrect entry that replaces buziness with the word, business.

9. Display the Word Count dialog box. How many words, characters without spaces, characters with spaces, paragraphs, and lines are in the document? Be sure to include footnote and endnote text in the statistics.

10. Check spelling of the document, displaying readability statistics. What are the Flesch-Kincaid Grade Level and the Flesch Reading Ease score? Modify the paper to increase the reading ease score. How did you modify the paper? What are the new statistics?

11. If requested by your instructor, change the student name at the top of the paper to your name, including the last name in the header.

12. Save the revised document with the file name, Extend 2-1 Databases Paper Modified, and then submit it in the format specified by your instructor.

13. If you have an Internet connection, translate the research paper into a language of your choice using the Translate button (Review tab | Language group), as shown in Figure 2–80. Submit the translated document in the format specified by your instructor. Use the Mini Translator to hear how to pronounce three words in your paper.

14. Select the entire document and then change the documentation style from MLA to APA. Save the APA version of the document with a new file name. Compare the APA version to the MLA version. If you have a hard copy of each and your instructor requests it, circle the differences between the two documents.

15. ✸ Answer the questions posed in #4, #5, #9, and #10. Where did you insert the second footnote and why?

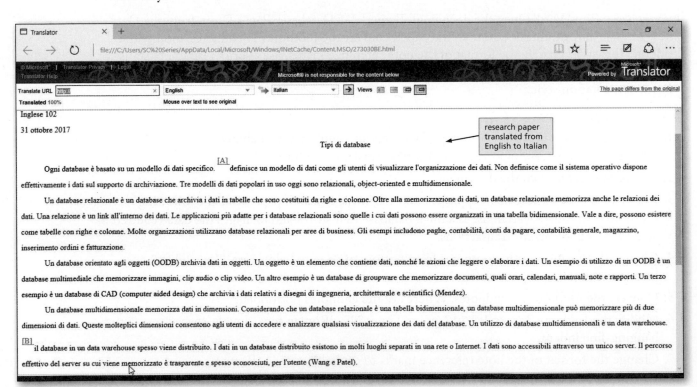

Figure 2–80

Expand Your World

Create a solution that uses cloud or web technologies by learning and investigating on your own from general guidance.

Using an Online Bibliography Tool to Create a List of Sources

Instructions: Assume you are using a computer or mobile device that does not have Word but has Internet access. To make use of time between classes, you use an online bibliography tool to create a list of sources that you can copy and paste into the Works Cited pages of a research paper that is due tomorrow.

Perform the following tasks:

1. Run a browser. Search for the text, online bibliography tool, using a search engine. Visit several of the online bibliography tools and determine which you would like to use to create a list of sources. Navigate to the desired online bibliography tool.

2. Use the online bibliography tool to enter list of sources shown below (Figure 2–81):

Alverez, Juan and Tracy Marie Wilson. *Radon in the Home.* Chicago: Martin Publishing, 2017. Print.

Buchalski, Leonard Adam. *Radon and Your Health.* Los Angeles: Coastal Works, 2017. Print.

Johnson, Shantair Jada. "Radon Facts." *Environment Danger* Aug. 2017. Web. 31 Aug. 2017.

Slobovnik, Vincent Alexander. *The Radon Guide.* Aug. 2017. Course Technology. Web. 18 Sept. 2017.

Wakefield, Ginger Lynn and Bethany Olivia Ames. "Radon Removal Systems." *Living Well Today* Aug. 2017. Web. 3 Oct. 2017.

Zhao, Shen Li. *Radon Testing Procedures.* Sept. 2017. Course Technology. Web. 8 Sept. 2017.

3. If requested by your instructor, replace the name in one of the sources above with your name.

4. Search for another source that discusses radon issues in the home. Add that source.

5. Copy and paste the list of sources into a Word document.

6. Save the document with the file name, Expand 2-1 Radon Issues Sources. Submit the document in the format specified by your instructor.

7. ✺ Which online bibliography tools did you evaluate? Which one did you select to use and why? Do you prefer using the online bibliography tool or Word to create sources? Why? What differences, if any, did you notice between the list of sources created with the online bibliography tool and the lists created when you use Word?

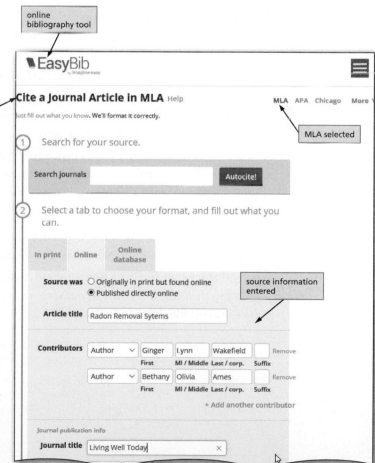

Figure 2–81

In the Labs

Design, create, modify, and/or use a document following the guidelines, concepts, and skills presented in this module. Labs 1 and 2, which increase in difficulty, require you to create solutions based on what you learned in the module; Lab 3 requires you to apply your creative thinking and problem-solving skills to design and implement a solution.

Lab 1: **Preparing a Short Research Paper**

Problem: You are a college student currently enrolled in an introductory English class. Your assignment is to prepare a short research paper (300–350 words) in any area of interest to you. The requirements are that the paper be presented according to the MLA documentation style and have three references. At least one of the three references must be from the web. You prepare the paper shown in Figure 2–82, which discusses wearable devices.

Perform the following tasks:

1. Run Word. If necessary, display formatting marks on the screen.

2. Modify the Normal style to the 12-point Times New Roman font.

3. Adjust line spacing to double.

4. Remove space below (after) paragraphs.

5. Update the Normal style to reflect the adjusted line and paragraph spacing.

6. Create a header to number pages.

7. Type the name and course information at the left margin. If requested by your instructor, use your name and course information instead of the information shown in Figure 2–82a. Center and type the title.

8. Set a first-line indent to one-half inch for paragraphs in the body of the research paper.

9. Type the research paper as shown in Figures 2–82a and 2–82b. Change the bibliography style to MLA. As you insert citations, enter their source information (shown in Figure 2–82c). Edit the citations so that they are displayed according to Figures 2–82a and 2–82b.

10. At the end of the research paper text, press the ENTER key and then insert a manual page break so that the Works Cited page begins on a new page. Enter and format the works cited title (Figure 2–82c). Use Word to insert the bibliographical list (bibliography).

11. Check the spelling and grammar of the paper at once.

12. Save the document using the file name, Lab 2–1 Wearable Devices Paper. Submit the document, shown in Figure 2–82, in the format specified by your instructor.

13. ✳ Read the paper in Print Layout view. Switch to Read mode and scroll through the pages. Do you prefer reading in Print Layout view or Read mode? Why? In Read mode, which of the page colors do you like best and why?

Hakimi 1

Farrah Iman Hakimi

Mr. Danshov

English 103

November 15, 2017

Wearable Devices

A wearable device or wearable is a small, mobile computing device designed to be worn by a consumer. These devices often communicate with a mobile device or computer using Bluetooth. Three popular types of wearable devices are activity trackers, smartwatches, and smart glasses.

An activity tracker is a wearable device that monitors fitness-related activities such as distance walked, heart rate, pulse, calories consumed, and sleep patterns. These devices typically sync, usually wirelessly, with a web or mobile app on your computer or mobile device to extend the capability of the wearable device (Pappas 32-41).

A smartwatch is a wearable device that, in addition to keeping time, can communicate wirelessly with a smartphone to make and answer phone calls, read and send messages, access the web, play music, work with apps such as fitness trackers and GPS, and more. Most include a touch screen (Carter and Schmidt).

Smart glasses, also called smart eyewear, are wearable head-mounted eyeglass-type devices that enable the user to view information or take photos and videos that are projected to a miniature screen in the user's field of vision. For example, the device wearer could run an app while wearing smart glasses that display flight status information when he or she walks into an airport. Users control the device through voice commands or by touching controls on its frame. Some smart glasses also include mobile apps, such as fitness trackers and GPS (Yazzie).

Figure 2–82a

Continued >

In the Labs *continued*

Hakimi 2

Activity trackers, smartwatches, and smart eyewear are available from a variety of manufacturers. Before making a purchase, consumers should research costs and features of all options to determine the device that best suits their requirements.

Figure 2–82b

Hakimi 3

Works Cited

Carter, Calvin J. and Karl Hans Schmidt. "Smartwatch Review." *Technology Trends* Aug. 2017:

n. pag. Web. 12 October 2017.

Pappas, Anastasia Maria. *Activity Trackers and Other Wearable Devices*. Dallas: Western Star

Publishing, 2017. Print.

Yazzie, Nina Tamaya. *Evaluating Today's Smart Glasses*. 25 Aug. 2017. Course Technology.

Web. 25 Sept. 2017.

Figure 2–82c

Lab 2: **Preparing a Research Report with a Footnote**

Problem: You are a college student enrolled in an introductory technology class. Your assignment is to prepare a short research paper (350–400 words) in any area of interest to you. The requirements are that the paper be presented according to the MLA documentation style, contain at least one note positioned as a footnote, and have three references. At least one of the three references must be from the web. You prepare a paper about two-step verification (Figure 2–83).

Perform the following tasks:
1. Run Word. Modify the Normal style to the 12-point Times New Roman font. Adjust line spacing to double and remove space below (after) paragraphs. Update the Normal style to include the adjusted line and paragraph spacing. Create a header to number pages. Type the name and course information at the left margin. If requested by your instructor, use your name and course information instead of the information shown in Figure 2–83a. Center and type the title. Set a first-line indent for paragraphs in the body of the research paper.
2. Type the research paper as shown in Figures 2–83a and 2–83b. Insert the footnote as shown in Figure 2–83a. Change the Footnote Text style to the format specified in the MLA documentation

Wagner 1

Bryan Wagner

Dr. Rosenberg

Technology 104

October 27, 2017

Two-Step Verification

In an attempt to protect personal data and information from online thieves, many

organizations, such as financial institutions or universities, that store sensitive or confidential

items use a two-step verification process. With two-step verification, a computer or mobile

device uses two separate methods, one after the next, to verify the identity of a user.

ATMs (automated teller machines) usually require a two-step verification. Users first

insert their ATM card into the ATM (Step 1) and then enter a PIN, or personal identification

number, (Step 2) to access their bank account. If someone steals these cards, the thief must enter

the user's PIN to access the account (Tanaka).

Another use of two-step verification requires a mobile phone and a computer or mobile

device.[1] When users sign in to an account on a computer or mobile device, they enter a user

name and password (Step 1). Next, they are prompted to enter another authentication code (Step

2), which is sent as a text or voice message or via an app on a smartphone. This second code

generally is valid for a set time, sometimes only for a few minutes or hours. If users do not sign

in during this time limit, they must repeat the process and request another verification code

---

[1] According to Moore and O'Sullivan, users should register an alternate mobile phone

number, landline phone number, email address, or other form of contact beyond a mobile phone

number so that they still can access their accounts even if they lose their mobile phone (54).

Figure 2–83a

Wagner 2

(Marcy). Microsoft and Google commonly use two-step verification when users sign in to these

websites (Moore and O'Sullivan).

Some organizations use two separate methods to verify the identity of users. These two-

step verification procedures are designed to protect users' sensitive and confidential items from

online thieves.

Figure 2–83b

Continued >

In the Labs *continued*

style. Change the bibliography style to MLA. As you insert citations, use the following source information, entering it according to the MLA style:

a. Type of Source: Article in a Periodical
   Author: Hana Kei Tanaka
   Article Title: Safeguards against Unauthorized Access and Use
   Periodical Title: Technology Today
   Year: 2017
   Month: Sept.
   Pages: no pages used
   Medium: Web
   Year Accessed: 2017
   Month Accessed: Oct.
   Day Accessed: 3

b. Type of Source: Web site
   Author: Fredrick Lee Marcy
   Name of webpage: Two-Step Verification
   Year/Month/Date: none given
   Production Company: Course Technology
   Medium: Web
   Year Accessed: 2017
   Month Accessed: Sept.
   Day Accessed: 18

c. Type of Source: Book
   Author: Aaron Bradley Moore and Brianna Clare O'Sullivan
   Title: Authentication Techniques
   Year: 2017
   City: Detroit
   Publisher: Great Lakes Press
   Medium: Print

3. At the end of the research paper text, press the ENTER key once and insert a manual page break so that the Works Cited page begins on a new page. Enter and format the works cited title. Use Word to insert the bibliographical list.

4. Check the spelling and grammar of the paper.

5. Save the document using the file name, Lab 2–2 Two-Step Verification Paper. Submit the document, shown in Figure 2–83, in the format specified by your instructor.

6. ✳ This paper uses web sources. What factors should you consider when selecting web sources?

Lab 3: **Consider This: Your Turn**

Create a Research Paper about Wireless Communications

Note: To complete this assignment, you will be required to use the Data Files. Please contact your instructor for information about accessing the Data Files.

Problem: As a student in an introductory computer class, your instructor has assigned a brief research paper that discusses wireless communications.

Perform the following tasks:

Part 1: The source for the text in your research paper is in a file called Lab 2–3 Consider This Your Turn Wireless Communications Notes, which is located in the Data Files. If your instructor requests, use the Insights task pane to obtain information from another source and include that information as a note positioned as a footnote in the paper, along with entering its corresponding source information as appropriate. Add an AutoCorrect entry to correct a word you commonly mistype. If necessary, set the default dictionary. Add one of the source last names to the dictionary.

Using the concepts and techniques presented in this module, organize the notes in the text in the file on the Data Files, rewording as necessary, and then create and format this research paper according to the MLA documentation style. Be sure to check spelling and grammar of the finished paper. Submit your assignment and answers to the critical thinking questions in the format specified by your instructor.

Part 2: ✳ You made several decisions while creating the research paper in this assignment: how to organize the notes, where to place citations, how to format sources, and which source on the web to use for the footnote text (if requested by your instructor). What was the rationale behind each of these decisions? When you proofread the document, what further revisions did you make and why?

3 Creating a Business Letter with a Letterhead and Table

Objectives

You will have mastered the material in this module when you can:

- Change margins
- Insert and format a shape
- Change text wrapping
- Insert an online picture and format it
- Insert a symbol
- Add a border to a paragraph
- Clear formatting
- Convert a hyperlink to regular text

- Apply a style
- Set and use tab stops
- Insert the current date
- Create, modify, and insert a building block
- Insert a Word table, enter data in the table, and format the table
- Address and print an envelope

Introduction

In a business environment, people use documents to communicate with others. Business documents can include letters, memos, newsletters, proposals, and resumes. An effective business document clearly and concisely conveys its message and has a professional, organized appearance. You can use your own creative skills to design and compose business documents. Using Word, for example, you can develop the content and decide on the location of each item in a business document.

Project — Business Letter with a Letterhead and Table

At some time, you more than likely will prepare a business letter. Contents of business letters include requests, inquiries, confirmations, acknowledgements, recommendations, notifications, responses, thank you letters, invitations, offers, referrals, complaints, and more.

The project in this module follows generally accepted guidelines for writing letters and uses Word to create the business letter shown in Figure 3–1. This business

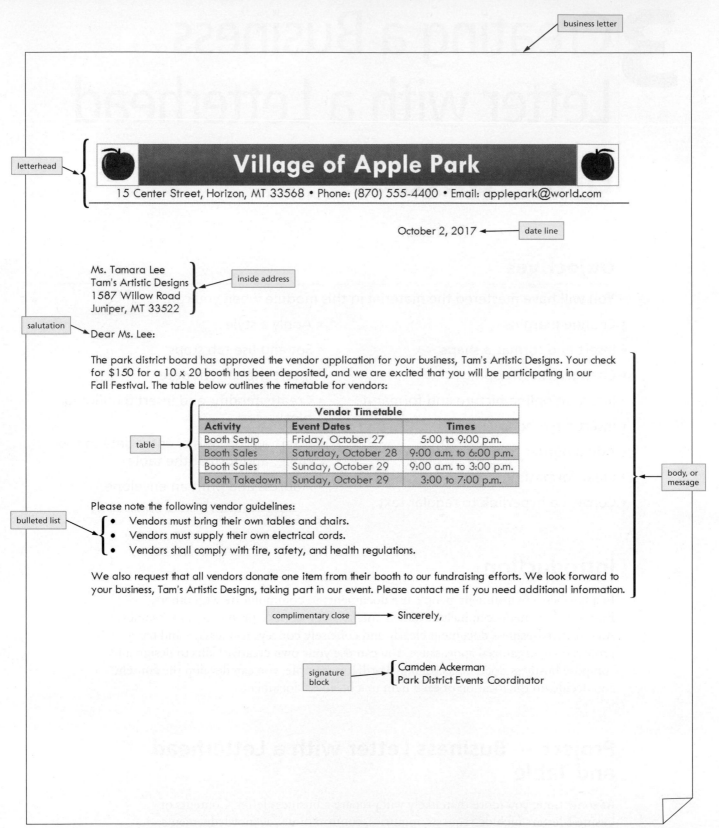

Figure 3–1

letter is a letter from the park district events coordinator at the Village of Apple Park that confirms a vendor application to participate in its community event. The letter includes a custom letterhead, as well as all essential business letter components: date line, inside address, salutation, body, complimentary close, and signature block. To easily present the vendor timetable during the event, the letter shows this information in a table. The vendor guidelines appear in a bulleted list.

In this module, you will learn how to create the letter shown in Figure 3–1. The following roadmap identifies general activities you will perform as you progress through this module:

1. CREATE AND FORMAT a LETTERHEAD WITH GRAPHICS.
2. SPECIFY the LETTER FORMATS according to business letter guidelines.
3. INSERT a TABLE in the letter.
4. FORMAT the TABLE in the letter.
5. INSERT a BULLETED LIST in the letter.
6. ADDRESS an ENVELOPE for the letter.

To Run Word and Change Word Settings

If you are using a computer to step through the project in this module and you want your screens to match the figures in this book, you should change your screen's resolution to 1366 × 768. For information about how to change a computer's resolution, refer to the Office and Windows module at the beginning of this book.

The following steps run Word, display formatting marks, and change the zoom to page width.

1 Run Word and create a blank document in the Word window. If necessary, maximize the Word window.

2 If the Print Layout button on the status bar is not selected (shown in Figure 3–2), click it so that your screen is in Print Layout view.

3 If the 'Show/Hide ¶' button (Home tab | Paragraph group) is not selected already, click it to display formatting marks on the screen.

4 To display the page the same width as the document window, if necessary, click the Page Width button (View tab | Zoom group).

For an introduction to Windows and instructions about how to perform basic Windows tasks, read the Office and Windows module at the beginning of this book, where you can learn how to resize windows, change screen resolution, create folders, move and rename files, use Windows Help, and much more.

For an introduction to Office and instructions about how to perform basic tasks in Office apps, read the Office and Windows module at the beginning of this book, where you can learn how to run an application, use the ribbon, save a file, open a file, print a file, exit an application, use Help, and much more.

To Change Margin Settings

1 CREATE & FORMAT LETTERHEAD WITH GRAPHICS | 2 SPECIFY LETTER FORMATS
3 INSERT TABLE | 4 FORMAT TABLE | 5 INSERT BULLETED LIST | 6 ADDRESS ENVELOPE

Word is preset to use standard 8.5-by-11-inch paper, with 1-inch top, bottom, left, and right margins. The business letter in this module uses .75-inch left and right margins and 1-inch top and bottom margins. *Why? You would like more text to fit from left to right on the page.*

When you change the default (preset) margin settings, the new margin settings affect every page in the document. If you wanted the margins to affect just a portion of the document, you would divide the document into sections (discussed in a later module), which enables you to specify different margin settings for each section. The following steps change margin settings.

1

- Display the Layout tab.

- Click the Adjust Margins button (Layout tab | Page Setup group) to display the Adjust Margins gallery (Figure 3–2).

2

- Click Moderate in the Adjust Margins gallery to change the margins to the specified settings.

Q&A

What if the margin settings I want are not in the Adjust Margins gallery?

You can click Custom Margins in the Adjust Margins gallery and then enter your desired margin values in the top, bottom, left, and right boxes in the Page Setup dialog box.

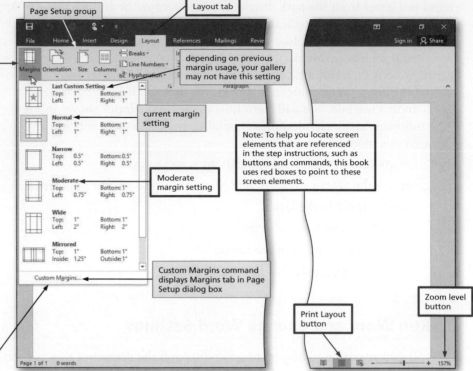

Figure 3–2

Other Ways

1. Position pointer on margin boundary on ruler; when pointer changes to two-headed arrow, drag margin boundary on ruler

Creating a Letterhead

The cost of preprinted letterhead can be high. An alternative is to create your own letterhead and save it in a file. When you want to create a letter at a later time, you can start by using the letterhead file. The following sections create a letterhead and then save it in a file for future use.

What is a letterhead?

A **letterhead** is the section of a letter that identifies an organization or individual. Often, the letterhead appears at the top of a letter. Although you can design and print a letterhead yourself, many businesses pay an outside firm to design and print their letterhead, usually on higher-quality paper. They then use the professionally preprinted paper for external business communications.

If you do not have preprinted letterhead paper, you can design a creative letterhead. It is important the letterhead appropriately represent the essence of the organization or individual (i.e., formal, technical, creative, etc.). That is, it should use text, graphics, formats, and colors that reflect the organization or individual. The letterhead should leave ample room for the contents of the letter.

When designing a letterhead, consider its contents, placement, and appearance.

- **Contents of letterhead.** A letterhead should contain these elements:
    - Complete legal name of the individual, group, or company
    - Complete mailing address: street address including building, room, suite number, or post office box, along with city, state, and postal code
    - Phone number(s) and fax number, if applicable
    - Email address

– Website address, if applicable

– Many letterheads also include a logo or other image; if an image is used, it should express the organization or individual's personality or goals

- **Placement of elements in the letterhead.** Many letterheads center their elements across the top of the page. Others align some or all of the elements with the left or right margins. Sometimes, the elements are split between the top and bottom of the page. For example, a name and logo may be at the top of the page with the address at the bottom of the page.

- **Appearance of letterhead elements.** Use fonts that are easy to read. Give the organization or individual name impact by making its font size larger than the rest of the text in the letterhead. For additional emphasis, consider formatting the name in bold, italic, or a different color. Choose colors that complement each other and convey the goals of the organization or individual.

When finished designing the letterhead, determine if a divider line would help to visually separate the letterhead from the remainder of the letter.

The letterhead for the letter in this module consists of the organization's name, appropriate graphics, postal address, phone number, and email address. The name and graphics are enclosed in a rectangular shape (shown in Figure 3–1), and the contact information is below the shape. You will follow these general steps to create the letterhead in this module:

1. Insert and format a shape.
2. Enter and format the organization name in the shape.
3. Insert, format, and position the images in the shape.
4. Enter the contact information below the shape.
5. Add a border below the contact information.

BTW
The Ribbon and Screen Resolution
Word may change how the groups and buttons within the groups appear on the ribbon, depending on the computer or mobile device's screen resolution. Thus, your ribbon may look different from the ones in this book if you are using a screen resolution other than 1366 x 768.

To Insert a Shape

1 CREATE & FORMAT LETTERHEAD WITH GRAPHICS | 2 SPECIFY LETTER FORMATS
3 INSERT TABLE | 4 FORMAT TABLE | 5 INSERT BULLETED LIST | 6 ADDRESS ENVELOPE

Word has a variety of predefined shapes, which are a type of drawing object, that you can insert in documents. A **drawing object** is a graphic that you create using Word. Examples of shape drawing objects include rectangles, circles, triangles, arrows, flowcharting symbols, stars, banners, and callouts. The following steps insert a rectangle shape in the letterhead. *Why? The organization's name is placed in a rectangle for emphasis and visual appeal.*

- Display the Insert tab.

- Click the 'Draw a Shape' button (Insert tab | Illustrations group) to display the Draw a Shape gallery (Figure 3–3).

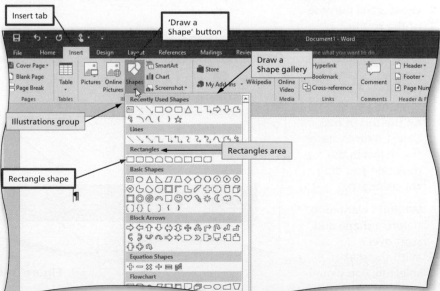

Figure 3–3

2

- Click the Rectangle shape in the Rectangles area in the Draw a Shape gallery, which removes the gallery.

Q&A What if I am using a touch screen?
The shape is inserted in the document window. Skip Steps 3 and 4, and proceed to Step 5.

- Position the pointer (a crosshair) in the approximate location for the upper-left corner of the desired shape (Figure 3–4).

Q&A What is the purpose of the crosshair pointer?
You drag the crosshair pointer from the upper-left corner to the lower-right corner to form the desired location and size of the shape.

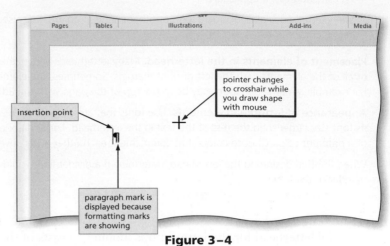

Figure 3–4

3

- Drag the mouse to the right and downward to form the boundaries of the shape, as shown in Figure 3–5. Do not release the mouse button.

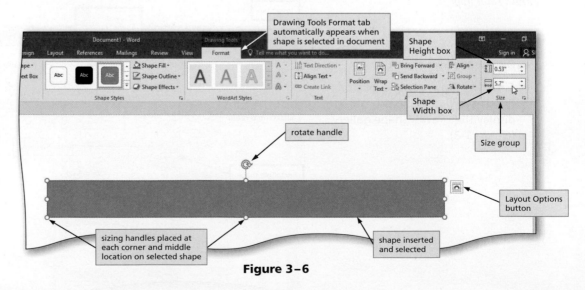

Figure 3–5

4

- Release the mouse button so that Word draws the shape according to your drawing in the document window.

5

- Verify your shape is the same approximate height and width as the one in this project by reviewing, and if necessary changing, the values in the Shape Height box and Shape Width boxes (Drawing Tools Format tab | Size group) to 0.53" and 5.7" by typing each value in the respective box and then pressing the ENTER key (Figure 3–6).

Q&A What is the purpose of the rotate handle?
When you drag an object's **rotate handle**, which is the white circle on the top of the object, Word rotates the object in the direction you drag the mouse.

What if I wanted to delete a shape and start over?
With the shape selected, you would press the DELETE key.

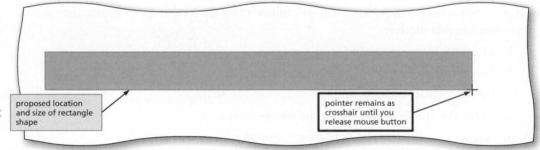

Figure 3–6

Floating versus Inline Objects

When you insert an object in a document, Word inserts it as either an inline object or a floating object. An **inline object** is an object that is part of a paragraph. With inline objects, you change the location of the object by setting paragraph options, such as centered, right-aligned, and so on. For example, when you inserted the picture of the surfer in Module 1, Word inserted it as an inline object. A **floating object**, by contrast, is an object that can be positioned at a specific location in a document or in a layer over or behind text in a document. The shape you just inserted is a floating object. You have more flexibility with floating objects because you can position a floating object anywhere on the page.

In addition to changing an object from inline to floating and vice versa, Word provides several floating options, which (along with inline) are called text wrapping options because they affect how text wraps with or around the object. Table 3–1 presents the various text wrapping options.

Table 3–1 Text Wrapping Options

Text Wrapping Option	Object Type	How It Works
In Line with Text	Inline	Object positioned according to paragraph formatting; for example, if paragraph is centered, object will be centered with any text in the paragraph.
Square	Floating	Text wraps around object, with text forming a box around the object.
Tight	Floating	Text wraps around object, with text forming to shape of the object.
Through	Floating	Object appears at beginning, middle, or end of text. Moving object changes location of text.
Top and Bottom	Floating	Object appears above or below text. Moving object changes location of text.
Behind Text	Floating	Object appears behind text.
In Front of Text	Floating	Object appears in front of text and may cover the text.

To Change an Object's Position

1 CREATE & FORMAT LETTERHEAD WITH GRAPHICS | 2 SPECIFY LETTER FORMATS
3 INSERT TABLE | 4 FORMAT TABLE | 5 INSERT BULLETED LIST | 6 ADDRESS ENVELOPE

You can specify an object's vertical position on a page (top, middle, bottom) and its horizontal position (left, center, right). The following steps change the position of an object, specifically, the rectangle shape. *Why?* *You want the shape to be centered at the top of the page in the letterhead.*

1

- With the shape still selected, click the Position Object button (Drawing Tools Format tab | Arrange group) to display the Position Object gallery (Figure 3–7).

Q&A What if the shape is not still selected?
Click the shape to select it.

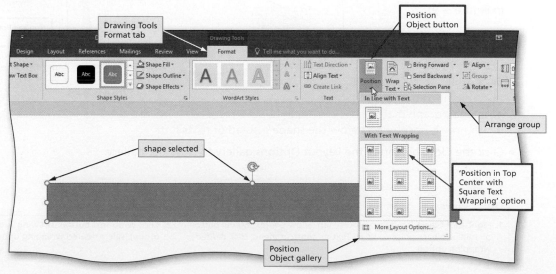

Figure 3–7

Experiment

- Point to various options in the Position Object gallery and watch the shape move to the selected position option.

❷

- Click 'Position in Top Center with Square Text Wrapping' in the Position Object gallery so that the object does not cover the document and is centered at the top of the document.

Other Ways

1. Click Layout Options button attached to graphic (shown in Figure 3–8), click See more link in Layout Options gallery, click Horizontal Alignment arrow and select alignment (Layout dialog box), click Vertical Alignment arrow and select alignment, click OK button

2. Click Advanced Layout: Size Dialog Box Launcher (Drawing Tools Format tab | Size group), click Position tab (Layout dialog box), click Horizontal Alignment arrow and select alignment, click Vertical Alignment arrow and select alignment, click OK button

To Change an Object's Text Wrapping

1 CREATE & FORMAT LETTERHEAD WITH GRAPHICS | 2 SPECIFY LETTER FORMATS
3 INSERT TABLE | 4 FORMAT TABLE | 5 INSERT BULLETED LIST | 6 ADDRESS ENVELOPE

When you insert a shape in a Word document, the default text wrapping is In Front of Text, which means the object will cover any text behind it. The previous steps, which changed the shape's position, changed the text wrapping to Square. In the letterhead, you want the shape's text wrapping to be Top and Bottom. *Why? You want the letterhead above the contents of the letter when you type it, instead of covering the contents of the letter.* The following steps change an object's text wrapping.

❶

- With the shape still selected, click the Layout Options button attached to the graphic to display the Layout Options gallery (Figure 3–8).

❷

- Click 'Top and Bottom' in the Layout Options gallery so that the object does not cover the document text (shown in Figure 3–9).

Q&A How can I tell that the text wrapping has changed?
Because the letter has no text, you need to look at the paragraph mark, which now is positioned below the shape instead of to its left.

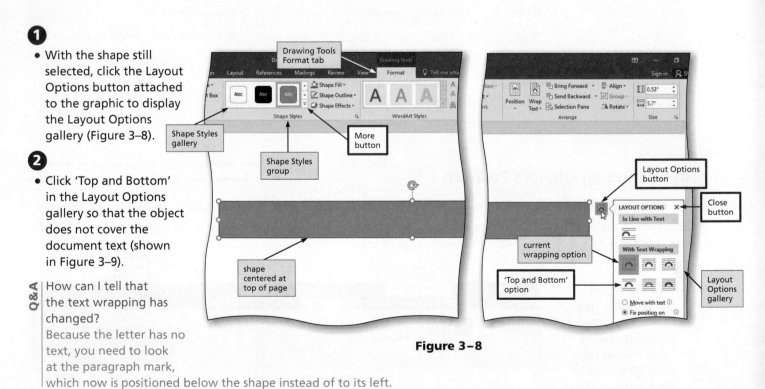

Figure 3–8

- Click the Close button in the Layout Options gallery to close the gallery.

Other Ways

1. Right-click object (or, if using touch, tap 'Show Context Menu' button on mini toolbar), point to Wrap Text on shortcut menu, click desired wrapping option

2. Click Wrap Text button (Drawing Tools Format tab | Arrange group), select desired wrapping option

1 CREATE & FORMAT LETTERHEAD WITH GRAPHICS | 2 SPECIFY LETTER FORMATS
3 INSERT TABLE | 4 FORMAT TABLE | 5 INSERT BULLETED LIST | 6 ADDRESS ENVELOPE

To Apply a Shape Style

Why apply a shape style? Word provides a Shape Styles gallery so that you easily can change the appearance of the shape. The following steps apply a shape style to the rectangle shape.

- With the shape still selected, click the More button (shown in Figure 3–8) in the Shape Styles gallery (Drawing Tools Format tab | Shape Styles group) to expand the gallery.

Q&A What if the shape no longer is selected?
Click the shape to select it.

- Point to 'Moderate Effect - Gray-50%, Accent 3' (fourth effect in fifth row) in the Shape Styles gallery to display a live preview of that style applied to the shape in the document (Figure 3–9).

Experiment

- Point to various styles in the Shape Styles gallery and watch the style of the shape change in the document.

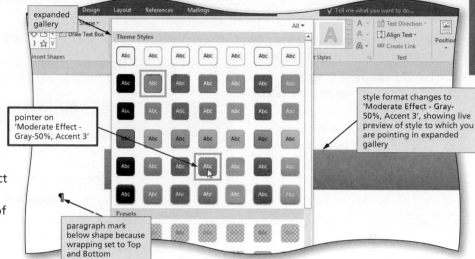

Figure 3–9

- Click 'Moderate Effect - Gray-50%, Accent 3' in the Shape Styles gallery to apply the selected style to the shape.

Other Ways

1. Right-click shape, click 'Shape Quick Styles' button on mini toolbar, select desired style
2. Click Format Shape Dialog Box Launcher (Drawing Tools Format tab | Shape Styles group), click 'Fill & Line' button (Format Shape task pane), expand Fill section, select desired colors, click Close button

To Add Text to a Shape

1 CREATE & FORMAT LETTERHEAD WITH GRAPHICS | 2 SPECIFY LETTER FORMATS
3 INSERT TABLE | 4 FORMAT TABLE | 5 INSERT BULLETED LIST | 6 ADDRESS ENVELOPE

The following steps add text (the organization name) to a shape. *Why? In the letterhead for this module, the name is in the shape. Similarly, an individual could put his or her name in a shape on a letterhead in order to create personalized letterhead.*

- Right-click the shape to display a mini toolbar and/or shortcut menu (Figure 3–10).

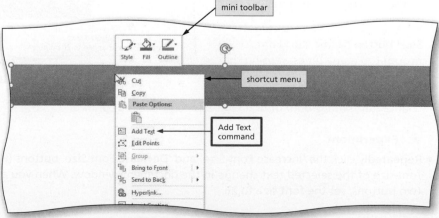

Figure 3–10

2

- Click Add Text on the shortcut menu to place an insertion point in the shape.

Q&A What if I am using a touch screen?
Tap the Edit Text button on the mini toolbar.

Why do the buttons on my mini toolbar differ?
If you are using a mouse in Mouse mode, the buttons on your mini toolbar will differ from those that appear when you use a touch screen in Touch mode.

- If the insertion point and paragraph mark are not centered in the shape, click the Center button (Home tab | Paragraph group) to center them.

- Type **Village of Apple Park** as the name in the shape (Figure 3–11).

If requested by your instructor, enter your name instead of the name shown in Figure 3–11.

text entered
and centered

Village·of·Apple·Park¶

Figure 3–11

To Use the 'Increase Font Size' Button

1 CREATE & FORMAT LETTERHEAD WITH GRAPHICS | 2 SPECIFY LETTER FORMATS
3 INSERT TABLE | 4 FORMAT TABLE | 5 INSERT BULLETED LIST | 6 ADDRESS ENVELOPE

In previous modules, you used the Font Size arrow (Home tab | Font group) to change the font size of text. Word also provides an 'Increase Font Size' button (Home tab | Font group), which increases the font size of selected text each time you click the button. The following steps use the 'Increase Font Size' button to increase the font size of the name in the shape to 26 point. ***Why?*** *You want the name to be as large as possible in the shape.*

1

- Drag through the text to be formatted (in this case, the name in the shape).

2

- If necessary, display the Home tab.

- Repeatedly click the 'Increase Font Size' button (Home tab | Font group) until the Font Size box displays 26 to increase the font size of the selected text (Figure 3–12).

Q&A What if I click the 'Increase Font Size' button (Home tab | Font group) too many times, causing the font size to be too big?
Click the 'Decrease Font Size' button (Home tab | Font group) until the desired font size is displayed.

Home tab
'Increase Font Size' button
'Decrease Font Size' button
Font Size box displays 26
Font group

Village·of·Apple·Park¶

selected text changed to 26 point

Figure 3–12

Experiment

- Repeatedly click the 'Increase Font Size' and 'Decrease Font Size' buttons (Home tab | Font group) and watch the font size of the selected text change in the document window. When you are finished experimenting with these two buttons, set the font size to 26.

Other Ways

1. Press CTRL+SHIFT+>

To Bold Selected Text

To make the name stand out even more, bold it. The following steps bold the selected text.

1 With the text selected, click the Bold button (Home tab | Font group) to bold the selected text (shown in Figure 3–13).

2 Click anywhere in the text in the shape to remove the selection and place the insertion point in the shape.

To Change the Document Theme

1 CREATE & FORMAT LETTERHEAD WITH GRAPHICS | 2 SPECIFY LETTER FORMATS
3 INSERT TABLE | 4 FORMAT TABLE | 5 INSERT BULLETED LIST | 6 ADDRESS ENVELOPE

A **document theme** is a coordinated combination of colors, fonts, and effects. The current default document theme is Office, which uses Calibri and Calibri Light as its font and shades of grays and blues primarily. The following steps change the document theme to Circuit for the letter in this module. *Why? You want to use shades of reds and oranges in the letterhead because those colors are associated with energy, success, creativity, and enthusiasm.*

1

- Display the Design tab.
- Click the Themes button (Design tab | Document Formatting group) to display the Themes gallery.
- Point to Circuit in the Themes gallery to display a live preview of that theme applied to the document (Figure 3–13).

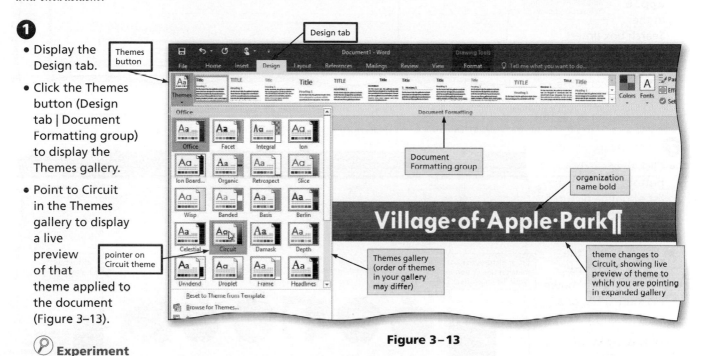

Figure 3–13

🔍 **Experiment**

- Point to various themes in the Themes gallery and watch the color scheme and font set change in the document window.

2

- Click Circuit in the Themes gallery to change the document theme.

To Insert an Online Picture

1 CREATE & FORMAT LETTERHEAD WITH GRAPHICS | 2 SPECIFY LETTER FORMATS
3 INSERT TABLE | 4 FORMAT TABLE | 5 INSERT BULLETED LIST | 6 ADDRESS ENVELOPE

Files containing graphics are available from a variety of sources. In the Module 1 flyer, you inserted a digital picture taken with a camera. In this project, you insert a picture from the web. Microsoft Office applications can access a collection of royalty-free photos and animations.

The letterhead in this project contains a picture of an apple (shown in Figure 3–1). *Why? Because the name of the organization is Village of Apple Park, an apple is an appropriate image for this letterhead.* The following steps insert an online picture in the document.

1

- If necessary, click the paragraph mark below the shape to position the insertion point where you want to insert the picture.

- Display the Insert tab.

- Click the Online Pictures button (Insert tab | Illustrations group) to display the Insert Pictures dialog box.

- Type **apple** in the Search box (Insert Pictures dialog box) to specify the search text, which indicates the type of image you want to locate (Figure 3–14).

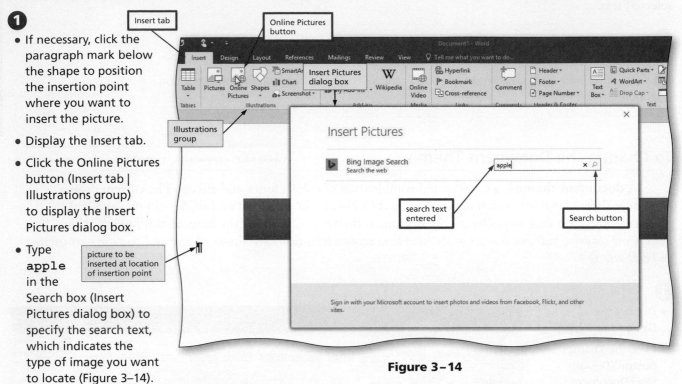

Figure 3–14

2

- Click the Search button to display a list of online pictures that matches the entered search text.

- Scroll through the list of pictures to locate the one shown in Figure 3–15, or a similar image.

Q&A

Why is my list of pictures different from Figure 3–15? The online images are continually updated.

What is Creative Commons? **Creative Commons** is a nonprofit organization that provides several standard licensing options that owners of creative works may specify when granting permission for others to use their digital content, such as the online pictures that appear in the Bing Image Search. Be sure to follow an image's guidelines when using it in a document.

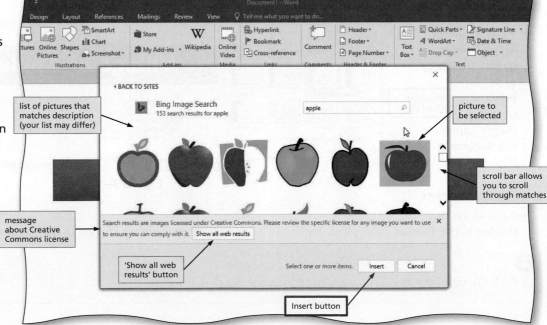

Figure 3–15

Q&A What if I cannot locate the image in Figure 3–15, and I would like to use that exact image?
The image is located in the Data Files. You can click the Cancel button and then click the From File button (Insert tab | Illustrations group), navigate to the file called apple-02.wmf in the Data Files, and then click the Insert button (Insert Picture dialog box).

3

- If necessary, click the 'Show all web results' button to display more images that match the search text.

- Click the desired picture to select it.

- Click the Insert button to insert the selected image in the document at the location of the insertion point. If necessary, scroll to display the image (picture) in the document window (Figure 3–16).

Figure 3–16

To Resize a Graphic to a Percent of the Original Size

1 CREATE & FORMAT LETTERHEAD WITH GRAPHICS | 2 SPECIFY LETTER FORMATS
3 INSERT TABLE | 4 FORMAT TABLE | 5 INSERT BULLETED LIST | 6 ADDRESS ENVELOPE

Instead of dragging a sizing handle to change the graphic's size, as you learned in Module 1, you can specify that the graphic be resized to a percent of its original size. In this module, the graphic is resized to 8 percent of its original size. **Why?** *The original size of the picture is too large for the letterhead.* The following steps resize a graphic to a percent of the original.

1

- With the graphic still selected, click the Advanced Layout: Size Dialog Box Launcher (Picture Tools Format tab | Size group) to display the Size sheet in the Layout dialog box.

 Q&A What if the graphic is not selected or the Picture Tools Format tab is not on the ribbon?
Click the graphic to select it or double-click the graphic to make the Picture Tools Format tab the active tab.

2

- In the Scale area (Layout dialog box), double-click the current value in the Height box to select it.

- Type 8 in the Height box and then press the TAB key to display the same percent value in the Width box (Figure 3–17).

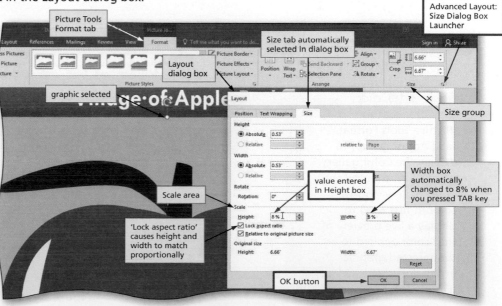

Figure 3–17

Q&A

Why did Word automatically fill in the value in the Width box?
When the 'Lock aspect ratio' check box (Layout dialog box) is selected, Word automatically maintains the size proportions of the graphic.

How do I know to use 8 percent for the resized graphic?
The larger graphic consumed too much room on the page. Try various percentages to determine the size that works best in the letterhead design.

❸

- Click the OK button to close the dialog box and resize the selected graphic.
- If necessary, scroll to display the top of the document
- Verify that the Shape Height and Shape Width boxes (Picture Tools Format tab | Size group) display 0.53". If they do not, change their values to 0.53" (Figure 3–18).

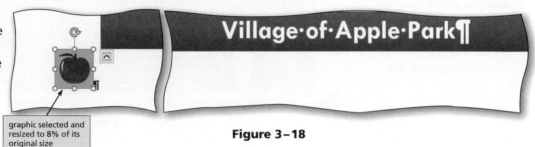

Figure 3–18

Other Ways

1. Click Layout Options button attached to graphic, click See more link in the Layout Options gallery, click Size tab (Layout dialog box), enter height and width values, click OK button

2. Right-click graphic, click 'Size and Position' on shortcut menu, enter height and width values (Layout dialog box), click OK button

To Change the Color of a Graphic

1 CREATE & FORMAT LETTERHEAD WITH GRAPHICS | 2 SPECIFY LETTER FORMATS
3 INSERT TABLE | 4 FORMAT TABLE | 5 INSERT BULLETED LIST | 6 ADDRESS ENVELOPE

In Word, you can change the color of a graphic. The apple image (graphic) currently is a bright red color. The following steps change the color of the graphic. *Why? Because the image in this project will be placed beside the rectangle shape, you prefer to use lighter colors.*

❶

- With the graphic still selected (shown in Figure 3–18), click the Color button (Picture Tools Format tab | Adjust group) to display the Color gallery.
- Point to Washout in the Color gallery (fourth color in first row) to display a live preview of that color applied to the selected graphic in the document (Figure 3–19).

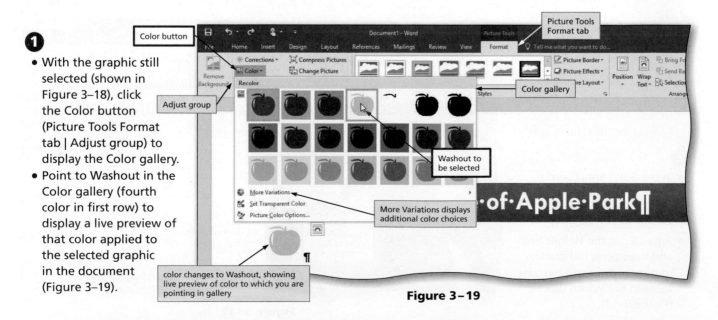

Figure 3–19

Experiment

- Point to various colors in the Color gallery and watch the color of the graphic change in the document.

2

- Click Washout in the Color gallery to change the color of the selected graphic.

Q&A How would I change a graphic back to its original colors?
With the graphic selected, you would click No Recolor, which is the upper-left color in the Color gallery.

Other Ways

1. Click Format Shape Dialog Box Launcher (Picture Tools Format tab | Picture Styles group), click Picture button (Format Picture task pane), expand Picture Color section, select desired options

2. Right-click graphic (or, if using touch, tap 'Show Context Menu' button on mini toolbar), click Format Picture on shortcut menu (or, if using touch, tap Format Object), click Picture button (Format Picture task pane), expand Picture Color section, select desired options

---

To Set a Transparent Color in a Graphic

1 CREATE & FORMAT LETTERHEAD WITH GRAPHICS | 2 SPECIFY LETTER FORMATS
3 INSERT TABLE | 4 FORMAT TABLE | 5 INSERT BULLETED LIST | 6 ADDRESS ENVELOPE

In Word, you can make one color in a graphic transparent; that is, you remove the color. You would make a color transparent if you wanted to remove part of a graphic or see text or colors behind a graphic. The following steps set the light green background around the apple in a transparent color. *Why? You prefer the light green color to be transparent.*

1

- With the graphic still selected, click the Color button (Picture Tools Format tab | Adjust group) to display the Color gallery (Figure 3–20).

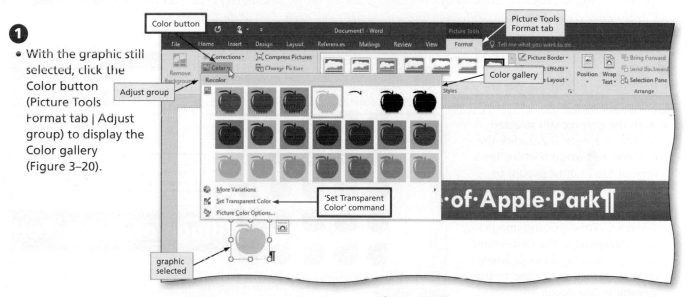

Figure 3–20

2

- Click 'Set Transparent Color' in the Color gallery to display a pen pointer in the document window.

Q&A What if I am using a touch screen?
You may need to use a stylus or mouse to perform these steps.

- Position the pen pointer in the graphic where you want to make the color transparent (Figure 3–21).

Q&A Can I make multiple colors in a graphic transparent?
No, you can make only one color transparent.

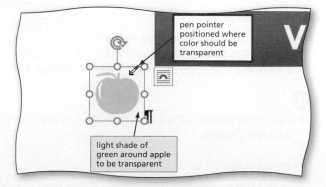

Figure 3–21

- Click the location in the graphic where you want the color to be transparent (Figure 3–22).

Q&A What if I make the wrong color transparent?
Click the Undo button on the Quick Access Toolbar, or press CTRL+Z, and then repeat these steps.

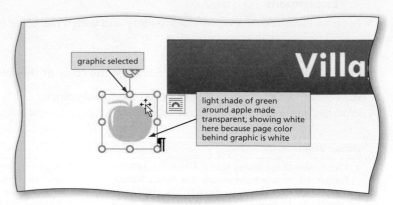

graphic selected

light shade of green around apple made transparent, showing white here because page color behind graphic is white

Figure 3–22

To Adjust the Brightness and Contrast of a Graphic

1 CREATE & FORMAT LETTERHEAD WITH GRAPHICS | 2 SPECIFY LETTER FORMATS
3 INSERT TABLE | 4 FORMAT TABLE | 5 INSERT BULLETED LIST | 6 ADDRESS ENVELOPE

In Word, you can adjust the brightness, or lightness, of a graphic and also the **contrast**, or the difference between the lightest and darkest areas of the graphic. The following steps decrease the brightness and contrast of the apple graphic, each by 20%. *Why? You want to darken the graphic slightly to increase its emphasis on the page and, at the same time, decrease the difference between the light and dark areas of the graphic.*

- If necessary, display the Picture Tools Format tab.

- With the graphic still selected (shown in Figure 3–22), click the Corrections button (Picture Tools Format tab | Adjust group) to display the Corrections gallery.

- Point to 'Brightness: -20% Contrast: -20%' (second image in second row) in the Corrections gallery to display a live preview of that correction applied to the graphic in the document (Figure 3–23).

 **Experiment**

- Point to various corrections in the Corrections gallery and watch the brightness and contrast of the graphic change in the document.

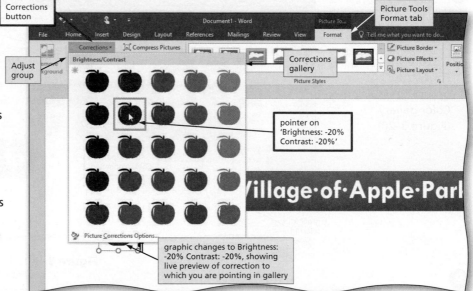

Corrections button

Picture Tools Format tab

Adjust group

Corrections gallery

pointer on 'Brightness: -20% Contrast: -20%'

graphic changes to Brightness: -20% Contrast: -20%, showing live preview of correction to which you are pointing in gallery

Figure 3–23

2

- Click 'Brightness: -20% Contrast: -20%' in the Corrections gallery to change the brightness and contrast of the selected graphic.

Other Ways

1. Click Format Shape Dialog Box Launcher (Picture Tools Format tab | Picture Styles group), click Picture button (Format Picture task pane), expand Picture Corrections section, select desired options

2. Right-click graphic (or, if using touch, tap 'Show Context Menu' button on mini toolbar), click Format Picture on shortcut menu (or, if using touch, tap Format Object on shortcut menu), click Picture button (Format Picture task pane), expand Picture Corrections section, select desired options

To Change the Border Color on a Graphic

The apple graphic currently has no border (outline). The following steps change the border color on the graphic. *Why? You would like the graphic to have a lime border so that it is in the same color family as the leaf on the apple.*

- Click the Picture Border arrow (Picture Tools Format tab | Picture Styles group) to display the Picture Border gallery.
- Point to 'Lime, Accent 1, Darker 25%' (fifth theme color in fifth row) in the Picture Border gallery to display a live preview of that border color around the picture (Figure 3–24).

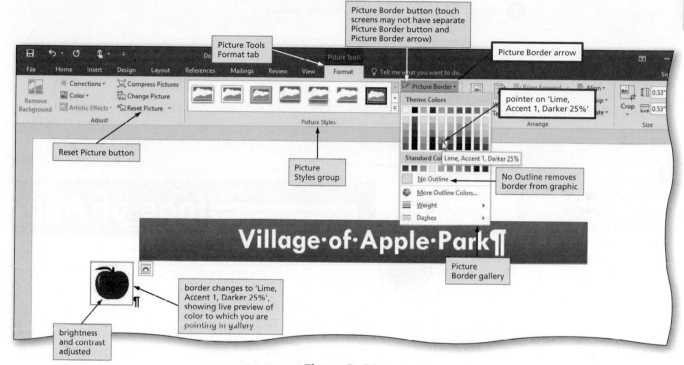

Figure 3–24

Q&A What if I click the Picture Border button by mistake?
Click the Picture Border arrow and proceed with Step 2.

Experiment

- Point to various colors in the Picture Border gallery and watch the border color on the graphic change in the document window.

- Click 'Lime, Accent 1, Darker 25%' in the Picture Border gallery to change the picture border color.

Q&A How would I remove a border from a graphic?
With the graphic selected, you would click No Outline in the Picture Border gallery.

Can I remove all formatting applied to a graphic and start over?
Yes. With the graphic selected, you would click the Reset Picture button (Picture Tools Format tab | Adjust group).

To Change an Object's Text Wrapping

The apple graphic is to be positioned to the left of the shape. By default, when you insert a picture, it is formatted as an inline graphic. Inline graphics cannot be moved to a precise location on a page. Recall that inline graphics are part of a paragraph and, thus, can be positioned according to paragraph formatting, such as centered or left-aligned. To move the graphic to the left of the shape, you format it as a floating object with In Front of Text wrapping. The following steps change a graphic's text wrapping.

1 If necessary, click the graphic to select it.

2 Click the Layout Options button attached to the graphic to display the Layout Options gallery.

3 Click 'In Front of Text' in the Layout Options gallery so that you can position the object on top of any item in the document, in this case, on top of the rectangular shape.

4 Click the Close button to close the gallery.

To Move a Graphic

1 CREATE & FORMAT LETTERHEAD WITH GRAPHICS | 2 SPECIFY LETTER FORMATS
3 INSERT TABLE | 4 FORMAT TABLE | 5 INSERT BULLETED LIST | 6 ADDRESS ENVELOPE

The following steps move a graphic. *Why? In this letterhead, the first apple graphic is positioned to the left of the shape.*

1

• Position the pointer in the graphic so that the pointer has a four-headed arrow attached to it (Figure 3–25).

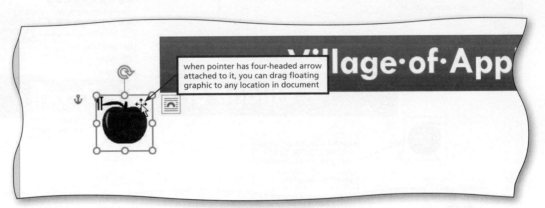

Figure 3–25

2

• Drag the graphic to the left of the shape, as shown in Figure 3–26.

Q&A

What if I moved the graphic to the wrong location?
Repeat these steps. You can drag a floating graphic to any location in a document.

Why do green lines appear on my screen as I drag a graphic?
You have alignment guides set, which help you line up graphics. To set alignment guides, click the Align Objects button (Picture Tools Format tab | Arrange group) and then click 'Use Alignment Guides'.

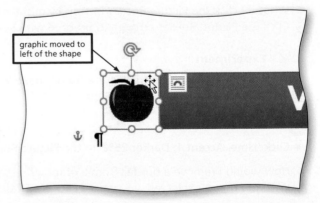

Figure 3–26

To Copy a Graphic

In this project, the same apple graphic is to be placed to the right of the shape. Instead of performing the same steps to insert and format a second identical apple graphic, you can copy the graphic to the Office Clipboard, paste the graphic from the Office Clipboard, and then move the graphic to the desired location.

You use the same steps to copy a graphic as you used in Module 2 to copy text. The following steps copy a graphic.

1 If necessary, click the graphic to select it.

2 Display the Home tab.

3 Click the Copy button, shown in Figure 3–27 (Home tab | Clipboard group), to copy the selected item to the Office Clipboard.

To Use Paste Options

1 CREATE & FORMAT LETTERHEAD WITH GRAPHICS | 2 SPECIFY LETTER FORMATS
3 INSERT TABLE | 4 FORMAT TABLE | 5 INSERT BULLETED LIST | 6 ADDRESS ENVELOPE

The following steps paste a graphic using the Paste Options gallery. *Why? Recall from Module 2 that you can specify the format of a pasted item using Paste Options.*

1

• Click the Paste arrow (Home tab | Clipboard group) to display the Paste gallery.

Q&A What if I accidentally click the Paste button?
Click the Paste Options button below the graphic pasted in the document to display a Paste Options gallery.

• Point to the 'Keep Source Formatting' button in the Paste gallery to display a live preview of that paste option (Figure 3–27).

Experiment

• Point to the two buttons in the Paste gallery and watch the appearance of the pasted graphic change.

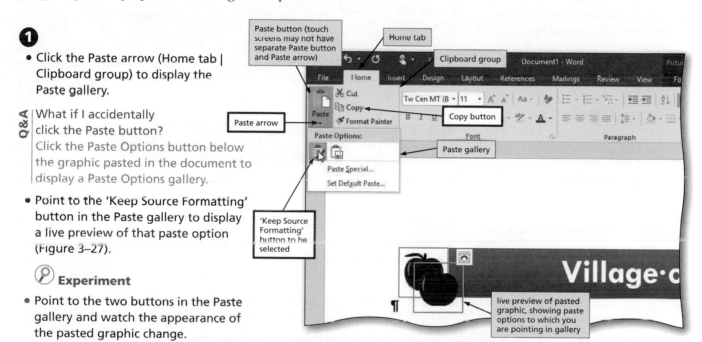

Figure 3–27

Q&A What do the buttons in the Paste gallery mean?
The 'Keep Source Formatting' button indicates the pasted graphic should have the same formats as it did in its original location. The Picture button removes some formatting from the graphic.

Why are these paste buttons different from the ones in Module 2?
The buttons that appear in the Paste gallery differ depending on the item you are pasting. Use live preview to see how the pasted object will look in the document.

2

• Click the 'Keep Source Formatting' button in the Paste gallery to paste the object using the same formatting as the original.

To Move a Graphic

The next step is to move the second apple graphic so that it is positioned to the right of the rectangle shape. The following steps move a graphic.

1 If you are using a mouse, position the pointer in the graphic so that the pointer has a four-headed arrow attached to it.

2 Drag the graphic to the location shown in Figure 3–28.

To Flip a Graphic

The following steps flip a graphic horizontally. *Why? In this letterhead, you want the leaves on the apple graphics to point toward the edge of the paper.*

- If necessary, display the Picture Tools Format tab.

- With the graphic still selected, click the Rotate Objects button (Picture Tools Format tab | Arrange group) to display the Rotate Objects gallery (Figure 3–28).

🔍 **Experiment**

- Point to the various rotate options in the Rotate Options gallery and watch the picture rotate in the document window.

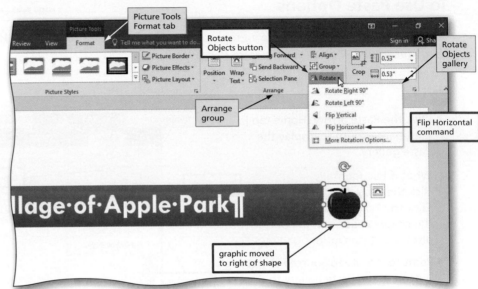

Figure 3–28

- Click Flip Horizontal in the Rotate Options gallery, so that Word flips the graphic to display its mirror image (shown in Figure 3–29).

Q&A | Can I flip a graphic vertically?
Yes, you would click Flip Vertical in the Rotate Options gallery. You also can rotate a graphic clockwise or counterclockwise by clicking 'Rotate Right 90°' and 'Rotate Left 90°', respectively, in the Rotate Options gallery.

- Save the letterhead on your hard drive, OneDrive, or other storage location using the file name, Apple Park Letterhead.

Q&A | Why should I save the letterhead at this time?
You have performed many tasks while creating this letterhead and do not want to risk losing work completed thus far.

To Format and Enter Text

The contact information for the letterhead in this project is located on the line below the shape containing the name. The following steps format and then enter the mailing address in the letterhead.

1 Position the insertion point on the line below the shape containing the name.

2 If necessary, display the Home tab. Click the Center button (Home tab | Paragraph group) to center the paragraph.

3 Click the 'Increase Font Size' button (Home tab | Font group) to increase the font size to 12 point.

4 Type `15 Center Street, Horizon, MT 33568` and then press the SPACEBAR (shown in Figure 3–29).

To Insert a Symbol from the Symbol Dialog Box

Word provides a method of inserting dots and other symbols, such as letters in the Greek alphabet and mathematical characters, that are not on the keyboard. The following steps insert a dot symbol, sometimes called a bullet symbol, in the letterhead. *Why? You want a visual separator between the mailing address and phone number in the letterhead and also between the phone number and email address.*

1

- If necessary, position the insertion point as shown in Figure 3–29.
- Display the Insert tab.
- Click the 'Insert a Symbol' button (Insert tab | Symbols group) to display the Insert a Symbol gallery (Figure 3–29).

Q&A What if the symbol I want to insert already appears in the Insert a Symbol gallery?
You can click any symbol shown in the Insert a Symbol gallery to insert it in the document.

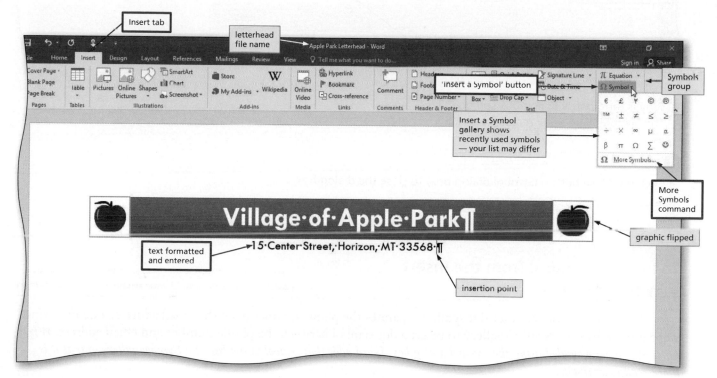

Figure 3–29

2

- Click More Symbols in the Insert a Symbol gallery to display the Symbol dialog box.
- If the font in the Font box is not (normal text), click the Font arrow (Symbol dialog box) and then scroll to and click (normal text) to select this font.
- If the subset in the Subset box is not General Punctuation, click the Subset arrow and then scroll and click General Punctuation to select this subset.
- In the list of symbols, if necessary, scroll to the dot symbol shown in Figure 3–30 and then click the symbol to select it.
- Click the Insert button (Symbol dialog box) to place the selected symbol in the document to the left of the insertion point (Figure 3–30).

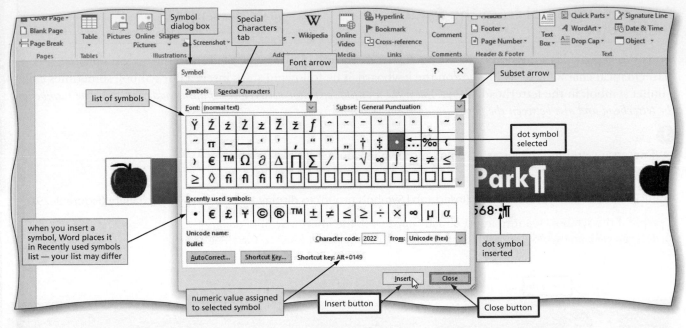

Figure 3–30

Why is the Symbol dialog box still open?
The Symbol dialog box remains open, allowing you to insert additional symbols.

 3

- Click the Close button (Symbol dialog box) to close the dialog box.

To Insert a Symbol from the Insert a Symbol Gallery

1 CREATE & FORMAT LETTERHEAD WITH GRAPHICS | 2 SPECIFY LETTER FORMATS

3 INSERT TABLE | 4 FORMAT TABLE | 5 INSERT BULLETED LIST | 6 ADDRESS ENVELOPE

In the letterhead, another dot symbol separates the phone number from the email address. The following steps use the Insert a Symbol gallery to insert a dot symbol between the phone number and email address. *Why? Once you insert a symbol using the Symbol dialog box, Word adds that symbol to the Insert a Symbol gallery so that it is more readily available.*

1

- Press the SPACEBAR, type **Phone: (870) 555-4400** and then press the SPACEBAR.

2

- Click the 'Insert a Symbol' button (Insert tab | Symbols group) to display the Insert a Symbol gallery (Figure 3–31).

Figure 3–31

Q&A | Why is the dot symbol now in the Insert a Symbol gallery?
When you insert a symbol from the Symbol dialog box, Word automatically adds the symbol to the Insert a Symbol gallery.

3

- Click the dot symbol in the Insert a Symbol gallery to insert the symbol at the location of the insertion point (shown in Figure 3–32).

To Enter Text

The following steps enter the email address in the letterhead.

1 Press the SPACEBAR.

2 Type `Email: applepark@world.com` to finish the text in the letterhead (Figure 3–32).

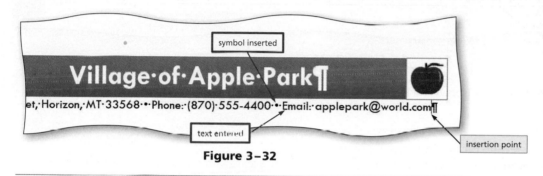

Figure 3–32

BTW
Inserting Special Characters
In addition to symbols, you can insert a variety of special characters, including dashes, hyphens, spaces, apostrophes, and quotation marks. Click the Special Characters tab in the Symbol dialog box (shown in Figure 3–30), click the desired character in the Character list, click the Insert button, and then click the Close button (Symbol dialog box).

To Bottom Border a Paragraph

1 CREATE & FORMAT LETTERHEAD WITH GRAPHICS | 2 SPECIFY LETTER FORMATS
3 INSERT TABLE | 4 FORMAT TABLE | 5 INSERT BULLETED LIST | 6 ADDRESS ENVELOPE

In Word, you can draw a solid line, called a **border**, at any edge of a paragraph. That is, borders may be added above or below a paragraph, to the left or right of a paragraph, or in any combination of these sides.

The letterhead in this project has a border that extends from the left margin to the right margin immediately below the mailing address, phone, and email address information. *Why? The horizontal line separates the letterhead from the rest of the letter.* The following steps add a bottom border to a paragraph.

1

- Display the Home tab.

- With the insertion point in the paragraph to border, click the Borders arrow (Home tab | Paragraph group) to display the Borders gallery (Figure 3–33).

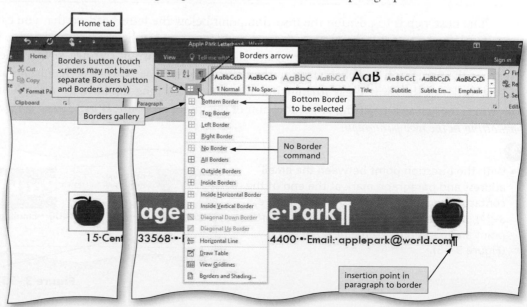

Figure 3–33

- Click Bottom Border in the Borders gallery to place a border below the paragraph containing the insertion point (Figure 3–34).

Figure 3–34

If the face of the Borders button displays the border icon I want to use, can I click the Borders button instead of using the Borders arrow?
Yes.

How would I remove an existing border from a paragraph?
If, for some reason, you wanted to remove a border from a paragraph, you would position the insertion point in the paragraph, click the Borders arrow (Home tab | Paragraph group), and then click No Border in the Borders gallery.

Other Ways

1. Click 'Borders and Shading' button (Design tab | Page Background group), click Borders tab (Borders and Shading dialog box), select desired border options, click OK button

To Clear Formatting

1 CREATE & FORMAT LETTERHEAD WITH GRAPHICS | 2 SPECIFY LETTER FORMATS
3 INSERT TABLE | 4 FORMAT TABLE | 5 INSERT BULLETED LIST | 6 ADDRESS ENVELOPE

The next step is to position the insertion point below the letterhead, so that you can type the contents of the letter. When you press the ENTER key at the end of a paragraph containing a border, Word moves the border forward to the next paragraph. The paragraph also retains all current settings, such as the center format. Instead, you want the paragraph and characters on the new line to use the Normal style: black font with no border.

Word uses the term, **clear formatting**, to refer to returning the formats to the Normal style. The following steps clear formatting at the location of the insertion point. *Why? You do not want to retain the current formatting in the new paragraph.*

- With the insertion point between the email address and paragraph mark at the end of the contact information line (as shown in Figure 3–34), press the ENTER key to move the insertion point and paragraph to the next line (Figure 3–35).

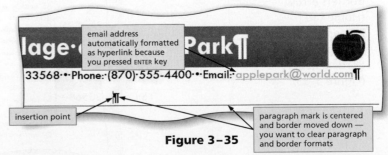

Figure 3–35

2

- Click the 'Clear All Formatting' button (Home tab | Font group) to apply the Normal style to the location of the insertion point (Figure 3–36).

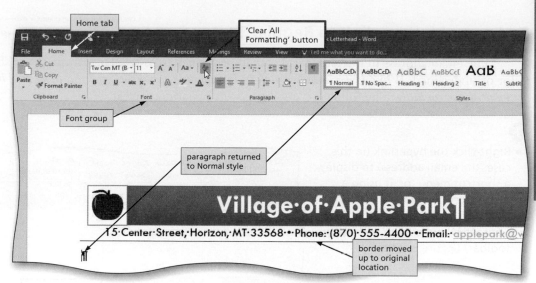

Figure 3–36

Other Ways

1. Click More button in Styles gallery (Home tab | Styles group), click Clear Formatting
2. Click Styles Dialog Box Launcher (Home tab | Styles group), click Clear All in Styles task pane
3. Select text, press CTRL+SPACEBAR, press CTRL+Q

AutoFormat As You Type

As you type text in a document, Word automatically formats some of it for you. For example, when you press the ENTER key or SPACEBAR after typing an email address or web address, Word automatically formats the address as a hyperlink, that is, in a different color and underlined. In Figure 3–35, for example, Word formatted the email address as a hyperlink because you pressed the ENTER key at the end of the line. Table 3–2 outlines commonly used AutoFormat As You Type options and their results.

Table 3–2 Commonly Used AutoFormat As You Type Options		
Typed Text	**AutoFormat As You Type Feature**	**Example**
Quotation marks or apostrophes	Changes straight quotation marks or apostrophes to curly ones	"the" becomes "the"
Text, a space, one hyphen, one or no spaces, text, space	Changes the hyphen to an en dash	ages 20-45 becomes ages 20–45
Text, two hyphens, text, space	Changes the two hyphens to an em dash	Two types--yellow and red becomes Two types—yellow and red
Web or email address followed by SPACEBAR OR ENTER key	Formats web or email address as a hyperlink	www.cengagebrain.com becomes www.cengagebrain.com
Number followed by a period, hyphen, right parenthesis, or greater than sign and then a space or tab followed by text	Creates a numbered list	1. Word 2. PowerPoint becomes 1. Word 2. PowerPoint
Asterisk, hyphen, or greater than sign and then a space or tab followed by text	Creates a bulleted list	* Home tab * Insert tab becomes • Home tab • Insert tab
Fraction and then a space or hyphen	Condenses the fraction entry so that it consumes one space instead of three	1/2 becomes ½
Ordinal and then a space or hyphen	Makes part of the ordinal a superscript	3rd becomes 3rd

To Convert a Hyperlink to Regular Text

The email address in the letterhead should be formatted as regular text; that is, it should not be a different color or underlined. *Why? Hyperlinks are useful only in online documents, and this letter will be printed instead of distributed electronically.* The following steps remove a hyperlink format.

- Right-click the hyperlink (in this case, the email address) to display a shortcut menu (or, if using a touch screen, press and hold the hyperlink and then tap the 'Show Context Menu' button on the mini toolbar) (Figure 3–37).

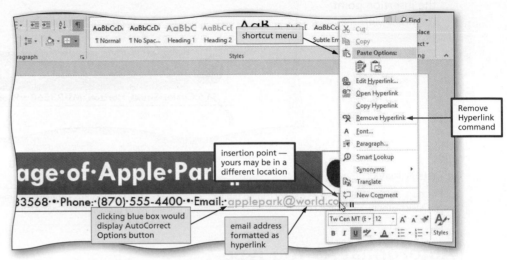

Figure 3–37

- Click Remove Hyperlink on the shortcut menu to remove the hyperlink format from the text.
- Position the insertion point on the paragraph mark below the border because you are finished with the letterhead (Figure 3–38).

Q&A Could I have used the AutoCorrect Options button instead of the Remove Hyperlink command?
Yes. Alternatively, you could have pointed to the small blue box at the beginning of the hyperlink, clicked the AutoCorrect Options button, and then clicked Undo Hyperlink on the AutoCorrect Options menu.

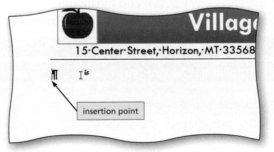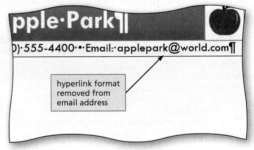

Figure 3–38

- Save the letterhead again on the same storage location with the same file name.

Other Ways

1. With insertion point in hyperlink, click 'Add a Hyperlink' button (Insert tab | Links group), click Remove Link button

---

Break Point: If you wish to take a break, this is a good place to do so. You can exit Word now. To resume at a later time, run Word, open the file called Apple Park Letterhead, and continue following the steps from this location forward.

Creating a Business Letter

With the letterhead for the business letter complete, the next task is to create the remainder of the content in the letter. The following sections use Word to create a business letter that contains a table and a bulleted list.

What should you consider when writing a business letter?
A finished business letter should look like a symmetrically framed picture with evenly spaced margins, all balanced below an attractive letterhead. The letter should be well written, properly formatted, logically organized, and use visuals where appropriate. The content of a letter should contain proper grammar, correct spelling, logically constructed sentences, flowing paragraphs, and sound ideas.

Be sure to include all essential elements, use proper spacing and formats, and determine which letter style to use.

- **Include all essential letter elements.** All business letters contain the same basic elements, including the date line, inside address, message, and signature block (shown in Figure 3–1 at the beginning of this module). If a business letter does not use a letterhead, then the top of the letter should include return address information in a heading.

- **Use proper spacing and formats for the contents of the letter below the letterhead.** Use a font that is easy to read, in a size between 8 and 12 point. Add emphasis with bold, italic, and bullets where appropriate, and use tables to present numeric information. Paragraphs should be single-spaced, with double-spacing between paragraphs.

- **Determine which letter style to use.** You can follow many different styles when creating business letters. A letter style specifies guidelines for the alignment and spacing of elements in the business letter.

If possible, keep the length of a business letter to one page. Be sure to proofread the finished letter carefully.

To Save a Document with a New File Name

The current open file has the name Apple Park Letterhead, which is the name of the organization letterhead. Because you want the letterhead file to remain intact so that you can reuse it, you save the document with a new file name. The following step saves a document with a new file name. For a detailed example of the procedure summarized below, refer to the Office and Windows module at the beginning of this book.

 Save the letter on your hard drive, OneDrive, or other storage location using a new file name, Lee Vendor Letter.

> **BTW**
> **Organizing Files and Folders**
> You should organize and store files in folders so that you easily can find the files later. For example, if you are taking an introductory technology class called CIS 101, a good practice would be to save all Word files in a Word folder in a CIS 101 folder. For a discussion of folders and detailed examples of creating folders, refer to the Office and Windows module at the beginning of this book.

To Apply a Style

1 CREATE & FORMAT LETTERHEAD WITH GRAPHICS | 2 SPECIFY LETTER FORMATS | 3 INSERT TABLE | 4 FORMAT TABLE | 5 INSERT BULLETED LIST | 6 ADDRESS ENVELOPE

Recall that the Normal style in Word places 8 points of blank space after each paragraph and inserts a vertical space equal to 1.08 lines between each line of text. You will need to modify the spacing used for the paragraphs in the business letter. *Why? Business letters should use single spacing for paragraphs and double spacing between paragraphs.*

Word has many built-in, or predefined, styles that you can use to format text. The No Spacing style, for example, defines line spacing as single and does not insert any additional blank space between lines when you press the ENTER key. To apply a style to a paragraph, you first position the insertion point in the paragraph. The following step applies the No Spacing style to a paragraph.

1

- With the insertion point positioned in the paragraph to be formatted, click No Spacing in the Styles gallery (Home tab | Styles group) to apply the selected style to the current paragraph (Figure 3–39).

Q&A

Will this style be used in the rest of the document?

Yes. The paragraph formatting, which includes the style, will carry forward to subsequent paragraphs each time you press the ENTER key.

Figure 3–39

Other Ways

1. Click Styles Dialog Box Launcher (Home tab | Styles group), click desired style in Styles task pane
2. Press CTRL+SHIFT+S, click Style Name arrow in Apply Styles task pane, click desired style in list

CONSIDER THIS

What elements should a business letter contain?

Be sure to include all essential business letter elements, properly spaced, in your letter:

- The **date line**, which consists of the month, day, and year, is positioned two to six lines below the letterhead.
- The **inside address**, placed three to eight lines below the date line, usually contains the addressee's courtesy title plus full name, job title, business affiliation, and full geographical address.
- The **salutation**, if present, begins two lines below the last line of the inside address. If you do not know the recipient's name, avoid using the salutation "To whom it may concern" — it is impersonal. Instead, use the recipient's title in the salutation, e.g., Dear Personnel Director. In a business letter, use a colon (:) at the end of the salutation; in a personal letter, use a comma.
- The body of the letter, the **message**, begins two lines below the salutation. Within the message, paragraphs are single-spaced with one blank line between paragraphs.
- Two lines below the last line of the message, the **complimentary close** is displayed. Capitalize only the first word in a complimentary close.
- Type the **signature block** at least four blank lines below the complimentary close, allowing room for the author to sign his or her name.

What are the common styles of business letters?

Three common business letter styles are the block, the modified block, and the modified semi-block. Each style specifies different alignments and indentations.

- In the block letter style, all components of the letter begin flush with the left margin.
- In the modified block letter style, the date, complimentary close, and signature block are positioned approximately one-half inch to the right of center or at the right margin. All other components of the letter begin flush with the left margin.
- In the modified semi-block letter style, the date, complimentary close, and signature block are centered, positioned approximately one-half inch to the right of center or at the right margin. The first line of each paragraph in the body of the letter is indented one-half to one inch from the left margin. All other components of the letter begin flush with the left margin.

The business letter in this project follows the modified block style.

Using Tab Stops to Align Text

A **tab stop** is a location on the horizontal ruler that tells Word where to position the insertion point when you press the TAB key on the keyboard. Word, by default, places a tab stop at every one-half inch mark on the ruler. You also can set your own custom tab stops. Tab settings are a paragraph format. Thus, each time you press the ENTER key, any custom tab stops are carried forward to the next paragraph.

To move the insertion point from one tab stop to another, press the TAB key on the keyboard. When you press the TAB key, a **tab character** formatting mark appears in the empty space between the tab stops.

When you set a custom tab stop, you specify how the text will align at a tab stop. The tab marker on the ruler reflects the alignment of the characters at the location of the tab stop. Table 3–3 shows types of tab stop alignments in Word and their corresponding tab markers.

Table 3–3 Types of Tab Stop Alignments			
Tab Stop Alignment	**Tab Marker**	**Result of Pressing TAB Key**	**Example**
Left Tab	L	Left-aligns text at the location of the tab stop	toolbar ruler
Center Tab	⊥	Centers text at the location of the tab stop	toolbar ruler
Right Tab	⅃	Right-aligns text at the location of the tab stop	toolbar ruler
Decimal Tab	⊥	Aligns text on decimal point at the location of the tab stop	15.72 223.75
Bar Tab	I	Aligns text at a bar character at the location of the tab stop	toolbar ruler

To Display the Ruler

One way to set custom tab stops is by using the horizontal ruler. Thus, the following steps display the ruler in the document window.

1 If the rulers are not showing, display the View tab.

2 Click the View Ruler check box (View tab | Show group) to place a check mark in the check box and display the horizontal and vertical rulers on the screen (shown in Figure 3–40).

To Set Custom Tab Stops

1 CREATE & FORMAT LETTERHEAD WITH GRAPHICS | 2 SPECIFY LETTER FORMATS
3 INSERT TABLE | 4 FORMAT TABLE | 5 INSERT BULLETED LIST | 6 ADDRESS ENVELOPE

The first required element of the business letter is the date line, which in this letter is positioned two lines below the letterhead. The date line contains the month, day, and year, and begins four inches from the left margin. ***Why?*** *Business letter guidelines specify to begin the date line approximately one-half inch to the right of center. Thus, you should set a custom tab stop at the 4" mark on the ruler.* The following steps set a left-aligned tab stop.

1

- With the insertion point on the paragraph mark below the border (shown in Figure 3–39), press the ENTER key so that a blank line appears above the insertion point.

- If necessary, click the tab selector at the left edge of the horizontal ruler until it displays the type of tab you wish to use, which is the Left Tab icon in this case.

- Position the pointer on the 4″ mark on the ruler, which is the location of the desired custom tab stop (Figure 3–40).

Q&A What is the purpose of the tab selector?
Before using the ruler to set a tab stop, ensure the correct tab stop icon appears in the tab selector. Each time you click the tab selector, its icon changes. The Left Tab icon is the default. For a list of the types of tab stops, see Table 3–3.

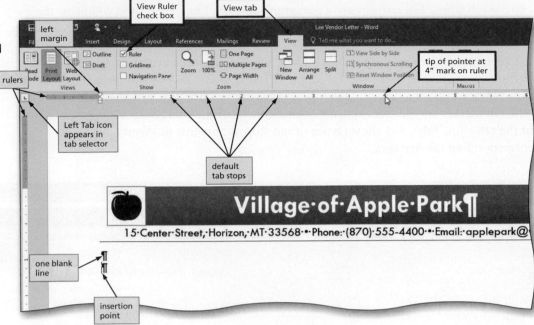

Figure 3–40

2

- Click the 4″ mark on the ruler to place a tab marker at that location (Figure 3–41).

Q&A What if I click the wrong location on the ruler?
You can move a custom tab stop by dragging the tab marker to the desired location on the ruler. Or, you can remove an existing custom tab stop by pointing to the tab marker on the ruler and then dragging the tab marker down and out of the ruler.

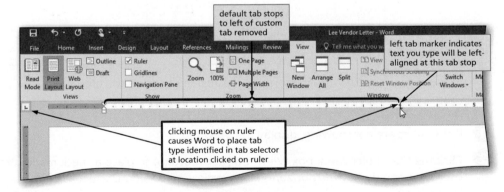

Figure 3–41

What if I am using a touch screen?
Display the Home tab, tap the Paragraph Settings Dialog Box Launcher (Home tab | Paragraph group), tap the Tabs button (Paragraph dialog box), type 4 in the Tab stop position box (Tabs dialog box), tap the Set button, and then tap the OK button to set a custom tab stop and place a corresponding tab marker on the ruler.

Other Ways

1. Click Paragraph Dialog Box Launcher (Home tab or Layout tab | Paragraph group), click Tabs button (Paragraph dialog box), type tab stop position (Tabs dialog box), click Set button, click OK button

To Insert the Current Date in a Document

The next step is to enter the current date at the 4" tab stop in the document. ***Why?*** *The date in this letter will be positioned according to the guidelines for a modified block style letter.* In Word, you can insert a computer's system date in a document. The following steps insert the current date in the letter.

1

- Press the TAB key to position the insertion point at the location of the tab stop in the current paragraph.

- Display the Insert tab.

- Click the 'Insert Date and Time' button (Insert tab | Text group) to display the Date and Time dialog box.

- Select the desired format (Date and Time dialog box), in this case October 2, 2017.

- If the Update automatically check box is selected, click the check box to remove the check mark (Figure 3–42).

Q&A Why should the Update automatically check box not be selected?

In this project, the date at the top of the letter always should show today's date (for example, October 2, 2017). If, however, you wanted the date always to change to reflect the current computer date (for example, showing the date you open or print the letter), then you would place a check mark in this check box.

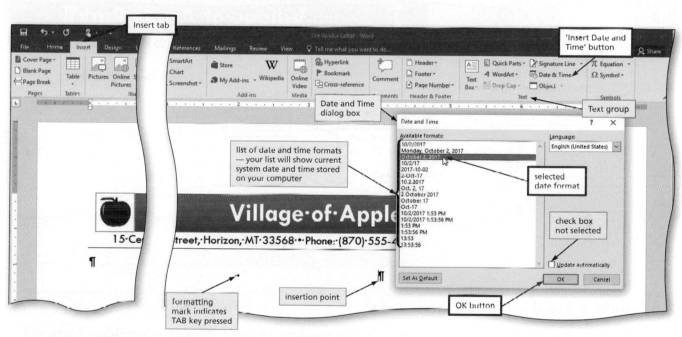

Figure 3–42

2

- Click the OK button to insert the current date at the location of the insertion point (Figure 3–43).

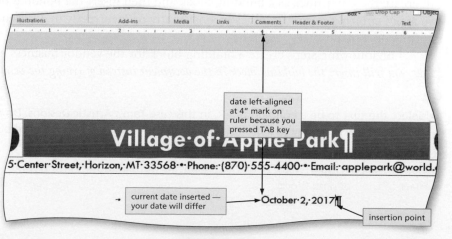

Figure 3–43

BTW
Tabs Dialog Box
You can use the Tabs dialog box to set, change the alignment of, and remove custom tab stops. To display the Tabs dialog box, click the Paragraph Settings Dialog Box Launcher (Home tab or Layout tab | Paragraph group) and then click the Tabs button (Paragraph dialog box). To set a custom tab stop, enter the desired tab position (Tabs dialog box) and then click the Set button. To change the alignment of a custom tab stop, click the tab stop position to be changed, click the new alignment, and then click the Set button. To remove an existing tab stop, click the tab stop position to be removed and then click the Clear button. To remove all tab stops, click the Clear All button in the Tabs dialog box.

To Enter the Inside Address and Salutation

The next step in composing the business letter is to type the inside address and salutation. The following steps enter this text.

1 With the insertion point at the end of the date (shown in Figure 3–43), press the ENTER key three times.

2 Type **Ms. Tamara Lee** and then press the ENTER key.

3 Type **Tam's Artistic Designs** and then press the ENTER key.

4 Type **1587 Willow Road** and then press the ENTER key.

5 Type **Juniper, MT 33522** and then press the ENTER key twice.

6 Type **Dear Ms. Lee:** to complete the inside address and salutation entries. Scroll up, if necessary (Figure 3–44).

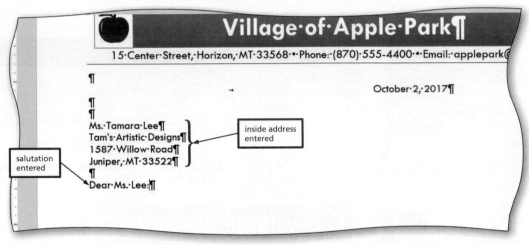

Figure 3–44

To Create a Building Block

1 CREATE & FORMAT LETTERHEAD WITH GRAPHICS | 2 SPECIFY LETTER FORMATS
3 INSERT TABLE | 4 FORMAT TABLE | 5 INSERT BULLETED LIST | 6 ADDRESS ENVELOPE

If you use the same text or graphic frequently, you can store the text or graphic as a **building block** and then insert the stored building block entry in the open document, as well as in future documents. That is, you can create the entry once as a building block and then insert the building block when you need it. In this way, you avoid entering text or graphics inconsistently or incorrectly in different locations throughout the same or multiple documents.

The following steps create a building block for the vendor business name, Tam's Artistic Designs. *Why? Later, you will insert the building block in the document instead of typing the vendor business name again.*

1
• Select the text to be a building block, in this case Tam's Artistic Designs. Do not select the paragraph mark at the end of the text because you do not want the paragraph to be part of the building block.

Q&A Why is the paragraph mark not part of the building block?
Select the paragraph mark only if you want to store paragraph formatting, such as indentation and line spacing, as part of the building block.

- Click the 'Explore Quick Parts' button (Insert tab | Text group) to display the Explore Quick Parts gallery (Figure 3–45).

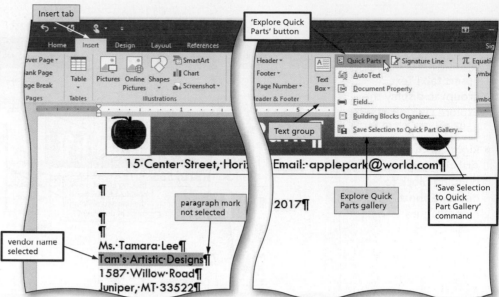

Figure 3–45

- Click 'Save Selection to Quick Part Gallery' in the Explore Quick Parts gallery to display the Create New Building Block dialog box.

- Type **tad** in the Name text box (Create New Building Block dialog box) to replace the proposed building block name (Tam's Artistic, in this case) with a shorter building block name (Figure 3–46).

- Click the OK button to store the building block entry and close the dialog box.

- If Word displays another dialog box, click the Yes button to save changes to the building blocks.

Figure 3–46

Q&A Will this building block be available in future documents?
When you exit Word, a dialog box may appear asking if you want to save changes to the building blocks. Click the Save button if you want to use the new building block in future documents.

To Modify a Building Block

1 CREATE & FORMAT LETTERHEAD WITH GRAPHICS | 2 SPECIFY LETTER FORMATS
3 INSERT TABLE | 4 FORMAT TABLE | 5 INSERT BULLETED LIST | 6 ADDRESS ENVELOPE

When you save a building block in the Explore Quick Parts gallery, the building block is displayed at the top of the Explore Quick Parts gallery. When you point to the building block in the Explore Quick Parts gallery, a ScreenTip displays the building block name. If you want to display more information when the user points to the building block, you can include a description in the ScreenTip.

The following steps modify a building block to include a description and change its category to AutoText. *Why? Because you want to reuse this text, you place it in the AutoText gallery, which also is accessible through the Explore Quick Parts gallery.*

- Click the 'Explore Quick Parts' button (Insert tab | Text group) to display the Explore Quick Parts gallery.

- Right-click the Tam's Artistic Design building block to display a shortcut menu (Figure 3–47).

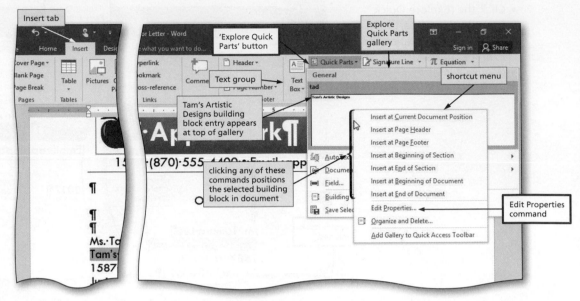

Figure 3–47

- Click Edit Properties on the shortcut menu to display the Modify Building Block dialog box, filled in with information related to the selected building block.

- Click the Gallery arrow (Modify Building Block dialog box) and then click AutoText to change the gallery in which the building block will be placed.

- Type **Event Vendor** in the Description text box (Figure 3–48).

- Click the OK button to store the building block entry and close the dialog box.

- Click the Yes button when asked if you want to redefine the building block entry.

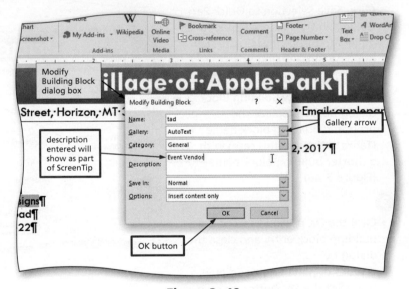

Figure 3–48

To Insert a Building Block

1 CREATE & FORMAT LETTERHEAD WITH GRAPHICS | 2 SPECIFY LETTER FORMATS | 3 INSERT TABLE | 4 FORMAT TABLE | 5 INSERT BULLETED LIST | 6 ADDRESS ENVELOPE

The vendor business name, Tam's Artistic Designs, appears in the first sentence in the body of the letter. You will type the building block name, tad, and then instruct Word to replace this building block name with the stored building block entry, Tam's Artistic Designs. The following steps insert a building block. *Why? Instead of typing the name, you will insert the stored building block.*

- Click to the right of the colon in the salutation and then press the ENTER key twice to position the insertion point one blank line below the salutation.

- Type the beginning of the first sentence as follows, entering the building block name as shown: **The park district board has approved the vendor application for your business, tad** (Figure 3–49).

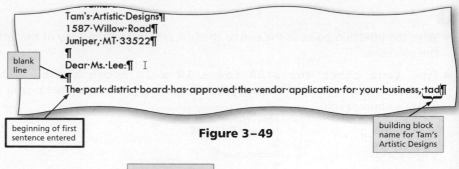

Figure 3–49

2

- Press the F3 key to instruct Word to replace the building block name (tad) with the stored building block entry (Tam's Artistic Designs).

- Press the PERIOD key (Figure 3–50).

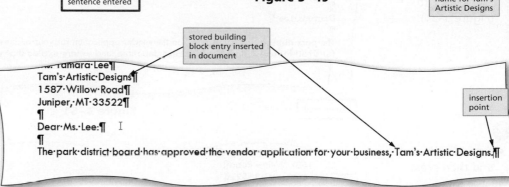

Figure 3–50

Other Ways

1. Click 'Explore Quick Parts' button (Insert tab | Text group), if necessary point to AutoText, select desired building block

2. Click 'Explore Quick Parts' button (Insert tab | Text group), click Building Blocks Organizer, select desired building block, click Insert button

---

Building Blocks versus AutoCorrect

In Module 2, you learned how to use the AutoCorrect feature, which enables you to insert and create AutoCorrect entries, similarly to how you created and inserted building blocks in this module. The difference between an AutoCorrect entry and a building block entry is that the AutoCorrect feature makes corrections for you automatically as soon as you press the SPACEBAR or type a punctuation mark, whereas you must instruct Word to insert a building block. That is, you enter the building block name and then press the F3 key, or click the Explore Quick Parts button and select the building block from one of the galleries or the Building Blocks Organizer.

To Insert a Nonbreaking Space

1 CREATE & FORMAT LETTERHEAD WITH GRAPHICS | 2 SPECIFY LETTER FORMATS
3 INSERT TABLE | 4 FORMAT TABLE | 5 INSERT BULLETED LIST | 6 ADDRESS ENVELOPE

Some compound words, such as proper nouns, dates, units of time and measure, abbreviations, and geographic destinations, should not be divided at the end of a line. These words either should fit as a unit at the end of a line or be wrapped together to the next line.

Word provides two special characters to assist with this task: the nonbreaking space and the nonbreaking hyphen. A **nonbreaking space** is a special space character that prevents two words from splitting if the first word falls at the end of a line. Similarly, a **nonbreaking hyphen** is a special type of hyphen that prevents two words separated by a hyphen from splitting at the end of a line.

The following steps insert a nonbreaking space between the two words, Fall Festival. *Why? You want these two words to appear on the same physical line.*

- With the insertion point at the end of the first sentence in the body of the letter (as shown in Figure 3–50), press the SPACEBAR.

- Type `Your check for $150 for a 10 x 20 booth has been deposited, and we are excited that you will be participating in our Fall` and then press CTRL+SHIFT+SPACEBAR to insert a nonbreaking space after the entered word (Figure 3–51).

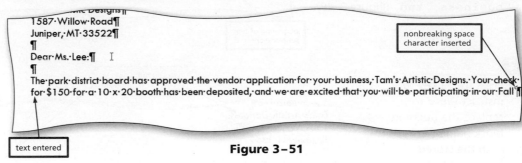

Figure 3–51

- Type `Festival` and then press PERIOD key (Figure 3–52).

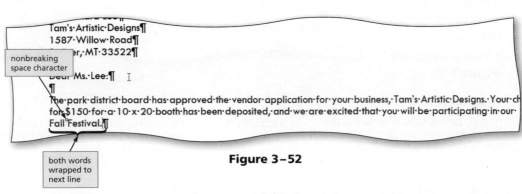

Figure 3–52

Other Ways

1. Click 'Insert a Symbol' button (Insert tab | Symbols group), click More Symbols, click Special Characters tab (Symbol dialog box), click Nonbreaking Space in Character list, click Insert button, click Close button

---

BTW
Nonbreaking Hyphen
If you wanted to insert a nonbreaking hyphen, you would press CTRL+SHIFT+HYPHEN.

To Enter Text

The next step in creating the letter is to enter the rest of the text in the first paragraph. The following steps enter this text.

1 Press the SPACEBAR.

2 Type this sentence: `The table below outlines the timetable for vendors:`

3 Press the ENTER key twice to place a blank line between paragraphs (shown in Figure 3–53).

Q&A | Why does my document wrap on different words?
Differences in wordwrap may relate to the printer connected to your computer. Thus, it is possible that the same document could wordwrap differently if associated with a different printer.

4 Save the letterhead again on the same storage location with the same file name.

Break Point: If you wish to take a break, this is a good place to do so. You can exit Word now. To resume at a later time, run Word, open the file called Lee Vendor Letter, and continue following the steps from this location forward.

Tables

The next step in composing the business letter is to place a table listing the vendor timetable (shown in Figure 3–1). A Word **table** is a collection of rows and columns. The intersection of a row and a column is called a **cell**, and cells are filled with data.

The first step in creating a table is to insert an empty table in the document. When inserting a table, you must specify the total number of rows and columns required, which is called the **dimension** of the table. The table in this project has three columns. You often do not know the total number of rows in a table. Thus, many Word users create one row initially and then add more rows as needed. In Word, the first number in a dimension is the number of columns, and the second is the number of rows. For example, in Word, a 3 × 1 (pronounced "three by one") table consists of three columns and one row.

To Insert an Empty Table

1 CREATE & FORMAT LETTERHEAD WITH GRAPHICS | 2 SPECIFY LETTER FORMATS
3 INSERT TABLE | 4 FORMAT TABLE | 5 INSERT BULLETED LIST | 6 ADDRESS ENVELOPE

The next step is to insert an empty table in the letter. The following steps insert a table with three columns and one row at the location of the insertion point. *Why? The first column will identify the activity, the second will identify the event dates, and the third will identify the activity times. You will start with one row and add them as needed.*

1

- Scroll the document so that you will be able to see the table in the document window.
- Display the Insert tab.
- With the insertion point positioned as shown in Figure 3–53, click the 'Add a Table' button (Insert tab | Tables group) to display the Add a Table gallery (Figure 3–53).

 Experiment

- Point to various cells on the grid to see a preview of various table dimensions in the document window.

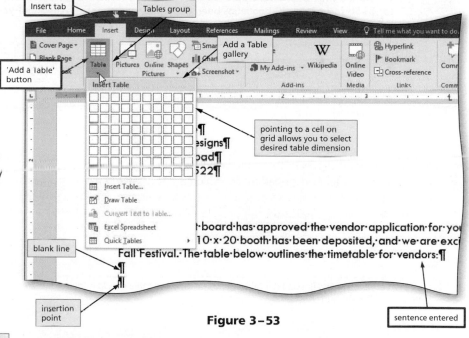

Figure 3–53

2

- Position the pointer on the cell in the first row and third column of the grid to preview the desired table dimension in the document (Figure 3–54).

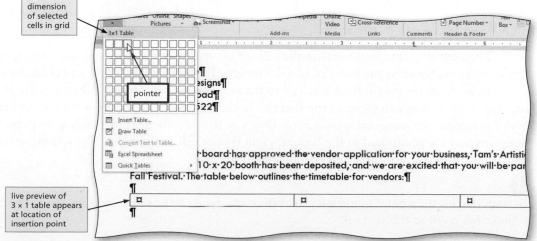

Figure 3–54

- Click the cell in the first row and third column of the grid to insert an empty table with one row and three columns in the document.

- If necessary, scroll the document so that the table is visible (Figure 3–55).

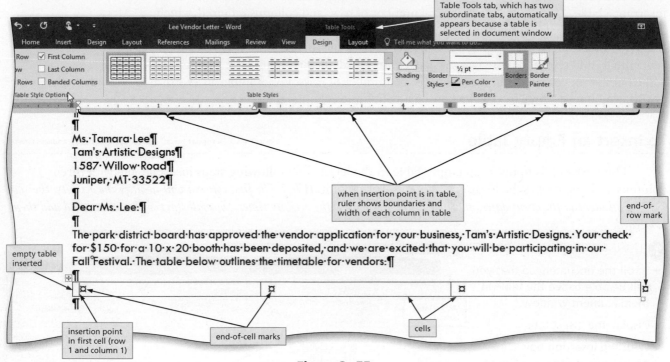

Figure 3–55

◁ What are the small circles in the table cells?
Q&A Each table cell has an **end-of-cell mark**, which is a formatting mark that assists you with selecting and formatting cells. Similarly, each row has an **end-of-row mark**, which you can use to add columns to the right of a table. Recall that formatting marks do not print on a hard copy. The end-of-cell marks currently are left-aligned, that is, positioned at the left edge of each cell.

Other Ways

1. Click 'Add a Table' button (Insert tab | Tables group), click Insert Table in Add a Table gallery, enter number of columns and rows (Insert Table dialog box), click OK button

To Enter Data in a Table

1 CREATE & FORMAT LETTERHEAD WITH GRAPHICS | 2 SPECIFY LETTER FORMATS
3 INSERT TABLE | 4 FORMAT TABLE | 5 INSERT BULLETED LIST | 6 ADDRESS ENVELOPE

The next step is to enter data in the cells of the empty table. The data you enter in a cell wordwraps just as text wordwraps between the margins of a document. To place data in a cell, you click the cell and then type.

To advance rightward from one cell to the next, press the TAB key. When you are at the rightmost cell in a row, press the TAB key to move to the first cell in the next row; do not press the ENTER key. *Why? The ENTER key is used to begin a new paragraph within a cell.* One way to add new rows to a table is to press the TAB key when the insertion point is positioned in the bottom-right corner cell of the table. The following step enters data in the first row of the table and then inserts a blank second row.

- With the insertion point in the left cell of the table, type **Activity** and then press the TAB key to advance the insertion point to the next cell.

- Type **Event Dates** and then press the TAB key to advance the insertion point to the next cell.
- Type **Times** and then press the TAB key to add a second row at the end of the table and position the insertion point in the first column of the new row (Figure 3–56).

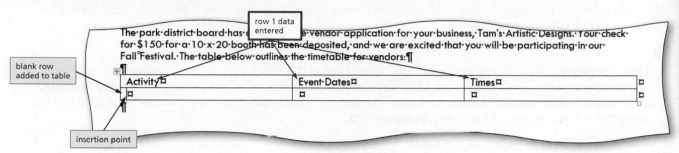

Figure 3–56

Q&A | How do I edit cell contents if I make a mistake?
Click in the cell and then correct the entry.

To Enter More Data in a Table

The following steps enter the remaining data in the table.

1 Type **Booth Setup** and then press the TAB key to advance the insertion point to the next cell. Type **Friday, October 27** and then press the TAB key to advance the insertion point to the next cell. Type **5:00 to 9:00 p.m.** and then press the TAB key to add a row at the end of the table and position the insertion point in the first column of the new row.

2 In the third row, type **Booth Sales** in the first column, **Saturday, October 28** in the second column, and **9:00 a.m. to 6:00 p.m.** in the third column. Press the TAB key to position the insertion point in the first column of a new row.

3 In the fourth row, type **Booth Sales** in the first column, **Sunday, October 29** in the second column, and **9:00 a.m. to 3:00 p.m.** in the third column. Press the TAB key.

4 In the fifth row, type **Booth Takedown** in the first column, **Sunday, October 29** in the second column, and **3:00 to 7:00 p.m.** in the third column (Figure 3–57).

BTW

Tables
For simple tables, such as the one just created, Word users often select the table dimension in the Add a Table gallery to create the table. For a more complex table, such as one with a varying number of columns per row, Word has a Draw Table feature that allows users to draw a table in the document using a pencil pointer. To use this feature, click the 'Add a Table' button (Insert tab | Tables group) and then click Draw Table on the Add a Table menu.

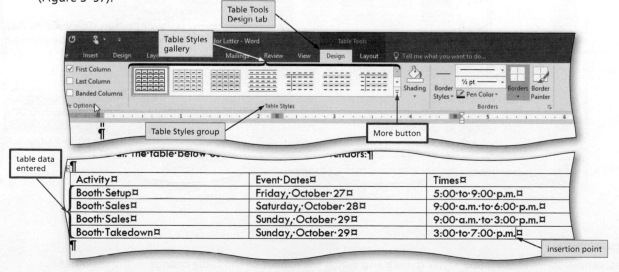

Figure 3–57

To Apply a Table Style

Word provides a gallery of more than 90 table styles, which include a variety of colors and shading. ***Why?*** *Table styles allow you to change the basic table format to a more visually appealing style.* The following steps apply a table style to the table in the letter.

- If the First Column check box in the Table Style Options group (Table Tools Design tab) contains a check mark, click the check box to remove the check mark because you do not want the first column in the table formatted differently from the rest of the table. Be sure the remaining check marks match those in the Table Style Options group (Table Tools Design tab) as shown in Figure 3–58.

Q&A What if the Table Tools Design tab no longer is the active tab?
Click in the table and then display the Table Tools Design tab.

What do the options in the Table Style Options group mean?
When you apply table styles, if you want the top row of the table (header row), a row containing totals (total row), first column, or last column to be formatted differently, select those check boxes. If you want the rows or columns to alternate with colors, select Banded Rows or Banded Columns, respectively.

- With the insertion point in the table, click the More button in the Table Styles gallery (Table Tools Design tab | Table Styles group), shown in Figure 3–57, to expand the gallery.

- Scroll and then point to 'Grid Table 6 Colorful - Accent 3' in the Table Styles gallery to display a live preview of that style applied to the table in the document (Figure 3–58).

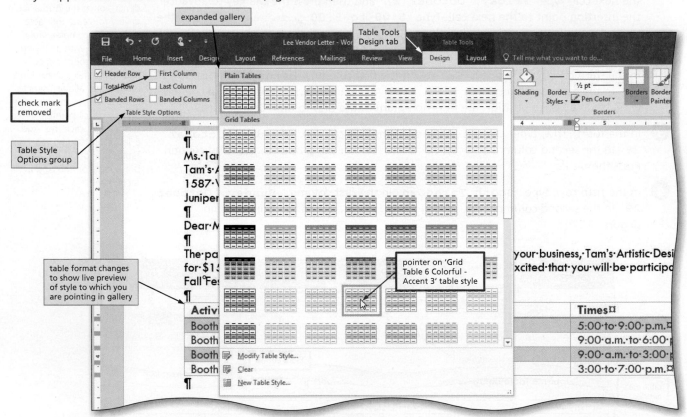

Figure 3–58

Experiment

- Point to various styles in the Table Styles gallery and watch the format of the table change in the document window.

3

- Click 'Grid Table 6 Colorful - Accent 3' in the Table Styles gallery to apply the selected style to the table. Scroll up, if necessary (Figure 3–59).

🔍 **Experiment**

- Select and remove check marks from various check boxes in the Table Style Options group and watch the format of the table change in the document window. When finished experimenting, be sure the check marks match those shown in Figure 3–58.

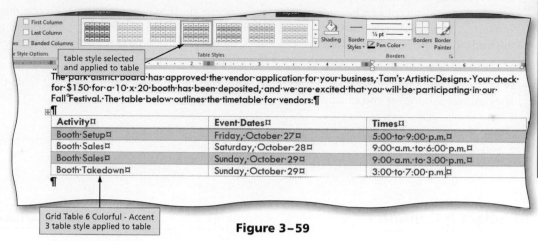

Figure 3–59

To Resize Table Columns to Fit Table Contents

1 CREATE & FORMAT LETTERHEAD WITH GRAPHICS | 2 SPECIFY LETTER FORMATS
3 INSERT TABLE | 4 FORMAT TABLE | 5 INSERT BULLETED LIST | 6 ADDRESS ENVELOPE

The table in this project currently extends from the left margin to the right margin of the document. The following steps instruct Word to fit the width of the columns to the contents of the table automatically. *Why? You want each column to be only as wide as the longest entry in the table. That is, the first column must be wide enough to accommodate the words, Booth Takedown, and the second column should be only as wide as the words, Saturday, October 28, and so on.*

1

- With the insertion point in the table, display the Table Tools Layout tab.

- Click the AutoFit button (Table Tools Layout tab | Cell Size group) to display the AutoFit menu (Figure 3–60).

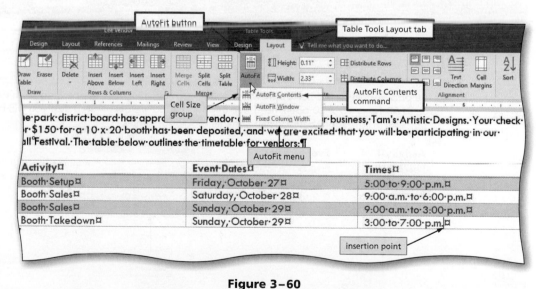

Figure 3–60

2

- Click AutoFit Contents on the AutoFit menu, so that Word automatically adjusts the widths of the columns based on the text in the table (Figure 3–61).

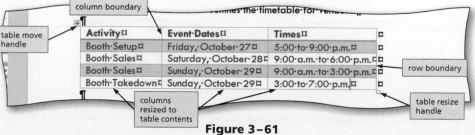

Figure 3–61

Q&A

Can I resize columns manually?

Yes, you can drag a **column boundary**, the border to the right of a column, until the column is the desired width. Similarly, you can resize a row by dragging the **row boundary**, the border at the bottom of a row, until the row is the desired height. You also can resize the entire table by dragging the **table resize handle**, which is a small square that appears when you point to a corner of the table.

What causes the table move handle and table resize handle to appear and disappear from the table?

They appear whenever you position the pointer in the table.

Other Ways

1. Double-click column boundary

To Select a Column

1 CREATE & FORMAT LETTERHEAD WITH GRAPHICS | 2 SPECIFY LETTER FORMATS
3 INSERT TABLE | 4 FORMAT TABLE | 5 INSERT BULLETED LIST | 6 ADDRESS ENVELOPE

The next task is to change the alignment of the data in cells in the third column of the table. To do this, you first must select the column. *Why? If you want to format the contents of a single cell, simply position the insertion point in the cell. To format a series of cells, you first must select them.* The following step selects a column.

- Position the pointer at the boundary above the column to be selected, the third column in this case, so that the pointer changes to a downward pointing arrow and then click to select the column (Figure 3–62).

Q&A

What if I am using a touch screen?

Position the insertion point in the third column, tap the Select Table button (Table Tools Layout tab | Table group), and then tap Select Column on the Select Table menu.

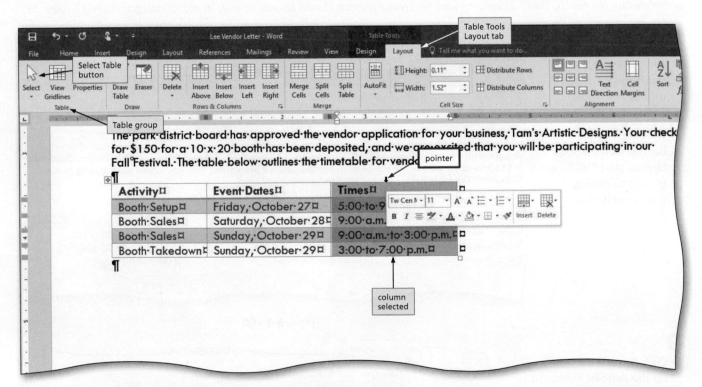

Figure 3–62

Other Ways

1. Click Select Table button (Table Tools Layout tab | Table group), click Select Column in Select Table gallery

Selecting Table Contents

When working with tables, you may need to select the contents of cells, rows, columns, or the entire table. Table 3–4 identifies ways to select various items in a table.

Table 3–4 Selecting Items in a Table	
Item to Select	**Action**
Cell	Point to left edge of cell and then click when the pointer changes to a small solid upward angled pointing arrow. Or Position insertion point in cell, click Select Table button (Table Tools Layout tab | Table group), and then click Select Cell on the Select Table menu.
Column	Point to border at top of column and then click when the pointer changes to a small solid downward-pointing arrow. Or Position insertion point in column, click Select Table button (Table Tools Layout tab | Table group), and then click Select Column on the Select Table menu.
Row	Point to the left of the row and then click when pointer changes to a right-pointing block arrow. Or Position insertion point in row, click Select Table button (Table Tools Layout tab | Table group), and then click Select Row on the Select Table menu.
Multiple cells, rows, or columns adjacent to one another	Drag through cells, rows, or columns.
Multiple cells, rows, or columns not adjacent to one another	Select first cell, row, or column (as described above) and then hold down CTRL key while selecting next cell, row, or column.
Next cell	Press TAB key.
Previous cell	Press SHIFT+TAB
Table	Point somewhere in table and then click table move handle that appears in upper-left corner of table (shown in Figure 3-63). Or Position insertion point in table, click Select Table button (Table Tools Layout tab | Table group), and then click Select Table on the Select Table menu.

BTW

Word Help
At any time while using Word, you can find answers to questions and display information about various topics through Word Help. Used properly, this form of assistance can increase your productivity and reduce your frustrations by minimizing the time you spend learning how to use Word. For instructions about Word Help and exercises that will help you gain confidence in using it, read the Office and Windows module at the beginning of this book.

To Align Data in Cells

1 CREATE & FORMAT LETTERHEAD WITH GRAPHICS | 2 SPECIFY LETTER FORMATS
3 INSERT TABLE | 4 FORMAT TABLE | 5 INSERT BULLETED LIST | 6 ADDRESS ENVELOPE

The next step is to change the alignment of the data in cells in the third column of the table. In addition to aligning text horizontally in a cell (left, center, or right), you can align it vertically within a cell (top, center, bottom). When the height of the cell is close to the same height as the text, however, differences in vertical alignment are not readily apparent, which is the case for this table. The following step centers data in cells. *Why?* *The column containing the times would look better if its contents are centered.*

1

- With the cells (column) selected, as shown in Figure 3–62, click the desired alignment, in this case the 'Align Top Center' button (Table Tools Layout tab | Alignment group) to center the contents of the selected cells (Figure 3–63).

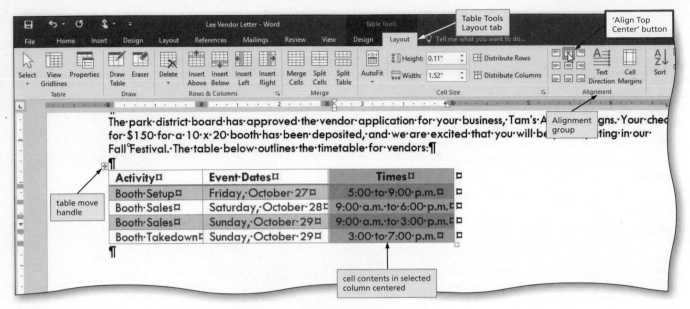

Figure 3–63

To Center a Table

1 CREATE & FORMAT LETTERHEAD WITH GRAPHICS | 2 SPECIFY LETTER FORMATS
3 INSERT TABLE | 4 FORMAT TABLE | 5 INSERT BULLETED LIST | 6 ADDRESS ENVELOPE

When you first create a table, it is left-aligned; that is, it is flush with the left margin. In this letter, the entire table should be centered between the margins of the page. To center a table, you first select the entire table. The following steps select and center a table using the mini toolbar. *Why? Recall that you can use buttons and boxes on the mini toolbar instead of those on the ribbon.*

1

- Position the pointer in the table so that the table move handle appears (shown in Figure 3–63).

Q&A What if the table move handle does not appear?
You also can select a table by clicking the Select Table button (Table Tools Layout tab | Table group) and then clicking Select Table on the menu.

2

- Click the table move handle to select the entire table (Figure 3–64).

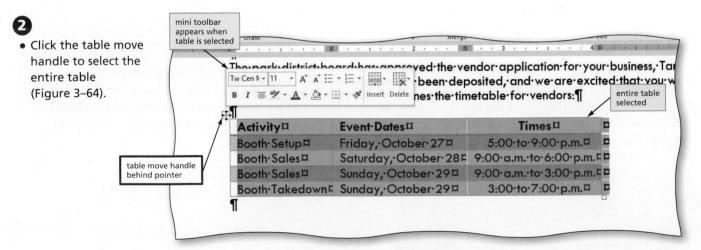

Figure 3–64

What if I am using a touch screen?
Tap the Select Table button (Table Tools Layout tab | Table group) and then tap Select Table on the Select Table menu to select the table.

3

- Click the Center button on the mini toolbar to center the selected table between the left and right page margins (Figure 3–65).

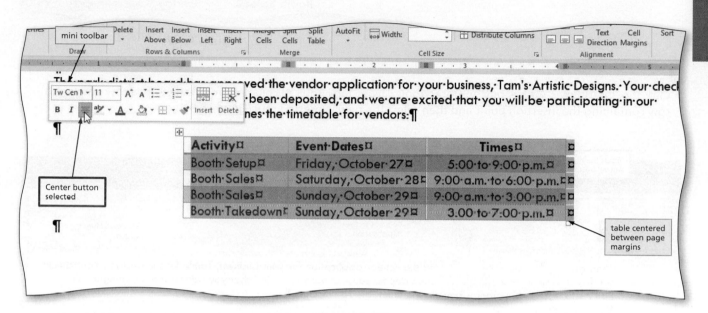

Figure 3–65

Could I have clicked the Center button on the Home tab?
Yes. If the command you want to use is not on the currently displayed tab on the ribbon and it is available on the mini toolbar, use the mini toolbar instead of switching to a different tab. This technique minimizes mouse movement.

What if I am using a touch screen?
Display the Home tab and then tap the Center button (Home tab | Paragraph group) to center the table.

To Insert a Row in a Table

1 CREATE & FORMAT LETTERHEAD WITH GRAPHICS | 2 SPECIFY LETTER FORMATS
3 INSERT TABLE | 4 FORMAT TABLE | 5 INSERT BULLETED LIST | 6 ADDRESS ENVELOPE

The next step is to insert a row at the top of the table. *Why? You want to place a title on the table.* As discussed earlier, you can insert a row at the end of a table by positioning the insertion point in the bottom-right corner cell and then pressing the TAB key. You cannot use the TAB key to insert a row at the beginning or middle of a table. Instead, you use the 'Insert Rows Above' or 'Insert Rows Below' command (Table Tools Layout tab | Rows & Columns group) or the Insert Control (shown in Figure 3–70). The following steps insert a row at the top of a table.

- Position the insertion point somewhere in the first row of the table because you want to insert a row above this row (Figure 3–66).

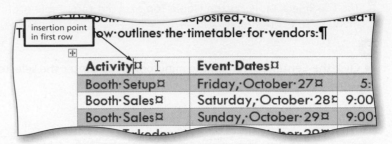

Figure 3–66

- Click the 'Insert Rows Above' button (Table Tools Layout tab | Rows & Columns group) to insert a row above the row containing the insertion point and then select the newly inserted row (Figure 3–67).

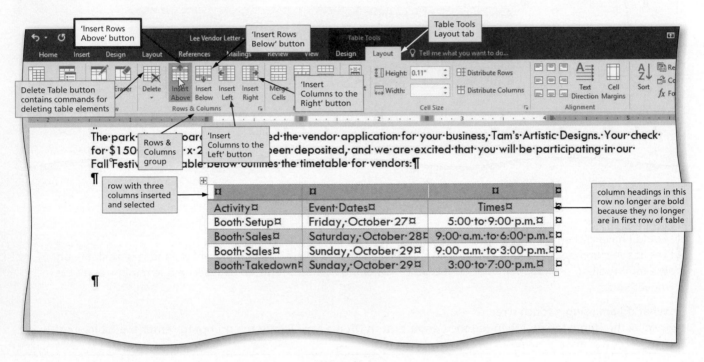

Figure 3–67

Do I have to insert rows above the row containing the insertion point?

No. You can insert below the row containing the insertion point by clicking the 'Insert Rows Below' button (Table Tools Layout tab | Rows & Columns group).

Why did the colors in the second row change?

The table style specifies to format the header row differently, which is the first row.

Other Ways

1. Point to the left of the table and click the desired Insert Control

2. Right-click row, point to Insert on shortcut menu (or, if using touch, tap Insert Table button on mini toolbar), click desired option on Insert submenu

TO INSERT A COLUMN IN A TABLE

If you wanted to insert a column in a table, instead of inserting rows, you would perform the following steps.

1. Point above the table and then click the desired Insert Control.

or

1. Position the insertion point in the column to the left or right of where you want to insert the column.
2. Click the 'Insert Columns to the Left' button (Table Tools Layout tab | Rows & Columns group) to insert a column to the left of the current column, or click the 'Insert Columns to the Right' button (Table Tools Layout tab | Rows & Columns group) to insert a column to the right of the current column.

or

1. Right-click the table, point to Insert on the shortcut menu (or, if using touch, tap Insert Table button on the mini toolbar), and then click 'Insert Columns to the Left' or 'Insert Columns to the Right' on the Insert submenu (or, if using touch, tap Insert Left or Insert Right).

BTW

Resizing Table Columns and Rows
To change the width of a column or height of a row to an exact measurement, hold down the ALT key while dragging markers on the ruler. Or, enter values in the 'Table Column Width' or 'Table Row Height' boxes (Table Tools Layout tab | Cell Size group).

To Merge Cells

1 CREATE & FORMAT LETTERHEAD WITH GRAPHICS | 2 SPECIFY LETTER FORMATS
3 INSERT TABLE | 4 FORMAT TABLE | 5 INSERT BULLETED LIST | 6 ADDRESS ENVELOPE

The row just inserted has one cell for each column, in this case, three cells (shown in Figure 3–67). The top row of the table, however, is to be a single cell that spans all rows. *Why?* *The top row contains the table title, which should be centered above the columns of the table.* Thus, the following steps merge the three cells into a single cell.

- With the cells to merge selected (as shown in Figure 3–67), click the Merge Cells button (Table Tools Layout tab | Merge group) to merge the selected cells into a single cell (Figure 3–68).

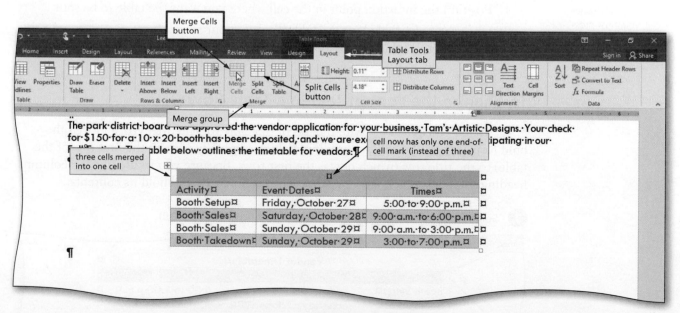

Figure 3–68

2

- Position the insertion point in the first row and then type **Vendor Timetable** as the table title (Figure 3–69).

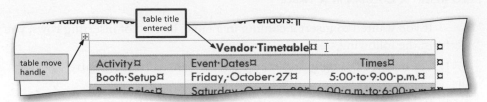

Figure 3–69

Other Ways

1. Right-click selected cells (or, if using touch, tap 'Show Context Menu' button on mini toolbar), click Merge Cells on shortcut menu

BTW
Moving Tables
If you wanted to move a table to a new location, you would point to the upper-left corner of the table until the table move handle appears (shown in Figure 3–69), point to the table move handle, and then drag it to move the entire table to a new location.

To Split Table Cells

Instead of merging multiple cells into a single cell, sometimes you want to split a single cell into multiple cells. If you wanted to split cells, you would perform the following steps.

1. Position the insertion point in the cell to split.
2. Click the Split Cells button (Table Tools Layout tab | Merge group) (or, if using touch, tap 'Show Context Menu' button on mini toolbar), or right-click the cell and then click Split Cells on the shortcut menu, to display the Split Cells dialog box.
3. Enter the number of columns and rows into which you want the cell split (Split Cells dialog box).
4. Click the OK button.

BTW
Tab Character in Tables
In a table, the TAB key advances the insertion point from one cell to the next. To insert a tab character in a cell, you must press CTRL+TAB.

To Split a Table

Instead of splitting table cells into multiple cells, sometimes you want to split a single table into multiple cells. If you wanted to split a table, you would perform the following steps.

1. Position the insertion point in the cell where you want the table to be split.
2. Click the Split Table button (Table Tools Layout tab | Merge group) to split the table into two tables at the location of the insertion point.

To Change the Font of Text in a Table Row

When you added a row to the top of the table for the title, Word moved the bold format from the column headings (which originally were in the first row of the table) to the title row (which now is the first row). Because you would like the columns headings bold also, the following steps select a table row and bold its contents.

1 Select the row containing the column headings (Figure 3–70).

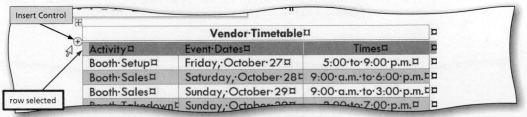

Figure 3–70

2 With the text selected, click the Bold button (Home tab | Font group) to bold the selected text.

Q&A What is the symbol that appeared to the left of the table?
When you select a row or column in a table, Word displays an Insert Control. You can click the **Insert Control** to add a row or column to the table at that location.

Deleting Table Data

If you want to delete row(s) or delete column(s) from a table, position the insertion point in the row(s) or column(s) to delete, click the Delete Table button (Table Tools Layout tab | Rows & Columns group), and then click Delete Rows or Delete Columns on the Delete Table menu. Or, select the row or column to delete, right-click the selection, and then click Delete Rows or Delete Columns on the mini toolbar or shortcut menu.

To delete the contents of a cell, select the cell contents and then press the DELETE or BACKSPACE key. You also can drag and drop or cut and paste the contents of cells. To delete an entire table, select the table, click the Delete Table button (Table Tools Layout tab | Rows & Columns group), and then click Delete Table on the Delete Table menu. To delete the contents of a table and leave an empty table, you would select the table and then press the DELETE key.

To Add More Text

The table now is complete. The next step is to enter text below the table. The following steps enter text.

1 Position the insertion point on the paragraph mark below the table and then press the ENTER key.

2 Type **Please note the following vendor guidelines:** and then press the ENTER key (shown in Figure 3–71).

BTW

AutoFormat Options
Before you can use them, AutoFormat options must be enabled. To check if an AutoFormat option is enabled, click File on the ribbon to open the Backstage view, click the Options tab in the Backstage view, click Proofing in the left pane (Word Options dialog box), click the AutoCorrect Options button, click the AutoFormat As You Type tab, select the appropriate check boxes, and then click the OK button in each open dialog box.

To Bullet a List as You Type

1 CREATE & FORMAT LETTERHEAD WITH GRAPHICS | 2 SPECIFY LETTER FORMATS
3 INSERT TABLE | 4 FORMAT TABLE | 5 INSERT BULLETED LIST | 6 ADDRESS ENVELOPE

In Module 1, you learned how to apply bullets to existing paragraphs. If you know before you type that a list should be bulleted, you can use Word's AutoFormat As You Type feature to bullet the paragraphs as you type them (see Table 3–2 shown earlier in this module). *Why? The AutoFormat As You Type feature saves you time because it applies formats automatically.* The following steps add bullets to a list as you type.

1
- Press the ASTERISK key (*) as the first character on the line (Figure 3–71).

2
- Press the SPACEBAR to convert the asterisk to a bullet character.

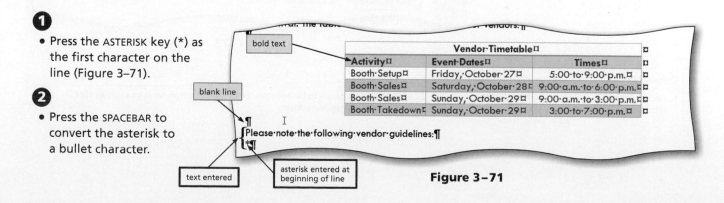

Figure 3–71

What if I did not want the asterisk converted to a bullet character?
You could undo the AutoFormat by clicking the Undo button; pressing CTRL+Z; clicking the AutoCorrect Options button that appears to the left of the bullet character as soon as you press the SPACEBAR and then clicking Undo Automatic Bullets on the AutoCorrect Options menu; or clicking the Bullets button (Home tab | Paragraph group).

3

- Type **Vendors must bring their own tables and chairs.** as the first bulleted item.
- Press the ENTER key to place another bullet character at the beginning of the next line (Figure 3–72).

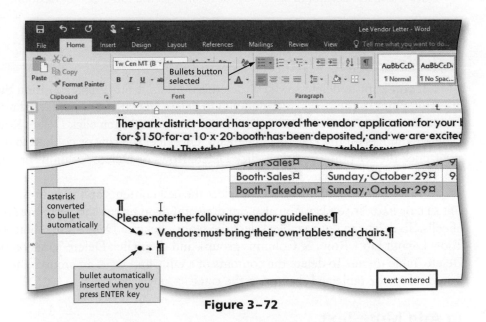

Figure 3–72

4

- Type **Vendors must supply their own electrical cords.** and then press the ENTER key.
- Type **Vendors shall comply with fire, safety, and health regulations.** and then press the ENTER key.
- Press the ENTER key to turn off automatic bullets as you type (Figure 3–73).

Why did automatic bullets stop?
When you press the ENTER key without entering any text after the automatic bullet character, Word turns off the automatic bullets feature.

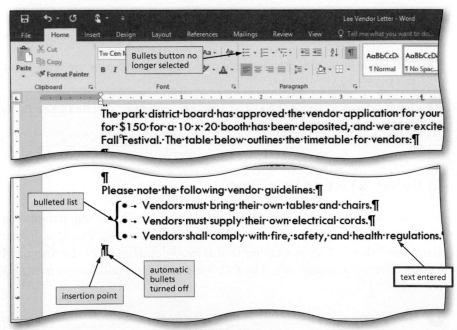

Figure 3–73

Other Ways

1. Click Bullets arrow (Home tab | Paragraph group), click desired bullet style
2. Right-click paragraph to be bulleted, click Bullets button on mini toolbar, click desired bullet style, if necessary

To Enter More Text and then Save and Print the Letter

The following steps enter the remainder of text in the letter.

1 With the insertion point positioned on the paragraph below the bulleted list, press the ENTER key and then type the paragraph shown in Figure 3–74, making certain you use the building block name, tad, to insert the organization name.

2 Press the ENTER key twice. Press the TAB key to position the insertion point at the tab stop set at the 4" mark on the ruler. Type **Sincerely,** and then press the ENTER key four times.

3 Press the TAB key to position the insertion point at the tab stop set at the 4" mark on the ruler. Type **Camden Ackerman** and then press the ENTER key.

If requested by your instructor, enter your name instead of the name stated above.

4 Press the TAB key to position the insertion point at the tab stop set at the 4" mark on the ruler. Type **Park District Events Coordinator** to finish the letter. Scroll up, if necessary (Figure 3–74).

5 Save the letter again on the same storage location with the same file name.

6 If requested by your instructor, print the letter.

BTW

Conserving Ink and Toner

If you want to conserve ink or toner, you can instruct Word to print draft quality documents by clicking File on the ribbon to open the Backstage view, clicking the Options tab in the Backstage view to display the Word Options dialog box, clicking Advanced in the left pane (Word Options dialog box), scrolling to the Print area in the right pane, placing a check mark in the 'Use draft quality' check box, and then clicking the OK button. Then, use the Backstage view to print the document as usual.

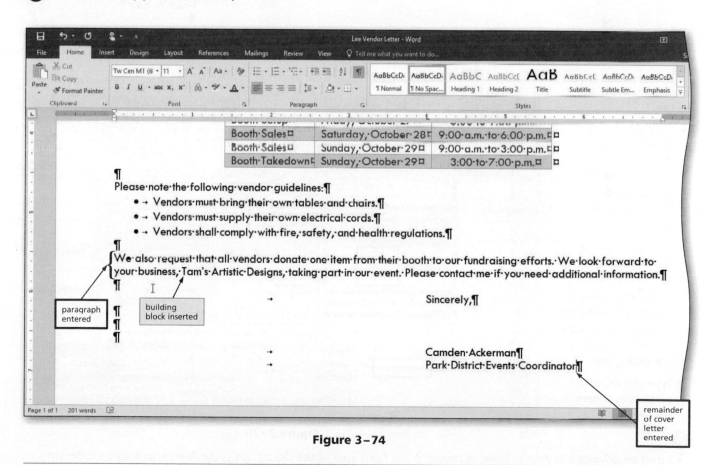

Figure 3–74

Addressing and Printing Envelopes and Mailing Labels

With Word, you can print mailing address information on an envelope or on a mailing label. Computer-printed addresses look more professional than handwritten ones.

To Address and Print an Envelope

1 CREATE & FORMAT LETTERHEAD WITH GRAPHICS | 2 SPECIFY LETTER FORMATS

3 INSERT TABLE | 4 FORMAT TABLE | 5 INSERT BULLETED LIST | **6 ADDRESS ENVELOPE**

The following steps address and print an envelope. If you are in a lab environment, check with your instructor before performing these steps. *Why? Some printers may not accommodate printing envelopes; others may stop printing until an envelope is inserted.*

- Scroll through the letter to display the inside address in the document window.
- Drag through the inside address to select it (Figure 3–75).

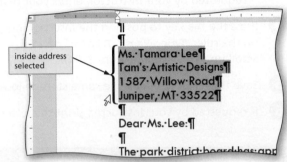

Figure 3–75

- Display the Mailings tab.
- Click the Create Envelopes button (Mailings tab | Create group) to display the Envelopes and Labels dialog box.
- If necessary, click the Envelopes tab (Envelopes and Labels dialog box), which automatically displays the selected delivery address in the dialog box.
- Type the return address as shown in Figure 3–76.

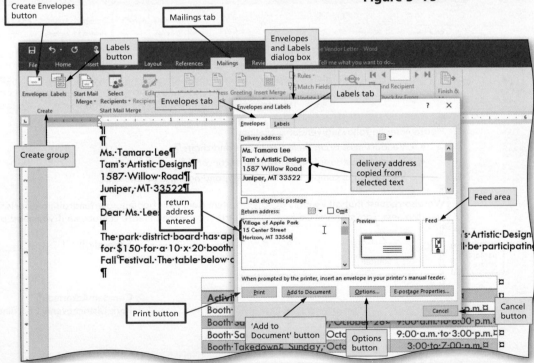

Figure 3–76

- Insert an envelope in your printer, as shown in the Feed area of the dialog box (your Feed area may be different depending on your printer).
- If your printer can print envelopes, click the Print button (Envelopes and Labels dialog box) to print the envelope; otherwise, click the Cancel button to close the dialog box.
- Because the project now is complete, you can exit Word.

Envelopes and Labels

Instead of printing the envelope immediately, you can add it to the document by clicking the 'Add to Document' button (Envelopes and Labels dialog box) (shown in Figure 3–76). To specify a different envelope or label type (identified by a number on the box of envelopes or labels), click the Options button (Envelopes and Labels dialog box) (shown in Figure 3–76).

Instead of printing an envelope, you can print a mailing label. To do this, click the Labels button (Mailings tab | Create group) (shown in Figure 3–76) and then type the delivery address in the Delivery address box. To print the same address on all labels on the page, select the 'Full page of the same label' option button in the Print area. Click the Print button (Envelopes and Labels dialog box) to print the label(s).

Summary

In this module, you have learned how to use Word to change margins, insert and format a shape, change text wrapping, insert and format a picture, move and copy graphics, insert symbols, add a border, clear formatting, convert a hyperlink to regular text, set and use tab stops, insert the current date, create and insert building blocks, insert and format tables, and address and print envelopes and mailing labels.

BTW

Distributing a Document

Instead of printing and distributing a hard copy of a document, you can distribute the document electronically. Options include sending the document via email; posting it on cloud storage (such as OneDrive) and sharing the file with others; posting it on social media, a blog, or other website; and sharing a link associated with an online location of the document. You also can create and share a PDF or XPS image of the document, so that users can view the file in Acrobat Reader or XPS Viewer instead of in Word.

What decisions will you need to make when creating your next business letter?

Use these guidelines as you complete the assignments in this module and create your own business letters outside of this class.

1. Create a letterhead.

   a) Ensure that the letterhead contains a complete legal name, mailing address, phone number, and if applicable, fax number, email address, web address, logo, or other image.

   b) Place elements in the letterhead in a visually appealing location.

   c) Format the letterhead with appropriate fonts, font sizes, font styles, and color.

2. Compose an effective business letter.

   a) Include a date line, inside address, message, and signature block.

   b) Use proper spacing and formats for letter contents.

   c) Follow the alignment and spacing guidelines based on the letter style used (i.e., block, modified block, or modified semi-block).

   d) Ensure the message is well written, properly formatted, and logically organized.

CONSIDER THIS: PLAN AHEAD

BTW

Saving a Template

As an alternative to saving the letterhead as a Word document, you could save it as a template. To do so, click File on the ribbon to open the Backstage view, click the Export tab to display the Export gallery, click 'Change File Type', click Template in the right pane, click the Save As button, enter the template file name (Save As dialog box), if necessary select the Templates folder, and then click the Save button in the dialog box. To use the template, tap or click File on the ribbon to open the Backstage view, click the New tab to display the New gallery, click the PERSONAL tab in the New gallery, and then click the template icon or file name.

STUDENT ASSIGNMENTS

Apply Your Knowledge

Reinforce the skills and apply the concepts you learned in this module.

Working with Tabs and a Table

Note: To complete this assignment, you will be required to use the Data Files. Please contact your instructor for information about accessing the Data Files.

Instructions: Run Word. Open the document called Apply 3–1 Fall Semester Schedule Draft located on the Data Files. The document is a Word table that you are to edit and format. The revised table is shown in Figure 3–77.

Fall Semester Schedule

Class/Activity	Monday	Tuesday	Wednesday	Thursday	Friday	Saturday
ENG 101	9:30-11:00 a.m.		9:30-11:00 a.m.			
COM 110		12:30-2:00 p.m.		12:30-2:00 p.m.		
MAT 120	1:00-2:00 p.m.		1:00-2:00 p.m.		1:00-2:00 p.m.	
CHM 102	3:30-5:00 p.m.		3:30-5:00 p.m.		3:00-5:00 p.m.	
MUS 152		9:30-11:00 a.m.		9:30-11:00 a.m.		
Yoga	6:00-7:00 p.m.			3:00-4:00 p.m.		8:00-9:00 a.m.
Work		4:00-8:00 p.m.			8:00-11:00 a.m.	1:00-4:00 p.m.

Figure 3–77

Perform the following tasks:

1. Change the document theme to Organic.
2. In the line containing the table title, Fall Semester Schedule, remove the tab stop at the 1" mark on the ruler.
3. Set a centered tab at the 3" mark on the ruler. Move the centered tab stop to the 3.5" mark on the ruler.
4. Bold the characters in the title. Use the 'Increase Font Size' button to increase their font size to 14. Change their color to Red, Accent 4, Darker 25%.
5. In the table, delete the row containing the HIS 107 class.
6. In the table, delete the Sunday column.

7. Insert a column between the Monday and Wednesday columns. Fill in the column as follows:

   Column Title – Tuesday

   COM 110 – 12:30-2:00 p.m.

   MUS 152 – 9:30-11:00 a.m.

   If the column heading, Tuesday, is not bold, apply the bold format to the text in this cell.

8. Insert a new row at the bottom of the table. In the first cell of the new row, enter the word, Work, in the cell. If this cell's contents are bold, remove the bold format. Fill in the cells in the remainder of the row as follows:

   Tuesday – 4:00-8:00 p.m.

   Friday – 8:00-11:00 a.m.

   Saturday – 1:00-4:00 p.m.

9. In the Table Style Options group (Table Tools Design tab), ensure that these check boxes have check marks: Header Row, Banded Rows, and First Column. The Total Row, Last Column, and Banded Columns check boxes should not have check marks.

10. Apply the Grid Table 5 Dark - Accent 4 style to the table.

11. Select the entire table. Click the 'Decrease Font Size' button once to decrease the font size of all characters in the table to 10 point.

12. Make all columns as wide as their contents (AutoFit Contents). Note that you may need to perform this step a couple of times to achieve the desired results.

13. Align center left all cells in the first column.

14. Align center the column headings containing the weekday names.

15. Align center right all cells containing times.

16. Center the table between the left and right margins of the page.

17. If requested by your instructor, enter your name on the line below the table.

18. Save the document using the file name, Apply 3–1 Fall Semester Schedule Modified, and submit the document (shown in Figure 3–77) in the format specified by your instructor.

19. ✳ If you wanted to add a row to the middle of the table, how would you add the row?

Extend Your Knowledge

Extend the skills you learned in this module and experiment with new skills. You may need to use Help to complete the assignment.

Working with Formulas, Graphics, Sorting, Picture Bullets, and Mailing Labels

Note: To complete this assignment, you will be required to use the Data Files. Please contact your instructor for information about accessing the Data Files.

Instructions: Run Word. Open the document called Extend 3–1 Donation Letter Draft located on the Data Files. You will use the Format Picture task pane, group objects, enter formulas in the table, change the table style, sort paragraphs, use picture bullets, move tabs, and print mailing labels.

Perform the following tasks:

1. Use Help to learn about grouping objects, entering formulas, sorting, picture bullets, and printing mailing labels.

Continued >

Extend Your Knowledge *continued*

2. Select the graphic of the globe in the hand, click the Format Shape Dialog Box Launcher (Picture Tools Format tab | Picture Styles group) to display the Format Picture task pane, and then click the Picture button in the task pane (Figure 3–78). Experiment with all the buttons in the task pane and modify the look of the graphic to your preferences.

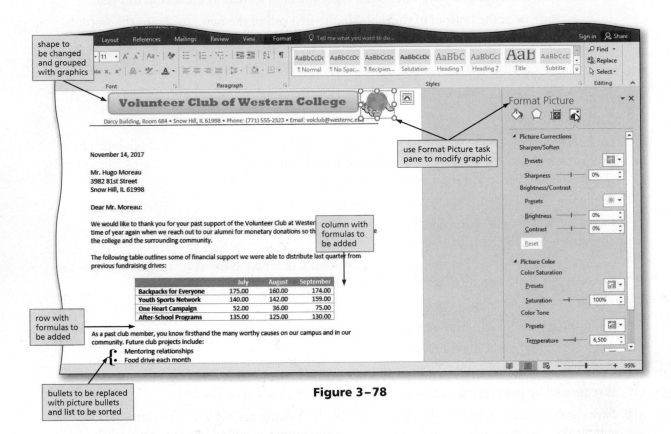

Figure 3–78

3. Select the shape around the Volunteer Club of Western College title and then use the Edit Shape button (Drawing Tools Format tab | Insert Shapes group) to change the shape to your preference. Position the globe in the hand graphic in the desired location to the right of the shape.

4. Copy and paste the modified globe in the hand graphic, flip it horizontally, and then position it on the opposite site of the shape. Group the two globe in hand graphics with the shape at the top of the letterhead. Change the text wrapping of the grouped shape to Top and Bottom.

5. Add a row to the bottom of the table. Insert the word, Total, in the first column of the new row. In the cell to contain the total for September, use the Formula dialog box to insert a formula that adds the cells in the column so that the total amount is displayed; in the dialog box, select a number format so that the total displays with dollar signs. *Hint:* Click the Formula button (Table Tools Format tab | Data group). Repeat this process for the August and July totals. Which formula did you use? Which number format?

6. Add a column to the right of the table. Insert the word, Total, as the column heading for the new column. Use the Formula dialog box to insert a formula that adds the cells each row so that the total amount is displayed. Use the same number format as you used in the previous step. Which formula did you use? What is the grand total for the quarter?

7. Position the insertion point in the table and one at a time, select and deselect each check box in the Table Style Options group. What are the functions of each check box: Header Row, Total Row, Banded Rows, First Column, Last Column, and Banded Columns? Select the check boxes you prefer for the table.

8. Sort the paragraphs in the bulleted list.

9. Change the bullets in the bulleted list to picture bullets.

10. Set a tab stop for the date line at the 4" mark on the ruler. Move the tab stops in the complimentary close and signature block from the 3.5" mark to the 4" mark on the ruler.

11. If requested by your instructor, change the name in the signature block to your name.

12. Save the revised document using the file name, Extend 3–1 Donation Letter Modified, and then submit it in the format specified by your instructor.

13. If requested by your instructor, print a single mailing label for the letter and then a full page of mailing labels, each containing the address shown in Figure 3–78.

14. ✸ Answer the questions posed in #5, #6, and #7. Why would you group objects? Which picture bullet did you use and why?

Expand Your World

Create a solution that uses cloud or web technologies by learning and investigating on your own from general guidance.

Using Google Docs to Upload and Edit Files

Notes:

- To complete this assignment, you will be required to use the Data Files. Please contact your instructor for information about accessing the Data Files.

- To complete this assignment, you will use a Google account, which you can create at no cost. If you do not have a Google account and do not want to create one, read this assignment without performing the instructions.

Instructions: You have created a letter in Word at your office and want to proofread and edit it at home. The problem is that you do not have Word at home. You do, however, have an Internet connection at home. Because you have a Google account, you upload your Word document to Google Drive so that you can view and edit it later from a computer that does not have Word installed.

Perform the following tasks:

1. In Word, open the document, Expand 3–1 Inquiry Letter in Word, from the Data Files. Look through the letter so that you are familiar with its contents and formats. If desired, print the letter so that you easily can compare it to the Google Docs converted file. Close the document.

2. Run a browser. Search for the text, google docs, using a search engine. Visit several websites to learn about Google Docs and Google Drive. Navigate to the Google website. Read about how to create files in Google Docs and upload files to Google Drive. If you do not have a Google account and you want to create one, follow the instructions to create an account. If you do not have a Google account and you do not want to create one, read the remaining instructions without performing them. If you have a Google account, sign in to your account.

3. If necessary, display Google Drive. Upload the file, Expand 3–1 Inquiry Letter in Word, to Google Drive.

Continued >

STUDENT ASSIGNMENTS

Expand Your World *continued*

4. Rename the file on Google Drive to Expand 3–1 Inquiry Letter in Google. Open the file in Google Docs (Figure 3–79). What differences do you see between the Word document and the Google Docs converted document?

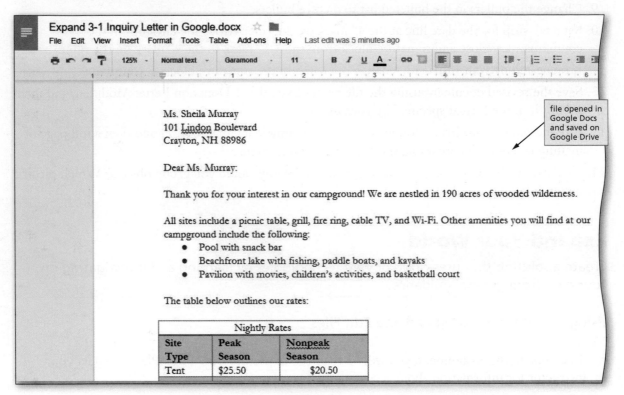

Figure 3–79

5. Fix the document in Google Docs so that it looks appealing, based on the concepts and techniques learned in this module. Add another item to the bulleted list: Fully-stocked camp store with attached laundry facilities. Add a row to the table: Pavilion, $20.00, $40.00. Insert a horizontal line below the line containing the mailing address.

6. If requested by your instructor, change the name in the signature block to your name.

7. Download the revised document to your local storage media, changing its format to Microsoft Word. Submit the document in the format requested by your instructor.

8. ☀ What is Google Drive? What is Google Docs? Answer the question posed in #4. Do you prefer using Google Docs or Word? Why?

In the Labs

Design, create, modify, and/or use a document following the guidelines, concepts, and skills presented in this module. Labs 1 and 2, which increase in difficulty, require you to create solutions based on what you learned in the module; Lab 3 requires you to apply your creative thinking and problem-solving skills to design and implement a solution.

Lab 1: **Creating a Letter with a Letterhead**

Problem: As a junior at your school, you are seeking a summer internship. One letter you prepare is shown in Figure 3–80.

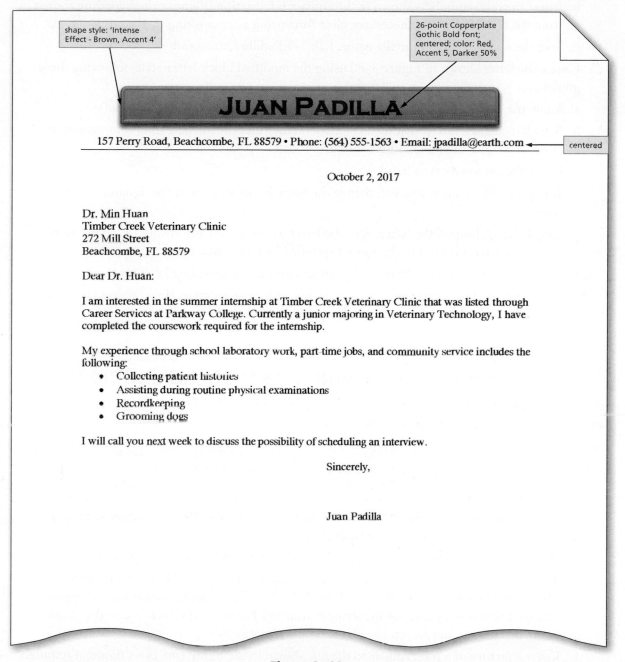

shape style: 'Intense Effect - Brown, Accent 4'

26-point Copperplate Gothic Bold font; centered; color: Red, Accent 5, Darker 50%

JUAN PADILLA

157 Perry Road, Beachcombe, FL 88579 • Phone: (564) 555-1563 • Email: jpadilla@earth.com

centered

October 2, 2017

Dr. Min Huan
Timber Creek Veterinary Clinic
272 Mill Street
Beachcombe, FL 88579

Dear Dr. Huan:

I am interested in the summer internship at Timber Creek Veterinary Clinic that was listed through Career Services at Parkway College. Currently a junior majoring in Veterinary Technology, I have completed the coursework required for the internship.

My experience through school laboratory work, part-time jobs, and community service includes the following:
- Collecting patient histories
- Assisting during routine physical examinations
- Recordkeeping
- Grooming dogs

I will call you next week to discuss the possibility of scheduling an interview.

Sincerely,

Juan Padilla

Figure 3–80

Perform the following tasks:

1. Run Word. Create a new blank document. Change the theme to Slate.

2. Create the letterhead shown at the top of Figure 3–80, following these guidelines:

   a. Insert the Rounded Same Side Corner Rectangle shape at an approximate height of 0.53" and width of 5.4". Change position of the shape to 'Position in Top Center with Square Text

Continued >

In the Labs continued

Wrapping'. Change the text wrapping for the shape to Top and Bottom. Add the student name, Juan Padilla, to the shape. Format the shape and its text as indicated in the figure.

b. Insert the dot symbols as shown in the contact information. Remove the hyperlink format from the email address. If necessary, clear formatting after entering the bottom border.

c. Save the letterhead with the file name, Lab 3–1 Padilla Letterhead.

3. Create the letter shown in Figure 3–80 using the modified block letter style, following these guidelines:

a. Apply the No Spacing Quick Style to the document text (below the letterhead).

b. Set a left-aligned tab stop at the 3.5" mark on the ruler for the date line, complimentary close, and signature block. Insert the current date.

c. Bullet the list as you type it.

d. If requested by your instructor, change the name in the shape and the signature block to your name.

e. Check the spelling of the letter. Save the letter with Lab 3–1 Internship Letter as the file name and then submit it in the format specified by your instructor.

4. If your instructor permits, address and print an envelope or a mailing label for the letter.

5. ✹ The letter in this assignment uses the modified block letter style. If you wanted to use the modified semi-block letter style, what changes would you make to this letter?

Lab 2: **Creating a Letter with a Letterhead and Table**

Note: To complete this assignment, you may be required to use the Data Files. Please contact your instructor for information about accessing the Data Files.

Problem: As the community education class coordinator, you are responsible for sending class registration confirmation letters. You prepare the letter shown in Figure 3–81.

Perform the following tasks:

1. Run Word. Create a new blank document. Change the theme to Berlin. Change the margins to 1" top and bottom and .75" left and right (Moderate).

2. Create the letterhead shown at the top of Figure 3–81, following these guidelines:

a. Insert the Horizontal Scroll shape at an approximate height of 0.74" and width of 6.32". Change the position of the shape to 'Position in Top Center with Square Text Wrapping'. Change the text wrapping for the shape to Top and Bottom. Add the name to the shape. Format the shape and its text as indicated in the figure.

b. Insert a picture of a rose, similar to the one shown in the figure (the exact figure, if required, is located in the Data Files). Resize the picture, change its text wrapping to In Front of Text, and move it to the left on the shape. Change its color tone to Temperature: 4700K. Copy the picture and move the copy of the image to the right on the shape, as shown in the figure. Flip the copied image horizontally.

c. Insert the small open diamond symbols as shown in the contact information. Remove the hyperlink format from the email address. If necessary, clear formatting after entering the bottom border.

d. Save the letterhead with the file name, Lab 3–2 Rosewood Letterhead.

3. Create the letter shown in Figure 3–81, following these guidelines:

a. Apply the No Spacing Quick Style to the document text (below the letterhead).

b. Set a left-aligned tab stop at the 4" mark on the ruler for the date line, complimentary close, and signature block. Insert the current date.

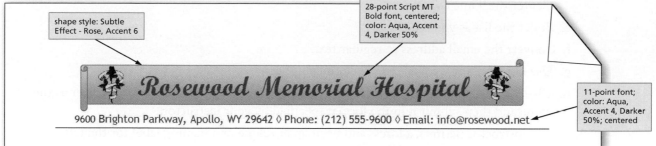

shape style: Subtle Effect - Rose, Accent 6

28-point Script MT Bold font, centered; color: Aqua, Accent 4, Darker 50%

11-point font; color: Aqua, Accent 4, Darker 50%; centered

9600 Brighton Parkway, Apollo, WY 29642 ◊ Phone: (212) 555-9600 ◊ Email: info@rosewood.net

October 16, 2017

Ms. Natalia Zajak
88 Sycamore Street
Apollo, WY 29642

Dear Ms. Zajak:

Thank you for your interest in our community education classes. We look forward to seeing you! The table below confirms the classes in which you are registered during November:

November Class Registration Confirmation			
Class	**Date**	**Time**	**Location**
Diabetes Risk Assessment	November 6	5:00 to 6:00 p.m.	Suite 101
First Aid and CPR	November 11	9:00 a.m. to 3:00 p.m.	Suite 220
Healthy Cooking	November 14	4:00 to 5:00 p.m.	Suite 203
Basics of Meditation	November 17	11:00 a.m. to 12:30 p.m.	Suite 124

bold text

table style: Grid Table 5 Dark - Accent 4; table style options: Header Row and Banded Rows

Please note the following:
- Arrive 10 minutes early for all classes.
- No outside food or drink allowed in classrooms.
- Kindly give 48-hour cancellation notice.

If you have any questions, please contact me via email at jgreen@rosewood.net or phone at 212-555-9612.

Sincerely,

Jerome Green
Community Education Class Coordinator

Figure 3–81

Continued >

In the Labs *continued*

   c. If requested by your instructor, change the name in the inside address and salutation to your name.

   d. Insert and center the table. Format the table as specified in the figure. Make all columns as wide as their contents (AutoFit Contents). Left-align the Class, Date, and Location columns. Center the Time column.

   e. Bullet the list as you type it.

   f. Convert the email address to regular text.

   g. Use nonbreaking hyphens in the phone number.

   h. Check the spelling of the letter. Save the letter with Lab 3–2 Confirmation Letter as the file name and then submit it in the format specified by your instructor.

4. If your instructor permits, address and print an envelope or a mailing label for the letter.

5. ✺ What is the purpose of the nonbreaking hyphens in this letter? Why do you think the picture in this letter used a text wrapping of In Front of Text? If the table used banded columns instead of banded rows, how would its appearance change?

Lab 3: **Consider This: Your Turn**

Create a Letter to a Potential Employer

Note: To complete this assignment, you may be required to use the Data Files. Please contact your instructor for information about accessing the Data Files.

Problem: As an intern in the career development office at your school, your boss has asked you to prepare a sample letter to a potential employer. Students seeking employment will use this letter as a reference document when creating their own letters.

Perform the following tasks:

Part 1: Using your name, mailing address, phone number, and email address, create a letterhead for the letter. Once the letterhead is designed, write the letter to this potential employer: Ms. Latisha Adams, Personnel Director, Cedar Plank Hotels, 85 College Grove Lane, P.O. Box 582, Gartner, TX 74812.

The draft wording for the letter is as follows:

First paragraph:
I am responding to your advertisement in the Texas Post for the Assistant Manager position. I have the credentials you are seeking and believe I can be a valuable asset to Cedar Plank Hotels.

Second paragraph:
In May, I will be earning my bachelor's degree in Hospitality Management from Greenville College. My relevant coursework includes the following:

Below the second paragraph, insert the following table:

Restaurant management	18 hours
Nutrition	15 hours
Tourism management	12 hours
Hotel management	12 hours

Third paragraph:
  In addition to my college coursework, I have the following experience:

Below the third paragraph, insert the following items as a bulleted list:
  Assistant to school cafeteria director; Volunteer in Hope Mission kitchen; Developed website and Facebook page for local cafe.

Last paragraph:
  I look forward to hearing from you to schedule an interview and to discuss my career opportunities at Cedar Plank Hotels.

The letter should contain a letterhead that uses a shape and picture(s); a table with an appropriate table title, column headings, and table style applied (unformatted table shown above); and a bulleted list (to present the experience). Insert nonbreaking spaces in the company name. Create a building block for the company name, edit the building block so that it has a ScreenTip, and insert the building block whenever you have to enter the company name.

Use the concepts and techniques presented in this module to create and format a letter according to a letter style, creating appropriate paragraph breaks and rewording the draft as necessary. The unformatted paragraphs in the letter are in a file called Lab 3-1 Letter Paragraphs, which is located on the Data Files. If you prefer, you can copy and paste this text into your letter instead of typing the paragraphs yourself. Use your name in the signature line in the letter. Be sure to check the spelling and grammar of the finished letter. Submit your assignment in the format specified by your instructor.

Part 2: ☀ You made several decisions while creating the letter in this assignment: where to position elements in the letterhead, how to format elements in the letterhead, which graphics to use in the letterhead, which theme to use in the letter, which font size to use for the letter text, which table style to use, and which letter style to use. What was the rationale behind each of these decisions?

Index